AF605887

The Mother of All Tableaux

Advances in Optimality Theory
Series Editors: Vieri Samek-Lodovici, University College London and Birgit Alber, Free Univerity of Bozen-Bolzano

Optimality Theory is an exciting new approach to linguistic analysis that originated in phonology but was soon taken up in syntax, morphology, and other fields of linguistics. Optimality Theory presents a clear vision of the universal properties underlying the vast surface typological variety in the world's languages. Cross-linguistic differences once relegated to idiosyncratic language-specific rules can now be understood as the result of different priority rankings among universal, but violable constraints on grammar.

Advances in Optimality Theory is designed to stimulate and promote research in this provocative new framework. It provides a central outlet for the best new work by both established and younger scholars in this rapidly moving field. The series includes studies with a broad typological focus, studies dedicated to the detailed analysis of individual languages, and studies on the nature of Optimality Theory itself. The series publishes theoretical work in the form of monographs and coherent edited collections as well as pedagogical texts and reference texts that promote the dissemination of Optimality Theory.

Consultant Board:

Published:

Blocking and Complementarity in Phonological Theory
Eric Baković

Conflicts in Interpretation
Petra Hendriks, Helen de Hoop, Irene Krämer, Henriätte de Swart and Joost Zwarts

Harmonic Grammar and Harmonic Serialism
Edited by John J. McCarthy and Joe Pater

Hidden Generalizations
Phonological Opacity in Optimality Theory
John J. McCarthy

Inflectional Morphology in Harmonic Serialism
Gereon Müller

Interactions of Vowel Quality and Prosody in East Slavic
Janina Mołczanow

Layering and Directionality
Metrical Stress in Optimality Theory
Brett Hyde

Linguistic Derivations and Filtering
Minimalism and Optimality Theory
Edited by Hans Broekhuis and Ralf Vogel

Modeling Ungrammaticality in Optimality Theory
Edited by Curt Rice and Sylvia Blaho

Optimality Theory, Phonological Acquisition and Disorders
Edited by Daniel A. Dinnsen and Judith A. Gierut

Phonological Argumentation
Essays in Evidence and Motivation
Edited by Steve Parker

Prosody Matters
Essays in Honor of Elisabeth Selkirk
Edited by Toni Borowsky, Shigeto Kawahara, Takahito Shinya and Mariko Sugahara

The Phonology of Contrast
Anna Łubowicz

Understanding Allomorphy
Perspectives from Optimality Theory
Edited by Eulàlia Bonet, Maria-Rosa Lloret and Joan Mascaró

The Mother of All Tableaux

Order, Equivalence, and Geometry in the Large-scale Structure of Optimality Theory

Nazarré Merchant and Alan Prince

SHEFFIELD UK BRISTOL CT

Published by Equinox Publishing Ltd.
UK: Office 415, The Workstation, 15 Paternoster Row, Sheffield, South Yorkshire S1 2BX
USA: ISD, 70 Enterprise Drive, Bristol, CT 06010

www.equinoxpub.com

First published 2023

British Library Cataloguing-in-Publication Data

A catalogue record for this book is available from the British Library.

ISBN-13 978 1 78179 899 7 (hardback)
978 1 78179 900 0 (ePDF)
978 1 80050 359 5 (ePub)

Library of Congress Cataloging-in-Publication Data

Names: Merchant, Nazarré, author. | Prince, Alan, author.
Title: The mother of all tableaux : order, equivalence, and geometry in the large-scale structure of optimality theory / Nazarré Merchant and Alan Prince.
Description: Sheffield, South Yorkshire ; Bristol, CT : Equinox Publishing Ltd, 2023. | Series: Advances in optimality theory | Includes bibliographical references and index. | Summary: "Through the MOAT ("Mother of All Tableaux"), Optimality Theoretic (OT) constraints rate entire grammars against each other within a typology, imposing a structure of order and equivalence on them. An associated geometry views grammars as regions, with properties determined at their borders, using the same data that gives rise to the MOAT. These structures delimit what can and cannot be an OT typology, how typologies can be represented in Violation Tableaux, and how grammar-regions can merge to classify concrete and abstract languages"-- Provided by publisher.
Identifiers: LCCN 2022051994 (print) | LCCN 2022051995 (ebook) | ISBN 9781781798997 (hardback) | ISBN 9781781799000 (ePDF) | ISBN 9781800503595 (ePub)
Subjects: LCSH: Optimality theory (Linguistics)
Classification: LCC P158.42 .M47 2023 (print) | LCC P158.42 (ebook) | DDC 410.1/822--dc23/eng/20230227
LC record available at https://lccn.loc.gov/2022051994
LC ebook record available at https://lccn.loc.gov/2022051995

Typeset by Sparks – www.sparkspublishing.com

Silent, upon a peak in Darien.

Contents

Acknowledgments

The authors' names are arranged in alphabetical order. We would like to thank Birgit Alber and Natalie DelBusso for detailed helpful comments on several versions of the manuscript. Two very thorough and helpful reviewers from Equinox Press had a wide impact on revisions. We are grateful to Nick Kalivoda for extensive work on the manuscript and many sharp observations which have improved it in numerous respects. Vieri Samek-Lodovici has overseen the editorial process from top to bottom with unfailing tact and close support. We thank Tom Fryer of Sparks Publishing Services Ltd for his transformative work on the proofs. We thank Giorgio Magri for inviting us to present this work in its original form at CNRS (Paris) in 2017, including its now much-modified technical core. To Nick Danis, Luca Iacoponi, Hope McManus, Kevin Thielen, Tonia Krueger, Erin Griesenauer, and Jane Grimshaw we are grateful for much discussion of related issues. We have profited from interaction with audiences at Rutgers, UCSC, MIT, Stanford, OCP 2014 (Leiden), and the Workshop on the Formal Structure of OT Typologies (2015), where aspects of this work were presented and discussed. Prince would like to thank the School of Arts and Sciences at Rutgers, The State University of New Jersey and especially Dean Douglas Greenberg for support during the initial stages of this work. Merchant's work on this project was supported in part by NSF Grant #1823827.

Introduction

OT GRAMMARS ARISE from the comparison of candidates over a set of constraints. An OT *typology*, we show, implicitly compares entire grammars over the same set of constraints. From the details of this comparison, each constraint can be seen in its essential form as an order and equivalence structure on grammars. At this level, a *constraint* is no longer a function penalizing concrete linguistic structures and mappings, but a more abstract order and equivaence structure on grammars that we call an EPO, an 'Equivalence-augmented Privileged Order'. The collection of the EPOs, each one representing a single constraint, forms the MOAT, the 'Mother of All Tableaux', which holds the relational essence of the entirety of CON for the system under scrutiny. The unique MOAT of a typology is instantiated in every Violation Tableau (VT) that gives rise to that typology.

With this new characterization of *typology* in hand, we can pose and answer fundamental questions about the structure imposed by OT on its grammars.

(1) Typological status. Since a typology must have a well-formed MOAT, we can assess whether a given collection of grammars constitutes an OT typology. Simply dividing the set of all rankings into individually well-formed grammars is not guaranteed to produce a legitimate typology. Failures are detected by the appearance of cycles in what should be the EPO graphs of the MOAT. Cycles indicate that it is impossible to realize the graphs as OT constraints assigning violations in a consistent manner. Concomitantly, we can determine which Violation Tableau (VT) representations are equivalent in the sense that they yield the same typology.

(2) Classification. Within a typology, MOAT structure determines whether a collection of grammars can be classified together as a kind of super-grammar within a valid, coarser typology, one that retains their shared linguistic patterns while abstracting away from their differences. This contributes to the foundations of the broader analysis of OT typologies developing under the name of Property Theory (Alber & Prince 2015–16, 2021, in prep.).

(3) Geometry. The relations in the MOAT arise from a notion of adjacency between constraint orders ('rankings'). Rendered graphically, this notion leads to the permutohedron, a geometric figure familiar from combinatorics, in which each vertex corresponds to an order. Grammars are spherically convex regions on the permutohedron (Riggle 2012), an important result that MOAT theory is used to prove. Further, if each grammar is shrunk to a single point, then a typology is associated with an object that represents the relations between its grammars: the typohedron. The super-grammars that coarsen typologies appear as regions on the typohedron.

The argument proceeds in both concrete and abstract terms. We pursue the main line of analysis by examining the Elementary Syllable Theory (EST) of Prince & Smolensky (1993/2004), which presents the basic issues accessibly and allows for thorough application of the ideas and techniques developed here. We also look at instructive typologies that are not as obviously rooted in language-based issues. Proceeding more abstractly, we provide fine-grained formal analysis. In investigations of this nature, where broad claims are advanced and truth is at issue, it is not possible to rest on anecdote, and we have introduced formal apparatus and methods of proof that allow us to state, establish, and illuminate claimed results. Not every reader will wish to examine every proof, but the leading ideas are built from a formal and graphical vocabulary familiar from linguistic analysis and worked out through concrete examples, so that they should be accessible in essence and in detail. The sequence and structure of the formal analysis is, we have found, illuminating rather than merely a 'verification of details' and it is placed centrally, where it is preceded by concrete exposition of the ideas it appeals to and followed by concrete applications, concluding with a geometric rendition of the results of the investigation, also intended to be accessible in the main.

For those interested in higher resolution of the landscape, we provide the following more fine-grained summary, in hopes that it may be useful as either prospectus or review.

We begin (§1) by fixing the fundamental notions of OT that play a role throughout. A foundational step is conceiving of a grammar as the set of all linear orders on the assumed constraint set ('rankings', or 'legs' in the terminology introduced here) that yield the same optima. A typology is then the set of all grammars. From that base, we move on to review the three key problems we address, enumerated above. We sketch their solutions in terms of the MOAT.

The familiar typology of Elementary Syllable Theory (EST) is used as our touchstone and stalking horse, so we take some care in laying it out (§2).

The concept of the MOAT is then developed concretely through analysis of EST (§3).

The key notion of the *border point pair* is introduced with reference to the grammars of EST (§3.2). A border point pair consists of two linear orders on the constraint set, each of which belongs to a different grammar and which are *adjacent* in the sense that they differ minimally: they are identical except for a single local transposition of two constraints. From the simple internal structure of the border point pair, order and equivalence relations between grammars emerge, populating the EPOs of the MOAT, which completely determine the possible numerical representations of a typology in VTs.

With the fundamental concepts in view, formal analysis begins (§4). The order and equivalence relations of the MOAT are developed from the information inherent in border point pairs and shown to be numerically instantiated in VTs. We extricate ourselves from the plentiful non-uniqueness of the VTs giving rise to a typology by identifying a way of filtering *grammars* that perfectly mirrors the familiar OT filtration of VTs. This leads immediately to another way of defining relations between grammars, paralleling those of MOAT. Using these tools, we show that the MOAT *characterizes* a typology, in the sense that any two typologies with the same MOAT are the same typology (§4.7). We then go on to demonstrate that a partition of all linear orders on a given Con is an OT typology if and only if its border-point-derived relations yield an acyclic structure – a valid MOAT (§4.8).

A striking conclusion of this investigation is that all information about the structure of a grammar is derivable from its *border* – the linear orders in a grammar that are each adjacent to a linear order *not* in the grammar. In this context, the 3-valued ERC is replaced by the 4-valued 'ERCoid', which exactly represents the relational content of a single border point pair. We examine the conjecture that canonical ERC grammars can be derived directly from border ERCoids using the familiar Fusional Reduction Algorithm (Brasoveanu & Prince 2005/11).

With the main results established, we return to the concrete via scrutiny of a self-contained EST subsystem, deriving its MOAT and showing how node merger in the MOAT graph parallels grammar union in the typology, illustrating how the MOAT functions as tool of typological analysis (§5).

Discussion then takes a mildly abstract turn toward the issue of coexistence of grammars within a single typology. Examples are presented which illustrate how the MOAT determines the typological compatibility of grammars, and how MOAT structure relates to the join of grammars into supergrammars (§6).

We conclude with a discussion of the remarkably well-behaved geometry of OT typologies, which makes graphically concrete the minimal-change relation that defines the border point pair. A typology can be usefully represented on the permutohedron, a figure representing the set of linear orders (permutations) on a set, with a linear order at each vertex, introduced into linguistic discourse by Riggle (2010). This representation then reduces to the *typohedron*, a structure in which each vertex represents an entire grammar. We complete the discussion by offering proofs of several striking results announced by Jason Riggle, showing that grammars are connected regions, that there is a notion of distance between linear orders, and that grammars are convex regions analogous to the disks and balls of the familiar Euclidean world (§7).

The narrative arc thus proceeds from the essential premises of OT to an examination of its central object, the typology. We aim to find and relate ways of characterizing the typology that open up its intrinsic properties to analysis. Multiple perspectives are explored, tied together by the properties and uses of the MOAT.

Chapter 1

Overview

Chapter contents

A *FACTORIAL TYPOLOGY* COMES INTO EXISTENCE whenever we specify an OT system as a set of constraints and the candidates they evaluate. The content of the typology follows from these assumptions, whether or not we endeavor to familiarize ourselves with it. Experience tells us that a typology comes with ways of classifying its languages in terms of linguistic patterns and their correlated ranking relations. Again, this is a fact of logic, not a modification of the theory, revealing structures that inhere in forms and rankings.

The Basic Syllable Theory of Prince & Smolensky (P&S:1993/2004:105–118), for example, defines a certain set of admitted inputs, outputs, candidates, candidate sets, and constraints. The resulting factorial typology of the system distinguishes languages in terms of output types like 'onset required' and 'coda allowed' as well as by characteristic input-output relations of epenthesis, deletion, and faithfulness, each of which follows from specific ranking conditions playing out over the admitted forms (P&S:116). In the same way, a stress typology may predict dozens or even hundreds of languages, but still categorize them neatly into 'iambic' and 'trochaic', 'left-aligned', and 'right-aligned', or into more complex classes that devolve from its defining assumptions. With this in mind, Alber & Prince (2015–16 *et seq.*) launch the Classification Program for typologies, proposing an articulated account (*Property Theory*) of the ranking relations (*properties*) that determine the structural and grammatical patterns (*traits*), analyzing a variety of systems abstracted from linguistic phenomena ranging from basic phonology to syllable structure, stress, and accent. Resolving these relations is essential if we wish to understand how the fundamental assumptions of OT, through constraint interaction, organize data into principled classes.

Here we identify and study key formal properties that underlie the linguistic macro-structure imposed by OT. We identify an invariant that is shared by all violation-tableau representations of the same typology: the MOAT ('Mother of All Tableaux'), which therefore gives status to the typology as a formal object independent of its implementation in linguistic substance. The MOAT contains the linguistically relevant order and equivalence information that must be present in *every* Violation Tableau (VT) that generates the same typology. Composed of numerical penalties assigned by the constraints to particular candidates, a given VT contains values that may or may not determine crucial ranking relations. The MOAT generalizes away from relational artifacts introduced by the use of numbers. It represents each constraint more abstractly, recording only the information relevant to ranking and filtration in the grammars of the typology. Each such representation of a constraint we call an EPO ('Equivalence-augmented Privileged Order'). The MOAT of a typology, composed of EPOs, one for each constraint, is the abstract analog of a concrete VT composed of constraint columns containing numbers. From the MOAT, we can determine when two different representations of a typology are equivalent, whether a given collection of grammars forms a typology, and how the grammars of a typology can be classified together in all the ways that respect their typological status.

We aim to keep both the concrete and the abstract in view as we proceed. The MOAT concept is developed through particular typologies with a firm and familiar linguistic basis. The principal burden will be borne by Elementary Syllable Theory (EST), the version of the Basic Syllable Theory (BST) which unifies the two anti-insertion faithfulness constraints f.depV and f.depC into a single constraint f.dep (P&S:106).[1]

We begin by laying out and refining the key concepts of OT (§§1.1–2). With the foundation in place, we state the three fundamental questions that the MOAT answers (§1.3). We then see in overview how the MOAT answers those questions (§§1.4–6).

---

[1] In P&S, f.depV is called FILL^{Nuc} and f.depC is called FILL^{Ons} (P&S: §6, p.115). With the advent of correspondence theory (McCarthy & Prince 1995), they became DEPV and DEPC. Following modern best practices, they are explicitly typed as faithfulness constraints by the prefix 'f'.

The body of the work begins with a specification of EST (§2). The principles of MOAT construction are then developed concretely in the EST context (§3) and the properties of the MOAT are established through formal analysis (§4). We then revisit EST to analyze in systematic detail the subtypology that deals with the fate of consonants (§5). Turning to a pair of somewhat more abstract cases, we examine how MOAT structure restricts the co-occurrence of grammars within a typology (§6). We conclude by developing a geometrical perspective that illuminates aspects of the MOAT concept and the intrinsic organization of OT typologies (§7), introducing an object, the *typohedron*, that carries the geometric relations between grammars.

1.1 Language, grammar, typology

In linguistic analysis, a factorial typology is calculated from a collection of candidate sets, each from a different input, each giving information about the treatment of the various structural issues implicit in the languages of the typology. Let us clarify the concepts that underlie this practice (see Prince 2015a for development).

First, all typological discussion takes place within the context of a fully specified OT system *S*. This requires definitions of *S*.GEN and *S*.CON sufficiently precise to delimit these objects without ambiguity. The most familiar example may be the Basic Syllable Theory (BST, P&S:115ff). BST.GEN and BST.CON are specified in P&S:106–111. Observe that *S*.GEN can be given by any mode of definition and need not involve a procedure of some sort.

In spelling out what we mean by an OT *system*, we cast the net wide, in anticipation of casting it yet wider. We count as a system $S = \langle S.\text{GEN}, S.\text{CON}\rangle$ any specification whatever of candidates and candidate sets (*S*.GEN), and any specification of a constraint set (*S*.CON) which characterizes each constraint as a function from candidates to the set of non-negative integers $\mathbb{N} = \{0, 1, 2, ...\}$. This way of defining a system we will call 'Concrete OT' (COT), because it deals with candidates and the constraints that evaluate them. We diverge somewhat from one form of familiar usage, in that we regard such an *S* as a closed, fully articulated formal system and not as a piece of a larger something that is only partially defined. This allows us to say true things about *S* that are not contingent upon other things not specified or specifiable. The Basic Syllable Theory, for example, stands on its own and is not to be understood as a fragment of something else, a brick in a monumental edifice perpetually under construction. To advance beyond it, we propose other systems which may expand on it, contract it, or differ from it in various ways. On this view, the project of developing a theory is carried out by analyzing a growing body of limited, inter-related, well-defined *systems* rather than by programmatic conjecture in which large-scale ambitions dominate the discourse.

1.1.1 Concrete OT

The conceptual infrastructure we need involves the notions *ranking, optimality, language, grammar, typology.* It will prove worth our while to be clear about these five basic notions. If we err in defining them, the structures inherent in the theory will be obscured or disappear entirely. We'll spend the most time here on the central notion of a *grammar*, which receives limited attention in much of the literature.

☐ By ***a ranking*** we will always mean a single linear order on the whole set *S*.CON. As usual, the notation $C_j \gg C_k$ means that C_j *dominates* or *is ranked above* C_k. To specify the set of linear orders G of which this holds, it is useful to write $C_j \gg_G C_k$. The subscript G is customarily omitted when its reference is clear. The global structure of the system is determined by the set of all the linear orders it provides, which we denote Ord(*S*.CON).

☐ The notion of ***optimality*** distinguishes certain candidates from others, given a ranking. This is defined within a *candidate set* ('cset'), a collection of all competing candidates. Each candidate of *S* is associated by *S*.GEN with a unique candidate set.

There are a couple of ways of thinking about optimality, both of which are important in this work. A constraint can be used as a filter, selecting a nonempty subset of its input, ejecting all others from consideration. The constraint-as-filter selects those candidates to which it assigns a minimal violation value. A ranking then filters sequentially, with each constraint taking as input the candidates selected by the previous filtration in the order. Forms are optimal in their candidate set, with respect to a ranking λ, if they survive filtration by every constraint in λ.

A constraint can also be understood as a comparator, determining which of a set of competing candidates are 'better' than the others. Given that we know how each constraint compares, we still need to be able to combine the set of such judgments, so that we know how an entire ranking compares. To arrive at OT, we can say that in a ranking, the better-than/worse-than candidate comparisons left open by the topmost constraint are submitted for refinement to the rest of the hierarchy (thinking recursively), or to the next constraint in the ranking (thinking iteratively), and so on down the line. 'Optimal' means being the best of the best... and so on, through the entire ranking. This imposes an order relation on candidates which goes by the name of 'lexicographic' because it resembles the way that words are ordered in a dictionary.[2] The ultimate evolution of this idea breaks down the comparison process as far as possible, building it from comparisons between just two candidates, one of which is nominated for optimality. One candidate is 'better' than another if filtering the pair would select it rather than its competitor. A candidate, from this point of view, is optimal with respect to a given ranking if it is better on that ranking than *every* violation-distinct competitor in its candidate set.

Optimality can be defined concisely in a single mouthful: a candidate q is ***optimal*** in its candidate set K with respect to a ranking λ, if and only if for every candidate z in K, the highest-ranked constraint C in λ which distinguishes q and z by assigning different violation values to them is one for which the value assigned to q is less than the value assigned to z. The more leisurely and analytical approaches just sketched, explicitly using notions of filtration and order, provide superior tools for handling the theory.

Optimality depends only on the values assigned by constraints and is blind to all structural differences that the constraints do not evaluate. The term *violation profile* refers to the entire collection of values assigned to a candidate by the constraints of *S*.Con (Samek-Lodovici & Prince 2005:1). If two candidates have identical violation profiles, there is no constraint on which they differ and they are indistinguishable with respect to every ranking: if one is optimal, so is the other. Similarly, if two candidates have *distinct* violation profiles and one is optimal under a given ranking, the other cannot be: there must be at least one constraint on which they differ, and the highest-ranked distinguishing constraint will decide between them.

□ A ***language*** of *S* is the collection of all optima for some ranking λ, drawn from every candidate set admitted by *S*.Gen. When we wish to emphasize the status of a *language* as a collection of linguistic objects, we will use the term *extensional language*. Each linear order, each ranking, on *S*.Con is thus associated with an extensional language. As is well known from descriptive practice, and as will be abundantly exemplified below, it often happens that more than one ranking delivers the same optima: in such a case, multiple (linear) rankings each yield the same extensional language.

---

[2] One word precedes another if the first letter of the one precedes the first letter of the other in the alphabetical order; if their first letters are the same, we examine the second letter under the same rubric, and so on (thinking iteratively), or the rest of the word, and so on (thinking recursively).

□ This leads directly to the notion of a ***ranking grammar***: the collection of *all* rankings that produce the same extensional language. A *ranking grammar* may be fully characterized by a set of Elementary Ranking Conditions (ERCs: Prince 2002ab), yielding an ***ERC grammar***, discussed directly below.

□ A ***typology***, construed extensionally, is the collection of all the languages of a system. Since each language has a unique grammar associated with it, a typology may also be understood intensionally as the collection of all *grammars* of a system. This is the conception that we regard as truly fundamental. Since grammars are sets of rankings, a typology in the grammatical sense is a collection of disjoint sets of rankings which exhaust the set of all rankings: a *partition* of Ord(*S*.CON).[3] If a grammar is viewed as a set of ERCs, then a grammatical typology consists of a collection of distinct, mutually inconsistent ERC sets.

The ERC develops the binary-comparative conception of optimality outlined above. Here is a brief account. An *Elementary Ranking Condition* or ERC (Prince 2002ab) is an expression derived from the comparison of two candidates, let's say *q* and *z*, typically denoted [*q* ~ *z*]. The ERC gives the ranking requirements that must prevail for the first candidate, *q*, to best the second, *z*, in their competition. The ERC is particularly useful when you have fixed an optimum and wish to obtain the set of rankings that will deliver it.

An ERC is represented by a list ('vector') of characters or '(comparative) values' W, L, *e*, one value for each constraint in *S*.CON. These are typically written out sequentially, but order of presentation is arbitrary; all ranking information is in the values. The value W indicates that the constraint favors the first of the competitors; L indicates that the constraint favors the second; and *e* indicates that the constraint does not distinguish them because both receive the same penalty. From this perspective, a 'constraint' is a function from pairs of candidates to {W, L, *e*}.

When an ERC contains both W and L, it imposes restrictions on ranking order. The ranking condition associated with it – the 'Elementary Ranking Condition' proper – requires that *some* constraint assessing W of the competing pair dominate *every* constraint assessing L of the pair. Under any ranking that satisfies this condition, the highest-ranked constraint that

[3] Formally, a partition of a set S is a collection of pairwise disjoint nonempty subsets of S that unions to S; equivalently, a collection of 'nonempty subsets of S such that every member of S belongs to exactly one of these subsets.' The members of a partition of S are called 'parts', 'cells', or 'blocks'; we will use the last of these terms. See Partition of a set, Wikipedia.

distinguishes the two competitors will favor the first, in the sense that it will assign fewer violations to the first than to the second.

Here's an example of pairwise competition from the syllable theory investigated below (EST). The order of columns in a tableau is *not* presumed here or anywhere else in this book to reflect a ranking order. (See Prince 2017 for the inutility of this common presupposition.) The brackets [...] indicate that the enclosed string forms a syllable. Indices mark input-output correspondence. For visibility, an epenthetic segment is shown unsubscripted.

(1) Faithful vs. Epenthetic mappings in Elementary Syllable Theory: VT

Input	Output	m.Ons	m.NoCoda	f.dep	f.max	Remarks
V_1	a. $[V_1]$	1	0	0	0	*faithful*
	b. $[CV_1]$	0	0	1	0	*epenthetic*

If the faithful map (1a) is asserted to be better than the epenthetic map (1b), the following ERC emerges, presented as a 'comparative tableau' (CT).

(2) When Faithful bests Epenthetic: CT

a ~ b	m.Ons	m.NoCoda	f.dep	f.max	Remarks
$\langle V_1 \rightarrow [V_1]\rangle \sim \langle V_1 \rightarrow [CV_1]\rangle$	**L**	*e*	**W**	*e*	*faithf.~epen.*

In this simple case, with one W and one L, the interpretation of 'some W dominates every L' is just f.dep ≫ m.Ons. In each of the 12 rankings that meet this requirement, the faithful candidate (1a) bests the epenthetic candidate (1b), as desired.

If we swap desired winner and loser, we obtain the following, exchanging W and L.

(3) Epenthetic bests Faithful: CT

b ~ a	m.Ons	m.NoCoda	f.dep	f.max	Remarks
$\langle V_1 \rightarrow [CV_1]\rangle \sim \langle V_1 \rightarrow [V_1]\rangle$	**W**	*e*	**L**	*e*	*epen.~faithf.*

Ecologically, as any practitioner can verify, ERCs with many Ws and Ls are common, reflecting the complexities of explanation where many factors are involved.

Optimality may also be defined in terms of ERCs. A candidate *q* is optimal under some ranking λ if and only if λ satisfies *every* ERC that compares *q* with another candidate in its cset.[4] The ERC notion supports a full theory of ranking in OT and the logic of ranking plays out in manipulation of ERC vectors. See Prince 2002ab, 2006, 2008, 2009, as well as Brasoveanu & Prince 2005/2011, for discussion. The ERC representation also supports the Join operation (Merchant 2008, 2011), which plays an important role in typological structure, as we will see below (§6). ERCs are logical expressions and therefore may stand on their own, without candidate data, to express ranking relations. The ERC set is therefore the standard valid representation of a grammar (Prince 2017).

A couple of ERC set representations have priority: the Most Informative Basis (MIB) and the Skeletal Basis (SKB) of Brasoveanu & Prince 2005/11. These are maximally concise, as indicated by the term 'basis', both using the same minimal number of ERCs. The MIB represents all consequence of transitivity; the SKB represents none, and is the incidence matrix of the hypergraph that represents the grammar. OTWorkplace (Prince, Merchant, and Tesar 2007–2021) uses the Fusional Reduction Algorithm (FRed) of Brasoveanu & Prince to calculate both of these for use by the grammatical and typological analyst.

An OT grammar as defined here is an *antimatroid*, a type of order structure that generalizes the more familiar partial order.[5] Just as we speak of the set of linear orders consistent with a given partial order as the *linear extensions* of that order, so may we speak of a ranking grammar G_R as the set of linear extensions of an ERC grammar G_E. With this in mind, we introduce the acronym ***leg*** ('**l**inear **e**xtension of a **g**rammar') to refer to a ranking, and we will speak of the ***legs*** or ***leg set*** of an ERC grammar to refer to the rankings associated with it. The notions 'ranking grammar' and 'ERC grammar' are equivalent in the following sense: every leg set of an

---

[4] This alternate definition of optimality is equivalent to the one given above. For discussion, see 'RCD – the Movie.' (Prince 2009). Follow the 'Optimality' link in the TOC, continuing to the worksheet 'Challenge'.

[5] On the equivalence of ERC sets and antimatroids, see Riggle (2010:13), and Merchant & Riggle (2016) for proof. So what is an *antimatroid*? The most accessible characterization may well be this: a set of linear orders delimited by an ERC set. All partial orders are antimatroids; some antimatroids are not partial orders. If the Skeletal Basis or Most Informative Basis of the grammar (Brasoveanu & Prince 2005/11) contains an ERC with two or more Ws, the grammar is properly antimatroidal and not representable as a partial order. Multiple Ws indicate disjunctive ranking requirements. See Prince (2006/7:13), ex. (32) ff,. and Prince (2017) for further discussion.

ERC grammar is a ranking grammar; every ranking grammar is the leg set of an ERC grammar.

A point of usage: the term *grammar* is sometimes used in the literature to refer to a single ranking or leg. For us, *grammar* always refers to either a *ranking grammar* – the *set* of rankings that yield the same extensional language – or to an *ERC grammar*, its characterization by a set of ERCs. These are the linguistically significant objects. The single ranking is a poor candidate for special recognition, since it almost always contains artifacts: ranking relations that arise not from the data, but from the fact that it is a total order on the constraint set. Thus, if the data requires exactly A ≫ C and B ≫ C, any leg will nevertheless contain either A ≫ B or B ≫ A, neither of which is supported by data.

1.1.2 *Abstract OT*

Toto, I have a feeling we're not in Kansas anymore.

Exactly as elsewhere in generative linguistics, the notion of a *grammar* disconnects us from the concrete. By shifting focus from the extensional language composed of concrete optimal candidates to the set of rankings that yield those optima, we characterize the extensional language *intensionally*, in the terminology of Alber & Prince (2015). This marks a consequential step into abstraction.

Two languages in completely unrelated Concrete OT systems S_1 and S_2 may have structurally identical grammars, in the sense that there's a 1:1 mapping between their constraint rankings, even though their concrete content diverges wildly. For example, in the Elementary Syllable Theory examined below, there is a ranking grammar that consists of the two linear extensions, *legs*, of the following partial order:

(4) Grammar of (C)V.del from EST

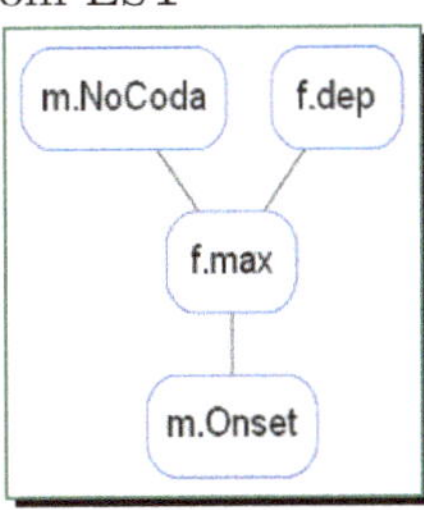

Given EST.Gen and EST.Con, this yields the extensional language (C)V.del, in which all outputs consist of open syllables that may or may not have onsets, and in which the output pattern is achieved through deletion of refractory underlying material. Compare this with the grammar of voicing systems like that of Polish, from Lombardi's voicing typology (Lombardi 1999). The linguistic generalization is that obstruents in clusters take on the underlying voicing value of a cluster's head, if it has one, and are otherwise voiceless.[6] This is a substantively different pattern, but the ranking structure is identical.

(5) Polish in the typology of Lombardi 1999

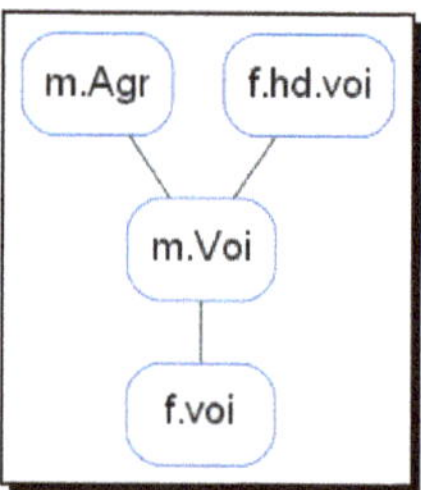

Both exemplify the following Y-shaped ranking structure, appropriately identifying constraints across systems:

(6) Y-ranking

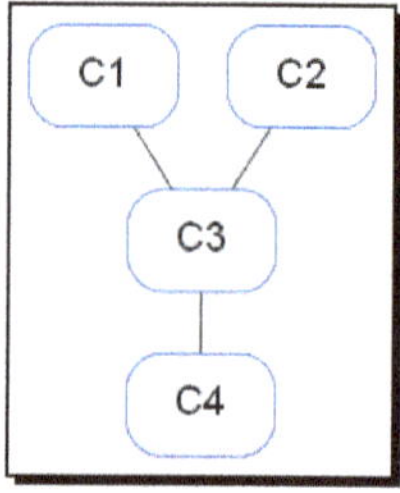

An ERC grammar of ex. (6), exactly mirroring those of exx. (4) and (5), is given below as a comparative tableau (CT). It is the Skeletal Basis for these grammars.

---

[6] To cover all the cases, think of a 'cluster' as consisting of *one or more* obstruents. A cluster is 'headed' if it precedes a vowel; the prevocalic obstruent is its head. In this rendition of Lombardi's constraint system, the constraint m.Agr penalizes adjacent obstruents that differ in voicing; f.voi penalizes disparity in voicing between corresponding input and output obstruents; f.hd.voi penalizes such disparity only when the output correspondent is in head position; and m.Voi penalizes all output voiced obstruents.

(7) ERC grammar of Y

C_1	C_2	C_3	C_4
W	*e*	**L**	*e*
e	**W**	**L**	*e*
e	e	**W**	**L**

Grammars like the three just cited must share all properties that follow from their identical ranking structure. This is true even if they are relevant to entirely incommensurable domains – one may be about syllables, the other about consonant voicing, as here, or their domains may even be further apart: managing an ecosystem, making a legal decision, making a choice of any kind. This realization leads to the notion of **Abstract OT** (AOT): the study of ranking structures in themselves, without calling on concrete candidates and constraints to generate them.

☐ As with *grammar*, so with *typology*. The extensional typology of a given concrete S is the collection of its extensional languages. The *intensional typology* of S is the set of grammars of its extensional languages. The intensional typology provides the natural setting for the study of Abstract OT. AOT is possible because both grammars and typologies are well-defined formal objects with an intrinsic structure that determines key aspects of their confrontation with the empirical. In AOT, any logically consistent ERC set is an ERC grammar, and any set of rankings that can be exactly delimited by a consistent ERC set is a ranking grammar. One of the main goals of this work is to characterize when a collection of grammars, or more broadly a partition of the set of rankings on S.Con, constitutes a valid typology.

Concrete OT relies on S.Gen and S.Con to produce the violation tableaux and comparative tableaux that determine the grammars of S. Abstract OT at its most concrete starts with the VTs, without regard to possible origins, and explicates their properties through the definitions of *optimality, language, grammar, typology.* Optimality doesn't see structures, only violation profiles. Abstract OT therefore can start from arrays of integers (or entities ordered like them) – VTs – to generate the grammars that are its province. And as more emerges in this work about the defining characteristics of grammars and typology, even VTs will shift to the background. From this point of view, a Concrete OT system $S = \langle S.\text{Gen}, S.\text{Con}\rangle$ which gives rise to a typology of languages always realizes an Abstract OT typology. All concrete typologies that realize the same abstract typology will be intensionally equivalent, in the sense that their ranking grammars are isomorphic, whether they are about prosody, conflict of laws, or ecological management. Everything that is true at the abstract level – and this investigation is dedicated to showing that there is much to be found there – must also be true of any of its realizations in the concrete. In practical analytical terms, we can access the properties of Abstract OT at the level of formal structure, or through its realizations; we'll do both here.

This distinction between a concrete system and the abstract principles that inform it pervades all forms of what Chomsky used to call 'rational inquiry' (see Chomsky 1988:41, for example). Perhaps mere ubiquity has diminished its role in familiar linguistic discourse: what we are doing here amounts to little more than insisting on it.

To encourage a sense of the relation, we cite a few striking examples. The principles behind the efficient stacking of oranges at the produce stand are the same as those behind designing an error-free code for transmitting pictures of distant planets.[7] Tree structure expresses constituency in phonology and syntax. String theory was invented to describe the strong force, was rousted from there by the quark, and re-emerged to dominate thinking about elementary particles that aspires to include gravitation.[8] Lexicographic optimization has uses ranging from linguistics to vehicle control, land planning, and psychological models of decision-making. Sports and politics often attract the same analysts because the relevant abstract principles of statistics are instantiated in both: to understand either baseball or politics, one must turn away from the balls, bats, and ballot boxes to grasp the disembodied principles that shape the outcomes.[9] There is, therefore, every reason to welcome the distinction between abstract and concrete and to embrace the techniques of analysis that allow us to see things from multiple perspectives.

The grammars that make up an intensional typology may be understood as either ranking grammars or ERC grammars. The ranking grammars of a typology partition the set of all possible rankings: they divide the set of all rankings into non-overlapping subsets.

A ranking grammar in Concrete OT is the set of all linear orders, legs, that give the same optima – those of the extensional language for which it

---

[7] Discussed in Wolchover 2013.

[8] This example has an interesting twist: it shows that understanding the abstract principles that animate a theory can be valuable even when a given concrete application of the theory falls short.

[9] Hence FiveThirtyEight, a premier site at this writing for sophisticated analysis of both. The always present, sometimes vitalizing tension between the abstract and the concrete, as well as between their practitioners, often turns on the validity of substantive premises. See e.g. Atkin (2014), Krugman (2014), Silver (2016).

is the grammar. Each leg determines a language in its entirety. From this, it follows that a given leg can belong to only one grammar. To see this, notice that if grammars share a leg, they share the extensional language, and they are therefore the same grammar, sharing *all* legs. Furthermore, every ranking must belong to some grammar. This means that the study of typologies is the study of certain kinds of partitions.

On the ERC side, the grammars of a typology are pairwise inconsistent: for any two grammars, each satisfies some ranking condition that contradicts a condition on the other, distinguishing their languages and guaranteeing that no leg can satisfy the ERC sets of both. Two grammars may share many ERCs, as well – for example, one language may be iambic, the other trochaic, while they are identical in every other respect. This means that the study of typologies is the study of certain families of ERC sets that cannot be conjoined together without incurring contradiction.

Just as with individual grammars, the notion of an intensional typology sets us loose from the linguistic substance that it aims to explicate. Our focus is to understand central properties that all concrete typologies must have by virtue of their being instances of abstract typologies, revealing the large-scale emergent consequences of the way optimality is defined in OT.

1.2 One tableau suffices

An extensional language is *finitely determined*: even when it contains an infinite number of optima, a well-chosen finite sample will fix all further choices. There may, of course, be many such determinative finite samples. Even when a single input yields, under *S*.GEN, an infinite number of violation profiles, only a finite number of them can be optimal. Finite determination follows from the finitude of the number of rankings, which provides a sharp upper bound for the number of grammars. Any finite collection of finite candidate sets that determines an extensional language will also determine the grammar of that language. Grammars are therefore also finitely determined. The study of grammar is the study of finite sets of rankings, or of finite sets of the ERCs that define them, deriving from a finite set of finite violation tableaux.

So: finitude everywhere outside *S*.GEN. But we can go further. From these observations, as well as from the empirical practice of Concrete OT, one might gather the impression that a number of different candidate sets, perhaps large (if finite), will be generally required to determine a typology. In some cases we can come up with a single input of sufficient complexity to generate the entire typology, one that manages to concatenate or otherwise contain all the relevant configurations. But there's no guarantee in Concrete

OT that this must happen. For example, in stress theory it is typically the case that inputs of different lengths must be examined – odd and even, or perhaps a monosyllable as well as longer lengths. But we will never be able to construct a string that is both odd and even in length, or both monosyllabic and polysyllabic.

If we attend to the *grammars* rather than to the languages, positioning ourselves within Abstract OT, the need for multiplicity of candidate sets disappears. Prince 2015b shows that any intensional typology – a collection of grammars, not languages – can always be characterized by a single violation tableau, which is of course finite.

Let's narrow our focus, then, without loss of generality, to a certain kind of typology-generating tableau, which we will call a 'Unitary Violation Tableau' or UVT. A UVT is minimal, in that its rows stand in a 1:1 relation with the grammars of the typology it generates, and vice versa. Thus, we require that each row of a UVT give rise to a distinct grammar, and we require that each grammar of a UVT's typology be associated with a unique row. From the filtration point of view, the grammar associated with a row – the grammar it 'gives rise to' – is the set of all legs that select that row as optimal. From the ERC point of view, the grammar associated with a row is the ERC set obtained by comparing that row against all the others. No row of a UVT can be harmonically bounded, because a bounded row does not give rise to a *grammar* – a non-empty leg set, or a logically consistent ERC set.

We may think of a UVT as containing a single abstract candidate set. Each 'language' consists of a single candidate. Each 'candidate' – each violation profile occupying a row of the UVT – is associated with a grammar, and each grammar with a candidate. Asserting a row as optimal yields the entirety of its associated grammar. In Abstract OT, a 'typology' is any collection of grammars produced from a UVT.

Any VT in which all the rows are distinct possible optima competing against each other can be interpreted as a UVT. To denote the typology associated with a UVT U, we will write T_U. To denote the set of all UVTs that produce a given typology T, we will write $\mathcal{U}(T)$.

(8) **Definition. Unitary Violation Tableau (UVT).** A Unitary Violation Tableau, abbreviated UVT, is a violation tableau with no duplicate or harmonically bounded rows, in which therefore each row, when taken as the designated optimum competing against the other rows, gives rise to a distinct grammar.

A formal definition is provided in ex. (7), §4.1. As noted, limiting the study of the notion 'intensional typology' to the collection of grammars derived from a single UVT places no restriction at all on our object of study, because of the following result.

(9) **Theorem. One tableau suffices.** Every intensional OT typology may be derived from a UVT.

Proof. See Prince 2015b.

In sum, each row of a UVT gives a distinct grammar of the typology; the entire set of rows gives the entire collection of grammars that comprise the typology. A grammar, by definition, contains all the legs that select the optima of that grammar's language. Thus, each leg of a given grammar selects from any one of its UVTs, by the usual filtration of VTs, the row that yields the grammar.

Here's an example, with arbitrarily named constraint columns and candidate rows.

(10) Specimen UVT

T	A	B	C
r	0	1	1
s	1	0	1
t	2	0	0

There is no implication as to what structures might be involved in concrete realizations of the typology; they needn't even be linguistic. And there is no sense of structure-detecting constraints that might produce the numbers, which are *just there*. Nevertheless, grammars are generated by the usual definition of optimality. If we wish for example to assert row *r* as optimal, the result is the following collection of ERCs, presented as a comparative tableau (CT).

(11) CT from (10) with *r* asserted as optimal

r as opt.	A	B	C
r~ *s*	**W**	**L**	*e*
r~ *t*	**W**	**L**	**L**

This CT tells us that one of the grammars of the intensional typology, the ranking grammar of row *r*, has the form $\mathrm{G_R}(r) = \{$A≫B≫C, A≫C≫B$\}$, which is exactly the set of two legs that satisfy the requirement 'A dominates both

B and C.' The ranking condition is given concisely by an ERC grammar $G_E(r) = \{WLL\}$, which contains the non-redundant content of the CT (11).[10]

To bring this example closer to the common experience of dealing with many candidate sets at once, we note that the very same grammar is produced by the following pair of csets, which indeed deliver the entire typology.

(12) Two csets yielding the typology T

T	cand	A	B	C
cset I	*a*	0	0	1
	b	1	0	0
cset II	*c*	0	1	1
	d	1	0	0

The grammar {WLL} of row *r* is obtained by choosing *a* and *c* as optima, which supply the ERCs W*e*L and WLL respectively. As the reader may verify, the comparison [*a* ~ *b*] delivers the ERC W*e*L, and the comparison [*c* ~ *d*] delivers WLL, which reduce logically to WLL, the content of CT (11). Numerous other equivalents exist as well: for example, if constraint B is modified by changing the value 0 to 1 in cset I, so that B(*a*) = B(*b*) = 1, the same grammars will result.[11]

This simple example illustrates the fact that any intensional typology whatever, constructed from no matter how many distinct csets, can always be exactly represented as a single VT, with just one abstract cset, as asserted in Theorem (9). Any row of such a UVT, when asserted to be optimal, generates the grammar of a unique language in the typology. **Therefore, understanding the grammatical structure of typologies reduces entirely to the study of typologies generated by a UVT.**

The preceding notions allow us to define precisely what we mean by 'typology', given only the OT notion of optimality. Consider the entire set of linear orders on a constraint set *S*.Con, which we have denoted by Ord(*S*.Con). A typology must partition Ord(*S*.Con). But not every such partition

---

[10] The original set {WL*e*, WLL} is also an ERC grammar of the same language. The ERC WL*e* is *entailed* by WLL by virtue of 'L-retraction', the ERC manipulation that mirrors the inference rule 'and-out', (p & q) ⊨ p. See Prince (2002a:7). The ERC WL*e* is therefore omitted in non-redundant representations of the grammar.

[11] It is reasonable to ask why csets I and II do not together generate 4 grammars, one for each possible pair of cset optima. Observe that the pair {*b*, *c*} is inconsistent: [*b* ~ *a*] = LeW and [*c* ~ *d*] = WLL, requiring both C≫A and A≫C. In terms of ERC logic, they *fuse* to LLL, indicating inconsistency: the impossibility of mutual satisfaction.

qualifies as a typology, either because some block of the partition is not a grammar, or because the grammars can't coexist in the same typology (§6 below). We don't need to clarify these failures before we define our object of study. A typology, in our sense, is *a partition of* Ord(*S*.CON) *which can be derived from a UVT*. This gives us a place to stand, which we will leverage to unfold the structures inherent in the definition of optimality.

(13) **Definition. Typology.** Given a set of constraints *S*.CON, a partition of the set of all orders on *S*.CON is a typology T iff there is a UVT U, with columns that correspond 1:1 to the constraints of *S*.CON and rows that correspond 1:1 to the grammars of T, such that each block in the partition T is the ranking grammar of a row in U.

1.3 Problems, problems, problems

Three basic structural questions arise from the abstract characterization of a typology as a set of grammars and from the availability of UVT representations. Here we outline the questions and indicate the answers. We then give an overview of the order and equivalence structure that we call a 'MOAT' and show how it resolves them.

Problem 1. Typological equivalence of UVTs

Any intensional typology can be derived from a UVT. But optimality depends on the relations between the entries, not their numerical values. Consequently, it will always be the case that many UVTs, with different numbers in them, produce the same intensional typology. They are *typologically equivalent*. What do these UVTs have in common?

Status: solved by the MOAT. The MOAT of a typology T identifies exactly those order and equivalence relations that each constraint must impose to produce the grammars of T. Every intensional typology has one and only one MOAT. And every MOAT is associated with one and only one intensional typology. This is the force of Theorem (155), §4.7. The order and equivalence relations in a typology's unique MOAT determine all of its possible numerical representations.

Problem 2. Compatibility of grammars within a typology

What conditions on mutual compatibility are imposed by a typology on its constituent grammars? An intensional typology turns out to be more than a set of pairwise disjoint ranking grammars, more than (equivalently) a set of pairwise inconsistent ERC grammars, exhausting Ord(*S*.CON). We must therefore ask: what conditions must a typology meet that a general partition of the ranking set doesn't have to?

Status: solved by the MOAT. A partition of the ranking set is a typology if and only if it has a well-formed MOAT (§4.8: Theorem (183)). Partitions that fail this condition may even consist of well-formed grammars (§6). Abstractly, this gives a formal characterization of the notion 'typology', paralleling the way that the notion 'grammar' is definable as an antimatroid, or as the set of linear extensions of an ERC set. Concretely, this finding provides a valuable tool which we will immediately make use of in dealing with the third problem.

Problem 3. Classification of languages and grammars

Classification and ranking. ERC grammars in a typology are pairwise inconsistent because they contradict one another on *some* ranking requirement. But even as grammars differ, they may also share other requirements, leading to groupings of languages that have ranking restrictions in common. The nature of these groupings is the central focus of Alber & Prince (2015–16 *et seq.*), under the Classification Program articulated there. In EST (Elementary Syllable Theory), for example, which will be studied in some detail below, EST.Con contains the markedness constraints m.Ons, m.NoCoda and the faithfulness constraints f.max and f.dep. One language may require f.dep ≫ f.max, another f.max ≫ f.dep. Of the eight languages in the typology, four share the first requirement, and four share the second. This kind of intensional patterning is native to Abstract OT; it can be discerned without any grasp of concrete particulars, and will of course be inherited in the concrete instances of an abstract typology. Considered intensionally, EST realizes an abstract four-constraint typology that has certain patterns of ranking relations defining its grammars.

On the extensional side, the *languages* of a typology will share and be distinguished by patterns of linguistic structure. In Elementary Syllable Theory, for example, one may observe that some languages require onsets in every syllable, and that others allow onsetless syllables under certain conditions; that some admit deletion and others epenthesis in the input-output mapping, and so on. In a typical stress typology, languages will differ in the size and shape of admissible feet: of the various types iambic, trochaic, unary, binary, some may be disallowed, some limited to certain positions; and so on. These shared and distinguishing traits are due to shared and distinguishing conditions on ranking. The Classification Program aims to explicate how intensional groupings, based on ranking patterns, impose a linguistically significant classification on the languages of a typology.

Consider the intensional contrast in EST between grammars requiring f.dep ≫ f.max and those requiring f.max ≫ f.dep. Concretely, the first ranking condition identifies the extensional languages where deletion rather than insertion appears in optima to avoid certain structural configurations; the second identifies those with insertion, not deletion. A complete *property analysis* in the Alber-Prince sense will reconstruct the entire typology in terms of the interactions of the ranking conditions that define its classes.

Such a ranking-based analysis not only gives insight into the functioning of the system $S = \langle S.\text{Gen}, S.\text{Con}\rangle$; it also resolves ambiguities that the plethora of extensional correlations may leave open. Going the other way, the possible extensional classes in a concrete instance of an abstract typology, determined by structural considerations, limit ambiguities in intensional analysis. A complete analysis of a typology mates intensional with extensional, giving an account of the way that ranking structure classifies the languages of the typology, relating theory (ranking patterns) to the data (patterns of linguistic structure). As Alber and Prince observe, it *is* the 'OT analysis' of the languages of a typology.

A class of grammars is associated with the union of individual ranking grammars of the class. From this perspective, a *class* of grammars is just another set of rankings.

Our goal in approaching Problem 3 is to resolve a fundamental formal question that underlies the Classification Program. In Abstract OT, any consistent ERC set defines a grammar. Therefore any *class* of grammars which can be delimited by a consistent ERC set is itself, formally, a *grammar*. In our EST example, the ranking condition 'f.dep ≫ f.max' is encodable as the ERC set {WL*ee*}, taking the constraints f.dep and f.max as the first two in the listing of EST.Con. Ranking-wise, this abstract grammar – this *class* – contains 12 of the 24 linear orders on EST.Con. Every ranking belongs to the grammar that shares its defining ERC set and to no others. There is no guarantee that abstract grammars of this sort will have a concrete instantiation in terms of concrete candidate sets made available by *S*.Gen for any particular system *S*. *But they are grammars nonetheless.* When a class of grammars is characterizable by a set of ERCs, we will call it a ***grammatical class***, meaning that it has formal status as a grammar. We can think of such a grammar as a generalization of the grammars that it is constructed from.

In EST, the insertion class is likewise given by an ERC set, namely {LW*ee*}, representing the condition 'f.max ≫ f.dep'. It is therefore also a grammatical class. The two classes taken together have an additional property: not only do they partition the set of rankings of *S*.Con into two disjoint subsets, each containing 12 rankings; it also happens that the partition they impose is abstractly a *typology*. Recall that an abstract typology is any collection of grammars derivable from a UVT. These two classes of EST, which we may call *Ins* and *Del*, are easily shown to meet the definition (13), which requires the existence of a witnessing UVT, provided here.

(14) Insertion/Deletion in EST: the two-language abstract typology 'Ins/Del'

Ins/Del	f.dep	f.max	m.Ons	m.NoCoda	Remarks
Ins	0	1	0	0	*Ins* optimal ⇔ f.dep ≫ f.max
Del	1	0	0	0	*Del* optimal ⇔ f.max ≫ f.dep

It may be directly verified that choice of the row labeled *Del* as optimal yields the deletional grammar {WL*ee*}, while choice of *Ins* yields the insertional grammar {LWee}, as promised. From the perspective of EST, the classes consist of all those grammars that delete problematic C/V and all those that epenthesize to support them syllabically.[12]

This example illustrates an entirely general phenomenon. Just as the amalgamation of several grammars can lead to an abstract *grammar* that represents their shared properties, so too can the amalgamation of grammars within a specific typology lead to another abstract *typology* which represents not just the properties of various sets of grammars, but also the ways that they are distinct from each other.[13] In example (14), we have constructed the abstract typology 'Ins/Del' which generalizes EST by amalgamating all inserting languages (pooling their legs) into one super-grammar and all deleting languages into the other. In cases like this, where amalgamations result in a well-formed typology, we will call any resulting generalized grammar a ***typological class***. What our example shows, in these terms, is that in EST there are typological classes 'inserter' and 'deleter', each of which generalizes over a subset of the languages in the typology of EST, producing

[12] In this simple case we can find an input from EST.GEN that produces the result, namely /C/. If we restrict *S*.GEN to provide just the one input /C/ while setting *S*.CON = EST.CON, then *S* will have exactly the typology (14), which divides the set of rankings into two classes. In this case, the cset derived from the input /C/ has only two possible optimal outputs, $[CV]_\sigma$ with epenthesis, and ε, the empty string, arrived at by deletion. This concretely instantiates the abstract typology 'Ins/Del'. In this fortuitous case, the concrete leads directly to the abstract. Generically, more subtle tools are needed.

[13] Formally, this is connected with the fact that the set of all possible typologies on *n* constraints is a lattice under refinement/coarsening (Prince 2013, 2015b). It is not a *sublattice* of the partition lattice because sups/joins may differ due to the extra requirements that a typology (as opposed to a generic partition) must meet.

a generalized typology that expresses this classification. The (moderately) abstract typology (14) classifies concrete EST along one of its structural dimensions.

With the notion of a typological class in place, we stand on the threshold of the first formal step in the Classification Program: obtaining the typological classes of a typology. To advance, we need to know when a collection of languages within a typology constitutes a typological class.

Our specific goal, then, is to answer the following question: under what conditions can several grammars in a given typology be amalgamated into a single more general grammar within a generalized typology?

Status: solved by the MOAT. Since every typology has a MOAT, amalgamation must produce a new MOAT. When it produces a structure that does not qualify as a MOAT, the resulting classes do not constitute a (generalized) typology.[14] When it does, they do.

With the three motivating questions now on display, we proceed to an overview of their treatment in the following sections (§1.4, §1.5, §1.6), introducing the MOAT concept in terms of a simple example. Our aim is to show how the MOAT is used to resolve the three questions. Details of MOAT construction will be pursued in the sections following, through a more complete contemplation of EST.

1.3.1 *Typological equivalence*

Problem 1. ***E Pluribus Unum.*** Every grammatical typology comes from a UVT. But many numerically distinct UVTs deliver the same typology. There is an algorithm ('Minkowski summation', as shown in Prince 2015b) that produces a single UVT from any set of VTs. That UVT is provably equivalent to the entire original VT collection, in the sense that they have exactly the same grammars. We refer to UVTs that produce the same typology as 'typologically equivalent'.

---

[14] The details can be given in the following concise form. The MOAT is a set of order and equivalence structures, EPOs, each of which represents the essential content of a single constraint. A UVT relates language to language, grammar to grammar. The MOAT delimits every UVT that yields the same typology. An EPO is representable by a kind of augmented Hasse-like diagram which marks equivalence as well as order. Whether or not a set of languages in a typology can be amalgamated into a typological class is determined by the structure of the EPO diagrams in its MOAT. The union of grammars into a class corresponds to merging their nodes in the MOAT to produce a modified graph of their relations. If merger produces a well-formed MOAT, then a generalized typology results, corresponding to that MOAT and consisting of valid typological classes that analyze the original typology. If not, then not. Graphically, as we will see shortly, this boils down to whether node merger introduces order-involving directed cycles (fatal) or retains the acyclic character of the EPOs in a legitimate MOAT.

(15) **Definition. Typologically equivalent.** Two UVTs based on the same constraint set are *typologically equivalent* if the typologies associated with each are identical.

A typology can typically be derived from many different collections of candidate sets, and the Minkowski sum algorithm will produce typologically equivalent UVTs from all of them. Thus, from concrete considerations alone, given a typical unbounded linguistic object as our target, we are already guaranteed an unlimited number of distinct UVTs grounded in linguistic fact. If we step away from concrete linguistic analysis, we will find many more UVTs – taken as arrays of integers – which produce any given typology. What is it that all these UVTs have in common which ties them to the same typology? The MOAT gives the answer.

Abstractly put, but with the specificity of an example, let's return to the UVT of example (10) above, with the rows labeled r and t swapped positionally for convenience, retaining the labels. We will display other UVTs that produce the same ranking typology, and then see how their shared patterns of equivalence and order are represented in a MOAT diagram.

(16) Specimen UVT

T	A	B	C
t	2	0	0
s	1	0	1
r	0	1	1

This yields a 3-grammar typology which we'll call 'T'. Certain numerical properties are accessible from experience with OT analysis: for example, we *cannot* change any of the 0s here, leaving the other numbers in place, without altering the ranking structure.[15] But further questions arise:

Q1. Consider the numerically-based order relations between languages in column A. Using functional notation to denote the values assigned by the constraint A, we have $\mathsf{A}(r) < \mathsf{A}(s) < \mathsf{A}(t)$. Any UVT with the same order relations in A will yield the same treatment of candidates by A, and therefore

[15] Consider the total order C≫A≫B. This selects t. If we modify the C value of t to 1, then this total order now selects r, which is no longer ejected at the first step of filtration. In the case at hand, as the reader may verify, none of the 0's may be altered without crucially altering the filtration patterns, and therefore the grammars of the typology. For further analysis, see §4.5.4 and especially Theorem (84), 'Filtration Uniformity'.

the same ranking information. Must these order relations be respected in *every* typologically equivalent UVT? Answer: ***Yes.***

Q2. Consider the relation between r and s in column C. Because $\mathsf{C}(r) = \mathsf{C}(s) = 1$, row r is treated as equivalent to row s with respect to C. The same holds for any UVT in which r and s assume identical values, so long as they are greater than zero. But must this equality be respected in *every* typologically equivalent UVT? Answer: ***No.***

We sketch here how all such questions can be comprehensively settled.

To begin with, and to dispel the air of pure formality, we will concretize within an OT system that makes direct contact with known linguistics.

Let's simplify a theory of stress patterns, following Alber & Prince (2015–2016, 2021). Let an input be a string of syllables, treated as unanalyzed atomic units as they are in the 'quantity insensitive' prosodic regime. For outputs, let feet of one or two syllables distribute freely anywhere throughout the string, with the proviso that at least one foot must be present. That's it: no further gradations of stress degrees, no syllable quantity, no deletion or insertion. (Many languages in the literature are in fact described as having stress patterns of this type.) This gives us the system nGX; the acronym refers to a 'new' definition of Iamb and Trochee constraints,[16] the use of Generalized Alignment, and the presence of stress (X) in every word.

To simplify yet further, let's drop one alignment constraint, leaving only AFL 'All Feet Left', and drop one foot-type constraint, leaving only Iamb. This leaves us with nGX.IL, nGX-Iambic-Left, simple but not trivial. The constituency can be rendered in the 'OTWorkplace notation' by writing 'X' for the head of a foot, 'u' for the nonhead of a foot, and 'o' for an unfooted syllable, with feet separated by periods. Here's a sample of admitted candidates, not all of which are possible optima, chosen to give the flavor of the system:

[16] The definitions of Iamb and Trochee are 'new' in that they each penalize not just the binary foot of opposite headedness but also the unary foot, which is therefore neither 'iambic' nor 'trochaic', as opposed to the paleoclassical conception in which the unary foot is both. See Alber & Prince (2017, 2021, in prep) for discussion.

(17) nGX.IL candidates (sample)

/σσσ/ →	.uX.o
	o.uX.
	.o.o.X.
	X.X.X.
	etc.
/σσσσσ/→	.uX.uX.o.
	.uX.o.uX.
	.X.uX.uX.
	.uX.o.o.o.
	etc.

The 3 constraints of nGX.IL are Parse-σ, AFL, and Iamb. In the interests of adhering to the demands of OT, we spelled out the system in the canonical *S*.GEN-*S*.CON fashion.

(18) nGX.IL.GEN

i. A *candidate* consists of an *input* and an *output*.

ii. An *input* is a sequence of *syllables* σ^n, $n \geq 1$, where σ is a primitive.

iii. Cset: an input σ^n with outputs being all admitted prosodic parses of *n* syllables.

iv. A *prosodic parse* of σ^n consists of a single Prosodic Word embracing the whole string, with the PrWd node dominating *at least one foot* (F) and perhaps many feet, which need not be sequential.

v. A *foot* contains one or two syllables, and has one head.

The three constraints of nGX.IL may be specified as follows:

(19) nGX.IL.CON

Parse-σ	*o	=	card{σ ∈ out(ϰ) | σ ∉ F}
Iamb	$*[_F\, \sigma'$	=	card{ $[_F\, \sigma'$ ∈ out(ϰ)}
AFL	*(σ,F): σ...F	=	card{(σ,F) ∈ out(ϰ) | σ precedes F}

Notation. The head of a foot is written σ′. We use the OT * operator to define constraints: *x:P(x) takes a candidate κ as its argument (left implicit) and returns the number of matches to the pattern P(x), running over all occurrences of P(x) in the candidate κ. We recruit '∈' to denote any relevant version of 'belongs to', and we write '...' to express linear precedence. The formulation of the alignment constraint All-Feet-Left, abbreviated AFL, adapts Hyde 2012.

Thus defined, nGX.IL is a Concrete OT system. Its typology is provably determined by the 5-syllable candidate set, which has 3 optima, listed here. (See Alber & Prince *op. cit.* for the richer system nGX, which contains the symmetrically defined constraints Trochee and AFR. See Alber, DeBusso, and Prince 2016 for general characterization of the candidate sets that suffice to generate the whole typology.)

(20) Optima of thc 5σ csct of nGX.IL

5σ					
Input	output	Parse-σ	Iamb	AFL	Class name
σσσσσ	.uX.o.o.o.	3	0	0	sparse (sp)
	.uX.uX.o.	1	0	2	weakly dense (WD)
	.X.uX.uX.	0	1	4	strongly dense (SD)

Comparison with the abstract specimen UVT (16) shows some numerical divergences. These do not affect the intensional typology generated, as may be readily calculated. Thus, nGX.IL provides a concrete instance of T.

Each of these optima belongs to a structural class, schematized here with 'F' for bisyllabic foot:

i. **Sparse** (sp), taking the form Fo^n, with one foot per word.
ii. **Weakly Dense** (WD), taking the from $F^n(o)$.
iii. **Strongly Dense** (SD), taking the form $(X)F^n$.

These easily recognizable structural types suggest, correctly, that we are looking at a useful simplification of the richer and more symmetrical system nGX. The 5-syllable candidate set does the work of finding a single, typology-generating VT, without further calculation. Below we re-label it '**X**' as a UVT for the system. Constraint names are prefixed with 'uvt' to emphasize that they no longer refer to the familiar functions defined above, as they now assign values to abstract candidates rather than linguistic forms.

(21) UVT X of T = nGX.IL with language names

X	uvt.Parse-σ	uvt.Iamb	uvt.AFL
sp	3	0	0
WD	1	0	2
SD	0	1	4

Now we step away from the specifics and assemble some VTs that produce exactly the same set of grammars. Particularly striking are the differences in the uvt.AFL column, boxed, where the relationship between the non-zero values runs through all the order possibilities. Since we have several UVTs at play, we switch to a row-labeling notation that is easy to compare across UVTs.

(22) Another UVT for T

U	uvt.Parse-σ	uvt.lamb	uvt.AFL
u_1	3	0	0
u_2	1	0	4
u_3	0	1	2

(23) And another UVT for T

V	uvt.Parse-σ	uvt.lamb	uvt.AFL
v_1	3	0	0
v_2	2	0	2
v_3	1	2	4

(24) And another

W	uvt.Parse-σ	uvt.lamb	uvt.AFL
w_1	7	7	0
w_2	5	7	2
w_3	3	18	2

We can sensibly compare the typologies of these UVTs because they correlate columns by constraint name; and rows are arranged so that the same grammar correlates with serial position. For example, sp ~ u_1 ~ v_1~ w_1 in that all yield identical grammars, and so on.

To see that the UVTs are typologically equivalent, as claimed, note first that uvt.Parse-σ and uvt.lamb impose the same order relations on cognate rows in all UVTs. Since OT comparison works on order, not quantity, the relevant relations between the candidates filter identically in each UVT on these two constraints.

By contrast, the values assigned by uvt.AFL all differ in **U**, **V**, and **W** (22)–(24). Were the differences typologically significant, they would distinguish the 2nd and 3rd rows from each other in some filtration. But this does not happen: no matter where it appears in a leg, uvt.AFL *never* decides the pair {WD, SD} or any of its cognates $\{u_2, u_3\}$, $\{v_2, v_3\}$, $\{w_2, w_3\}$.

To see this, suppose first that uvt.AFL is the top-ranked constraint in some leg: in this case it ejects both, which then simultaneously vanish from the filtration sequence. Now suppose the top-ranked constraint is uvt.Parse-σ or uvt.lamb. Each of these distinguishes between u_2/u_3, v_2/v_3, w_2/w_3, ejecting one of them. In this case, uvt.AFL never sees the entire pair.

What, then, do all these typologically equivalent UVTs have in common? To obtain the answer, we must attend to those relations that have impact on selecting optima. Since the numerical values are integers, there are only two kinds of relevant relations that can hold between them: equivalence (equality) and order (greater than, less than).

In uvt.AFL, concrete WD and its abstract cognates u_2, v_2, w_2 stand variously in every possible relation with their competitors SD, u_3, v_3, w_3.

(25) Numerical relations within the constraint uvt.AFL

UVT	uvt.AFL			Ref
X	WD	<	SD	(21)
U	u_2	>	u_3	(22)
V	v_2	<	v_3	(23)
W	w_2	=	w_3	(24)

Because all four UVTs are known to be typologically equivalent, this unstable relationship can have no impact on the filtration of the candidate set.

Finding stability across the set of all UVTs is what's necessary. Heuristically, we can observe that certain orders and equalities hold in the sample that we've amassed.

(26) Some stable relations in the sample

uvt.Parse-σ	**uvt.lamb**	**uvt.AFL**
WD < sp	WD = sp	sp < WD
$u_2 < u_1$	$u_2 = u_1$	$u_2 < u_1$
$v_2 < v_1$	$v_2 = v_1$	$v_2 < v_1$
$w_2 < w_1$	$w_2 = w_1$	$w_2 < w_1$

We wish to conclude that these relations appear in *all* UVTs of the typology: but this requires more than citing a few favorable instances. A brute force attack would simply enumerate tableaux containing every possible order/equality relation between the entries in each column and check to see which of them give rise to the targeted typology. This method is, of course, computational in the least interesting sense, since it offers no insight into any aspect of typological structure: we cite it only to abandon it.

It is far more instructive focus on the grammars themselves, construed as leg sets. The fundamental relationship turns out to be the one between 'adjacent' or minimally different legs. For our purposes, any linear order on all the constraints of any *S*.CON can be parsed like this: PXYQ, where X, Y are distinct individual constraints and P, Q are sequences of constraints, possibly empty. Every leg has this form, assuming *S*.CON has more than one constraint.

We will say that PXYQ is 'adjacent' to PYXQ, a leg identical to it except for a flip in the order of the two neighboring constraints X and Y (underlined for emphasis). This notion defines a skein of adjacencies that encompasses the entire leg set: it is possible to move between any two arbitrary legs along a path between them that consists of pairwise of adjacent legs (see §7 below for further discussion and analysis).

Leg adjacency gives rise to grammar adjacency. Two *grammars* are adjacent if one contains a leg PXYQ, the other a leg PYXQ. These form a 'border point pair', and yield the information that the ranking relation X ≫ Y plays a crucial role in one of the grammars, and Y ≫ X in the other.[17] Further information is contained in the prefix P: in filtration by either leg, both grammars must successfully pass through all the constraints in P, in which case both must receive the same value on each constraint in P.

The information about a constraint that derives from border point pairs is recorded in its EPO, the 'Equivalence-augmented Privileged Order' structure which represents the order and equivalence relations that any instantiation of the constraint will impose. The MOAT collects the EPO of each constraint.

Here and in the following two introductory sections, we present EPOs as given objects, illustrating how their structure contributes to solutions of the three central problems: typological equivalence, compatibility of grammars within a typology, classification of grammars. The order relations in an EPO are 'privileged' in that they derive ultimately from adjacent grammars and play a crucial role in resolving the grammar-compatibility problem. How information from adjacent grammars is used to construct EPOs will be examined concretely through examples in §3.2 and §3.3 below, and studied in detail in §4.

The EPO is a relational structure, and as such can be portrayed as a graphical object with directed and undirected edges. An EPO diagram is similar to but richer than the ubiquitous Hasse diagram, in that it represents two distinct relations; we will therefore term it a 'bigraph'. In an EPO bigraph, we mark the *order* relations (directed) with single-headed red arrows and the *equivalence* relations (undirected) with double blue lines. Under these conventions, the MOAT for the simplified stress theory nGX.IL looks like this:

---

[17] The role may be as a disjunct, as in 'X ≫ Y *or* Z ≫ Y', a condition of the form ...WLW... .

(27) MOAT(nGX.IL)

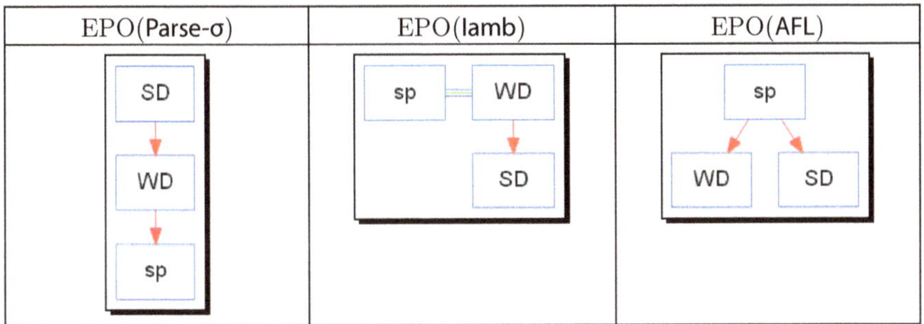

To represent the portrayed relations symbolically, we will write $<^{\text{bp.C}}$ for the order, and $\sim^{\text{bp.C}}$ for the equivalence, signaling their border-point origins. The cited diagram for EPO(Parse-σ) tells us immediately that SD $<^{\text{bp.Parse-}\sigma}$ WD and WD $<^{\text{bp.Parse-}\sigma}$ sp.

The EPO for Parse-σ indicates, exactly as we've claimed, that the order relations implicit in the violation values assigned by Parse-σ in the VT (21) are universally required. Qualitatively speaking, the Parse-σ EPO indicates that SD is better parsed than sp and WD, and that WD is in turn better parsed than sp. As it happens, grammars SD and sp are adjacent, but as in Hasse diagrams, the order between them is not shown explicitly because it can be derived from transitivity of the order relation.[18] In the lingo, a Hasse diagram is said to be *transitively reduced*, and we follow this practice in representing the orders in an EPO diagram.[19]

Although these judgments pertain to entire grammars rather than to linguistic forms, they are not shocking. In a Strongly Dense language, with optima (X)F^n, for F bisyllabic, *every* output is fully parsed, with no violations of Parse-σ in any form. In Weakly Dense, with optima F^n(o), all *even* forms are fully parsed, but odd forms of length 3 or greater have one unparsed syllable, earning one violation of Parse-σ. And in Sparse, with optima Fo^n, all forms 3 syllables or longer have $1, 2, \ldots$ unparsed syllables, with length n having $n-2$ of them, earning $n-2$ violations of Parse-σ. For any given form, then, it is literally true that SD is equally (even lengths) or better parsed (odd lengths) than WD, which is equally (lengths 3σ and less)

---

[18] Adjacency: SD contains a leg Parse-σ ≫ AFL ≫ lamb and sp contains the adjacent leg AFL ≫ Parse-σ ≫ lamb.

[19] See e.g. the article Hasse diagram in Wikipedia.

or better parsed (4σ and longer) than sp. Note that in each case, there are forms where the inequalities are strict.[20]

This pattern reflects the general situation. If two grammars are ordered in the EPO for a constraint, that ordering cannot be numerically reversed in any cset of their associated languages, where optima from the corresponding languages are compared (Theorem (160), §4.7). By contrast, if two grammars are *equivalent* in an EPO for a constraint C, not only must the entire corresponding languages be equal on C in each UVT; the *optima* of associated concrete languages must be evaluated as equal by C within their csets in any concrete instantiation of the typology, indeed in any collection of csets that delivers the grammars of the typology, whether or not the csets have a concrete interpretation (Theorem (159), §4.7). EPO relations hold in every UVT that yields a given typology, and they impose structure on multiple candidate set decompositions of the typology as well. This gives local content to the notion that one grammar can, in its entirety, be better than or equivalent to another.

As noted, the EPO diagram of Parse-σ, as presented here, does not explicitly indicate that there is a *privileged relation* between SD and sp, because that relation follows by transitivity. If we include transitively derivable information in order to better display the underlying adjacency structure, we obtain the following, which violates the norms of the Hasse diagram.

---

[20] These observations allow us to make precise sense of the intuitive idea that one language can be better parsed than another. Enumerate the candidate sets of nGX.IL in some way. The language we have called SD can be thought of as a (longish) list or vector **SD** with the optimum of candidate set k sitting in component k of **SD**, and similarly for the other languages.

Let a given constraint, for example Parse-σ, written in this guise as *ps*, evaluate the vector of optima **SD** at each component, producing a numerical vector, call it $ps(\mathbf{SD})$, and so on for the other constraints. For any C, these numerical vectors $c(\mathbf{SD})$ can be ordered componentwise. In this order, which we'll notate as $<_{coord}$, we have in the case of nGX.IL that $ps(\mathbf{SD}) <_{coord} ps(\mathbf{WD})$, because at each component n, we have numerically $ps(\mathbf{SD})[n] \leq ps(\mathbf{WD})[n]$ and at some component k, $k > 1$ and odd, we have $ps(\mathbf{SD})[k] < ps(\mathbf{WD})[k]$. This is the sense in which the language SD is *better parsed* than the language WD. Writing G_i for the grammar and $\mathbf{L}_i$ for its vector of optima, in the general case we have, with respect to the order $<^{bp.C}$ in the EPO of C, that $G_i <^{bp.C} G_j \Rightarrow c(\mathbf{L}_i) <_{coord} c(\mathbf{L}_j)$. EPO equivalence implies equality, so that $G_i \sim^{bp.C} G_j \Rightarrow c(\mathbf{L}_i) = c(\mathbf{L}_j)$. An example is provided by lamb in MOAT (27). See also p. 171 below.

Observe, however, that the converse does not hold. For example, it's true that for every input, the SD optimum is equally or worse *left-aligned* then the WD optimum – the odd lengths of SD have that extra unary foot, the even lengths are parsed identically. Thus, $afl(\mathbf{WD}) <_{coord} afl(\mathbf{SD})$. But, as we've seen, the numerical relations between WD and SD on AFL play no role in filtration and therefore no role in determining the ranking structure of the grammars. Consequently, WD and SD are *not* ordered in the EPO of AFL, as shown in (27). OT filtration works by lexicogaphic order, and this has effects beyond those of componentwise order.

(28) Adjacency-faithful EPO Representation of EPO(Parse-σ), *deprecated in this work.*

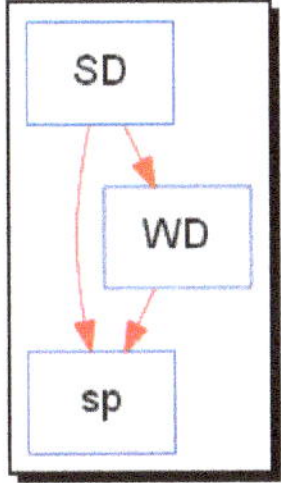

This fuller representation supports exactly the same inferences about orders as the transitively reduced one, so we eschew its full portrayal of adjacency, because it plays no role in the analysis developed here, even if it may conceivably prove useful or instructive in other circumstances.

With the MOAT (27) lodged in mind, let's go all the way back to our starting point in Concrete OT, the 5σ cset of nGX.IL. We can now disentangle the necessary relations from the artifacts of concreteness.

(29) UVT from a single input for nGX.IL

5σ	Output	Parse-σ	lamb	AFL
σσσσσ	.uX.o.o.o. (sp)	3	0	0
	.uX.uX.o. (WD)	1	0	2
	.X.uX.uX. (SD)	0	1	4

Let's compare these values with the demands imposed by each EPO.

(30) EPO(Parse-σ) of nGX.IL

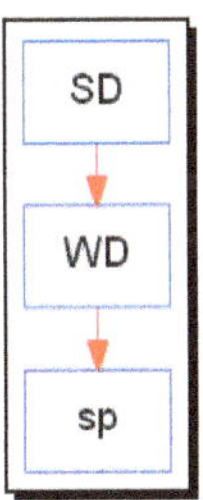

The EPO(Parse-σ) requirements are instantiated in the values in VT (29) as follows.[21]

i. SD $<^{\text{bp.Parse-}\sigma}$ WD $0 < 1$
ii. WD $<^{\text{bp.Parse-}\sigma}$ sp $1 < 3$

The cited numerical order relations are all necessary, though of course the values in (29) are determined by concrete considerations: any strictly increasing numerical triple will produce the same rankings.

(31) EPO(Iamb) of nGX.IL

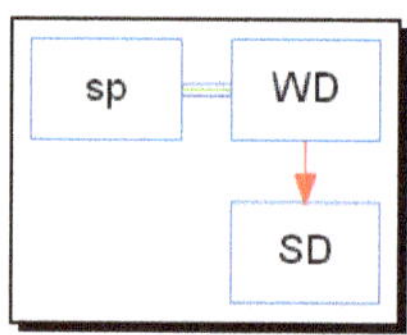

The EPO(Iamb) requirements are instantiated in VT (29) as follows:

i. sp $\sim^{\text{bp.Iamb}}$ WD $0 = 0$
ii. WD $<^{\text{bp.Iamb}}$ SD $0 < 1$

In terms of the cset decomposition of the concrete grammars, it follows that competing Sparse and Weakly Dense optima must always have the same value on Iamb. In concrete reality, Sparse and Weakly Dense optima are shaped Fo^n and F^no, where F is a binary iambic foot. These forms never have feet that are non-iambic, always being evaluated at 0 by the constraint Iamb. Furthermore, in any UVT the shared value of their cognates must be strictly less than that of the cognate of Strongly Dense. In the concrete world of csets, even-length Strongly Dense optima are identical to even-length Weakly Dense optima, with both shaped F^n, weighing in iambically at 0. But odd-length Strongly Dense forms X-F^n always display a single monosyllabic foot, defined as non-iambic, earning the evaluation of 1 on Iamb. This exemplifies the fact that an EPO order relation can never be reversed in any cset that is part of a multi-cset rendering of a typology, as shown below in Theorem (160), §4.7.3.

[21] An account of the details of relational instantiation is provided in definitions (17) and (18), §4.3.3, p. 96.

(32) EPO(AFL) of nGX.IL

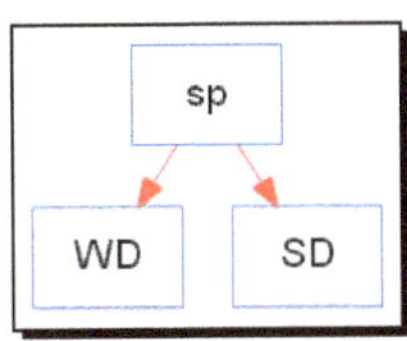

The EPO(AFL) requirements are instantiated in VT (29) as follows:

i. sp $<^{\text{bp.AFL}}$ WD $0 < 2$

ii. sp $<^{\text{bp.AFL}}$ SD $0 < 4$

Because evaluation lives among the integers, a further relation is forced on us: $2 < 4$. This exceeds the requirements of EPO(AFL). The appearance of order between WD and SD languages in the values of VT (29) is artifactual from the grammatical point of view. It holds in some of the concrete instantiations of the intensional typology, of which the 5σ cset of nGX.IL is just one. As noted at the outset of this discussion, AFL values are never called on to choose between WD and SD. In the concrete world of nGX.IL, the WD violations of AFL incurred by optima are always equal to (even forms) or less than (odd forms) those of SD, but this has – perhaps unexpectedly – no effect on the functioning of the grammar. Consequently, as we've seen in UVTs (21)–(24), there exist renderings of the typology in which the cognates of WD and SD stand in any relation whatever with respect to AFL.

We conclude with a note on the nature of privilege. EPO(lamb) given in (31) imposes just two numerical relations, writing lamb(L) to signify the value lamb assigns to L:

lamb(sp) = lamb(WD)
lamb(WD) < lamb(SD)

It follows arithmetically that lamb(sp) < lamb(SD) – and this holds of the corresponding languages in all UVTs of nGX.IL. But *no relation* between sp and SD is included in EPO(lamb). Only 'privileged' orders appear in an EPO, and privileged status develops from a pairwise relation between legs of adjacent grammars (§3.2), with transitivity imposed on it to produce a partial order, which is represented graphically as it is in a Hasse diagram. The EPO does not recognize any interaction between equivalence and order; this involves a further consideration, 'hypertransitivity' in our terminology, which is examined in detail in §4. Continuing our focus on the properties of the EPO object, we observe that different privileged relations may define the very same numerical instantiations. For example, the following valid EPO structures sponsor exactly the same numerical realizations for the constraints they epitomize, but will appear in different typologies with distinct UVTs.

(33) Distinct EPO structures

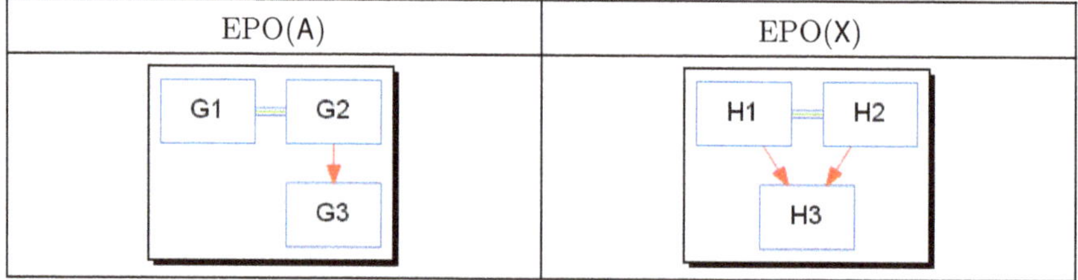

For example, the following UVTs generate EPO(A) and EPO(X), respectively, with grammars coindexed to rows.

U	A	B	C
u_1	0	0	2
u_2	0	1	1
u_3	1	1	0

V	X	Y	Z
v_1	0	0	2
v_2	0	1	1
v_3	1	0	0

The UVTs differ critically in columns B and Y.

As we will see in §1.3.3, this distinction in privilege has important consequences for the classification of the participating languages. In particular, EPO(A) obstructs the amalgamation of G_3 and G_1 as a typological class, allowing only G_2 and G_3 to merge, while EPO(X) obstructs the amalgamation of H_3 with H_2 as well as with H_1. This effect is examined in the discussion of ex. (36) below.

1.3.2 Compatibility of grammars within a typology

Johnson could see no bicycle would go.
'You bear yourself, and the machine as well.'
– Empson

Problem 2. ***Why can't we all just get along?*** An intensional typology is a collection of grammars. But not every collection of grammars is a typology. We know that any typology must be generable by a UVT, so that lack of a generating UVT is fatal. The issue then becomes: what properties of a collection of ranking grammars will prevent it from having a UVT?

Recall that no two grammars in a typology can share a leg, because each leg of a grammar delivers all of its optima. By definition, same optima implies same grammar. Nor can there be a ranking that is not assigned to a grammar in the typology. A typology, as we have noted, is therefore minimally a partition of the set of all rankings, which divides the set into non-overlapping subsets. Necessarily, then, each ranking grammar in a typology is a block in a partition of Ord(S.CON), the entire set of possible rankings on the constraints of S.

A partition can fail to be a typology for two reasons. First, a block of the partition may not be a grammar. This happens when the set of linear orders constituting the block is not characterizable by an ERC set. Second, and perhaps in defiance of naïve intuition, a partition may consist of well-formed grammars but still fail to be a typology.

To see how a partition can fail to consist of grammars, consider a simple Abstract OT system with three constraints X, Y, Z. Partition the set of 6 rankings into two blocks. Let the first block be {XYZ, YXZ}, where (as usual in this work) sequencing notates ranking order. The legs of this block are delimited by the requirement that both X and Y dominate Z. For this reason, we can call it ZBot, indicating that Z is at the bottom of every ranking in the grammar and no other conditions apply. Its complement 'co-ZBot' contains all the other rankings. It is delimited by the condition 'Z ≫ X *or* Z ≫ Y', as may be ascertained through logic or through inspection of its contents: co-ZBot = {ZXY, ZYX, YZX, XZY}.

The ZBot block has a familiar ranking pattern given by the ERC set {WeL, eWL}, assuming the constraints are listed in alphabetical order. Grammars of this form were originally noticed in subsystems of Elementary Syllable Theory (see P&S:112ff). In the form of {f.max, f.dep} ≫ m.Ons, 'Ons-Bot' in our terms, the grammar yields the no-deletion, no-insertion languages in which onsetless syllables are allowed in optima because no breach of faithfulness can be called on to avoid them. Symmetrically, the grammar {f.max, m.Ons} ≫ f.dep, 'Dep-Bot', yields 'Onset Required' languages where insertion eliminates the possibility of onsetless syllables. And {f.dep, m.Ons} ≫ f.max, 'Max-Bot', yields 'Onset Required' languages where deletion is called on to deliver onsetted syllables.

VTs like those in which m.Ons (or m.NoCoda) contends with f.dep and f.max assume the following shape. For perspicuity, we have named the rows after the grammars they deliver.

(34) The 3 Bots

3 Bots	X	Y	Z
ZBot	0	0	1
YBot	0	1	0
XBot	1	0	0

The crisis comes when we try to implant ZBot in a typology with just one other block, co-ZBot, which is the union of the legs associated with XBot and YBot. No ERC or set of ERCs can represent the condition 'Z≫X *or* Z≫Y'.[22] The block co-ZBot is not ERC-characterizable and hence not a grammar. The two-block partition {ZBot, co-ZBot} is not a typology for the most elemental reason: it does not consist of grammars.

Let's now turn to the second, subtler shortfall in which a partition consists of grammars but fails to be a typology.[23] There will be no UVT that generates it, even though each block is a grammar and can appear in some other typology. The simplest cases show up in systems with 4 constraints and will be examined below in §6.2. Being together in a typology thus requires a certain kind of compatibility between grammars. Two fundamental questions then arise. Suppose $\mathcal{P}$ is a collection of grammars that partitions the set of all rankings of some constraint set:

i. Is $\mathcal{P}$ a typology?
ii. If $\mathcal{P}$ is a typology, which UVTs produce it?

Both are resolved by the MOAT. The principles of MOAT construction (§3.2) can be applied to any partition of the ranking set. If a well-formed MOAT results, we have not just a partition composed of grammars, but a partition that is guaranteed to be a typology (§4.8, (183)). Furthermore, as

---

[22] It can't be {LLW} – 'Z dominates *both* X and Y'. It can't be {LeW, eLW}, which is equivalent to {LLW}. Observe that no one constraint is subordinated in the rankings of co-ZBot: X, Y, Z all appear top-ranked in some leg. Therefore, no ERC that describes the typology can contain an L in any constraint, which would require that it be subordinated in every leg of the grammar. The only grammar that this set belongs to is the trivial grammar that includes all rankings. See §6 for calculation of this fact via the *join*, an ERC-logic based operation introduced in Merchant (2008).

[23] Every grammar belongs to *some* typology. We can take an ERC grammar represented in a CT and mechanically construct a VT according to the following recipe. First, add a row containing only 1s, representing the target grammar. Then for each ERC, add a row, using these numerical values: set W = 2, L = 0, *e* = 1. Comparing the first row, having all 1s, with each subsequent row recreates the ERCs in the original CT. The typology of the constructed VT contains the target grammar.

we have emphasized, *all* UVTs that produce the typology are determined by the order and equivalence relations represented in the EPOs of the MOAT (§4.7, Theorem (152), 'Instantiating the MOAT'). Conversely, failure to produce a well-formed MOAT signals that the collection of blocks is not a typology.

To see how this works, consider first the Bot/coBot partition on three constraints. Using the techniques that will be developed in §3.2, we find that it sponsors the relations portrayed in (35) below.

(35) Bigraphs of the Bot/coBot typology

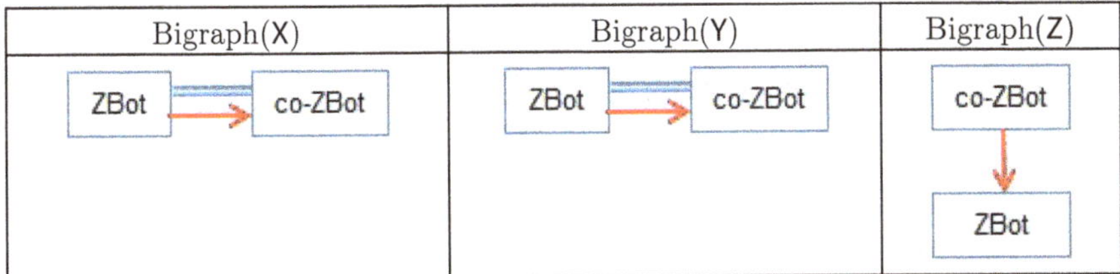

Because these take us outside of what a UVT can produce, they exhibit relations that are not found in EPOs. Nevertheless, the bigraph notation developed for the EPO is exactly what we need to diagnose a non-typological partition.

Objects that involve a set with an equivalence relation on it are known as 'setoids' or 'E-sets'.[24] An EPO is a setoid that also carries a partial order. The more general structure that arises from partitions like Bot/coBot is also a setoid, but its second relation needn't be a partial order; and even if it is one, it needn't behave well in combination with the first. We examine the more general setoids that arise in partitioning the set of all rankings in §4.4 under the name GEPO for *Generalized* EPO. We write bigraph(X) or GEPO(X) to label a representation of the setoid associated with constraint X. Example (35) collects the bigraphs for each constraint in the 3-constraint partition Bot/co-ZBot.

The bigraphs (GEPO diagrams) of constraints X and Y indicate that they cannot be instantiated in a UVT. Each incoherently demands that the value assigned to ZBot be *equal* to that assigned to co-ZBot, shown by the blue double line, and at the same time strictly *less than* that assigned co-ZBot, shown by the red arrow. You can do many things with numbers, but not this. The bigraph of Z represents a proper EPO, but the damage has been done.

---

[24] See e.g. Setoid, Wikipedia.

Graphically, the fatal configuration is a *cycle*. Intuitively, a cycle is a configuration which can be traversed back to the point of departure. More specifically: in a graph, *edges* connect pairs of *vertices* (sometimes called *nodes* or *points*). If the pair is unordered, the edge is *undirected* and typically represented by a line. If the pair is ordered, the edge (or *arc*) is *directed* and is represented as an arrow pointing from one node to another. A *trail* is a sequence of distinct edges joining a sequence of vertices. A *directed trail* is a trail in which all edges are oriented in the same direction. A *cycle* is a trail with a repeated node.[25] In this work, we will not distinguish between a trail and a *path* proper, in which all nodes are distinct.

A bigraph has the further complexity of including both directed and undirected edges, where the directed edges (*arcs*) are shown as arrows, and the undirected edges as double lines. The relevant notion of path in the bigraph respects the directional status of the arcs: in proceeding from node to node along a path, the direction of the arrows must be followed, but the double lines may be traversed either way. As always, any path that proceeds from a node to itself counts as a cycle. In a bigraph, we defined a *directed cycle* to be a cycle that *contains* a directed arc. Since directed cycles in this sense are the critical structures in the theory of OT, we will simply refer to them here as *cycles*. A bigraph that contains a (directed) cycle will be termed *cyclic*; a bigraph that does not is *acyclic.*[26]

The cycles in the X and Y bigraphs of (35) mix arrows and double lines: order and equivalence. A cycle may consist entirely of arrows, arising without need for equivalences between any of its members. One such case derived from nGX.IL is examined below in ex. (40). Another (the 'Contradictory Snake') is examined in §6.2.2, and pictured in ex. (27) of that section.

The GEPOs for any partition are produced by the same kind of analysis that produces the EPOs of the MOAT for a valid typology. When legitimate grammars can't coexist in the same typology (§6.2), they reveal their incompatibility through participation in cycles.

---

[25] For details, see Path (graph theory) and Cycle (discrete mathematics), Wikipedia.

[26] To explicate this further, we can define the notion 'cycle' by taking the formal step of regarding equivalent nodes as being literally the same node – 'identifying equivalents'. This maneuver yields a structure B~ from a bigraph B, in which every set of nodes in B connected by double lines is represented in B~ as a single node. B~ is just an ordinary directed graph, and we can apply familiar definitions to it. If there is a directed cycle in B~, we say that B is cyclic; if not, acyclic. In our example, bigraph(X)~ and bigraph(Y)~ will each have the single node obtained by identifying the ZBot and co-ZBot nodes. In these derived structures, there's a loop – the smallest kind of cycle – connecting this single node to itself.

In sum: cycles in a bigraph indicate that it cannot come from an EPO. Any partition of Ord(*S*.Con) with a cyclic bigraph isn't a typology.

1.3.3 Classification

Problem 3. ***Us vs. Them.*** A typology implicitly classifies its languages both intensionally and extensionally. Grammars are intensionally groupable by shared and distinguishing ranking relations; languages are extensionally groupable by structural traits. Understanding how the theory characterizes data requires aligning these conceptually distinct modes of categorization (Alber & Prince *op. cit.*).

This is not just a matter of annotating some prior correlational analysis of data. Extensional grouping may be non-unique in purely extensional terms, so that reference to ranking structure is required to decide the validity of proposed classes. Under Generalized Alignment (McCarthy & Prince 1993), for example, X-F^n and F^n-o are regarded as better *left*-aligned for any given $n > 0$ than their respective competitors F^n-X and o-F^n; but within iterative theories, X-F^n parallels o-F^n (Crowhurst & Hewitt 1995; Alber 2005:491; cf. also Mester & Padgett 1994:81, ex. (5)).[27] Extensionally, we have a free choice between positing data classes {F^n-o, X-F^n}, predicted by Generalized Alignment, and {o-F^n, X-F^n}, predicted by directional iteration, as Alber & Prince observe. Which classification is deemed grammatically meaningful depends on the theory that generates it; which is correct depends on the world. Alber 2005, for example, constructs a prosodic theory that relies crucially on the Generalized Alignment grouping to obtain observed left-right/iambic-trochaic asymmetries in the distribution of stress patterns. Similarly, intensional classification will often admit alternatives, and disambiguation may require reference to the structure of the traits that are to be explicated. See Alber & Prince (*op. cit.*) for further discussion.

The structure of typologies, construed in this way, does not appear to be entirely trivial. Therefore, an attack on the problem requires levels of development. We aim here to establish the groundwork for a basic mode of intensional classification. Following §1.3 above, we take this to be founded on the notion of a typological class. Within a target typology, a *typological class* of grammars is a set of grammars that is itself not only a grammar, but also a grammar within an abstract typology that generalizes the original target typology. A typology *generalizes* a target typology if it consists

---

[27] Absent from SPE, iterative rules were introduced into generative phonology by C. Douglas Johnson (1972) and Irwin Howard (1972). After a period of stout resistance, they made a quick transition from abominable to obvious. *We've always been at war with Eastasia.*

of grammars and unions of grammars from the target.[28] In this case, we will follow the terminology of partition theory and say that the more general typology *coarsens* the target typology, and that the target *refines* the more general typology.[29]

Let's apply this mode of analysis to nGX.IL. To discover its typological classes, we consult its MOAT, reproduced below.

(36) MOAT(nGX.IL)

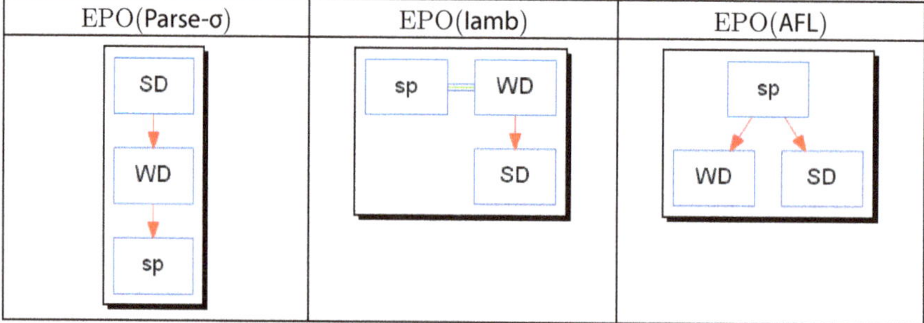

Amalgamating a set of grammars in a typology – forming the union of their legs – is equivalent to merging their nodes in each EPO of the MOAT. We'll write the result of the merger of nodes A and B as A•B.

Let us first ask if there is a typological class 'dense' in nGX.IL, consisting of WD and SD taken together. Such a class would include the grammars of languages that have any multi-foot optima, abstracting away from the weak/strong difference that contrasts FF.o, o.FF with X.FF, FF.X, and so on, in odd-length forms. The dense class would stand in opposition to *sparse*, whose members have optima that contain one foot per word regardless of length, following the patterns F^{n}o and o^{n}F. *Dense* is extensionally definable; is it also a typological class?

---

[28] a Prince (2015b) shows that the set of all typologies on n constraints forms a lattice, a subset of the lattice of partitions of the set all permutations of n objects. It is not a sublattice because joins in the typology lattice needn't be the same as in the general lattice. The order relation in the lattice is *coarsening* (dually *refinement*). See Prince (2013) [Youtube] for discussion.

[29] The qualitive sense of the terminology is this: (proper) refinement breaks up a block of a partition into smaller pieces, introducing further distinctions within that block. Coarsening goes in the opposite direction, amalgamating blocks into larger pieces, losing distinctions. For example, the grades A, B, C, D, F distinguish academic performance, as do Pass and Fail. Pass/Fail coarsens the grading partition by amalgamating A through D. Similarly, the A, B, C, D, F system *refines* the Pass/Fail system by dividing the Pass category into four subcategories, while identifying the Fail category with F. Strictly speaking, we need only describe a coarsened typology as consisting of unions, allowing for union of a block with itself.

To determine the answer, we examine the effect of merging the nodes in the MOAT. With the relevant nodes labeled SD and WD, their merger SD•WD corresponds to the union of legs SD∪WD. We engage in a mild abuse of notation, using the same names for nodes in EPO bigraphs as for the grammars themselves, allowing context to distinguish them. To emphasize the distinction where it is most critical, we take care to distinguish node merger '•' from set union '∪'. Consider the bigraph 'nGX.IL/D' produced by this merger.

(37) nGX.IL/D

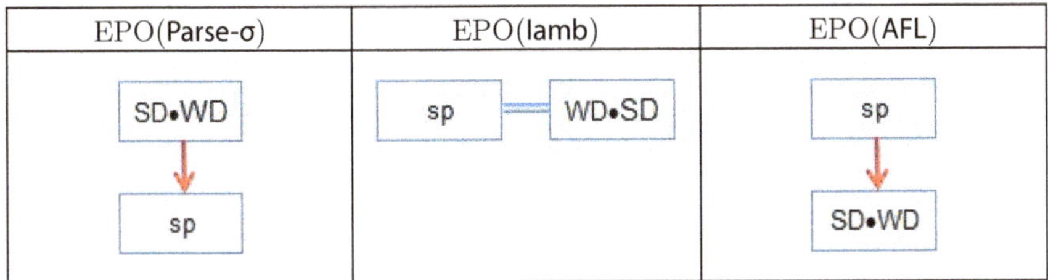

All external relations of the merging nodes are preserved. These are the equivalence and privileged order relations that hold between any participant in the merger and any node not participating in the merger. In the case of the lamb EPO (central cell), for example, the nGX.IL equivalence between sp and WD is inherited by the merged node WD•SD. But there is no relation between sp and SD in the lamb EPO of nGX.IL, either of equivalence or of privileged order, so there is nothing to preserve. In the merger, any internal relation – here, the order between nodes WD and SD – is lost. This explains the structure of the MOAT (37) which represents the result of merging WD and SD in MOAT (36).

The results can be tabulated as follows:

(38) Inheritance of component relations in EPO mergers

Constraint	Derived relations	Source in nGX.IL	
Parse-σ	SD•WD → sp	SD, WD → sp	in Parse-σ bigraph
lamb	SD•WD = sp	WD = sp	in lamb bigraph
AFL	sp → SD•WD	sp → WD, SD	in AFL bigraph

These graphical effects parallel the relations determined by examination of the legs. Anticipating §3.1, ex. (12), and the formal development of §4.3.4, we use the symbols $<^{bp.C}$ and $\sim^{bp.C}$ to indicate the inter-grammar relations which make up the content of the EPO setoids. The prefix *bp* signals that the relations are derived from facts about *b*order *p*oint pairs.

(39) Reasoning from MOAT(nGX.IL): EPO by EPO

Constraint	Grammar relations	Component relations
Parse-σ	SD ∪ WD $<^{\text{bp.Parse-}\sigma}$ sp	SD $<^{\text{bp.Parse-}\sigma}$ sp *and* WD $<^{\text{bp.Parse-}\sigma}$ sp
Iamb	SD ∪ WD $\sim^{\text{bp.Iamb}}$ sp	WD $\sim^{\text{bp.Iamb}}$ sp
AFL	sp $<^{\text{bp.AFL}}$ SD ∪ WD	sp $<^{\text{bp.AFL}}$ WD *and* sp $<^{\text{bp.AFL}}$ SD

In each case, the algebraic analysis based on union of leg sets exactly mirrors the results of the graphical operation of node merger. MOAT (37) is also identical to what would be obtained directly from analyzing the partition of the ranking set into the two blocks sp and D = WD∪SD. However derived, the partition {Sparse, Dense} has a well-formed MOAT: there are no cycles in any EPO. We are therefore licensed to conclude that the partition {Sparse, Dense} is a typology – an intensional typology of Abstract OT, strictly coarser than nGX.IL. It follows that Dense, the union of WD and SD, is a *typological class*.

There's another way of classifying the three grammars of nGX.IL: merge Sparse and Strongly Dense, contrasting them jointly with Weakly Dense. The informal names of the grammars prejudice us against this breakdown, but words may fail. There's even an extensional rationale for the classification: WD forms have exactly one unparsed syllable in odd-length forms of length greater than one syllable; the others do not. Does this hypothesized generalization yield a typological class {sp, SD} in nGX.IL? We do not need to enumerate and analyze the leg sets. With the MOAT of nGX.IL in hand, we can test the status of the proposed generalization through graphical merger. The result is a collection of bigraphs: but only one of them is a valid EPO.

(40) Partition {WD, SD∪sp}

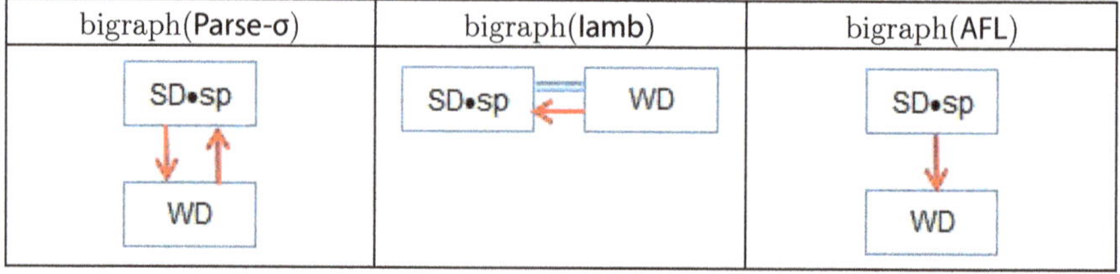

This bigraph set fails to attain MOAThood: the first two GEPOs show cycles, implying contradictory requirements that cannot be realized in any structure ordered like the integers. We may parse the components as follows, showing how the relations in the amalgamated structure follow from the equivalence and privileged order relations in the unamalgamated EPOs of nGX.IL.

(41) Partition {WD, SD∪sp}, bigraph by bigraph

Constraint	Merger Relations in (40)	Component relations in nGX.IL (36)
Parse-σ	SD•sp → WD	SD → WD
	WD → SD•sp	WD → sp
lamb	SD•sp = WD	sp = WD
	SD•sp → WD	WD → SD
AFL	SD•sp → WD	sp → WD

On Parse-σ, qualitatively speaking, the amalgam SD•sp is *better parsed* than WD because its component SD is better parsed than WD, while at the same time SD•sp is *worse parsed* than WD because its component sp is worse parsed than WD. On lamb, SD•sp submits to a similar analysis. Only on AFL is coherence maintained.

We conclude that {SD, sp} is not a *typological class* of nGX.IL. In this case, the failure comes about because SD∪sp is not a grammar: its leg set is not ERC-characterizable. In §6.2 we look at two subtler examples, in which legitimate grammars cannot coexist within a typology because the local relations between them cannot be realized as globally consistent orders and equivalences.

Main classification result. A partition of the set of all rankings is a typology if and only if it has a MOAT (see Theorem (183), §4.8). The MOAT is determined from the partition. Union of blocks in a partition corresponds exactly to merging the corresponding nodes in the EPO bigraphs. The typological status of a partition $\mathcal{P}$ that is arrived at by the union of some grammars of a typology T can be evaluated by an effective calculation on the MOAT of T. It is only necessary to check that each of the bigraphs associated with $\mathcal{P}$ has no cycles and is therefore a well-formed EPO. Any hypothesis that a set of grammars is a typological class can therefore be verified or falsified by a simple calculation.

The MOAT solves the typological class problem, and it solves the grammatical class problem as well whenever the two notions coincide. When they do not, other techniques are available, using the *join* of ERC sets (Merchant 2008, 2011), discussed in §6.1.

The notions *typological class* and *grammatical class* initiate the enterprise of classification but do not end it. Consider the 'Onset Required' set of languages within Elementary Syllable Theory. As discussed above in relation to the bigraph example, this class has no ERC set characterization, since it involves an irreducible disjunction among the necessarily dominated constraints. An ERC requires conjunction across its dominated constraints.

'Onset Required' comes from *either* m.Ons ≫ f.dep *or* m.Ons ≫ f.max: therefore, no grammar. The two subcases 'enforced by deletion' and 'enforced by insertion' cannot be merged into a grammatical class, and so *a fortiori* cannot be merged into a typological class.

To recognize 'Onset Required' as a coherent, ranking-defined class requires further conceptual development that generalizes the ERC and the ERC set, introduced by Alber & Prince (*op. cit.*) under the name of 'Property Theory' and currently under vigorous exploration.[30] The richer predicates of Property Theory can take account of symmetries in the behavior of disparate constraints, recognizing classes of constraints as well as classes of grammars, and introducing two operators that choose from the constraint class to define ranking conditions that generalize the ERC. In the 'Onset Required' case, the set of faithfulness constraints functions as a grammatically significant class, and in an OR grammar, every leg must meet the condition that the *lowest ranked member* of that class dominates m.Ons. In the grammars of the complement class OLA, the opposite ranking holds: m.Ons must dominate the lowest ranked member of the faithfulness constraint class. Together, these two opposing conditions constitute a formal 'property', the object after which the theory is named. The goal of property analysis is to resolve a typology into a set of properties, such that each of its grammars is completely defined by a choice of ranking conditions from them.

We are assured, then, that there is structure in typologies that lies beyond the immediate reach of the concepts developed here. But we can see it most clearly, and extend analysis to it, only when we understand the ground it stands on. Our strategy, then, is to focus on the groundwork, so that further structure may be soundly built upon it.[31]

---

[30] Alber & Prince (2019), ch. 2, includes a full analysis of EST. For a broader view, the reader may wish to consult such works as Alber (2017), Alber, DelBusso & Prince (2016), Alber & Prince (2021, 2022), Bennett & DelBusso (2017, 2018), Danis (2017), DelBusso (2016, 2018), McManus (2016), Merchant (2018), Merchant & Krämer (2018).

[31] καὶ πᾶς ὁ ἀκούων μου τοὺς λόγους τούτους καὶ μὴ ποιῶν αὐτοὺς ὁμοιωθήσεται ἀνδρὶ μωρῷ ὅστις ᾠκοδόμησεν αὐτοῦ τὴν οἰκίαν ἐπὶ τὴν ἄμμον…

Chapter 2

The EST typology

Chapter contents

LET'S DEVELOP THE CENTRAL IDEAS in the context of an example: Elementary Syllable Theory (EST). In §5 below, we will also explore its reduced cousin, the C-System of EST, which deals only with the disposition of consonants.

2.1 Definition of EST

In the first version of syllable theory laid out in P&S:104–115, epenthetic differences between V and C are conflated, with both handled by a single constraint, FILL. This system we will call *Elementary Syllable Theory* (EST), as distinct from Basic Syllable Theory (BST: P&S:115ff), in which FILL is split into two faithfulness constraints, one that detects epenthesis of vowels (FILL^{Nuc}) and the other, epenthesis of consonants (FILL^{Ons}). The containment-based system of P&S will be adapted to post-P&S correspondence theory (McCarthy & Prince 1995).

A Concrete OT system *S* must articulate *S*.GEN and *S*.CON. Since predictive consequences, reified in the system's typology, follow necessarily, it will be worth our while to be clear at the definitional stage. We first present the definitions descriptively and then conclude with a compact formal statement of their contents.

S.GEN for any system S spells out what a candidate of S is, and what its candidate set is, within which comparison takes place. For EST.GEN, as is typical in phonological analysis, a candidate consists of an input, an output, and a correspondence relation between them.

Input. EST.GEN accepts as inputs non-empty strings of arbitrary length composed of the characters C and V, called *segments*.

Output. EST.GEN accepts as the outputs for any input all syllabically parsed arbitrary-length strings of C and V, including the empty string. *Syllabically parsed* means that each segment belongs to a syllable. A *syllable* has exactly one V; at most one C preceding the vowel; and at most one C following the vowel. Syllable boundaries will be denoted by square brackets. A prevocalic C is termed the *onset* of the syllable; a postvocalic C is termed the *coda* of a syllable. These terms are descriptive of string position and do not name constituents in syllable structure, as they do in P&S:110.[1]

Correspondence. Segments in the input may be associated with segments in the output in a *correspondence* relation. We limit this in EST.GEN so that an input segment has at most one correspondent output segment, and vice versa. In addition, C may correspond only to C; V only to V. The linear order of segments in the input is maintained in the order of their correspondents in the output. Crucially, a segment in the input need not have a correspondent in the output, a state of affairs representing deletion; and a segment in the output need not have an input correspondent, representing epenthesis.

These considerations may be spelled exactly in the following terms. The notation Σ^*, where Σ is a set of strings, denotes the set of all strings concatenating members of Σ any number of times, including none. Σ^+ is defined similarly, but omits the empty string.

(1) EST.GEN: input, output, and correspondence

$$\text{IN} = \{C, V\}^+$$

[1] P&S allow for unsyllabified segments in the output, phonetically interpreted as deletion, and empty structural nodes, phonetically interpreted as insertion, following earlier works such as Steriade (1982) and Ito (1986, 1989). Correspondence theory represents deletion and insertion in the phonology itself. Thus EST.Gen imposes on phonology the output conditions that are met only after phonetic interpretation in P&S: exhaustive syllabification, and segmental saturation of all higher-order structural nodes (here just σ).

OUT = {[(C)V(C)]}*

Correspondence: Each input-output pair (*in*, *out*), where length(*in*) = *n* and length(*out*) = *m*, comes with a set of partial functions CORR.IO(*in*,*out*) defined as follows. First, the partial function and the conditions on it:

a) ${}_{p}f_{nm}$: **n** → **m**, where **n** = {1, 2,..., *n*}, **m** = {1, 2,..., *m*}, for **n** and **m** the ordinal positions of the characters in strings *in* ∈ IN and *out* ∈ OUT, with ${}_{p}f_{nm}$ a partial function on **n**.

b) LIN: $i < j \Rightarrow {}_{p}f_{nm}(i) < {}_{p}f_{nm}(j)$, for $i, j \in \mathbf{n}$, whenever both ${}_{p}f_{nm}(i)$ and ${}_{p}f_{nm}(j)$ are defined.

c) TYPE: ${}_{p}f_{nm}(i) = k \Rightarrow$ in[*i*] = out[*k*], ensuring that in[*i*] and out[*k*] have the same value. Here this means they are both C or both V.

Now, the set of all admitted correspondence relations between an IO pair:

CORR.IO(*in*, *out*) = $\{{}_{p}f_{nm} \mid {}_{p}f_{nm}$ satisfies LIN & TYPE, n = length(*in*), m = length(*out*), *in* ∈ IN, *out* ∈ OUT }.

The set of candidates admitted by EST.GEN, denoted EST.CAND, is then the following:

(2) EST.CAND = {⟨*in*, *out*, **c**⟩| *in* ∈ IN, *out* ∈ OUT, **c** ∈ CORR.IO(*in*, *out*)}
A *candidate set* is obtained by fixing the value of *in* in EST.CAND.

The correspondence relation is represented as a partial function from a set of indices on the segments of the input to a set of output indices. The indices simply give the ordinal position of characters in the strings. A *partial* function need not map every member of its domain to its co-domain. Here proper partiality represents deletion; epenthesis obtains when the co-domain contains indices not in the range of the function.

We define four constraints in EST.CON, each of which is a function from EST.CAND to ℕ, the set of non-negative integers {0, 1, 2,...}. Though modified in light of correspondence theory, these constraints operate very much as they do in P&S:106. Following OT best practices, we mark the type of each constraint by a prefix: 'm' for markedness, indicating the constraint only evaluates the output, and 'f' for faithfulness, indicating it requires the correspondence relation for its evaluation of input-output disparities. This makes it easy to track markedness-faithfulness relations. We reserve the right to omit the prefixes on occasion when other distinctions, in our judgment, deserve greater salience.

The constraints of EST.Con are four in number.

(3) EST.Con: verbose

m.Ons	returns the number of onsetless syllables in a candidate's output
m.NoCoda	returns the number of syllables that have a coda in a candidate's output
f.max	returns the number of input segments that lack output correspondents
f.dep	returns the number of output segments that lack input correspondents

To spell this out, we adopt a shorthand for substring containment, defining '$x \sqsubseteq s$' = 'x is a contiguous substring of the string s'. The notation 'card S' denotes the cardinality of the set S. The (partial) correspondence function is denoted c.

(4) EST.Con defined

m.Ons($\langle in, out, \mathsf{c}\rangle$)	$= \text{card}\{\, \text{'[V'} \sqsubseteq out\}$
m.NoCoda($\langle in, out, \mathsf{c}\rangle$)	$= \text{card}\{\, \text{'C]'} \sqsubseteq out\}$
f.max($\langle in, out, \mathsf{c}\rangle$)	$= \text{card}\{x \sqsubseteq in \mid x \in \{C, V\} \text{ and } \neg\exists y \sqsubseteq out, y = \mathsf{c}(x)\}$
f.dep($\langle in, out, \mathsf{c}\rangle$)	$= \text{card}\{y \sqsubseteq out \mid y \in \{C, V\} \text{ and } \neg\exists x \sqsubseteq in, y = \mathsf{c}(x)\}$

We define the constraints as explicit functions from EST.Cand to $\mathbb{N}$ to make clear the familiar desired interpretation of the * notation and its verbal paraphrases.

2.2 Three representations of a typology

Any well-defined theory will invariably give rise to multiple characterizations, each equally valid, each shining different light on the theory. OT is no different. In the typological realm we will be concerned with the extensional typology of languages, the intensional typology of ranking grammars, and the intensional typology of ERC grammars. The typology is determinable from a well-chosen set of inputs.

2.2.1 A universal support for EST

With EST.Gen and EST.Con in hand, the next typological question is this: which candidate sets determine the typology? A set of candidate sets that makes all possible distinctions for all languages in a typology we call a *universal support.* (See e.g. Prince 2015a.) Given any concrete instantiation of OT, typological claims can only be justified after a universal support has been identified (see Bane & Riggle 2012 for the unwelcome consequences of candidate omission). Below is a universal support for EST consisting of three candidate sets.[2] We write ε for the empty string, and indicate the correspondence relation with subscripts. For visibility, epenthetic segments are shown in a hollow font.

(5) A Universal Support for EST

input	output	m.Ons	m.NoCoda	f.dep	f.max	Type
V_1	$[V_1]$	1	0	0	0	F
	ε	0	0	0	1	del
	$[\mathbb{C}V_1]$	0	0	1	0	ins
C_1	ε	0	0	0	1	del
	$[C_1\mathbb{V}]$	0	0	1	0	ins
$C_1V_2C_3$	$[C_1V_2C_3]$	0	1	0	0	F
	$[C_1V_2]$	0	0	0	1	del
	$[C_1V_2]\ [C_3\mathbb{V}]$	0	0	1	0	ins

Notation in rightmost column: F = 'faithful', del = 'deletional', ins = 'insertional'.

Each cset in this universal support contains all and only the non-harmonically bounded candidates ('possible optima') for each of their respective inputs. For example, in the second cset, the input /C/ has only two possibly-optimal outputs. One lacks the C, resulting in the empty string as the output. The other contains an epenthetic V, forming a valid syllable. Further deletions can't happen: we've reached the zero lower bound. Further insertions merely worsen performance on **f.dep** and perhaps m.Ons and m.NoCoda.[3] Since further unfaithfulness is either impossible or lacking in benefit, no other

---

[2] P&S:112–114 deploy the first and third in their analysis of BST, delivering a typology that is coarser than the typology of the target system. Riggle (2004:108ff) recognizes that a telling candidate with a C that must be unfaithfully syllabified (for him, CCVVC) will refine the P&S typology to the BST as defined in P&S.

[3] See P&S:116–118 for the theory of optimal epenthesis sites in BST. The same mode of analysis applies to EST as studied here.

candidate can displace either of the two listed. Similar arguments hold for the other candidate sets.

Observe that /C/ must be unfaithfully mapped, as [C] is not a licit parse in EST: outputs are fully syllabified and syllables contain V. For outputs of /C/, EST.Gen only admits unfaithful candidates.

These three candidate sets provide a universal support for this typology since no additional candidate sets can induce further ranking distinctions in any language of EST, as may be shown by working through the predicted grammars with EST.Gen in mind.[4]

There are 8 languages in the typology of EST corresponding to the 8 viable selections of optima, one from each of the three candidate sets above. Even though there are 18 candidate languages – 3×2×3 combinations of candidates – 10 of these involve inconsistent rankings. For example, no ranking can deletionally map /V/ to ε while insertionally mapping /C/ to [C𝕍]. The first map requires f.dep ≫ f.max and the second f.max ≫ f.dep, an impossible requirement on any total order on the constraints.

2.2.2 *Extensional languages of EST*

The eight languages of EST are characterized extensionally in terms of three distinctions.

The determinative differences are these:

i. Onset Required (**OR**) *vs.* Onset Lack Allowed (**OLA**)
ii. Coda Prohibited (**CP**) *vs.* Coda Allowed (**CA**)
iii. Insertion *vs.* Deletion

As each language in EST must select one choice from these three binary distinctions, we can label the eight languages perspicuously by their selections, adapting the naming style of P&S:116. Below is a chart giving our labels of the eight, their possible outputs across the range of all inputs, and how input-output disparities in syllable structure are managed.

Recall that the notation {*string*}* indicates the set of all strings formed by concatentating repetitions of *string*, including the empty string, while {*string*}$^{+}$ has at least one instance of *string*. To diminish clutter, we omit set brackets around the output syllable canon.

[4] Alber, DelBusso, and Prince (2016) delimit all Universal Supports for nGX, providing formal proof.

(6) Languages of EST

Name	Outputs	IO	Onset	Coda
1:CV.del	[CV]*	deletion	OR	CP
2:(C)V.del	[(C)V]*		OLA	
3:CV.ins	$[CV]^+$	insertion	OR	
4:(C)V.ins	$[(C)V]^+$		OLA	
5:CV(C).del	[CV(C)]*	deletion	OR	CA
6:(C)V(C).del	[(C)V(C)]*		OLA	
7:CV(C).ins	$[CV(C)]^+$	insertion	OR	
8:(C)V(C).ins	$[(C)V(C)]^+$		OLA	

Even the languages OLA/CA, numbered 6 and 8, though they allow every admitted syllable shape, are distinguished by deletion vs. insertion. This is because inputs like /C/, which cannot be mapped faithfully, will nevertheless have an output and must obtain it through either insertion or deletion.

The inputs of the universal support map to their respective outputs in the individual languages as follows. We omit the correspondence indices to remove distraction from the structural patterns; because segment order is preserved, they are easily recovered.

(7) Input-Output map of the universal support for EST

Language Name	**/V/**	**/C/**	**/CVC/**
1:CV.del	ε	ε	[CV]
2:(C)V.del	[V]	ε	[CV]
3:CV.ins	[ℂV]	[C𝕍]	[CV] [C𝕍]
4:(C)V.ins	[V]	[C𝕍]	[CV] [C𝕍]
5:CV(C).del	ε	ε	[CVC]
6:(C)V(C).del	[V_1]	ε	[CVC]
7:CV(C).ins	[ℂV]	[C𝕍]	[CVC]
8:(C)V(C).ins	[V]	[C𝕍]	[CVC]

In sum, the three-fold binary nature of the eight languages leads to a natural grouping which is reflected in the universal support and in our naming practice.

i. **OR/OLA**. Onsets are required / allowed to be absent.
ii. **CP/CA**. Codas are prohibited / allowed.
iii. **ins/del**. Compliance with these and with GEN-imposed syllabification requirements is achieved by insertion / by deletion.

Compare the classification of BST in P&S:116. Simplifying the table found there, we have:

(8) Extensional categorization of EST languages

		Onset	
		Required	Lack Allowed
Coda	Prohibited	1:CV.del 3:CV.ins	2:(C)V.del 4:(C)V.ins
	Allowed	5:CV(C).del 7:CV(C).ins	6:(C)V(C).del 8:(C)V(C).ins

2.2.3 *Representations of the grammars of CV.del and (C)V.del*

Every extensional language is characterized intensionally by its ranking grammar, the set of total orders that select its optima. The ranking grammar of language 1:CV.del, describable as OR.CP.del, contains the following 6 legs:

(9) The ranking grammar of 1:CV.del

m.Ons	≫	m.NoCoda	≫	f.dep	≫	f.max
m.Ons	≫	f.dep	≫	m.NoCoda	≫	f.max
m.NoCoda	≫	m.Ons	≫	f.dep	≫	f.max
m.NoCoda	≫	f.dep	≫	m.Ons	≫	f.max
f.dep	≫	m.Ons	≫	m.NoCoda	≫	f.max
f.dep	≫	m.NoCoda	≫	m.Ons	≫	f.max

Gross enumerations like this are not linguistically informative. Inspection reveals that the set G_R(1:CV.del) consists of those rankings in which f.max is dominated by the other three constraints, which may occur in any order among themselves, hence the $6 = 3!$ legs. This generalization is represented directly in an ERC grammar G_E(1:CV.del).

(10) G_E(1:CV.del), OR.CP.del

m.Ons	m.NoCoda	f.dep	f.max
W			**L**
	W		**L**
		W	**L**

This tells us directly that m.Ons, m.NoCoda are maximally respected, leading to all syllables being onsetted and codaless, and that any and all compliance with the demands of EST.Gen and of markedness is obtained by deletion (violating f.max), rather than by insertion (violating f.dep).[5]

There is a precise relationship between the ranking grammar and the ERC grammar. The ERC grammar has a set of total orders that are consistent with it, its linear extensions or *legs*, in our acronym. Each total order of the ranking grammar must also be a leg of the ERC grammar, and there can be no legs of the ERC grammar that are not total orders of the ranking grammar. The legs of the ERC grammar are thus exactly the total orders of the ranking grammar.

The ranking grammar in the case of G_R(1:CV.del) consists of the linear extensions of a partial order. This partial order can be perspicuously displayed as a Hasse diagram.

(11) 1:CV.del, OR.CP.del

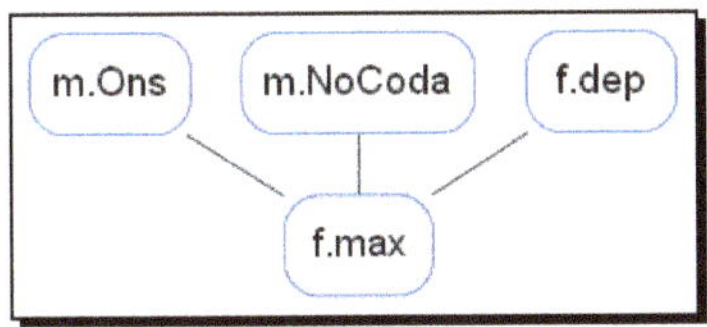

By contrast, the ranking grammar of 2:(C)V.del, OLA.CP.del, contains only two legs:

(12) Ranking grammar of 2:(C)V.del, OLA.CP.del

m.NoCoda	≫	f.dep	≫	f.max	≫	m.Ons
f.dep	≫	m.NoCoda	≫	f.max	≫	m.Ons

The linguistic generalizations inherent in this collection are represented in an ERC grammar below.

(13) ERC grammar for 2:(C)V.del, OLA.CP.del

ERC#	m.NoCoda	f.dep	f.max	m.Ons
1	**W**		**L**	
2		**W**	**L**	
3			**W**	**L**

[5] In this simple case, each ERC derives from a single winner-loser pair coming from a different input, as may be seen by analyzing the universal support VT (5).

Observe that ERC#2, requiring f.dep ≫ f.max, secures deletion as the mode of unfaithfulness. ERC#1 requires m.NoCoda ≫ f.max, ensuring that all optimal syllables are codaless. ERC#3 positions f.max with respect to m.Ons, leading to onsetless syllables in the output via faithful reproduction of the input sequences like /V/ and /CVV/.

Here too the legs linearly extend a partial order, yielding a Y-shaped Hasse diagram like Lombardi's Polish, shown in exx. (5) and (6) above, which can be displayed as follows:

(14) Hasse diagram of 2:(C)V.del, OLA.CP.del

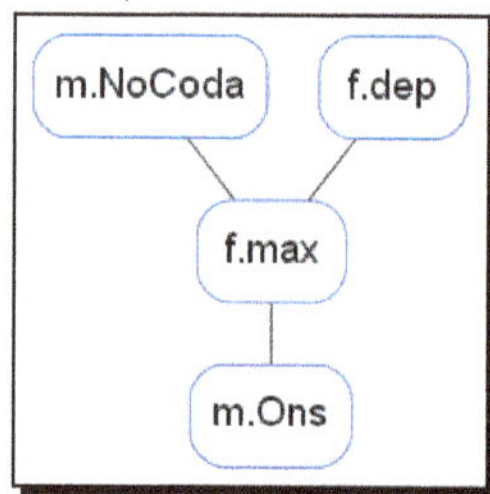

2.2.4 A Unitary VT for EST

The preceding exemplification of the grammars of EST can be fully projected from the three candidate sets given above in ex. (5), §2.2.1 Even so, this concrete instantiation of EST will not serve us well when we ask further questions about the typology. We must take a step away from the concrete. From Prince (2015b), we know that the Minkowski sum[6] of these three candidate sets provides a single Unitary VT (UVT), from which all 8 grammars can be produced. In this UVT, shown below, each row represents an entire language, and its grammar is determined by competing for optimality against the other languages.

---

[6] The Minkowski sum of two sets, often denoted by ⊕, is a set consisting of the sum of every pair of elements from the two sets, one from the first, the other from the second. Vectors sum componentwise: here, adding the violation values in each constraint. In short, $A \oplus B = \{\mathbf{a} + \mathbf{b} \mid \mathbf{a} \in A, \mathbf{b} \in B\}$, with $(\mathbf{a} + \mathbf{b})[i] = \mathbf{a}[i] + \mathbf{b}[i]$.

(15) A Unitary VT U for EST

U	m.Ons	m.NoCoda	f.dep	f.max	Grammar
u_1	0	0	0	3	CV.del
u_2	1	0	0	2	(C)V.del
u_3	0	0	3	0	CV.ins
u_4	1	0	2	0	(C)V.ins
u_5	0	1	0	2	CV(C).del
u_6	1	1	0	1	(C)V(C).del
u_7	0	1	2	0	CV(C).ins
u_8	1	1	1	0	(C)V(C).ins

With the UVT U in hand, we have transited to the abstract. Candidates no longer have the structure of ⟨*in*, *out*, **c**⟩ triples, but are violation profiles, labeled here in a way that conveniently identifies their concrete origins. Each constraint is newly reformulated as a function from abstract candidates u_k to $\mathbb{N} = \{0, 1, 2,...\}$. In the interests of simplicity, we continue with the same constraint names.

This UVT was produced from the three candidate sets above in ex. (5), §2.2.1, but other universal support candidate sets could have been chosen, resulting in different UVTs. The Minkowski sum algorithm, from various universal supports, will produce typologically equivalent UVTs, even if numerical equality is not guaranteed. In addition, there will be many UVTs that generate the typology but have no source in Minkowski summation of concrete VTs.

We are brought back to the first question raised above in §1.3, asked there of nGX.IL, now asked of EST. Which of the numerical relations in the UVT are linguistically meaningful, in that they recur in every UVT for the typology? Equivalently, which relations play a crucial role in the process of selecting optima? The MOAT provides the answer.

Chapter 3

EST: The MOAT and its EPOs

Chapter contents

THREE NOTIONS ARE CENTRAL to construction of the MOAT: order, equivalence, and privilege. Order and equivalence are singled out because of the way that OT chooses optima, privilege because of the way languages class together under typological coarsening. Every grammatical typology comes from many typologically equivalent UVTs, which differ numerically but give rise to identical grammars. The MOAT tells us exactly which order and equivalence relations must hold within any UVT that realizes the typology. The EPOs of a MOAT retain 'privileged' information from grammar adjacency that is crucial to typological classification.

This chapter contains example-based exposition of the key ideas and procedures associated with the MOAT, developing the basic technical apparatus and applying it. In §4, we move on to detailed formal analysis in the course of demonstrating the claims advanced here.

We begin with the order and equivalence relations that must be instantiated in all UVTs of the same typology (§3.1). We then show how these relations can be obtained from the grammars of the typology, construed as sets of legs (§3.2). The procedure relies on the notion of a *border point pair*, which consists of two maximally similar legs that belong to different grammars. These contain the data that the privileged order relations and the equivalences are built from. This information gives a complete account of the ranking and order relations shared across UVTs. The privileged order and equivalence relations for a single constraint are contained in the EPO ('Equivalence-augmented Privileged Order') of that constraint. The collection of EPOs, one for each constraint, is the MOAT of the typology. The MOAT is unique and free from the peculiarities of any individual UVT. In addition to delimiting the numerical possibilities of the UVTs, the MOAT determines the range of typological classifications based on unioning grammars to form an abstract typology coarser than the original.

We conclude (§3.3) by exploring how the distinction between privileged and non-privileged orders plays out concretely in the analysis of EST.

3.1 From order and equivalence to the EPO

OT filtration is famously sensitive only to the relations of equality and order between violation values, not to the magnitudes of the values themselves. If a given number is minimal for the set of candidates evaluated by a constraint in a ranking, then all candidates *not* assigned that value will be ejected.

Though the decision made by a constraint is binary – in / out – each constraint establishes order and equivalence relations among *all* competing candidates by virtue of its numerical assignments, simply because the integers have their own inescapable logic. These become crucial in the course of filtration when a constraint's top candidates are gone.

In Concrete OT, candidates are linguistic forms, typically input-output-correspondence triples, as in the treatment of EST in §2, ex. (2), and languages are collections of optimal candidates. In Abstract OT, the candidates are violation profiles, and there is no notion of 'language' in the concrete sense. When a UVT is constructed by Minkowski summation of multiple concrete VTs in a universal support, each of its rows – each abstract candidate – represents an entire language of the concrete typology by virtue of delivering (when asserted optimal) the grammar of that language. In this situation, the rows of the UVT can be identified with the corresponding languages of the typology. For convenience, at minor risk of ambiguity, UVT rows may be referred to as 'languages'.

Consider the EST languages as evaluated in a UVT by the constraint m.Ons. The relevant column from UVT (15), §2.2.4, is repeated here, with the rows rearranged to emphasize the behavior of interest.

(1) m.Ons in EST UVT U (15)

U	m.Ons	...	Grammar	Type
u_1	0	...	CV.del	OR
u_3	0	...	CV.ins	
u_5	0	...	CV(C).del	
u_7	0	...	CV(C).ins	
u_2	1	...	(C)V.del	OLA
u_4	1	...	(C)V.ins	
u_6	1	...	(C)V(C).del	
u_8	1	...	(C)V(C).ins	

Four languages receive '0'. In their concrete extensional correlates, every syllable in optimal outputs has an onset; these are of the type 'Onset Required (OR)'. The other four receive '1'. Concretely, some syllables in some of their optimal outputs are onsetless; in IO terms, neither insertion nor deletion is employed in the syllabification of input sequences VV or #V to evade the ill consequences of faithfulness. These we term 'Onset Lack Allowed' (OLA).

In this particular UVT, all languages of the set OR are given the same value on m.Ons, as are the members of the set OLA. Neither the languages nor their associated grammars are thereby rendered 'equal', because two things that are *equal* are just one thing. The values assigned by a constraint define an equivalence relation with respect to that constraint.

It is worth our while to spell this out as a transient step toward the relations we seek. We notate this equivalence as '$\approx^{U:C}$', indicating that it responds to the values assigned by C in the UVT U. Since grammars are the objects that intensional typologies consist of, and the languages or rows merely players in the drama that leads to them, we want the relation to hold of grammars, not languages. We notate the grammar corresponding to row u_k as G_k.

(2) UVT-induced equivalence relation. For UVT U and constraint C:

$$G_j \approx^{U:C} G_k \text{ iff } C(u_j) = C(u_k)$$

In U, the constraint m.Ons induces two equivalence classes on grammars, OR and OLA.

(3) Equivalence classes of m.Ons in UVT U (1)

OR: 1:CV.del $\approx^{U.Ons}$ 3:CV.ins $\approx^{U.Ons}$ 5:CV(C).del $\approx^{U.Ons}$ 7:CV(C).ins

OLA: 2:(C)V.del $\approx^{U.Ons}$ 4:(C)V.ins $\approx^{U.Ons}$ 6:(C)V(C).del $\approx^{U.Ons}$ 8:(C)V(C).ins

For conciseness, we will refer to languages by their position in the enumeration, bolded. We obtain the following equivalences.

(4) Equivalence classes of m.Ons in UVT U (1), concisely

OR: $\mathbf{1} \approx \mathbf{3} \approx \mathbf{5} \approx \mathbf{7}$

OLA: $\mathbf{2} \approx \mathbf{4} \approx \mathbf{6} \approx \mathbf{8}$

Along the same lines, the purely numerical relation $0 < 1$ leads to an abstract order relation '$\lessdot^{U:Ons}$' holding between the grammars of OR and those of OLA in UVT U.

(5) UVT-induced order relation. For UVT U and C,

$G_j \lessdot^{U:C} G_k$ iff $C(u_j) < C(u_k)$

We use special symbols $\lessdot^{U:C}$ and $\approx^{U:C}$ to demarcate these relations as clearly as possible. Both order and equivalence can be portrayed in a bigraph, which here amounts to a Hasse diagram augmented to show equivalence. As always, double blue lines indicate equivalence; red arrows, order.

(6) Bigraph induced by m.Ons in UVT (15), §2.2.4

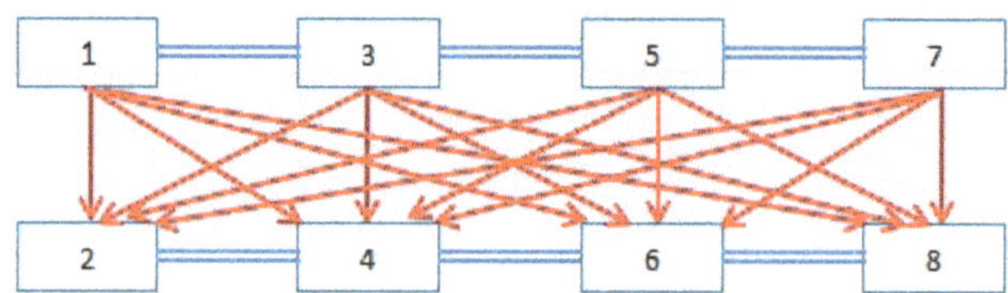

We may now ask which of these relations are necessary to produce the EST typology. For example, may we disrupt the equivalences of the bottom-dwelling OLA set {**2, 4, 6, 8**}? Suppose a different universal support had been used to construct a UVT for EST, or that we had simply managed to write down a UVT with a typology identical to that of EST. Could such a UVT **V** contain the following assignment of values by m.Ons?

(7) UVT **V**, attempted alternative version of EST UVT U (15), §2.2.4

V	m.Ons	...	**Intended Type**
v_1	0	...	OR
v_3	0	...	
v_5	0	...	
v_7	0	...	
v_2	1	...	OLA
v_4	2	...	
v_6	3	...	
v_8	4	...	

We assume that the entire **V** will have the same constraint names as **U**. This allows us to compare grammars across UVTs, in accord with the intuitive idea that different UVTs can deliver the same typology.

The numerical assignments in **V** represent one of the many possible ways of putting an order on the OLA class while retaining equivalence within the OR class (in which all evaluate to 0) as well as the order relations between the members of the two classes (0 being less than the positive integers assigned to OLA languages). This contemplated rendition of m.Ons gives rise to the following bigraph:

(8) Alternative m.Ons bigraph from UVT V, with equivalence abandoned in OLA

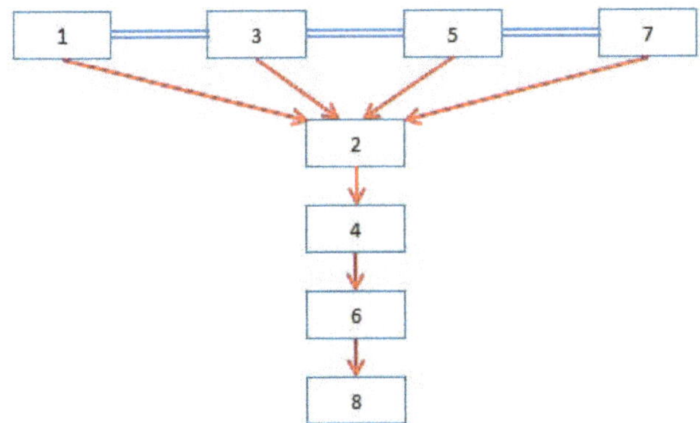

The shock is that this still works. In any UVT for EST, we can replace the entries in the m.Ons column with any numerical values that follow the order and equivalence relations in the bigraph (8), including of course those of ex. (7). No filtration ever depends upon distinguishing the members of the OLA class from each other by virtue of their performance on m.Ons. Concretely put, the members of OLA class do not show gradations in onsetlessness.[1]

May the equivalences in the OR class $\{\mathbf{1}, \mathbf{3}, \mathbf{5}, \mathbf{7}\}$ be similarly disrupted? Here's one way to do it, among many.

(9) UVT **W**, attempted alternative version of m.Ons (15), §2.2.4

W	'm.Ons'	...	Intended Type
w_1	0	...	OR
w_3	1	...	
w_5	2	...	
w_7	3	...	
w_2	4	...	OLA
w_4	4	...	
w_6	4	...	
w_8	4	...	

These assignments, as well as any that have the same order properties, induce the following bigraph:

(10) Bigraph for m.Ons in **W**, abandoning OR equivalence

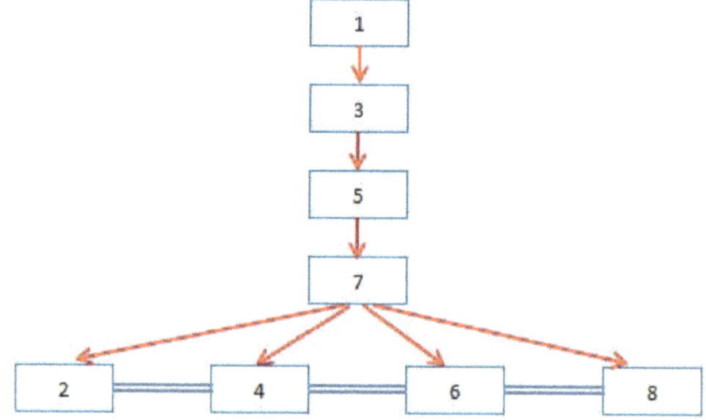

[1] To see this, return to UVT (15), §2.2.4, and contemplate any linear order selecting an OLA language (C)VX. Follow its filtration pattern. You will find that the decision between the OLA class members will be made before m.Ons has a chance to distinguish them. For example, consider Lg.#2 (C)V.del. One of the legs that selects it is m.NoCoda ≫ f.dep ≫ f.max ≫ m.Ons. Focus on its competitors in the OLA class. Top-ranked m.NoCoda ejects Lg.#6 (C)V(C).del and Lg.#8 (C)V(C).ins. Then f.dep ejects Lg.#4 (C)V.ins. At this point, all OLA languages except for Lg.#2 are gone, and m.Ons has no chance to compare them. All other legs selecting an OLA member behave similarly.

This fails radically and obviously. Suppose m.Ons stands first in a leg. There can be only one survivor of filtration by top-ranked m.Ons as rendered in UVT W (10), and that would be the row corresponding to the grammar 1:CV.del, the sole bearer of the value 0. But in the EST typology, all four OR grammars include legs with m.Ons in first position, and so *all* OR languages must pass through m.Ons together when it's initial in a linear order. Thus, in every UVT for EST, the m.Ons column must assign the same numerical value to all OR languages – and that value must be minimal. In general, the languages receiving the minimal value in any constraint (ecologically, often 0) *must* be equivalent, but relations among the non-minimals are dependent on what happens elsewhere. In sum, the UVT W simply cannot deliver the EST typology.

To understand the linguistically significant order and equivalence relations inherent in a UVT – those which determine its typology and therefore cannot be altered – we need to know which of them hold not just in that single UVT but in *every* UVT that yields the same typology. The route we will follow to obtain this information lies not in the UVTs themselves but in the grammars they sponsor, which are constant across the plethora of UVTs. Extracting the order and equivalence information latent in the border point pairs of the typology – pairs of legs $\{P\underline{XY}Q, P\underline{YX}Q\}$, where each lies in a distinct grammar – we will find that the m.Onset EPO takes on this form:

(11) EPO_{EST}(m.Ons)

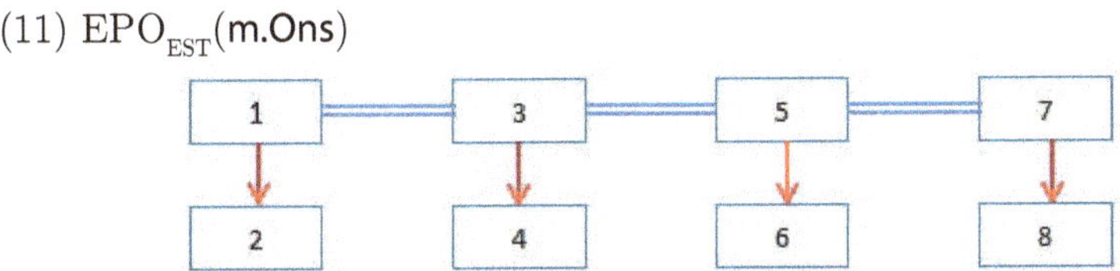

Recall that OR = $\{\mathbf{1}, \mathbf{3}, \mathbf{5}, \mathbf{7}\}$ and OLA = $\{\mathbf{2}, \mathbf{4}, \mathbf{6}, \mathbf{8}\}$. The privileged order relations in EPO(m.Ons), are between pairs of grammars which differ only along the dimension OR/OLA, holding constant the coda requirements and mode of faithfulness breach. To notate this, we introduce a special symbol for the privileged order relations, indicating both the constraint C and the origin of the relation in border point analysis: $<^{\text{bp.C}}$. Analogously, the EPO equivalence relation will notated $\sim^{\text{bp.C}}$. For typographical simplicity, the prefixes 'm' and 'f' that type constraints will be dropped in superscripts, leaving $<^{\text{bp.Ons}}$ to denote the EPO order relation with respect to m.Ons.

(12) EPO(C) Relation notation

i. Order: $<^{\mathrm{bp.C}}$

ii. Equivalence: $\sim^{\mathrm{bp.C}}$

With these conventions, the order relations in EPO(m.Ons) may be tabulated as follows:

(13) Privileged order relations in the m.Ons EPO

OR		OLA
1:CV.del	$<^{\mathrm{bp.Ons}}$	2:(C)V.del
3:CV.ins	$<^{\mathrm{bp.Ons}}$	4:(C)V.ins
5:CV(C).del	$<^{\mathrm{bp.Ons}}$	6:(C)V(C).del
7:CV(C).ins	$<^{\mathrm{bp.Ons}}$	8:(C)V(C).ins

As claimed, these pairs differ concretely only in treatment of onsets and agree on all other traits. The EPO provides only a proper subset of the order relations implied by the numerics: in this case, four out of the sixteen denoted by $\lessdot^{\mathrm{U:Ons}}$.

(14) All order relations implied by U

OR		OLA
1:CV.del	$\lessdot^{\mathrm{U:Ons}}$	2:(C)V.del, 4:(C)V.ins, 6:(C)V(C).del, 8:(C)V(C).ins
3:CV.ins	$\lessdot^{\mathrm{U:Ons}}$	2:(C)V.del, 4:(C)V.ins, 6:(C)V(C).del, 8:(C)V(C).ins
5:CV(C).del	$\lessdot^{\mathrm{U:Ons}}$	2:(C)V.del, 4:(C)V.ins, 6:(C)V(C).del, 8:(C)V(C).ins
7:CV(C).ins	$\lessdot^{\mathrm{U:Ons}}$	2:(C)V.del, 4:(C)V.ins, 6:(C)V(C).del, 8:(C)V(C).ins

The profuse relations $\lessdot^{\mathrm{U:Ons}}$ in (14) are exactly those displayed in bigraph (6). They must in fact occur in *every* UVT for EST, because the abstract relations $\lessdot^{\mathrm{U:C}}$ and $\approx^{\mathrm{U:C}}$ arise from numerical relations and lead back to them, where equality and not just equivalence is at play. In a UVT, the EPO order relation translates into ordinary numerical $<$ and the EPO equivalence relation translates into numerical $=$. Thus when we have among the abstract relations in EPO(Ons)

$\mathbf{1} \sim^{\mathrm{bp.Ons}} \mathbf{3}$

$\mathbf{3} <^{\mathrm{bp/Ons}} \mathbf{4}$,

we have numerically, as in U and indeed in every other UVT for EST,

$\mathsf{m.Ons}(\mathbf{1}) = \mathsf{m.Ons}(\mathbf{3})$

$\mathsf{m.Ons}(\mathbf{3}) < \mathsf{m.Ons}(\mathbf{4})$.

But it follows from this by arithmetic that $\mathsf{m.Ons}(\mathbf{1}) < \mathsf{m.Ons}(\mathbf{4})$ and it follows in every UVT. By definition of the relation $\lessdot^{\mathrm{U:Cons}}$, which translates UVT numerical inequalities into relations between grammars, we have then

1:CV.del $<^{\text{U:Ons}}$ 4:(C)V.ins

and by similar reasoning, all the other grammar relationships cited in (14) and portrayed in (6).

In the EPO relational system, we do *not* have **1** $<^{\text{bp.Ons}}$ **4**. That's because we have no guarantee that the grammar relations $\sim^{\text{bp.C}}$ and $<^{\text{bp.C}}$ combine like numerical $=$ and $<$. Nor do we wish them to. The order $<^{\text{bp.C}}$ is *privileged* in that it plays a role in determining the compatibility of grammars as typology-mates. We must protect privilege from equivalence so that the MOAT and its EPOs can be used to reckon typological classes of grammars.

When an abstract order relation does behave with respect to equivalence like $<$ behaves with respect to $=$, we will call it 'hypertransitive' (§4.3.5). Recall that transitivity is just the requirement on a relation $\rightsquigarrow$ that

i. $a \rightsquigarrow b \;\&\; b \rightsquigarrow c \Rightarrow a \rightsquigarrow c$

For example, numerical $<$ is transitive, so we may safely conclude from $1 < 2$ and $2 < 3$ that $1 < 3$.

Hypertransitivity requires analogously that, for an equivalence relation $\equiv$ and a relation $\rightsquigarrow$,

ii. $a \equiv b \;\&\; b \rightsquigarrow c \;\Rightarrow a \rightsquigarrow c$

iii. $a \rightsquigarrow b \;\&\; b \equiv c \;\Rightarrow a \rightsquigarrow c$

We can take a relation that is not transitive and replace it with one that includes it but *is* transitive by imposing (i), a process called 'transitive closure'. Similarly, we can form the 'hypertransitive closure' of a relation with respect to an equivalence relation by imposing (ii) and (iii). The hypertransitively closed expansion of $<^{\text{bp.C}}$, written $<^{\text{htc.bp.C}}$, obscures privilege, but, because of its concord with the UVT world, will prove essential in the course of the formal analysis in §4.

In sum, the EPO of a constraint is a kind of skeletal version of its relational structure. The EPO holds the core subset of privileged relations that restrict the content of every UVT and determine the joining of grammars into typological classes. Let us turn now to developing the EPO from the raw material of grammars, their legs and the border point pairs they participate in.

3.2 Building the MOAT & the EPO

The MOAT of a typology is derived not from the varying arithmetic of its UVTs, but from the grammars themselves, construed as collections of linear orders (*legs*).

Certain legs stand out as particularly informative: those that differ minimally in constraint ranking and belong to different grammars. Here's a typical *border point pair*, with the zone of minimal difference, in which two adjacent constraints transpose, typographically highlighted. We will mine it for information.

To keep track of the relevant memberships as we explore the cases, a leg of grammar *N* will be designated as ⟨*Nx*⟩, where *x* is an arbitrary alphabetical identifier distinguishing the legs of grammar *N*. A classified list of all the legs of EST is found in Appendix I.

(15) A border point pair (EST)

Leg	**P**	**X/Y**	**Q**	**Grammar**	**Type**
⟨7a⟩	f.max ≫	*m.Ons* ≫ **f.dep** ≫	m.NoCoda	**7**:CV(C).ins	OR.CA
⟨8a⟩	f.max ≫	**f.dep** ≫ *m.Ons* ≫	m.NoCoda	**8**:(C)V(C).ins	OLA.CA

Leg ⟨7a⟩ belongs to the grammar of **7**:CV(C).ins, which requires onsets (OR) in every syllable. Leg ⟨8a⟩ belongs to the grammar of **8**:(C)V(C).ins, in which lack of onset is allowed (OLA), indeed required when a syllable arises from an input vowel not preceded by a consonant. Otherwise, both grammars handle input configurations identically. Extensional considerations like these only hint at the nature of the relationship between these legs, which is revealed by attention to their form. The key is the notion of smallest possible significant difference as it manifests in the world of order and permutation.

Consider the generic border point pair: {P<u>XY</u>Q, P<u>YX</u>Q}, where X, Y are individual constraints and P, Q are sequences of constraints, possibly empty. We call the shared sequences P and Q the *prefix* and the *suffix* of the pair, respectively. The sequence <u>XY</u> is the *transposition* (as is <u>YX</u>), with its participating constraints underlined for visibility. We will abbreviate the name to BPP for occasional conciseness.

The members of a border point pair can be thought of as sitting next to each other graphically, if we construe each leg of Ord(*S*.Con) as corresponding to a point in the space of ranking possibilities, in which an adjacent transposition connects a point to a neighboring point.[2] On this view, a grammar turns out to be a contiguous region of such points, and grammars qua regions may also be construed as *adjacent*, by virtue of the adjacency of points they contain. It is natural therefore to speak of 'border points' which

[2] The use of transposition in this way is taken from the analysis of the 'symmetric group' S_n, the group of all permutations of a set S of *n* objects. Adjacent permutation is a generator for S_n and its Cayley graph is embodied in the permutohedron (§7).

inhabit the border region or boundary of a grammar, where a well-chosen minimal local change in constraint order occasions a higher-level change from one grammar to another. The term loses its metaphorical sheen completely in §7, where we examine the geometry behind it. As we will see, a grammar is entirely determined by its border; a typology is determined by the relations established at the borders of its constituent grammars.

The notion of the border point pair may be spelled out as follows:

(16) **Definition. Border Point Pair.** Let T = $\{G_1,..., G_n\}$ be a typology on a set of constraints T.Con, given as a set of ranking grammars $G_k = \{\lambda_i\}$, for some legs $\lambda_i \in$ Ord(T.Con). Let λ_1 = P<u>XY</u>Q and λ_2 = P<u>YX</u>Q, where P, Q are sequences of constraints from T.Con and X, Y ∈ T.Con. Let $G_j, G_k \in$ T, $G_j \neq G_k$. Then $\{\lambda_1, \lambda_2\}$ is a *border point pair* for G_j, G_k if $\lambda_1 \in G_j$ and $\lambda_2 \in G_k$.

Such pairs are unordered: transposition, like adjacency, has no inherent directional bias. A border point pair licenses EPO relations. In the border point pair below, repeated from above, information about grammars **7** and **8** is contributed to the EPOs of three different constraints.

(17) A border point pair (EST)

Leg	P	XY / YX	Q	**Grammar**
⟨7a⟩	f.max ≫	*m.Ons* ≫ **f.dep** ≫	m.NoCoda	**7**:CV(C).ins
⟨8a⟩	f.max ≫	**f.dep** ≫ *m.Ons* ≫	m.NoCoda	**8**:(C)V(C).ins

The structure of this pair is interpreted in EPO terms as follows:

i. Prefix P
   Both grammars pass through f.max.
   Therefore, they are equivalent on f.max. **7** $\sim^{\text{bp.max}}$ **8**
ii. Transposition <u>XY/YX</u>
   Leg ⟨7a⟩. Grammar **7** ejects grammar **8** on m.Ons.
   Therefore, **7** $<^{\text{bp.Ons}}$ **8**.
   Leg ⟨8a⟩. Grammar **8** ejects grammar **7** on f.dep.
   Therefore, **8** $<^{\text{bp.dep}}$ **7**.
iii. Suffix Q
   The suffix yields no information.

These findings may be tabulated as follows, using the notation laid out in (12).

(18) Relations from BPP (17)

Segment Type	Relevant segment	Relation	Relation Type	EPO
prefix	f.max ≫ ...	$7 \sim^{\text{bp.max}} 8$	equivalence	EPO(f.max)
⟨7a⟩ transposition	... m.Ons ≫ f.dep ...	$7 <^{\text{bp.Ons}} 8$	order	EPO(m.Ons)
⟨8a⟩ transposition	... f.dep ≫ m.Ons ...	$8 <^{\text{bp.dep}} 7$	order	EPO(f.dep)
suffix	... ≫ m.NoCoda		*no info*	

i. In the general case, for a transposition XY/YX, the leg PXYQ sponsors an order relation in EPO(X) that sets its grammar as $<^{\text{bp.X}}$ with respect to the grammar of PYXQ. Symmetrically, the leg PYXQ installs a relation $<^{\text{bp.Y}}$ in EPO(Y), reversing the order of the grammars.

ii. For every C in P, the grammars are equivalent in EPO(C), standing in the relation $\sim^{\text{bp.C}}$.

iii. Nothing is learned about any constraint D in Q, so that EPO(D) is determined by the role of D in the prefixes and transpositions of other border point pairs. See §4.3 for discussion.

These are abstract ascriptions, reflecting the order of constraints in legs at the border. But they are echoed in the way that candidates are filtered by the numerics of the UVTs: this gives them their interest and their potency. To see how it works, it is instructive to pursue the details of filtration by legs ⟨7a⟩ and ⟨8a⟩. Filtration within a UVT proceeds in exactly the same way as in familiar concrete OT. The top-ranked constraint accepts those candidates to which it gives the minimal value and disregards the rest. And so on down the hierarchy, at each step dealing in the same way with the survivors of the previous step. Since the candidates are rows ('languages'), filtration by a leg chooses a language as optimal and thereby assigns the filtering leg to the grammar of the language it selects. Let's examine the entire filtration, keeping an eye on the behavior of **7** and **8** as we proceed.

First up: f.max.

⟨7a⟩ = f.max ≫ ... ∈ **7**

⟨8a⟩ = f.max ≫ ... ∈ **8**

(19) Filtration map

Leg	Constraint	Input	Output	Survivor Type
⟨7a⟩	f.max	{**1**, **2**, **3**, **4**, **5**, **6**, **7**, **8**}	{**3**, **4**, **7**, **8**}	Σ.ins
⟨8a⟩	f.max	{**1**, **2**, **3**, **4**, **5**, **6**, **7**, **8**}	{**3**, **4**, **7**, **8**}	Σ.ins

The legs in the border point pair $\{\langle 7a\rangle, \langle 8a\rangle\}$ start off the same way. The grammars {**3**, **4**, **7**, **8**} all have legs beginning with f.max, and the other grammars do not. This is therefore the subset that survives filtration here, concretely the grammars of the insertional languages Σ.ins for syllable-shape Σ. The ejectees {**1**, **2**, **5**, **6**} at this step of filtration are the complement set of deleters Σ.del.

Languages **7** and **8**, whatever their numerical values, must both pass through f.max in order to show up as optimal in the final reckoning by legs ⟨7a⟩ and ⟨8a⟩ respectively. In UVT (15), §2.2.4, f.max(**7**) = f.max(**8**) = 0, the minimal value.

This is no quirk: equality must hold in *all* UVTs that deliver the EST typology. To test this claim, suppose that in some putative UVT, we found instead f.max(**7**) < f.max(**8**). In this case, language **8** would be ejected right away by any leg beginning with f.max, because **8** would bear a nonminimal value. But we know from the concrete EST that leg ⟨8a⟩ belongs to the grammar of **8**, so this inequality cannot be tolerated. Similarly, an inequality in the other direction ejects ⟨7a⟩ from grammar **7**. With neither inequality allowed, equality is the only remaining option.

When we add the abstract equivalence **7** $\sim^{\text{bp.max}}$ **8** to EPO(f.max), we may therefore rest secure in the knowledge that this relation will be instantiated as numerical equality in every UVT for EST, although we have looked at none of them.

Next up: m.Ons and **f.dep**. Here the transposition begins and the two legs differ.

⟨7a⟩ = f.max ≫ *m.Ons* ≫ ... ∈ **7**
⟨8a⟩ = f.max ≫ **f.dep** ≫ ... ∈ **8**

(20) Filtration map

Leg	Constraint	Input	Output	Survivor Type
⟨7a⟩	m.Ons	{**3**, **4**, **7**, **8**}	{**3**, **7**}	OR.ins
⟨8a⟩	f.dep	{**3**, **4**, **7**, **8**}	{**8**}	OLA.CA.ins

The survivor set is filtered down further on the second step in each leg.

On ⟨7a⟩, filtering by m.Ons, the inserters {**3**, **4**, **7**, **8**} shrink to the *Onset-Required* inserters {**3**,**7**}, concretely **3**:CV.ins and **7**:CV(C).ins, ejecting **8**:(C)V(C).ins as well as **4**:(C)V.ins.

By contrast, and more subtly, in ⟨8a⟩ the survivor set $\{\mathbf{3}, \mathbf{4}, \mathbf{7}, \mathbf{8}\}$ faces f.dep, which discriminates degrees of insertionality. All that remains is **8**:(C)V(C).ins, with **7**:CV(C).ins ejected along with **3**:CV.ins and **4**:(C)V.ins.[3]

MOATwise, we add to EPO(m.Ons) the relation: $\mathbf{7} <^{\text{bp.Ons}} \mathbf{8}$ and to EPO(f.dep) the relation $\mathbf{8} <^{\text{bp.dep}} \mathbf{7}$. Filtrationwise, narrowing our focus to just these two languages, these abstract order relations correlate with the following actions.

i. On ⟨7a⟩, m.Ons selects language **7** from the pair $\{\mathbf{7}, \mathbf{8}\}$ and ejects **8**.
ii. On ⟨8a⟩, f.dep selects language **8** from the pair $\{\mathbf{7}, \mathbf{8}\}$ and ejects **7**.

Looking back to the numbers in UVT (15), §2.2.4, we see that selection of **7** along with ejection of **8** by ⟨7a⟩ happens because numerically m.Ons(**7**) < m.Ons(**8**). Selection of **8** with ejection of **7** by ⟨8a⟩ is similarly due to the fact that f.dep(**8**) < f.dep(**7**). For thoroughness, let's confirm that these orderings must occur in every UVT for EST by running through – and dismissing – the alternatives.

Suppose first that the relative magnitudes were reversed: that m.Ons(**8**) < m.Ons(**7**) in some claimed UVT. Then **7** is going to be ejected by ⟨7a⟩ when m.Ons is reached in the filtration, because its value is nonminimal. According to this VT, ⟨7a⟩ ∉ **7**, contrary to the facts of EST. Fail! So this order can't be reversed.

Experimenting further, suppose that we were to set m.Ons(**7**) = m.Ons(**8**). Now m.Ons doesn't distinguish **7** from **8**. But this means that the entire transposition zone can't distinguish them either: in selecting from $\{\mathbf{7}, \mathbf{8}\}$, the ranking m.Ons ≫ f.dep gives the same result as f.dep ≫ m.Ons when m.Ons treats **7** and **8** as equal. Therefore, under this hopeless assumption, ⟨7a⟩ and ⟨8a⟩ would yield the same optimum, since the only difference between them has been erased. But in reality they give different results: a fact we cannot escape. Equality is out, and we must therefore have everywhere m.Ons(**7**) < m.Ons(**8**).

For parallel reasons, the f.dep EPO relation $\mathbf{8} <^{\text{bp.dep}} \mathbf{7}$ derived from border point analysis will correlate in every UVT with numerical f.dep(**8**) < f.dep(**7**).

[3] Because **8**:(C)V(C).ins admits both onsetless and codaic syllables, insertion is allowed only in the case of inputs like /C/, which contain consonants that always provoke a faithfulness breach. The other three inserters treat /C/ and its congeners the same way, but use insertion more profusely to deal with markedness requirements.

Next up: f.dep and m.Ons

⟨7a⟩ = f.max≫ *m.Ons* ≫ **f.dep** ≫ ... ∈ **7**

⟨8a⟩ = f.max ≫ **f.dep** ≫ *m.Ons* ≫ ... ∈ **8**

(21) Filtration map

Leg	Constraint	Input	Output	Survivor Type
⟨7a⟩	f.dep	{**3**, **7**}	{**7**}	OR.CA.ins
⟨8s⟩	m.Ons	{**8**}	{**8**}	OLA.CA.ins

There's nothing more to learn about relations between **7** and **8** from this border point pair, since each of them has been ejected from one of the survivor sets in the previous step. In the ongoing filtration, leg ⟨7a⟩ now faces the set {**3**,**7**}, ejecting **3**. At this point, leg ⟨8a⟩ sees only {**8**}, which passes through without competitors.

Last up: m.NoCoda.

⟨7a⟩ = f.max≫ *m.Ons* ≫ **f.dep** ≫ m.NoCoda ∈ **7**

⟨8a⟩ = f.max ≫ **f.dep** ≫ *m.Ons* ≫ m.NoCoda ∈ **8**

(22) Filtration map: final step

Leg	Constraint	Input	Output	Survivor Type
⟨7a⟩	m.NoCoda	{**7**}	{**7**}	OR.CA.ins
⟨8s⟩	m.NoCoda	{**8**}	{**8**}	OLA.CA.ins

As in the previous step, no further consequences follow since the set {**7**, **8**} was decided at the leading constraint of the transposition. Here the suffix contains but one item, but in the general case, we know that any permutation of suffixal constraints produces the same outcome and yields no relational information from the border point pair, because the decisions between the competing pair of languages have been made. This completes the analysis of BPP {⟨**7**a⟩, ⟨**8**a⟩}.

We have conducted this investigation among the particulars of UVT (15), §2.2.4, but in every case we are able to argue that the results apply generally across the entire set of UVTs. We know that each UVT for EST assigns the same legs to its grammars, by the definition of UVT. But the discussion has disclosed a pervasive broader generalization: every UVT for a given typology exhibits the same *filtration patterns*, working through each leg from the highest ranked constraint to lowest. To be more precise, by the *filtration pattern* of a ranking λ with respect to a collection of candidates, we mean the telescoping sequence of surviving subsets obtained in the course of filtering it by λ. As exemplified here and as is established for the general case in Theorem (84), §4.5.4, any change in filtration patterns, even at intermediate stages, will involve a reassignment of legs to grammars, yielding a different typology.

Even more strikingly, it turns out that to obtain the privileged relations between grammars, we need only attend to the border point pairs. To build the MOAT in its entirety, we examine every border point pair in the manner just laid out, gathering the relevant information for each EPO.

The border point pair {⟨7a⟩, ⟨8a⟩} gives a quantum of information about EPO(m.Ons). Let's now complete that EPO, examining first the following three border point pairs.

(23) Three BPPs in EST

Leg	**Border Point Pair**	**Grammar**	**Type**
	P — **XY/YX**		
⟨1a⟩	f.dep ≫ m.NoCoda ≫ *m.Ons* ≫ **f.max**	1:CV.del	OR.CP
⟨2a⟩	f.dep ≫ m.NoCoda ≫ **f.max** ≫ *m.Ons*	2:(C)V.del	OLA.CP
	P — **XY/YX**		
⟨3a⟩	m.NoCoda ≫ f.max ≫ *m.Ons* ≫ **f.dep**	3:CV.ins	OR.CP
⟨4a⟩	m.NoCoda ≫ f.max ≫ **f.dep** ≫ *m.Ons*	4:(C)V.ins	OLA.CP
	P — **XY/YX** — **Q**		
⟨5a⟩	f.dep ≫ *m.Ons* ≫ **f.max** ≫ m.NoCoda	5:CV(C).del	OR.CA
⟨6a⟩	f.dep ≫ **f.max** ≫ *m.Ons* ≫ m.NoCoda	6:(C)V(C).del	OLA.CA

The three pairs in (23), along with the pair {⟨7a⟩,⟨8a⟩} in (17), establish all four privileged order relations between the languages of EST on the constraint m.Ons.

(24) Privileged relations of EST on m.Ons

From {⟨**1**a⟩, ⟨**2**a⟩}: $\mathbf{1} <^{\text{bp.Ons}} \mathbf{2}$
From {⟨**3**a⟩, ⟨**4**a⟩}: $\mathbf{3} <^{\text{bp.Ons}} \mathbf{4}$
From {⟨**5**a⟩, ⟨**6**a⟩}: $\mathbf{5} <^{\text{bp.Ons}} \mathbf{6}$
From {⟨**7**a⟩, ⟨**8**a⟩}: $\mathbf{7} <^{\text{bp.Ons}} \mathbf{8}$

It remains to find the EPO equivalences of m.Ons. By examining other border point pairs which have prefixes containing m.Ons, we can cull those languages which must share an m.Ons value. The following three pairs will suffice. In each border point pair, the prefix preceding the transposition is boxed.

(25) Equivalences on m.Ons

Leg	Border Point Pair (Prefix Boxed)				Grammar	Type
⟨1b⟩	m.Ons ≫ m.NoCoda	≫ *f.dep*	≫ **f.max**		1:CV.del	OR.CP
⟨3b⟩	m.Ons ≫ m.NoCoda	≫ **f.max**	≫ *f.dep*		3:CV.ins	OR.CP
⟨5a⟩	f.dep ≫ m.Ons	≫ *f.max*	≫ **m.NoCoda**		5:CV(C).del	OR.CA
⟨1c⟩	f.dep ≫ m.Ons	≫ **m.NoCoda**	≫ *f.max*		1:CV.del	OR.CP
⟨7b⟩	m.Ons	≫ *f.max*	≫ **f.dep**	≫ m.NoCoda	7:CV(C).ins	OR.CA
⟨5b⟩	m.Ons	≫ **f.dep**	≫ *f.max*	≫ m.NoCoda	5:CV(C).del	OR.CA

The members of each competing pair of adjacent grammars register as equivalent on all constraints in the prefix. The pairs above license the following relations in EPO(m.Ons):

$\mathbf{1} \sim^{\text{bp.Ons}} \mathbf{3}$

$\mathbf{1} \sim^{\text{bp.Ons}} \mathbf{5}$

$\mathbf{5} \sim^{\text{bp.Ons}} \mathbf{7}$.

An equivalence relation is symmetric, reflexive, and transitive. Symmetry is guaranteed by prefixal status and by the fact that border point pairs are unordered, so that each of the above may be written the other way around, as e.g. $\mathbf{3} \sim^{\text{bp.Ons}} \mathbf{1}$. To achieve full-scale equivalence, the base border point relation must be augmented to the equivalence $\sim^{\text{bp.Ons}}$ by reflexive and transitive closure. Once this is done, it follows that the OR languages **1, 3, 5, 7** are all equivalent in EPO(m.Ons) to each other.

(26) EPO(m.Ons): equivalent languages

$\mathbf{1} \sim^{\text{bp.Ons}} \mathbf{3} \sim^{\text{bp.Ons}} \mathbf{5} \sim^{\text{bp.Ons}} \mathbf{7}$

Strikingly, there is no border point pair distinguishing **1** and **7** which has m.Ons in its prefix. Thus, **1** and **7** are Ons-equivalent, but only by transitivity. Nevertheless, we are certain of their relationship. Privilege, similarly, must be made transitive, though not hypertransitive, as noted.

In an EPO diagram, we do not attempt to represent the relation 'equivalent by virtue of some border point pair'. Equivalence, however derived, is portrayed in any of several convenient layouts, from which all further pairwise equivalences may be easily derived by transitivity. We repeat the EPO diagram given above for m.Ons, which lays out the equivalences and privileged relations just derived.

(27) EPO(m.Ons) of EST

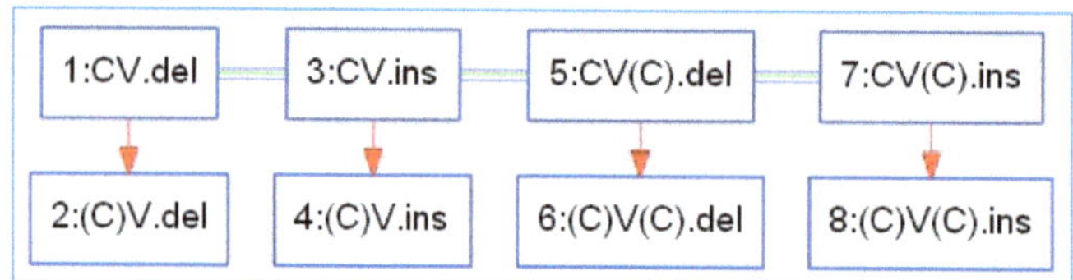

Note that 1:CV.del and 5:CV(C).del (top row) are in fact adjacent, as is shown by the existence of the second border point pair in (25) and graphically represented below in §7.2, diagrams (6) and (7). We take advantage of the transitivity of equivalence to simplify by omitting this connection in bigraph (27).

Continuing in this fashion, we can derive every EPO of EST. Here are the remaining three, completing the MOAT with one EPO for each constraint in the system.

(28) EPO(m.NoCoda) of EST

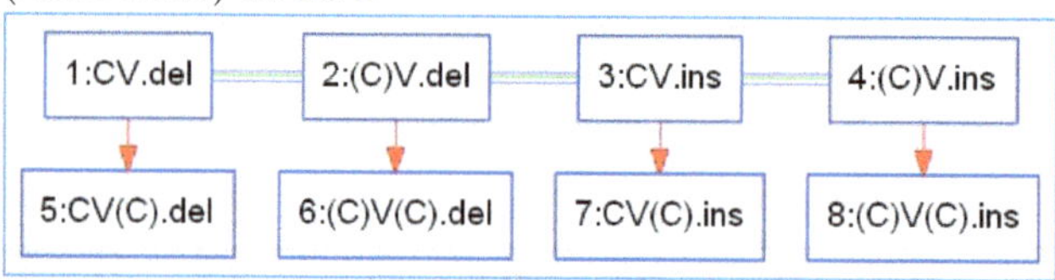

Note in (28) that the mentioned adjacency between 1:CV.del and 5:CV(C).del is manifest (far left).

(29) EPO(f.dep) of EST

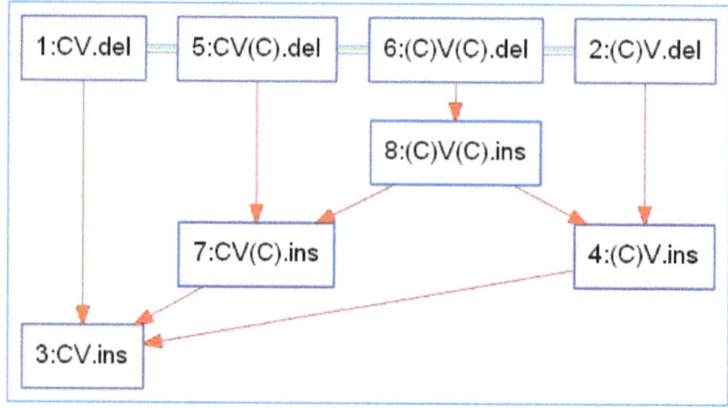

(30) EPO(**f.max**) of EST

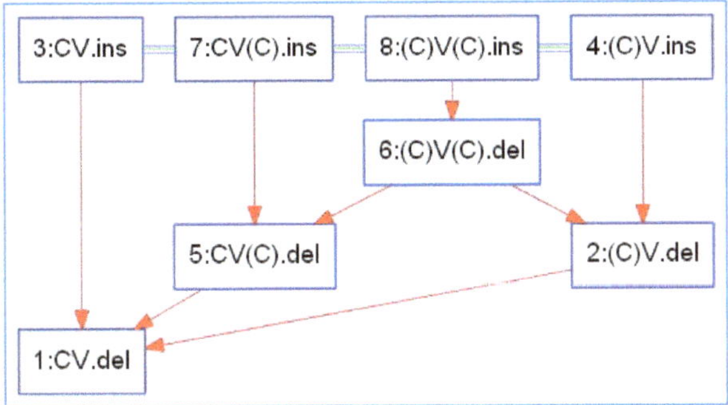

In contrast to the way equivalence is represented, without implication that the grammars adjacent in the bigraph are border-point adjacent, the order arrows connect only strictly adjacent grammars. Thus, in EPO(**f.dep**) and EPO(**f.max**) we have, respectively,

8:(C)V(C).ins $<^{\text{bp.dep}}$ 3:CV.ins (29)

6:(C)V(C).del $<^{\text{bp.max}}$ 1:CV.del (30)

But in neither case is the grammar on the one side of the relation *adjacent* to the grammar on the other. Both relations are derived by transitivity: see the center-right/far-left downward diagonal in (29) and (30).

With the full MOAT assembled, it becomes clear that there are striking symmetries in the structure of the typology. Visible in EPOs (27) and (28) is the parallelism between **m.Ons** and **m.NoCoda**. EPOs (29) and (30) show a similarly close relation between **f.dep** and **f.max**. Concretely, these graph isomorphisms are prefigured in the definitions of EST.Con, but the cooperation of EST.Gen is required to achieve the results.[4] EPO analysis tells us exactly how the definitional parallels play out in the typology and, in the general case, will identify symmetries that may not otherwise be perspicuous.

We conclude with an observation about structural properties of the EPO. Each EPO comes ultimately from the analysis of border point pairs. The assignment of legs to grammars comes from a UVT, via the general OT definition of optimality. As we have glimpsed in our example, and as we will show for the general case in §4.3.3, Lemma (25), the EPO relations are instantiated as numerical relations in UVTs. They must therefore be consistent with some partial order on the grammars, because they ultimately cash out as the ordered values of a UVT column. The local pairwise relations between grammars determined at their borders must extend to order and

[4] For details of these, see §2.1, exx. (1) and (4).

equivalence relations that combine together in a way that comports with the way numerical order and equality combine; see the build-up to Lemma (49), §4.3.5, for details. Graphically, then, a valid EPO cannot have cycles.

The *privileged* order relations that populate an EPO are all and only those order relations that come, directly or by transitivity, from border point pairs. A standard EPO *diagram*, like a Hasse diagram, elides order relations derivable from transitivity, for conciseness. Returning to our first example (27), §1.3.1 from the system nGX.IL, recall that the EPO diagram of Parse-σ omits the transitively derivable arrow, even though it represents a relation from the border of **SD** and **sp**.

(31) EPO(Parse-σ) in nGX.IL

Standard

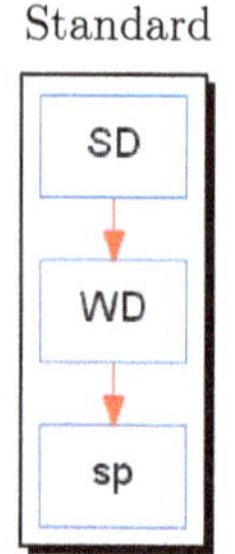

Unreduced

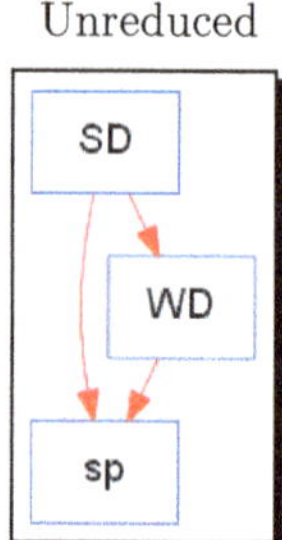

The link between **SD** and **sp** signals the existence of a border point pair spanning the languages. A little inspection shows it to be the following, in which P is empty.

(32) Border point pair, SD/sp in nGX.IL

X/Y				Q	
Parse-σ	≫	**AFL**	≫	lamb	∈ **SD**
AFL	≫	*Parse-σ*	≫	lamb	∈ **sp**

Both bigraphs in (31) represent the same order. Observe that there is no (directed) cycle in the unreduced version, since all arrows point in the same direction: downward.

In sum: an EPO is a certain kind of order structure derived from analysis of the border point pairs of a typology. It is represented by a bigraph. Since any UVT of a typology gives rise to the same grammars and therefore the same border point pairs, the EPO is invariant across all typologically equivalent UVTs. More than that, the EPO relations delimit the entire range of UVT possibilities. The EPO contains the privileged relations that lead to an order on the grammars of the typology; it must therefore be *acyclic*.

Acyclicity diagnoses whether a partition is a typology. Acyclicity and privilege determine the possible typological classes.[5]

3.3 Why privilege?

The privileged relations provide the data for determining typological classes from a MOAT. The non-privileged relations, which arise by combining order and equivalence information hypertransitively, are excluded from the MOAT because they do not obstruct the formation of typological classes. In this section, we examine cases that show the force of this crucial distinction.

As we've seen, a given numerical UVT will typically induce many pairwise relations of ordering. Some of these are arbitrary in the sense that there are other UVTs for the same typology that lack them. Others follow from the EPO relations of order and equivalence taken together, and will therefore hold across the set of all typologically equivalent UVTs. But if we want to use the MOAT for typological analysis, we must omit universally present but non-privileged relations from the EPO and disregard them in typological calculations.

To see why this must be so, it is instructive to re-examine EPO(m.Ons), repeated from (27).

(33) EPO(m.Ons) of EST

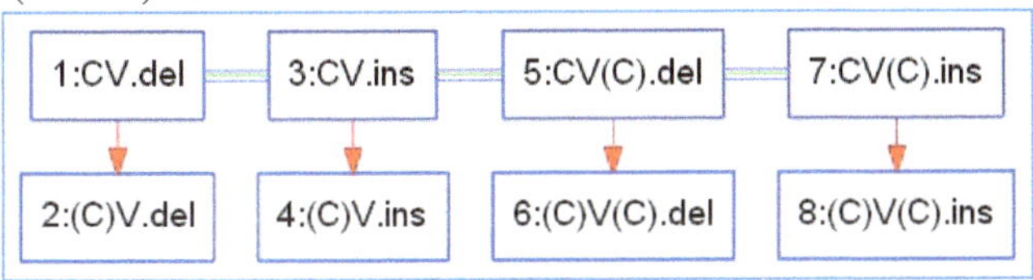

An EPO arrow shows a privileged order relation that arises directly from an extant border point pair. The instructive comparison is with a bigraph reflecting the full range of numerical order relations that hold between the first and second rows, as presented in table (14) above. These hold not just in the UVT U (15), §2.2.4, but in every UVT for EST.

---

[5] These assertions are demonstrated below. EPOs delimit: Theorems (155), (159), (160), §4.7. The privileged relations extend to an order on grammars: Lemma (28), §4.3.4. Acyclicity described: p. 35, §1.3.2; defined: Definition (170), §4.8. When a partition is a typology: Theorem (183), §4.8. On acyclicity and typological classification: see §6.

(34) Bigraph of m.Ons in all UVTs, including non-privileged orders

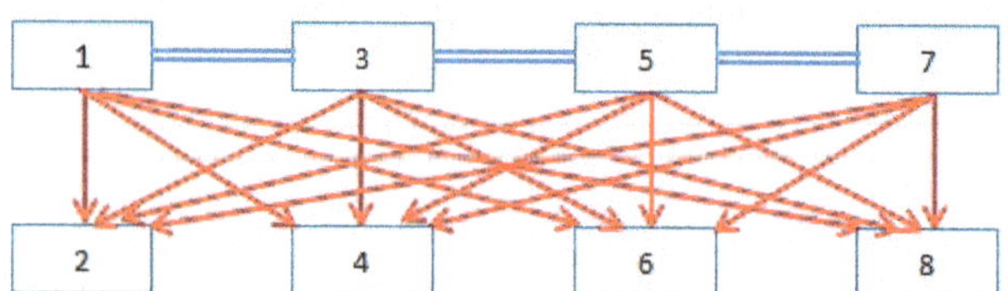

Equivalence holds in both bigraphs between grammars **1**, **3**, **5**, and **7**. These are the members of the class OR in which m.Ons is never violated in optima: concretely, every optimal form has only C-initial syllables. The order-contributing arrows in the bigraphs have a more interesting relationship. The privileged orders in EPO(m.Ons) are just four in number, but when combined with equivalence in the way that numerical '<' combines with '=' ('hypertransitively'), they yield the 16 pairwise orders of bigraph (34). Consequently, these 16 must be present in every UVT of EST.

To see how the privileged order $\mathbf{7} <^{\text{bp.Ons}} \mathbf{8}$ restricts typological classification, let's examine the effects of amalgamating **5**:CV(C).del (top row, penultimate position) with **8**:(C)V(C).ins in an ill-fated attempt to classify them together to the exclusion of all others.

In terms of ranking content, classifying a set of grammars together means unioning their legs. In the EPO bigraph, such a union corresponds to merging the nodes that bear the grammar names. The node **5•8** thus corresponds to a partition block that contains all and only the legs of grammars **5** and **8**, namely **5∪8**. As above, we write N•M for graphical merger of nodes labeled N and M, and N∪M for the union of the legs.[6] Graphical node merger retains all external edges that connect the merged nodes with other nodes, just as union of blocks retains all border points with grammars outside the union. We will see that scrutiny of the border point pairs involving **5∪8** confirms the graphical analysis conducted within the EPO.

The effect of merging **5** and **8** in EPO(m.Ons) is seen in the bigraph (35). It fails to support a UVT, because it has a cycle involving **7** and therefore fails to assert order and equivalence relations that can be realized numerically as order and equality. No constraint can assign the *same* number to **7** and **5•8** while at the same time assigning a smaller number to **7** than to **5•8.**

[6] We tolerate the mild ambiguity of letting the symbols N,M refer to nodes in N•M and leg sets in N∪M.

(35) A bigraph tangled by merger

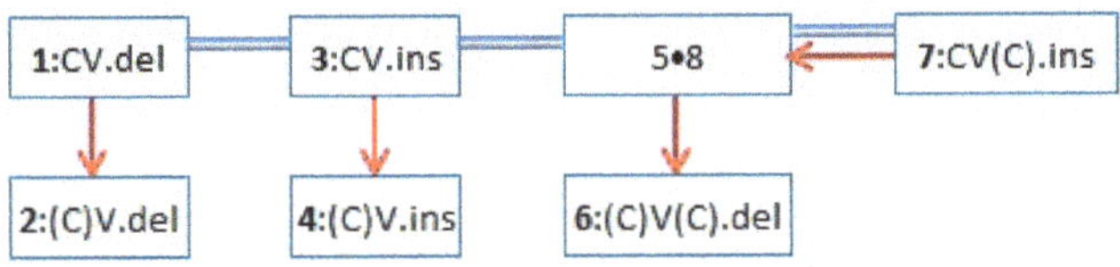

This merged bigraph visibly fails to represent an EPO, because of the relations between **5•8** and **7**. The cycle arises from the fact that **7** = **5** and **7** → **8**. The node **5•8** inherits both.

(36) Birth of a bigraph cycle

Relation in (35)	Source in EPO bigraph (33)	Source in EPO(m.Ons)
7 = **5•8**	**7** = **5**	**7** $\sim^{\text{bp.Ons}}$ **5**
7 → **5•8**	**7** → **8**	**7** $<^{\text{bp.Ons}}$ **8**

The class denoted by **5•8** acquires its equivalence with **7** because it incorporates **5**, which is equivalent to **7**. But from its **8** component, **5•8** acquires an order relation to **7**. This cycle defies numerical instantiation. Substantively, this tells us that **5**:CV(C).ins and **8**:(C)V(C).del, unioned, do not form a typological class, a super-grammar generalizing over its component grammars.

To see how border point analysis leads to the same result in the coarsened partition containing the unioned grammars, we list the legs of **5∪8**, which are simply those of **5** and **8** lumped together. Leg designations are retained from §3.2.

(37) All legs of **5∪8**, from **5**:CV(C).del and **8**:(C)V(C).ins

Name	Source	Leg
⟨**5∪8**.i⟩	⟨5a⟩	f.dep ≫ m.Ons ≫ f.max ≫ m.NoCoda
⟨**5∪8**.ii⟩	⟨5b⟩	m.Ons ≫ f.dep ≫ f.max ≫ m.NoCoda
⟨**5∪8**.iii⟩	⟨8a⟩	f.max ≫ f.dep ≫ m.Ons ≫ m.NoCoda
⟨**5∪8**.iv⟩	⟨8b⟩	f.max ≫ f.dep ≫ m.NoCoda ≫ m.Ons
⟨**5∪8**.v⟩	⟨8c⟩	f.dep ≫ m.Ons ≫ f.max ≫ m.NoCoda

Here are the two legs of **7**:

(38) Legs of **7**:CV(C).ins

Name	Source	Leg
⟨7a⟩	⟨7a⟩	f.max ≫ m.Ons ≫ f.dep ≫ m.NoCoda
⟨7b⟩	⟨7b⟩	m.Ons ≫ f.max ≫ f.dep ≫ m.NoCoda

To analyze the border point pairs linking **5∪8** and **7** requires little more than observing that **5∪8** simply inherits the relations with **7** that **5** and **8** have individually. *The legs that determine these relations are still there,* and still in border position. Thus:

The equivalence **5∪8** $\sim^{\text{bp.Ons}}$ **7** comes from the relation between ⟨7b⟩ and ⟨**5∪8**.ii⟩, also known as ⟨5b⟩. We've already encountered this in the border point analysis that established the m.Ons EPO, because ⟨5b⟩ and ⟨7b⟩ form a border point pair for EST, examined in ex. (15) and repeated here. The constraint m.Ons sits in the prefix.

(39) Equivalence on m.Ons: **5∪8**$\sim^{\text{bp.Ons}}$ **7**

Leg	Border Point Pair	Grammar
⟨5b⟩ = ⟨**5∪8**.ii⟩	m.Ons ≫ *f.dep* ≫ **f.max** ≫ m.NoCoda	**5**:CV(C).del
⟨7b⟩	m.Ons ≫ **f.max** ≫ *f.dep* ≫ m.NoCoda	**7**:CV(C).ins

The privileged relation **7** $<^{\text{m.Ons}}$ **5∪8** comes from the relation between ⟨8a⟩ = ⟨**5∪8**.iii⟩ and ⟨7a⟩, seen previously in the border point analysis of ⟨7a⟩, ⟨8a⟩, ex. (17). The constraint m.Ons now sits in the transposition zone.

(40) Order on m.Ons: **7** $<^{\text{m.Ons}}$ **5∪8**

Leg	Border Point Pair	Grammar
⟨7a⟩	f.max ≫ *m.Ons* ≫ **f.dep** ≫ m.NoCoda	**7**:CV(C).ins
⟨8a⟩ = ⟨**5∪8**.iii⟩	f.max ≫ **f.dep** ≫ *m.Ons* ≫ m.NoCoda	**8**:(C)V(C).ins

But here the equivalence $\sim^{\text{bp.X}}$ is not consistent with the order $<^{\text{bp.X}}$ when cashed out numerically. To track the dire consequences, we may explicitly perform the following deduction in the integers.

i.	Ons(**7**)	<	Ons(**5∪8**)	in every UVT
ii.	Ons(**5∪8**)	=	Ons(**7**)	in every UVT
iii.	∴ Ons(**7**)	<	Ons(**7**)	in every UVT, from i. & ii. Contradiction!

Because no integer is smaller than itself, conclusion iii. invalidates the premises.

Since the relation $<^{\text{bp.Ons}}$ established from the border point pairs of **5∪8** and **7** cannot be numerically instantiated along with $\sim^{\text{bp.Ons}}$, there is no UVT that yields a typology that is like that of EST except for containing **5∪8** in place of **5** and **8**. And thus, there is no such typology.

We have now shown this in two ways. First, by examining the bigraph created by *merging* **5** and **8** into **5•8.** Second, by directly analyzing the border points pairs on the coarsened partition that contains **5∪8**. Conclusion: **5∪8** is not a typological class.

What then of the non-privileged orders that frequently accompany the privileged orders? These do not come from border point pairs, but they are derivable from an EPO by combining equivalence and order information hypertransitively. To see how this works out, let's take another look at the **5-7-8** nexus.

It is assuredly the case that in every UVT Ons(**5**) < Ons(**8**) numerically. We now mark this in the following bigraph, which expands the EPO diagram. The dashed grey arrow indicates the non-privileged relation between **5** and **8**, which is derived numerically from the fact that m.Ons(**5**) = m.Ons(**7**) and m.Ons(**7**) < m.Ons(**8**) in every UVT.

(41) Bigraph of EPO(m.Ons) augmented to include some non-privileged information

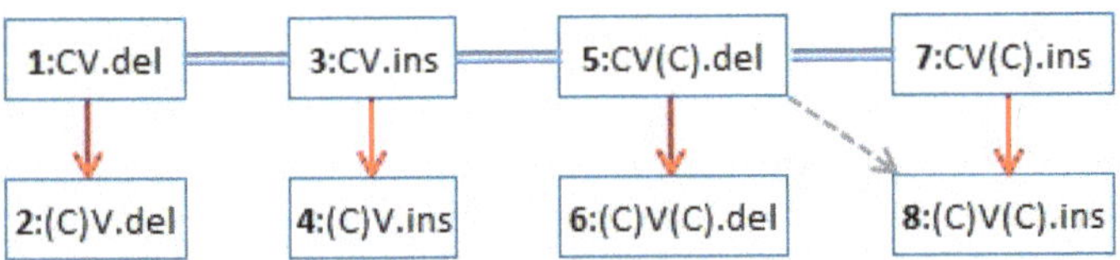

If the grey arrow were taken into account, it would obstruct the typological merger of **7** and **8** into the class **7•8**. In EST, this is the class CA.ins: codas allowed, with all unfaithfulness handled by insertion. It generalizes over **7**:CV(C).ins and **8**:(C)V(C).ins, abstracting away from the different treatment of onsets in the two languages (OR in **7**, OLA in **8**).

(42) Merger diagram preserving non-privileged information

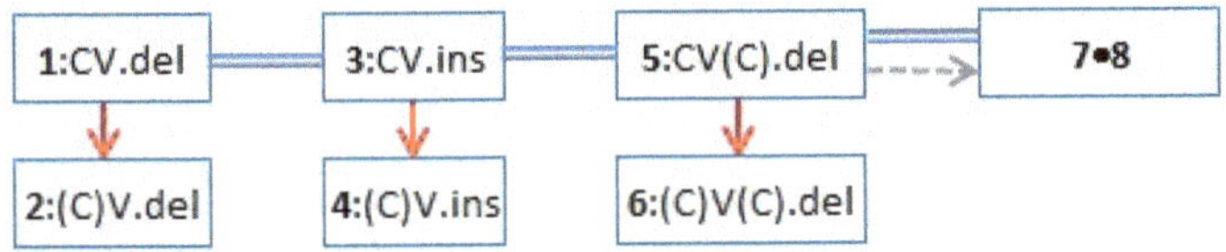

The cycle that appears between nodes **5** and **7•**8 is illusory. The grammatical class **7∪8** is a typologically valid union, and EPO(m.Ons) raises no objection. Note that the *red* arrow between **7** and **8** in (41) disappears when they merge. Without it, the grey-arrow relation between **5** and **8**, which depends on it, no longer exists. Unlike the privileged red-arrow relations, its existence is contingent upon configurations outside it that can vanish in a merger.

Compare the result of merging **7** and **8** in the actual EPO of m.Ons.

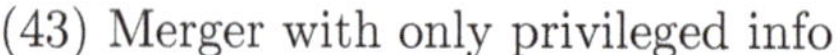
(43) Merger with only privileged info

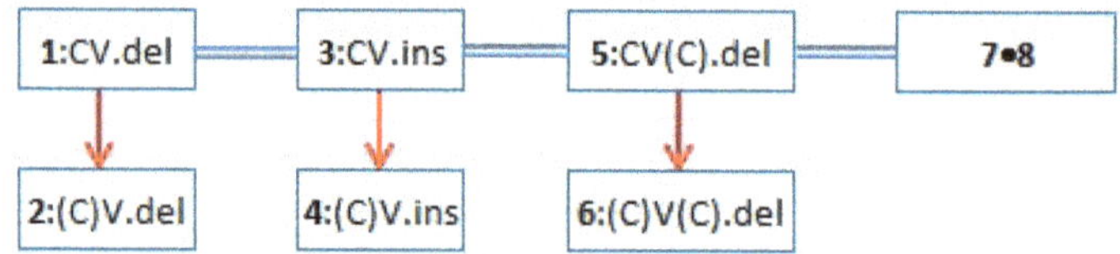

Because there is no border point between **5** and **8**, there is nothing about their relationship that is retained in the merger and everything runs smoothly. It is the lack of border-point based relational structure external to the merger that ensures the typological validity of the **7•8** class.[7]

Let's conclude the discussion by looking at potential mergers between nodes where only order is at play. The EPO of f.dep provides a worthy example.

(44) EPO(f.dep) of EST

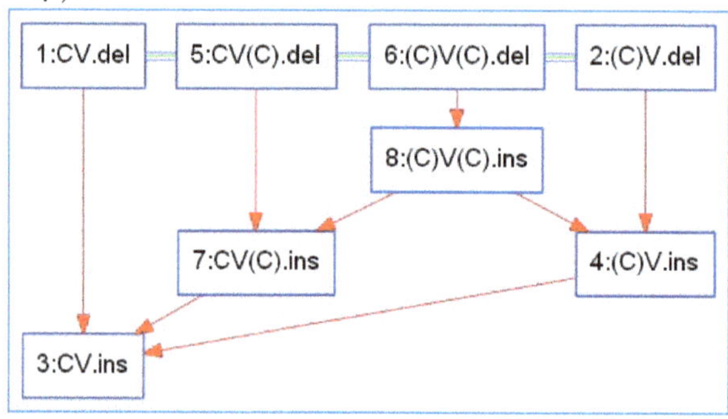

We'll focus on the sequences running down from **8** (center right) to **3** (lower left). These sit below the equivalence class of deleters in the top row and include all and only the members of the insertional class. There are 11 possible mergers among the four nodes **8**, **7**, **4**, **3**.[8] Of these, the following four 2-node mergers are fully legit:

---

[7] General bigraphs can contain more elaborate structures like A→B=C→D=E→F. Here, the merger A•F creates a cycle that is not instantiable in numbers. As expected, the path between A and F is external to the merger.

[8] For a set of 4 objects, we have $2^4 = 16$ subsets, but one of them is $\emptyset$ and four are singletons.

(45) Binary mergers producing typological classes

Merger	Union	Resulting Class	Insertion with:
8•7	**8**:(C)V(C).ins ∪ **7**:CV(C).ins	CA.ins	Coda allowed
8•4	**8**:(C)V(C).ins ∪ **4**:(C)V.ins	OLA.ins	Onset lack allowed
7•3	**7**:CV(C).ins ∪ **3**:CV.ins	OR.ins	Onset required
4•3	**4**:(C)V.ins ∪ **3**:CV.ins	CP.ins	Coda prohibited

As may be quickly checked on diagram (44), each of these mergers produces an acyclic bigraph from EPO(f.dep). To complete the argument that these are valid typological classes, their effects must be checked on all the other EPOs. EPO(f.max) is trivial, because the inserting group stands at the top, mutually equivalent, since its members allow no deletion at all. To facilitate readerly checking of the others, we reproduce EPO(m.Ons) and EPO(m. NoCoda) here.

(46) EPO(m.Ons)

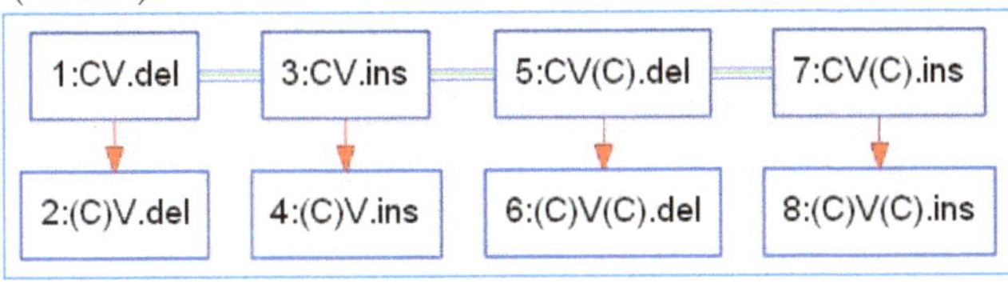

(47) EPO(m.NoCoda)

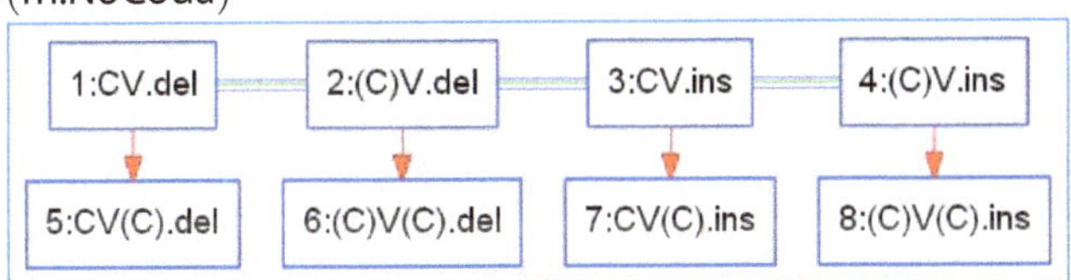

Returning to EPO(f.dep), we find that the binary merger **8•3** introduces, by contrast with those we've just examined, a nasty double cycle. Only the sub-bigraph involving the insertion grammars is displayed here.

(48) Typologically invalid merger **8•3**, from EPO(f.dep)

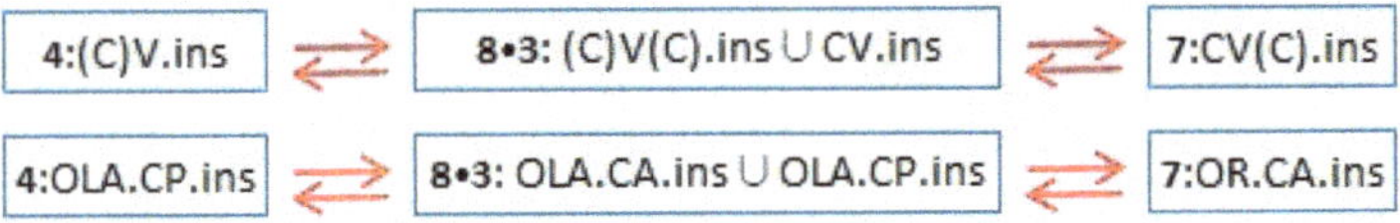

Both modes of descriptive labeling are shown, to make it easier to see how the formal cycle correlates with trait structure. Merged **8•3** requires both more epenthesis (3:OR.CP) and less (8:OLA.CA) than its flankers, while not admitting the middle level they allow.

The triple mergers **4•8•3**, amalgamating left and center in (48), and **7•8•3**, amalgamating center and right, fail for the same reason, since they each retain a cycle.

Even less fortunate is the remaining binary merger **4•7** of mid-level inserters, which – although it induces no cycles in EPO(f.dep), shown immediately below – goes awry elsewhere.

(49) 4•7 in EPO(f.dep), insertion grammars only

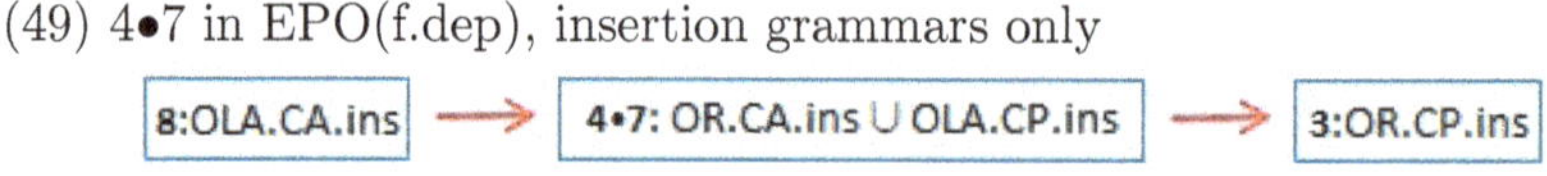

As the reader may wish to check, in EPO(m.Ons), repeated above in (46), the merger **4•7** would create an equivalence/order cycle involving **3**, paralleling the way that **5•8** tangles with **7**, as studied above in ex. (35).

In addition, the merger **4•7** interacts just as badly with **3** in EPO(m.NoCoda), also easily checked above in (47).

Along the same lines, the merger **4•7•8**, which includes all insertion grammars except for the least faithful 3:CV.ins, is well-behaved within EPO(f.dep), but once again runs afoul of EPO(m.Ons) and EPO(m.NoCoda), creating a cycle in both cases with respect to **3**.

By contrast, the final possible merger **3•4•7** introduces no cycles within EPO(f.dep) or anywhere else. As may be seen from the EPO(m.Ons) and EPO(m.NoCoda) in bigraphs (46) and (47), the relevant mergers are cleanly acyclic and the super-grammar **3∪4∪7** is therefore an authentic (if perhaps somewhat unexpected) typological class.

The merging of **3•4•7** has an interesting structure: it excludes only **8:(C)V(C).ins**, the least insertional of the inserters. This gives a glimpse into subtler aspects of how traits can be shared across and within grammars. The three languages in the typological class are these:

7:CV(C).ins	OR.CA
4:(C)V.ins	OLA.CP
3:CV.ins	OR.CP

It's striking that **7** (OR.CA) and **4** (OLA.CP) essentially share nothing at the level of distinguishing traits, while each overlaps in a different trait with **3** (OR.CP). This directly reflects the disjunctive character of the crucial

ERC in the grammar of **3U4U7**, which may be obtained from the *join* of their components.[9]

(50) Grammar of **3U4U7**

m.Ons	m.NoCoda	f.max	f.dep
W	**W**		**L**
		W	**L**

Observe that **8**, the only remaining member of the inserting class, has the following grammar, which like (50) enforces insertion through f.max≫f.dep, but otherwise exactly negates the ERC that determines the output syllable canon (first row).

(51) Grammar of **8**

m.Ons	m.NoCoda	f.max	f.dep
L	**L**		**W**
		W	**L**

The most basic property of ERCs, whereby dominators are disjunctive and subordinates conjunctive, thus lies behind this rather generous notion of sharing that enables **3U4U7**.

In sum, then: the privileged order relations arise from the structure of transpositions in border point pairs. EPO equivalences arise from the prefixes. The interaction of equivalence and order – 'hypertransitivity' – impacts numerical realization in UVTs, but is not privileged. Inclusion of non-privileged information in a bigraph, as we have seen, disables its relevance to typological classification. The privileged relations, along with the equivalences, suffice to exactly distinguish the cases in which merger leads to grammatical classes from those in which it leads to exit from the realm of typologies.

We now proceed to focused formal development, where the secrets all are told.

[9] On the join, see Merchant (2008, 2011) and in this work, §6.1, ex. (11) and discussion following.

Chapter 4

Analysis of the MOAT

Chapter contents

Next we provide a detailed contents listing all examples, intended for re-readers who wish to study the argument closely. Similar lists will also be found at the head of other subsections.

Detailed contents

4.0 Analysis of the MOAT: Overview

Above the forest of the parakeets,
A parakeet of parakeets prevails...
– Stevens (1923)

The UVTs of a typology differ numerically, but the MOAT is invariant: it derives from border point pairs, which are the same no matter what VT or VTs are used to produce the typology. A primary goal of this section, carried out from §4.1-§4.7, is to show that MOAT(T) is not merely unique for a given typology T, but that it *characterizes* T: if a typology has the same MOAT as another, then they are the same typology. This gives us license to argue, as we have done, from the properties of the MOAT to the properties of the typology it represents.

The MOAT derives from a subset of the legs of T, typically proper. Its constituent relations both lose and gain information, in that they abstract away from the details of the legs they are built from and yet contain inferences that go beyond the border point data. Crucially, however, the MOAT determines the full content of every grammar in T.

The analytical challenge is to connect the MOAT, derived by analysis of border point pairs, each consisting of just two adjacent legs, with the typology, which is defined by filtration of an entire UVT by single legs. Filtration to a UVT optimum involves a sequence of sets of rows, each row corresponding to a grammar, starting out from the entire set and telescoping down to a singleton. Border point analysis rests on a far more selective and local view of the typological data: at no point are more than two grammars under consideration, and those are adjacent; further relations are inferred from transitive closure. Nevertheless the data-impoverished construction of the MOAT yields a characterization of the same object as the relatively data-rich filtration process, and, precisely due to its narrow focus, gives even more information about the structure of that object, particularly as pertains to potential generalization of its grammars through union.

To bridge between the locally-derived relational structure of the MOAT and the global filtration process that defines a typology, we introduce another set of relations on grammars, which has the unexpected virtue of leaving the numerics of the UVT set behind while tracking filtration exactly. These call on the *prefixal* structure of the legs as the basis for relations. Broadly put, if grammars each contain some legs that begin with a prefix P, they will filter alike through P, yielding a notion of equivalence. If grammars contain legs that start out with P and some of them diverge thereafter, so that one set of grammars contains legs PC... and the other legs P... but no legs of the form PC..., the point of divergence marks a point of ejection in the filtration process, and at the same time supports a relation of the 'less than' type. These prefix-based relations give rise to a structure we call the PMOAT. Our line of attack on the characterization problem is to show that a relationally-enriched version of the MOAT is in fact identical to a relationally-enriched PMOAT, which allows for a chain of inferences leading from the assumption that two typologies have the same MOAT (defined via border points) to the conclusion that they must be the same typology (defined via filtration).

To accomplish this, we build up the MOAT relations from their origins in border points pairs while determining their relation to UVT numerics (§4.1-§4.3), do the same for the PMOAT relations (§4.6), and then bring them together to close the argument (§4.7). Along the way, we encounter some significant results that shed further light on the inner workings of OT.

□ If a candidate known to be optimal for *some* unspecified leg survives filtration by a particular prefix P, there will always be a leg-completing suffix Q such that the leg PQ selects that candidate as optimal. ('No Dead Man Walking', Theorem (65), §4.5.1). For OT, then, there is a sense in which,

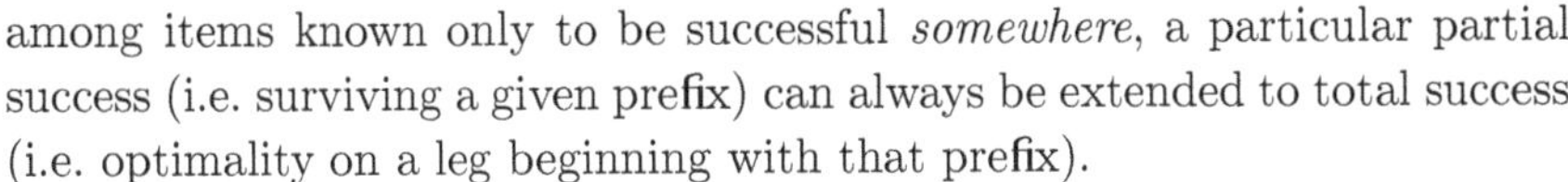

among items known only to be successful *somewhere*, a particular partial success (i.e. surviving a given prefix) can always be extended to total success (i.e. optimality on a leg beginning with that prefix).

□ Although UVTs for a given typology differ from each other, they not only choose the same grammars as optima, they agree on every detail of the entire filtration process ('Filtration Uniformity' (84), 'Co-Filtration Uniformity' (85), §4.5.4).

□ In addition, we find that the MOAT not only governs the structure of UVTs, it limits the numerical possibilities in *any* VT that belongs to a collection of VTs that gives rise to a typology. In this general, multiple-cset case, which is the typical one in concrete OT, MOAT equivalence requires numerical equality of constraint evaluation and MOAT 'less than' requires numerical 'less than or equal to' with strict 'less than' in at least one of the supporting VTs (Theorems (159) and (160), §4.7).

We take the MOAT concept a step further in §4.8. Not all partitions of Ord(*S*.Con) are typologies: far from it. How do we know whether a given partition is a typology? To satisfy the definition directly, we might aim to display a UVT that yields it. The method of border point analysis offers another avenue. It applies to any partition of Ord(*S*.Con) and yields a relational structure we call the Generalized MOAT or GMOAT, developed in §4.5 to parallel the MOAT to the extent possible. In §4.8, we show that *acyclicity* of the GMOAT is all that's needed to certify that its sponsoring partition is a typology. The typology qua abstract object is therefore a certain kind of order structure, above and beyond the numerics of the VT.

We conclude by extending ERC logic to interpret the border points of a grammar (§4.9). The members of a border point pair can be compared in much the same way as two candidates can. This comparison supplies the familiar ERC values for constraints appearing in the prefix (*e*) and the transposition (W, L) but yields no information at all about the ranking of suffixal constraints. This fourth, undetermined state we reify as a new value u, giving rise to the 4-valued *ERCoid*. Treating u as the identity for fusion, we show for various cases how the Fusional Reduction Algorithm (FRed: Brasoveanu & Prince 2005/2011) operates unmodified to produce ERC grammars from the richer ERCoid representation, suggesting that the procedure is efficacious in general.

Analysis of this type requires attention to the formal. Rigor does not preclude intuition or insight, however, and in this case the emergence of structure from the simple defining assumptions of OT can, we believe, be appreciated amid the detail. The basic analytic tools used throughout will be familiar from theoretical linguistics as it is often practiced, though they must be employed with more persistence than is customary. But we have aimed for a level of breadth, exemplification, and pace that (we hope) will make it possible for an audience wider than specialists to access the argument. The more concrete approach of §1-§3 resumes in §5.

4.1 Filtration

OT filtration is concisely celebrated in the slogan of Gigerenzer & Goldstein (1996): 'take the best, ignore the rest.' Because of its fundamental importance, it will be worth our while to spell out explicitly what this means and to note its basic properties. Filtration may be defined recursively: once we settle what it means to filter by a single constraint, we can handle general filtration by peeling off the constraints one at a time.

We refer to a linearly ordered set of constraints as a 'sequence' of constraints. We write C(k) for the numerical value assigned by constraint C to candidate k, and C[K] for the subset of the set of candidates K that is selected by C, and similarly P[K] for the subset of K selected by a sequence P.

If P is empty, i.e. contains no constraints, we define P[K] = K. Filtration of a set of candidates by a non-empty sequence of constraints is defined as follows.

(1) **Definition. Candidate filtration.** Let K be any non-empty set of candidates. Let C be any constraint, and P any sequence of one or more constraints.

i. $C[K] = \{k \in K \mid C(k) \leq C(x) \text{ for all } x \in K\}$
ii. $CP[K] = P[C[K]]$

This concise definition encodes the familiar constraint-by-constraint pattern of OT filtration.

By the first clause, C[K] is the (unique) subset of K whose members receive the *numerically minimal* value on the constraint C. Because C is a function to the non-negative integers, there is always and only one such value.

By the second clause, filtration by a sequence CP consists of filtering the set of candidates C[K], the 'survivors' of C, by the subsequence P. This is accomplished by reapplying the definition:

i. If P consists of a single constraint, then clause 1 may be re-applied, concluding the filtration.

ii. If P is more extensive, then clause 2 may itself be re-applied, since P itself is of the form one constraint + sequence-of-one-or-more-constraints.

The end result, spelled out, is a structure of composed functions, $C_n \circ C_{n-1} \circ \cdots \circ C[K]$. Helpfully, this implies that filtration by a whole hierarchy is itself a well-defined *function* with one determinate outcome, the set of candidates optimal under the hierarchy, whose members share identical violation profiles.

OT filtration has some basic properties familiar to practitioners. It is useful to recall and specify them.

Most basic, perhaps, is the **'forced choice'** property, whereby filtration always produces a result (Prince 2002a:iv). Put formally, we have $C[K] \neq \emptyset$ for every C and non-empty K; thus $P[K] \neq \emptyset$ for P any sequence of constraints. This follows from the definition because the value C(k) is a non-negative integer for candidate $k \in K$, and every set of non-negative integers has a least element. No matter how large a set of candidates K is, there is always some candidate $k \in K$, and possibly more than one, such that C(k) is the smallest among the values assigned by C.

A second important property is **'telescoping'**, whereby as filtration proceeds, the set of survivors shrinks, or (more exactly) never grows. Each successive step of filtration produces a non-empty subset of the output of the previous step, and more generally, the output of any initial subsequence of a hierarchy is a superset of the output of any longer sequence that it initiates.

(2) **Lemma. Telescoping property of candidate filtration.** $PQ[K] \subseteq P[K]$.

Proof. Filtration by a single C is defined in ex. (1) as yielding a subset. Spelled out, the recursive definition yields a sequence of single-C function applications: $(C_n(C_{n-1}(\cdots (C_1(K)) \cdots)$, the result of each application being a subset of the previous. Thus, since $PQ[K] = Q[P[K]]$ and $Q[P[K]] \subseteq P[K]$, have $PQ[K] \subseteq P[K] \subseteq K$. □

As shown below in §4.5 the filtration properties of OT selection will lead to a set of order and equivalence relations that parallel the order and equivalence relations derived from border points. We will find that filtration is a typological invariant (§4.5.4), in the sense that every UVT for a given typology has the same filtration pattern, permitting typological claims to be established via the order and equivalence relations deriving from filtration.

Further important properties involve the numerical relations that determine how a set of candidates is filtered. Once again, these are familiar to practitioners, but they play such a fundamental role in the argument that it is worth rehearsing them here.

Survivor sameness. Consider any set of candidates K. The survivors of filtration by some sequence P, namely the set $P[K] \subseteq K$, must all be assigned *equal values* by each constraint in P. These values need not be the same across the constraints in P, but for each constraint, the assigned value must be minimal.

Losers lose. At any stage of filtration, say by PC, the candidates from P[K] that survive filtration by PC[K], the candidates $k \in PC[K]$, will all have the same, minimal value on C, and all those from P[K] that are ejected at PC, namely those in $P[K] \setminus PC[K]$, will be assigned values on C *strictly greater* than the value assigned to the members of P[K].

We now list some key terms that will be used throughout.

(3) **Terminology: prefix, suffix; survive, pass through; eject.**

Given a total order on *n* constraints, a leg $\lambda = PQ$, where $P = C_1 ... C_j$ and $Q = C_{j+1} ... C_n$, we say that P is a *prefix* of λ and Q is a *suffix* of λ. A prefix is also permitted to be the empty sequence, as is a suffix.

We say a candidate $k \in K$ *survives filtration by prefix* P or *passes through the constraints of* P, if $k \in P[K]$. Candidate k is *ejected* by C if $k \in P[K]$ but $k \notin PC[K]$.

We conclude by using filtration to give simple and concise formal definitions of the key notions *optimality*, *grammar*, *typology*, and *UVT* as they apply to single VTs. A valid VT has columns labeled by all the constraints of some given set of constraints, T.Con. We construe a VT as a set of rows, so that we can sensibly write $v \in V$ for a row v in a VT V. A row is analogous to a 'candidate' in the sense of concrete OT, where a VT is derived from a candidate set. In a UVT, each 'language' has one candidate, the row associated with the language. A constraint C, applied to a row $v \in V$, with V a VT, returns the value C(v) occupying the column labeled C, the Cth component of the row.

(4) **Definition. Optimality, with respect to a VT.** Let V be a VT. A row $v \in V$ is optimal for a leg $\lambda \in \mathrm{Ord}(\mathrm{T.Con})$ if $v \in \lambda[V]$.

(5) **Definition. Grammar, with respect to a VT.** Let V be a VT. For each row $v \in V$, the grammar of v is the set of all linear orders on T.Con for which v is optimal.

$$G_v = \{\lambda \in \mathrm{Ord}(\mathrm{T.Con}) \mid v \in \lambda[V]\}$$

(6) **Definition. Typology of a VT.** Let V be a VT. The typology T_V of V is the set of all grammars of the rows of V.

$$T_V = \{G \subseteq \text{Ord}(\text{T.C{\scriptsize ON}}) \mid G = G_v \text{ for some } v \in V\}$$

Thus, in this context, a 'typology' is a set of grammars, as defined in (5), that derives from some VT, and crucially therefore partitions Ord(T.CON). We write '$\exists!$u' for 'there is a unique u'.

(7) **Definition. UVT for T.** Let T be a typology and U be a VT such that $T = T_U$. Then U is a Unitary Violation Tableau (UVT) for T if

i. $\forall G \in T\ \exists! u \in U$ such that $G = G_u$
ii. $\forall u \in U\ \exists G \in T$ such that $G = G_u$.

Verbosely, a UVT for T has exactly one row for each grammar of T, which is chosen as optimal by any leg of its corresponding grammar; and it has no other rows. In particular, it has no duplicate or harmonically bounded rows, as is explicitly asserted in the equivalent definition (8), §1.2. To give the results of filtration by a leg λ in a UVT U, we will allow ourselves to write λ[U] = u, rather than u ∈ λ[U], emphasizing the uniqueness of optima in a UVT.

We write $\mathcal{U}$(T) for the set of all UVTs for T.

4.2 Border point pairs

We now take a step away from the way OT is disclosed at the level of linguistic practice and consider individual linear orders on a constraint set, *legs*, as objects in themselves, rather than as filtration devices. Borrowing from the theory of permutations, we view two legs as *adjacent* if they differ only in a single adjacent transposition of constraints. Thus, legs P$\underline{\text{XY}}$Q and P$\underline{\text{YX}}$Q, where P and Q may be empty, are in this abstract sense adjacent; throughout we underline the locus of transposition to draw attention to it. Defined in this way, 'adjacency' is an algebraic relation between two structured objects. Although we will proceed algebraically in this chapter, it can be useful to have in mind a graphical representation in which adjacency is more literally interpreted. Here we sketch the basic picture; the idea is examined in detail in chapter 6.

If we lay out the set of legs as a graph, where each leg is represented as a point and adjacency is interpreted graphically as connection by an edge, it turns out that a grammar is a *region*, a connected set of points,[1] so that

[1] Riggle (2010) introduces this notion into the linguistic literature.

you can travel from any one leg-point in the grammar to another, hopping from point to adjacent point without leaving the region (see §7 below for further discussion). A typology is then a collection of such regions. We can lift the notion of adjacency from points to whole regions by declaring that a grammar-region is *adjacent* to another if there is a leg-point in one that is adjacent to a leg-point in the other. Thinking of a polity as a network of connected cities rather than as an expanse of territory, we can say that the US as a whole is adjacent to Mexico as a whole because e.g. the west Texas town of El Paso is adjacent to Ciudad Juárez. This way of thinking leads immediately to a key notion in the analysis of typological structure: the *border point pair*, which is just a pair of adjacent legs that gives witness to the adjacency of grammars. A border point pair is a pair of legs {P$\underline{XY}$Q, P$\underline{YX}$Q}, where each belongs to a different grammar. Graphically, a border point pair is an edge (an *edge* being formally nothing more than an unordered pair of vertices), and we will speak of such a pair as *connecting* two grammars.[2] Portrayed spatially and intuitively, the situation looks like this.

(8) Adjacent grammars sketched. G_1 and G_2 linked by a border point pair.

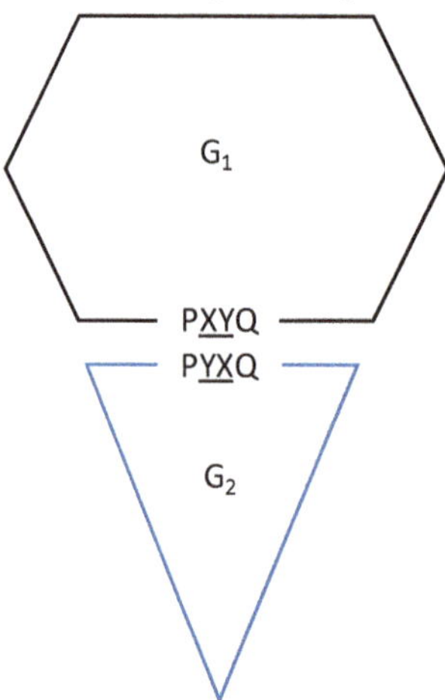

For a fully accurate and quite non-euclidean rendition of the notion 'border' for grammars on the permutohedron, see the three-dimensional structures portrayed in §7.1, especially exx. (2) and (3), as well as the two-dimensional structures in exx. (57)–(58), §4.4, and ex. (71), §4.5.2.

[2] In the theory of expander graphs, the set of border point pairs for a subset of the graph is known as its 'edge boundary' (Wikipedia).

Here is the definition that we will use throughout.

(9) **Definition. Border point pair.** Let T $=\{G_1,..., G_n\}$ be a typology on a set of constraints T.Con, given as a set of ranking grammars $G_k = \{\lambda_i\}$, for some legs $\lambda_i \in$ T.Con. Let $\lambda_1 = P\underline{XY}Q$ and $\lambda_2 = P\underline{YX}Q$, where P,Q are sequences of constraints from T.Con and X, Y $\in$ T.Con. Let $G_j, G_k \in T$, $G_j \neq G_k$. Then $\{\lambda_1, \lambda_2\}$ is a *border point pair* for G_j, G_k if $\lambda_1 \in G_j$ and $\lambda_2 \in G_k$.

We have approached the border point pair through what we might think of as the political geography of typologies, but the concept applies just as well to the blocks of any partition of a set of linear orders. In the general case of a partition of Ord(T.Con), the set of all orders on T.Con, a block is just a set, disjoint from other blocks, with no further structure guaranteed. In particular, there's no certainty that the blocks will be connected regions and in the general case there is no reason to expect them to be. Nevertheless we can think of any pair of blocks as 'adjacent' when they are connected by a border point pair, and non-adjacent when they are not. We take this up in §4.4 below.

Representing a typology as a partition of Ord(T.Con) presents no direct information about the violation values that its constraints might assign to candidates or, in the case of a UVT, whole languages. But under the notion of grammar adjacency, each border point pair {P$\underline{XY}$Q, P$\underline{YX}$Q} gives rise to abstract non-numerical order relations between the bordering grammars with respect to constraint X and, symmetrically, constraint Y. When the prefix P is nonempty, it also contains information about the abstract equivalence of the grammars on each of the constraints in P. These relations are unique for each typology, up to isomorphism, and form the base from which the structure of the typology can be derived.

In the situation portrayed in diagram (8), for example, we will find that with respect to the order relations that explicate constraint X, G_1 is abstractly *less than* G_2, while on the order relation relevant to constraint Y the opposite holds: G_2 is abstractly *less than* G_1. Further, G_1 and G_2 are equivalent on any constraint C in the prefix P. These abstract relations will be shown to constrain the ways that a given typology can be represented numerically, both in UVTs (§4.3.4) and in sets of VTs (§4.7), and to govern which partitions are and are not typologies (§4.8).

4.3 Relations derived from border point pairs

In this section, we construct the grammar-grammar relations that derive from their border point pairs. Each constraint participates in two types of 'base relations' which derive directly from border point pairs. One gives rise to an order relation when transitively closed. The other gives rise to an equivalence relation when transitively and reflexively closed. For each constraint, these are instantiated in the numerical relations of every UVT of the typology. These order and equivalence relations constitute the EPO for a constraint. For each constraint, we introduce the 'hypertransitive closure', a new order relation on the grammars of the typology, which combines the order and equivalence information in the EPO in much the same way that $<$ combines with $=$ among the integers. The hypertransitive closure will allow us to connect the EPO with relations derived from filtration patterns (§4.6).

4.3.1 Border point pairs and numbers

The members of a border point pair like {P<u>XY</u>Q, P<u>YX</u>Q} differ only in the relative order of X and Y, so it is natural to expect the difference in their filtration behavior to reside entirely in the behavior of XY and YX in the context P_Q. In particular, given a choice between u = P<u>XY</u>Q[U] and v = P<u>YX</u>Q[U], the constraint X must choose u over v, and Y must choose v over u, since everything else is the same, constraining the values assigned to u and v by X and Y. The details are worked out in the proof of the following lemma.

(10) **Lemma. Border points to numerical relations: BP → NR (Rows).** Let λ_x = P<u>XY</u>Q and λ_y = P<u>YX</u>Q be a border point pair $\{\lambda_{x,} \lambda_y\}$ in a typology T = $\{G_1,..., G_n\}$. Let U ∈ $\mathcal{U}$(T), with rows $u, v \in$ U such that $\lambda_x[U] = u$ and $\lambda_y[U] = v$. Then the following numerical relations hold in every U ∈ $\mathcal{U}$(T).

i. $C(u) = C(v)$ for every C in P.
ii. $X(u) < X(v)$
iii. $Y(v) < Y(u)$

Proof. Let U ∈ $\mathcal{U}$(T), with $u, v \in$ U such that u = P<u>XY</u>Q[U] and v = P<u>YX</u>Q[U]. From the telescoping property of filtration (2), we have $u \in$ PXY[U] ⇒ $u \in$ PX[U] ⇒ $u \in$ P[U], and similarly for v with respect to P<u>YX</u>Q. Thus $u, v \in$ P[U], so that $C(u) = C(v)$ for every C in P, establishing (a). We now move on to show that $X(u) < X(v)$ and, symmetrically, $Y(v) < Y(u)$.

Observe first that $X(u) \leq X(v)$ and $Y(v) \leq Y(u)$. If the first is false, then $X(u) > X(v)$, and $u \notin$ PX[U], because u loses to v at X, contradicting the assumption that P<u>XY</u>Q[U] = u. Similarly for $Y(v) \leq Y(u)$, because $Y(v) > Y(u)$ implies $v \notin$ PY[U], contradicting P<u>YX</u>Q[U] = v.

We now show that $X(u) < X(v)$. Suppose for purposes of contradiction that $X(u) = X(v)$. This now gives us $u, v \in$ PX[U]. But since $v \in$ PX[U], it can't be that $Y(v) < Y(u)$, because then $u \notin P\underline{XY}[U]$, falsely implying $P\underline{XY}Q[U] \neq u$. As noted, $Y(v) \leq Y(u)$. So it follows that $Y(v) = Y(u)$ as well. Thus $v \in P\underline{XY}[U]$ in addition to $v \in P\underline{YX}[U]$. This gives us $u, v \in P\underline{XY}[U]$ and $u, v \in P\underline{YX}[U]$. The only subsequence remaining to filter them appropriately is Q. But Q is a function and cannot give two distinct results when filtering the same set. Therefore, $X(u) \neq X(v)$.

The same argument holds for Y *mutatis mutandis*, establishing $Y(v) < Y(u)$. □

These relationships hold in all UVTs for a given typology T and associate the border point pairs of a typology with stable numerical relations, regardless of how the UVTs may otherwise differ. To see beyond the variety in the UVTs, we are interested in constructing abstract relations that hold not between rows of UVTs but between *grammars*, because there is one and only one set of grammars that defines a typology. Going from grammars to numbers therefore requires a mediating relation between grammars and the rows of a UVT.

Every UVT has a simple relationship with the grammars of its typology, required by definition (56): each row corresponds to one and only one grammar, and each grammar corresponds to one and only one row. This describes a natural bijection between a typology T and the rows of any $U \in \mathcal{U}(T)$.

To display it perspicuously, we adopt a subscripting system whereby each grammar bears the same index as its associated row. This system is notationally convenient, imposes no new restrictions on typologies or UVTs, and allows us to define the correspondence function directly.

(11) **Definition. Grammar-row bijection.** Let T be a typology consisting of a set of grammars $\{G_1, \ldots, G_n\}$. Let $U \in \mathcal{U}(T)$, and let the rows $u_1, \ldots, u_n$ of U be indexed such that for every $\lambda \in G_k$, $1 \leq k \leq n$, $u_k = \lambda[U]$. We define the bijection g_U as follows:

$$g_U : T \rightarrow U \text{ such that } g_U(G_k) = u_k$$

By the definition of UVT (7), for any $U \in \mathcal{U}(T)$ and an arbitrary grammar $G \in T$, every total order $\lambda \in G$ selects the same row, call it u_G, of U. Thus, in the definition (11), $u_k = \lambda[U]$ is well-defined and therefore the function g_U is well-defined.

This allows us to go easily from grammars to numbers via function composition, since constraints in the UVT context are functions from the rows of U to the non-negative integers $\mathbb{N}$.

The function $C \circ g_U$ thus assigns to each *grammar* G_k the numerical value in U that C assigns to its corresponding row u_k. With this technical assist, we may now re-state Lemma (10) BP → NR as involving border points pairs and the grammars they connect.

(12) **Lemma. BP → NR (Grammars).** Let $\lambda_x = \text{P}\underline{\text{XY}}\text{Q}$ and $\lambda_y = \text{P}\underline{\text{YX}}\text{Q}$ be a border point pair $\{\lambda_x, \lambda_y\}$ in a typology $\text{T} = \{\text{G}_1,..., \text{G}_n\}$. Let $\text{U} \in \mathcal{U}(\text{T})$, with $\text{u}_j, \text{u}_k \in \text{U}$ such that $\lambda_x[\text{U}] = \text{u}_j$ and $\lambda_y[\text{U}] = \text{u}_k$, where $\text{g}_\text{U}(\text{G}_j) = \text{u}_j$ and $\text{g}_\text{U}(\text{G}_k) = \text{u}_k$. Then the following numerical relations hold in every $\text{U} \in \mathcal{U}(\text{T})$.

i. $\text{C} \circ \text{g}_\text{U}(\text{G}_j) = \text{C} \circ \text{g}_\text{U}(\text{G}_k)$ for $\text{G}_j, \text{G}_k \in \text{T}$ and for all $\text{C} \in \text{P}$.

ii. $\text{X} \circ \text{g}_\text{U}(\text{G}_j) < \text{X} \circ \text{g}_\text{U}(\text{G}_k)$

iii. $\text{Y} \circ \text{g}_\text{U}(\text{G}_k) < \text{Y} \circ \text{g}_\text{U}(\text{G}_j)$

Proof. Follows directly from Lemma (10) 'BP → NR (Rows)', since $\text{C} \circ \text{g}_\text{U}(\text{G}_j) = \text{C}(\text{u}_j)$. □

With these numerical correlates in hand, we now develop relations between grammars that will prove central to relating EPO relations to filtration patterns.

4.3.2 Border point pairs and the base relations

We now construe the border point pair as the source of abstract relations between grammars. These relations are defined without reference to the integers. We will, however, call on the numerical implications recorded in Lemma BP → NR (Rows) (10) and its corollary Lemma (12) BP → NR (Grammars) to derive properties of the new relations. We begin with a relation $\prec^{\text{bp.X}}$ that holds between adjacent grammars connected by the border point pair {P<u>XY</u>Q, P<u>YX</u>Q}, such as those portrayed in diagram (8).

(13) **Definition. Base relation $\prec^{\text{bp.X}}$.** Given a typology $\text{T} = \{\text{G}_j\}$, for each $\text{X} \in \text{T.C}\textsc{on}$ we say $\text{G}_i \prec^{\text{bp.X}} \text{G}_k$ iff there is a border point pair {P<u>XY</u>Q, P<u>YX</u>Q}, with $\text{P}\underline{\text{XY}}\text{Q} \in \text{G}_i$ and $\text{P}\underline{\text{YX}}\text{Q} \in \text{G}_k$.

The base relation $\prec^{\text{bp.X}}$ will lead to an order relation between grammars. Accompanying it is a base relation $\equiv^{\text{bp.C}}$, which will lead to an equivalence relation between grammars.

(14) **Definition. Base relation $\equiv^{\text{bp.C}}$.** Given a typology $\text{T} = \{\text{G}_i\}$ and $\text{C} \in \text{T.C}\textsc{on}$, we say $\text{G}_j \equiv^{\text{bp.C}} \text{G}_k$ iff there is a border point pair {P<u>XY</u>Q, P<u>YX</u>Q} with $\text{P}\underline{\text{XY}}\text{Q} \in \text{G}_j$ and $\text{P}\underline{\text{YX}}\text{Q} \in \text{G}_k$, with C in the prefix P.

It is encouraging that the relation $\equiv^{\mathrm{bp.C}}$ comes with the property of symmetry, namely that $\mathrm{A} \equiv^{\mathrm{bp.C}} \mathrm{B} \Rightarrow \mathrm{B} \equiv^{\mathrm{bp.C}} \mathrm{A}$. But it is not reflexive, since it depends on the existence of a border point pair involving the two grammars it relates, and no grammar can be involved in a border point pair with itself. Nor is it guaranteed to be transitive. A little further work will therefore be required.

The relation $\prec^{\mathrm{bp.X}}$ underlies the *privileged relations* discussed in §3. For example, the grammars portrayed in sketch (8) above would appear in the bigraphs of §1 and §3 like this:

(15) Bigraph representation of $\mathrm{G}_1 \prec^{\mathrm{bp.X}} \mathrm{G}_2$

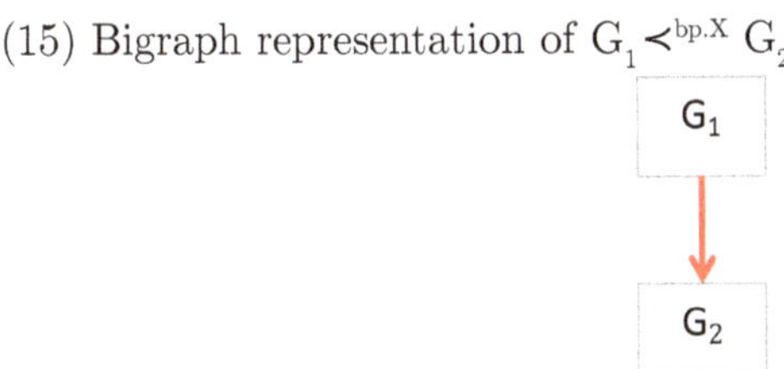

But the relation $\prec^{\mathrm{bp.C}}$ is by no means guaranteed to be a partial order. Its status depends entirely on whatever border point pairs happen to exist in the typology at hand. In this, the base relations $\prec^{\mathrm{bp.C}}$ and $\equiv^{\mathrm{bp.C}}$ differ notably from the integer relations $<$ and $=$. In particular, there is no guarantee that either abstract relation is *transitive*, since local versions of the long-range relational links may simply be absent. We may have, e.g., $\mathrm{G}_1 \prec^{\mathrm{bp.C}} \mathrm{G}_2$ and $\mathrm{G}_2 \prec^{\mathrm{bp.C}} \mathrm{G}_3$ from extant border point pairs, but there may be no border point pair that yields $\mathrm{G}_1 \prec^{\mathrm{bp.C}} \mathrm{G}_3$. The same remark holds for $\equiv^{\mathrm{bp.C}}$.

These two relations may, however, be extended without difficulty to a partial order and an equivalence relation, respectively, by defining new relations based on them, which are declared to have the desired properties: *transitively closing* them by fiat, and closing $\equiv^{\mathrm{bp.C}}$ reflexively as well. To show that this tactic is successful, we will rely on Lemma (10) 'From border points to numerical relations (rows)' and on Lemma (12) 'BP → NR (grammars)' to take advantage of the known order $<$ on the integers and the known equivalence relation $=$.

Bridging between the abstract relations on grammars and the more concrete relations on integers requires some attention to the way an abstract order or equivalence relation can correspond to its natural correlates on the integers. It's worthwhile at this point to develop concepts and terminology sufficient to our purposes.

A correspondence is a kind of function, and we are interested in the kind of function that respects relational structure, a *homomorphism*. We need something more general than mapping from order to order, or equivalence to equivalence, because the base relations just defined do not fall into these well-behaved classes. A standard notion is available for use: the *relational homomorphism.*

(16) **Definition. Relational homomorphism.** Given a binary relation R_A on a set A, a binary relation R_B on a set B, and a function f: A → B, the function f is a *relational homomorphism* with respect to R_A and R_B if for all $x, y \in A$, $x R_A y \Rightarrow f(x) R_B f(y)$.

Thus, if a pair of elements of a set A stand in a relation R_A, then their images in the set B stand in the relation R_B. These relations may be unrecognizably different on substantive grounds, but nevertheless share essential structural properties. For example, the relation 'child of' among people can be tied to the relation 'less than' among the integers by a suitable map of people to integers, even though the two types of entities are discernibly different in character. The utility of obtaining such a relation-between-relations is that properties that are already established on the one side, for example the integers, can be transported back to the other.

4.3.3 Instantiation

Since we focus on the integers, we limit our specific definitions to them, although the underlying concept is quite general, as we've just seen. When we have a function $f : S \rightarrow \mathbb{N}$ that behaves as in (16), we will say that the relation $R_{\mathbb{N}}$ on the integers *instantiates* the relation R_S on the set S. We will refer to the function f as an *instantiating* function with respect to the relation R_S.

Of interest to us are the standard integer relations $<$ and $=$. Thus, the following usages will be particularly prominent in subsequent discussion.

(17) **Definition. Instantiate a relation.** Given a relation R_S on a set S, the relation $<$ on $\mathbb{N}$, and a function $f: S \rightarrow \mathbb{N}$, if f is a relational homomorphism such that for all $x, y \in S$,

$$x R_S y \Rightarrow f(x) < f(y)$$

we say that f *instantiates* R_S *as* $<$.

Similarly, under the same assumptions, if f is a relational homomorphism such that for all $x, y \in S$,

$$x R y \Rightarrow f(x) = f(y)$$

we say that f *instantiates* R *as* $=$.

(18) **Definition. Instantiating function.** A function that instantiates a relation R_S on S as a relation $R_{\mathbb{N}}$ on the integers $\mathbb{N}$ will be termed an *instantiating function* for R_S.

(19) **Definition. Instantiable.** Given a relation R_S on a set S, if there is a function $f: S \rightarrow \mathbb{N}$ instantiating R_S as $<$, or instantiating R_S as $=$, then R is *instantiable as* $<$, or *as* $=$, respectively.

Many relations simply cannot be instantiated in this sense. For example, no reflexive or symmetrical relation can be instantiated in the integers as $<$. We have, in the first instance, $x R_S x$ for $x \in S$, but there is no instantiating function $f: S \rightarrow \mathbb{N}$ with $f(x) < f(x)$. Conversely, if a relation can be instantiated as $<$, it must be asymmetric.

(20) **Lemma. Asymmetry and instantiability**. If a relation R is instantiable as $<$, then R is asymmetric.

Proof. Assume R is instantiable as $<$ by a function f. Suppose for contradiction that R is not asymmetric. Then for some x, y, we have $x R y$ and $y R x$. But then we have both $f(x) < f(y)$ and $f(y) < f(x)$, an impossibility. Thus, R is asymmetric. □

The integer relation $<$ has the useful property that it can instantiate any finite partial order.

(21) Remark. Any finite partial order is instantiable as $<$.

Proof. Any finite strict *total* order R can be instantiated as $<$ in the integers. Any partial order can be linearly extended to a strict total order.[3]□

The integers may contain more structure than a relation that they instantiate. Returning to our example, given a set of people, we can instantiate the relation 'child of' in the integers as $<$, with the child assigned a smaller value than the parent. But 'child of' is not an *order* because although it is asymmetric like $<$, it is not transitive. You are the child of your mother, and she is the child of her mother, but you are not the child of your grandmother. Nevertheless, among the integers, for any function f that instantiates 'child of', f(child) $<$ f(grandparent of child). If we want an order relation that

---

[3] See Wikipedia, Linear extension. 'Given any partial orders $\leq$ and $\leq^*$ on a set X, $\leq^*$ is a linear extension of $\leq$ exactly when (1) $\leq^*$ is a total order and (2) for every x and y in X, if $x \leq y$, then $x \leq^* y$.'

includes 'child of', we can enlarge the original relation to obtain another relation properly including it, which carries the richer structure. In the example, we can replace 'child of' with 'descendant of', which is transitive, to obtain the desired order. This process is known as transitive closure.

The transitive closure of a relation R is obtained by defining a new relation, conventionally denoted R^+, which contains R but is in addition required to be transitive.[4]

(22) **Definition. Transitive closure R^+ of a relation R.**

i. $a \mathrm{R}\, b \Rightarrow a \mathrm{R}^+ b$ 'whatever is in R is also in R^+'

ii. $a \mathrm{R}^+ b \;\&\; b \mathrm{R}^+ c \Rightarrow a \mathrm{R}^+ c$ 'R^+ is transitive'

To apply this to the example: clause i. sets things going by informing us that if Alice is a child of Bob, then Alice is a *descendant* (child$^+$) of Bob. Thus, according to i., you are a descendant of your mother, and by the same token, she is a descendant of hers. By clause ii., you are therefore a descendant of your grandmother.

We will often make use of the fact that the transitively closed relation R^+ on a finite set can always be expressed in terms of its source relation R, in the following sense: if $a \mathrm{R}^+ b$, then there is a chain of pairs (x_i, x_{i+1}), each in the relation R, running between a and b. In terms of the example: for any (descendant, ancestor) pair, we can find a chain of 'child of' relations that links the two. Put more exactly, we can say that given $a\mathrm{R}^+ b$, there will always be some sequence $x_1,..., x_j, x_{j+1},..., x_n$, where $x_1 = a$ and $x_n = b$ and $x_k \mathrm{R}\, x_{k+1}$, $1 \leq k \leq n-1$. This fact is easily appreciated from a Hasse diagram of the order. We will call such a sequence an 'overlapping transitive chain' between a and b, and we will see many such as we proceed.

For our purposes, it is important that the transitive closure of an instantiable relation is also instantiable, a fact of sufficient utility that we record it in a lemma. This will be applied shortly to the transitive closure of the base relations $\prec^{\mathrm{bp.X}}$ and $\equiv^{\mathrm{bp.C}}$ as defined in (13) and (14).

(23) **Lemma. Instantiating the transitive closure.** If a relation R on a set S is instantiable as $<$, then its transitive closure R^+ is instantiable as $<$

[4] Wikipedia, Transitive closure, gives a clear example. 'For example, if X is a set of airports and $x\mathrm{R}y$ means "there is a direct flight from airport x to airport y" (for x and y in X), then the transitive closure of R on X is the relation R^+ such that $x\mathrm{R}^+y$ means "it is possible to fly from x to y in one or more flights". Informally, the transitive closure gives you the set of all places you can get to from any starting place.'

on ℕ. Furthermore, if $f : S \to \mathbb{N}$ instantiates R as $<$, then f also instantiates R^+. The same holds for $=$, *mutatis mutandis.*

Proof. If a relation R on a set S is instantiable as $<$, then by definition (19) there exists $f : S \to \mathbb{N}$, such that $a \, R \, b \Rightarrow f(a) < f(b)$ for all $a, b \in S$. Let R^+ be the transitive closure of R. Suppose $x R^+ y$ for some $x, y \in S$. If $x \, R \, y$, then $f(x) < f(y)$. If not, then there is a nonempty sequence of elements $z_1, \dots, z_n \in S$ with $x = z_1$ and $y = z_n$ such that $z_1 \, R \, z_2, \dots, z_{n-1} \, R \, z_n$, an overlapping transitive chain between x and y. By the instantiability of R, each intermediate relation in the chain is instantiated by f as $<$, so that $f(z_k) < f(z_{k+1})$. It follows then that $f(x) < f(y)$ because $<$ is transitive. Therefore, f instantiates R^+. The same argument holds for $=$. □

Worth noting is the contrapositive: if the transitive closure R^+ of a relation R is *not* instantiable as $<$, then R itself is not instantiable as $<$. We now go on to obtain the useful result that the transitive closure R^+ of a relation R instantiable as $<$ is guaranteed to be a (strict) partial order.

(24) **Lemma. Instantiability and order.** If a relation R is instantiable as $<$, then R^+ is a strict partial order.

Proof. Assume R instantiable as $<$. We need to show that R^+ is asymmetric and transitive. Transitive, we have by construction. We want asymmetry: namely, $x R^+ y \Rightarrow \neg \, y R^+ x$. Suppose for contradiction that R^+ is not asymmetric: that is, there are $x, y \in S$ such that $x R^+ y$ and $y R^+ x$. From Lemma (23), we know that R instantiable as $<$ implies R^+ instantiable as $<$. But there is no function f of any kind with range ℕ such that $f(x) < f(y)$ and $f(y) < f(x)$, because $<$ is asymmetric. Therefore, there is *a fortiori* no instantiating function and R^+ is not instantiable as $<$. Then, by contraposition of Lemma (23), R is not instantiable as $<$. Contradiction. □

We now turn to the specific instantiation properties of the base relations $\prec^{\text{bp.C}}$ and $\equiv^{\text{bp.C}}$.

(25) **Lemma. Universal instantiation of the base relations.** For every $U \in \mathcal{U}(T)$, the base relation $\prec^{\text{bp.C}}$ is instantiated as $<$, and the base relation $\equiv^{\text{bp.C}}$ as $=$, by the function $C \circ g_U$.

Proof. This is just a restatement of Lemma (12) in terms of the base relations. Let $U \in \mathcal{U}(T)$ and $G_i \prec^{\text{bp.C}} G_j$. Then there is a border point pair $(P\underline{CY}Q, P\underline{YC}Q)$ with $P\underline{CY}Q \in G_i$ and $P\underline{YC}Q \in G_j$. Lemma (12) 'BP → NR (Grammars)', which assumes the border point pair, may now be invoked. Its proof cites the instantiating function $f = C \circ g_U$, where $g_U : G_k \mapsto u_k$ as in definition (11). Thus, $f(G_i) < f(G_j)$. This means that the integer $<$ relation

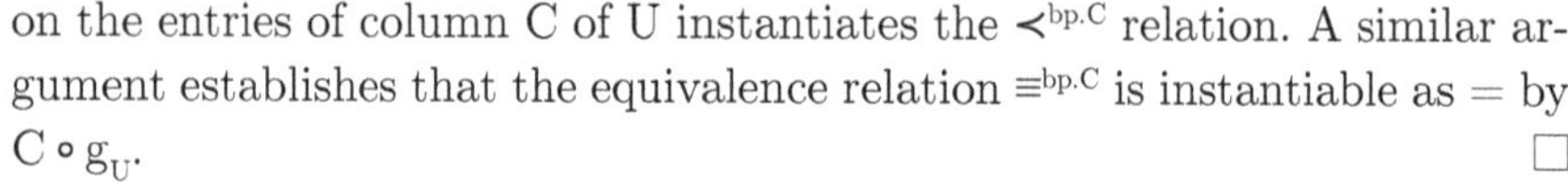
on the entries of column C of U instantiates the $\prec^{bp.C}$ relation. A similar argument establishes that the equivalence relation $\equiv^{bp.C}$ is instantiable as $=$ by $C \circ g_U$. □

4.3.4 The EPO relations

Our goal is to define the EPO of each constraint, and from that the MOAT which gathers them all. To reach it, we must construct the relations on a typology T that each EPO(C) contains, for C ∈ T.Con. We start out from the base relations and close them appropriately to arrive at order and equivalence relations.

(26) **Definition. The EPO order relation.** The relation $<^{bp.C}$ is the transitive closure of $\prec^{bp.C}$.

To rehearse the definition of transitive closure (22) in this context: we have, for any $G_1, G_2, H \in T$:

i. $G_1 \prec^{bp.C} G_2 \Rightarrow G_1 <^{bp.C} G_2$ '$\prec^{bp.C}$ is in $<^{bp.C}$'
ii. $G_1 <^{bp.C} H \;\&\; H <^{bp.C} G_2 \Rightarrow G_1 <^{bp.C} G_2$ '$<^{bp.C}$ is transitive'

(27) **Lemma. Universal instantiation of $<^{bp.C}$.** For every $U \in \mathcal{U}(T)$, the relation $<^{bp.C}$ is instantiated by the function $C \circ g_U$ as $<$.

Proof. By definition (26), the relation $<^{bp.C}$ is the transitive closure of the base relation $\prec^{bp.C}$, which is instantiated by $C \circ g_U$ as $<$ according to Lemma (25). By Lemma (23), its transitive closure, the relation $<^{bp.C}$, is also instantiated as $<$ by the same function that instantiates $\prec^{bp.C}$, namely $C \circ g_U$. □

Lemma (27) allows us to conclude that $<^{bp.C}$ is in fact the order relation we seek.

(28) **Lemma. EPO/PO.** The EPO relation $<^{bp.C}$ is a partial order on the grammars of a typology.

Proof. Because $\prec^{bp.C}$ is instantiable as $<$, and because $<^{bp.C}$ is the transitive closure of $\prec^{bp.C}$, by Lemma (24) the relation $<^{bp.C}$ is a (strict) partial order. □

(29) **Definition. The EPO equivalence relation.** The relation $\sim^{bp.C}$ is the transitive closure of the reflexive closure of $\equiv^{bp.C}$. Equivalently, $\sim^{bp.C}$ is the reflexive closure of the transitive closure of $\equiv^{bp.C}$.

The definition of $\sim^{\text{bp.C}}$ must include reflexive closure. As noted above, the base relation $\equiv^{\text{bp.C}}$ is nonreflexive because no grammar is connected by a border point pair to itself. Observe that the order of the closure operations does not matter. If reflexive closure comes first, producing R^{refl} from R, then an overlapping transitive chain of relations R^{refl} establishing the transitive relation $(R^{\mathit{refl}})^{+}$ between two objects may contain components like G R^{refl} G. But any such component may be simply removed without affecting the validity of the chain, reducing the chain to contain only relations R. The reflexive closure of the transitive closure, $(R^{+})^{\mathit{refl}}$, will include only those transitive chains based on R, but, as just seen, they suffice to yield $(R^{\mathit{refl}})^{+}$.

(30) **Lemma. The EPO equivalence relation.** The relation $\sim^{\text{bp.C}}$ is an equivalence relation on the grammars of T.

Proof. The relation $\sim^{\text{bp.C}}$ is reflexive and transitive by construction. It remains only to show that it is symmetrical. The base relation $\equiv^{\text{bp.C}}$ is clearly symmetrical. Its reflexive closure is also symmetrical. Now suppose $G_i \sim^{\text{bp.C}} G_j$. The relation $\sim^{\text{bp.C}}$ is the transitive closure of the reflexive closure of $\equiv^{\text{bp.C}}$ and therefore, since reflexive information of the form $G \sim^{\text{bp.C}} G$ adds nothing to a transitive chain, there will exist a sequence of distinct grammars $G_i = H_1, \ldots, H_n = G_j$ such that $H_k \equiv^{\text{bp.C}} H_{k+1}$, $1 \leq k < n$, in which each adjacent pair is symmetrical. Reverse them to create a transitive chain going the other way, establishing $G_j \sim^{\text{bp.C}} G_i$. □

(31) **Lemma. Universal instantiation of $\sim^{\text{bp.C}}$.** For every $U \in \mathcal{U}(T)$, the relation $\sim^{\text{bp.C}}$ is instantiated by the function $C \circ g_U$ as $=$.

Proof. By definition (29), the relation $\sim^{\text{bp.C}}$ is the reflexive closure of the transitive closure of the base relation $\equiv^{\text{bp.C}}$. By Lemma (25), $\equiv^{\text{bp.C}}$ is instantiated by $C \circ g_U$ as $=$. By Lemma (23), its transitive closure is also instantiated as $=$ by the same function. Clearly, if a relation is instantiable as $=$, its reflexive closure is instantiable as $=$ by the same function. □

We note in passing that the definition of the equivalence relation, unlike that of the order relation, does not depend on any special properties that distinguish a typology from a general partition. This becomes significant in §4.8 when we build the infrastructure that allows us to formally distinguish the class of typologies within the class of partitions.

(32) **Lemma. Double instantiation (EPO relations).** For every $U \in \mathcal{U}(T)$, the relations $<^{\text{bp.C}}$ and $\sim^{\text{bp.C}}$ are instantiated as $<$ and $=$, respectively, by the function $C \circ g_U$.

Proof. By Lemma (25), both base relations $\prec^{\text{bp.C}}$ and $\equiv^{\text{bp.C}}$ are instantiable as $<$ and $=$, respectively, by the function $\mathrm{C} \circ \mathrm{g}_{\mathrm{U}}$. By Lemma (23), their transitive closures are also instantiable by $\mathrm{C} \circ \mathrm{g}_{\mathrm{U}}$. Since instantiating a relation as $=$ also instantiates its reflexive closure, thc proof is complete, since $<^{\text{bp.C}}$ is the transitive closure of $\prec^{\text{bp.C}}$ and $\sim^{\text{bp.C}}$ is the reflexive closure of the transitive closure of $\equiv^{\text{bp.C}}$. □

The EPO for a constraint C is the following structure, a 'setoid' with an order relation, in the standard nomenclature,[5] which collects the grammars and the two relations $<^{\text{bp.C}}$ and $\sim^{\text{bp.C}}$.

(33) **Definition. $\mathbf{EPO_T(C)}$.** For a typology $\mathrm{T} = \{\mathrm{G}_1, \ldots, \mathrm{G}_n\}$, and $\mathrm{C} \in \mathrm{T.C{\small ON}}$,

$$\mathrm{EPO_T(C)} = \langle \mathrm{T}, <^{\text{bp.C}}, \sim^{\text{bp.C}} \rangle.$$

When the sponsoring typology is evident from context, we will often write simply EPO(C). The MOAT(T) collects the $\mathrm{EPO_T(C)}$ for every C in T.CON.

(34) **Definition. MOAT(T).** For a typology T,

$$\mathrm{MOAT(T)} = \{\mathrm{EPO_T(C)} \mid \mathrm{C} \in \mathrm{T.C{\small ON}}\}.$$

In light of these developments, it is convenient to extend the terminology of instantiation to whole EPOs and whole MOATs.

(35) **Definition. EPO instantiation.** A function $f_C : \mathrm{T} \rightarrow \mathbb{N}$ *instantiates* EPO(C) if f_C instantiates both relations of EPO(C).

(36) **Definition. MOAT instantiation.** The MOAT(T) is *instantiated* by a set S of functions $\{f_{\mathrm{C}} : \mathrm{T} \rightarrow \mathbb{N} \mid \mathrm{C} \in \mathrm{T.C{\small ON}}\}$ if for each constraint C, f_{C} instantiates EPO(C).

We have immediately that MOAT(T) is instantiated in every UVT U of T.

(37) **Lemma. Instantiating the MOAT.** For each $\mathrm{U} \in \mathcal{U}(\mathrm{T})$, $\mathrm{S_U} = \{\mathrm{C} \circ \mathrm{g_U} \mid \mathrm{C} \in \mathrm{T.C{\small ON}}\}$ instantiates MOAT(T).

Proof. Lemma (32) establishes that $\mathrm{S_U}$, $\mathrm{U} \in \mathcal{U}(\mathrm{T})$, instantiates the relations $<^{\text{bp.C}}$ and $\sim^{\text{bp.C}}$ of MOAT(T), satisfying definition (36). □

---

[5] See e.g. Wikipedia, Setoid.

Because S_U always instantiates MOAT(T), it is natural to broaden the usage even further and we will say of U itself that it *instantiates* MOAT(T), implicitly referring to S_U, and similarly that a column of U labeled by C *instantiates* EPO(C), implicitly referring to the instantiating function $C \circ g_U$. We will also allow the same usage with respect to other structures that parallel the EPO and the MOAT.

In sum: the $EPO_T(C)$ represents the essential order and equivalence relations inherent in C, those which are instantiated in every UVT for T and which therefore play a role in structuring the typology of the system in which C is defined. The MOAT(T) is thus an abstract version of T.Con, collecting all EPO(C) just as T.Con collects all the C.

4.3.5 Hypertransitivity

One final step is required to extract everything that we want from EPO(C). Because it contains two distinct relations, we need to ensure that they combine appropriately.

The two EPO relations $<^{bp.C}$ and $\sim^{bp.C}$ are developed from base relations that depend directly on border point pairs, but they come with no particular guarantee of how they relate to each other. The *integer* relations $<$ and $=$, by contrast, which instantiate $<^{bp.C}$ and $\sim^{bp.C}$ respectively, chain together nicely. If we have $a < b$ and $c < d$, then $b = c$ yields $a < d$, a point so obvious that it is rarely dwelt on.

For example, suppose we know only that $1 < 2^3$ and $8 < 9$. Once we grasp that $2^3 = 8$, we can be sure that $1 < 9$. This type of inference, however, does not hold for $<^{bp.C}$ and $\sim^{bp.C}$, because equivalence is not identity. We would like to build a new, richer order relation from $<^{bp.C}$ and $\sim^{bp.C}$ for which this type of inference is sound. In the general case, we have an order and an equivalence relation on a set, and we need the validity of what we will call *hypertransitive inference* involving the underlying order and equivalence relations.

Numerical $<$ and $=$ support hypertransitive inference, of course. To achieve this in the context of the EPO, we introduce a new relation: the *hypertransitive closure* (htc) of $<^{bp.C}$, written $<^{htc.bp.C}$, defined with respect to the equivalence relation $\sim^{bp.C}$.

(38) **Definition. Hypertransitive inference.** Let R and E be relations on any set S, with E an equivalence relation. Given elements $x_1,\ldots, x_n \in S$, the entailment

$$x_1 \mathcal{R} x_2,\ldots, x_{n-1} \mathcal{R} x_n \models x_1 \mathsf{R}\, x_n$$

where $\mathcal{R}$ is either R or E, and at least one $\mathcal{R}$ is R, will be termed *hypertransitive inference.*

For present purposes, suppose we have G_1 and G_n as the endpoints of a chain of relations $<^{\text{htc.bp.C}}$ and $\sim^{\text{bp.C}}$, of the form $G_1 \mathcal{R} G_2$, $G_2 \mathcal{R} G_3$, ..., $G_{n-1} \mathcal{R} G_n$, where each $\mathcal{R}$ is either $<^{\text{htc.bp.C}}$ or $\sim^{\text{bp.C}}$ and at least one of the $\mathcal{R}$ is $<^{\text{htc.bp.C}}$. From this, we want hypertransitive inference to yield $G_1 <^{\text{htc.bp.C}} G_n$.

Before laying out the relevant definitions, let's briefly recall why we need the hypertransitive relation $<^{\text{htc.bp.C}}$ even though the EPO itself is built on the *non*-hypertransitive relation $<^{\text{bp.C}}$. Recall the distinction between *privileged relations* which appear in the EPO and other order facts that follow from them. Consider, for example, the EPO diagram for m.Ons, repeated from §3.3, (27).

(39) EPO(m.Ons) of EST

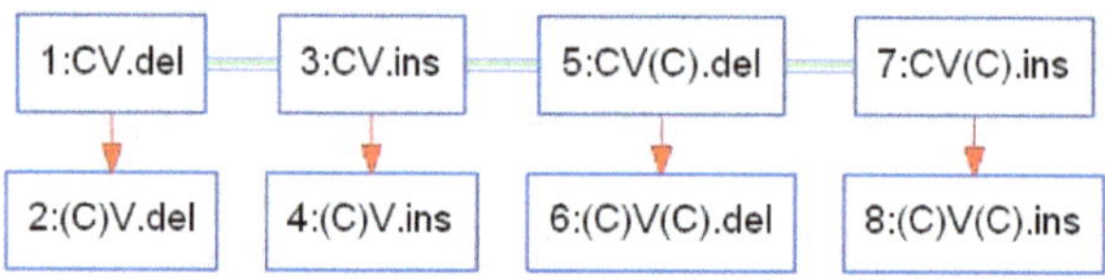

Red arrows indicate relations we denote as $<^{\text{bp.m.Ons}}$. (Indeed, they are also $\prec^{\text{bp.C}}$ because an EPO diagram is by convention transitively reduced.) Nevertheless, as observed in §3.3, other numerical order relations will be present in any UVT that instantiates this EPO. For example, any numerical value assigned to **5**:CV(C).del (top row) by m.Ons in any given UVT must be less than that assigned to **8**:(C)V(C).ins (far right, bottom row). This is because of the hypertransitive inference
[m.Ons(**5**) = m.Ons(**7**) & m.Ons(**7**) < m.Ons(**8**)] ⇒ [m.Ons(**5**) < m.Ons(**8**)], which is ordinary and unremarkable among the integers.

Nevertheless, when it comes to the question of which grammars may merge to produce a coarser typology, only the privileged relation $<^{\text{bp.m.Ons}}$ counts. There can be no typology in which grammars **5** and **8** merge, because of the cycle thereby induced. We repeat ex. (35) from §3.3.

(40) A bigraph tangled by merger

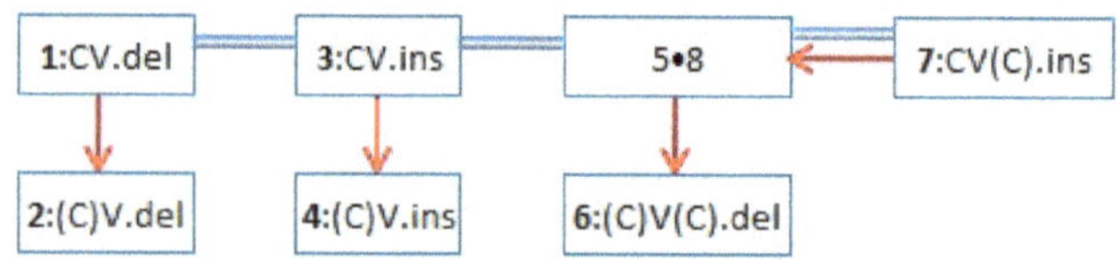

Notice that the crucial, merger-killing cycle itself requires hypertransitive inference to establish its non-instantiability. Nevertheless, non-privileged order relations deduced *only* via hypertransitivity in a valid EPO do not themselves obstruct merger. Suppose we were to include in a bigraph the information about the relation of **5** to **8**, which will appear numerically in every UVT, but is only hypertransitively derivable. We repeat ex. (41) from §3.3.

(41) EPO(m.Ons) augmented to include some non-privileged information

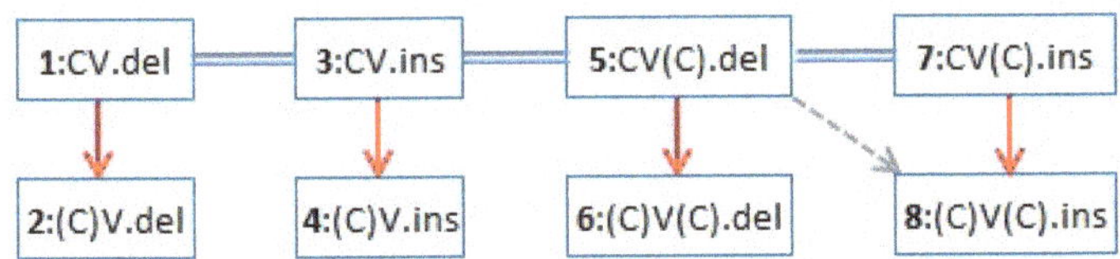

In this case, the merger of **7** and **8** is unobjectionable: the cycle is a graphical apparition, caused by retaining prior information that is no longer present after merger.

(42) Merger misleadingly including prior, non-privileged information

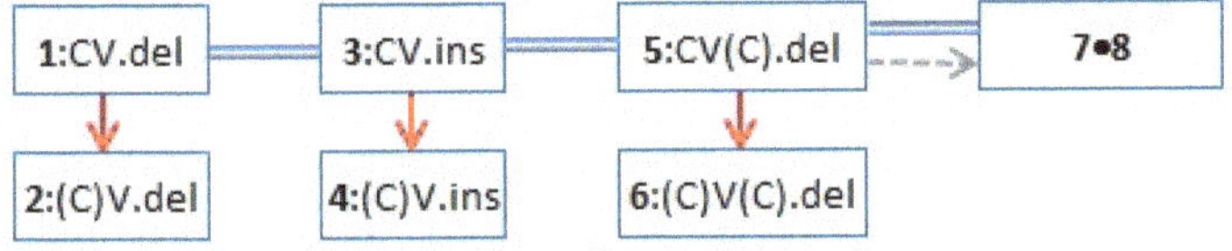

The coarsened partition is a fully legitimate typology. In it, there is no border point information to suggest the existence of the dotted, non-privileged arrow of diagrams (41) and (42). This is its actual, inoffensive EPO diagram, repeated from (43), §3.3.

(43) Merger with only privileged information

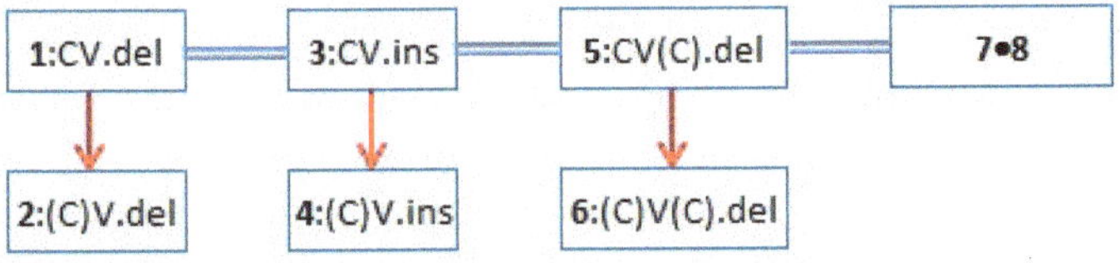

Thus, the hypertransitive relation $<^{\text{htc.bp.Ons}}$ is relevant to the status of a general partition as a typology: in every typological partition, this relation must be a partial order, as will be shown in Theorem (183). The non-hypertransitive EPO relation $<^{\text{bp.Ons}}$, in addition, determines the legitimacy of merger.

Broadly put, merger is allowed if it eliminates, as in (42), the border point pairs that give rise to the critical order relations in the pre-merger typology. For the EPO to serve as a representation displaying this information, it must respect border point pair structure in a way that hypertransitive closure does not. Thinking qualitatively in anticipation of the more precise geometric account in §7, this following kind of merger is allowed:

(44) Border-dissolving union of grammars

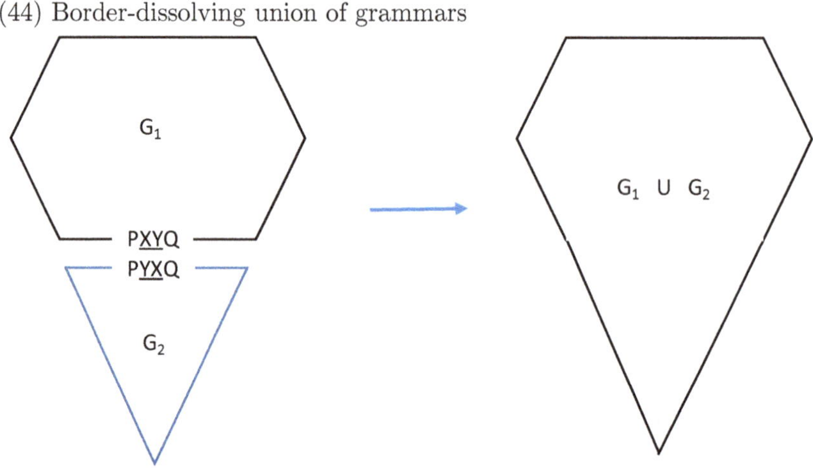

Let us now turn to defining the hypertransitive closure $<^{\text{htc.bp.C}}$. We use the same approach as in the definition of transitive closure in (22), augmenting the required conditions to take account of equality as well as order.

(45) **Definition. Hypertransitive closure (htc.bp).** Given a typology T and a constraint C ∈ T.Con, the hypertransitive closure of $<^{\text{bp.C}}$ is the relation $<^{\text{htc.bp.C}}$ on T, defined as follows.

For all $G_1, H, G_2 \in T$,

i.	$G_1 <^{\text{bp.C}} G_2$	$\Rightarrow G_1 <^{\text{htc.bp.C}} G_2$	'$<^{\text{bp.C}}$ is in $<^{\text{htc.bp.C}}$'
ii.	$G_1 <^{\text{htc.bp.C}} H$ and $H <^{\text{htc.bp.C}} G_2$	$\Rightarrow G_1 <^{\text{htc.bp.C}} G_2$	'$<^{\text{htc.bp.C}}$ is transitive'
iii.a	$G_1 \sim^{\text{bp.C}} H$ & $H <^{\text{htc.bp.C}} G_2$	$\Rightarrow G_1 <^{\text{htc.bp.C}} G_2$	'~ combines at the left'
iii.b	$G_1 <^{\text{htc.bp.C}} H$ & $H \sim^{\text{bp.C}} G_2$	$\Rightarrow G_1 <^{\text{htc.bp.C}} G_2$.	'~ combines at the right'

Observe that this definition does not rely on any properties that distinguish a typology from an unconstrained partition of Ord(*S*.Con), nor on any properties that distinguish a grammar from a block of an arbitrary partition. Its generality will become useful in §4.8, where we take up the issue of what it is exactly that makes a typology different from all other partitions.

Recall from (38) that *hypertransitive inference* means that if there is a sequence of overlapping pairwise relations involving equivalence E and another relation R, with one of the relations in the sequence being R, you may validly conclude that the first element in the sequence is R-related to the last.

(46) **Lemma. Hypertransitivity.** The relation $<^{\text{htc.bp.C}}$ supports hypertransitive inference with respect to the equivalence relation $\sim^{\text{bp.C}}$.

Proof. This follows directly from definition (45). Clauses (iii.a) and (iii.b) license the conflation of a sequence of adjacent equivalence relations $\sim^{\text{bp.C}}$ with a preceding or following order relation $<^{\text{htc.bp.C}}$. This leaves an overlapping sequence of relations $<^{\text{htc.bp.C}}$. This relation is transitive by construction. □

We may go one step farther, decomposing a relation involving $<^{\text{htc.bp.C}}$ into an overlapping chain of relations involving only the EPO relations $<^{\text{bp.C}}$ and $\sim^{\text{bp.C}}$.

(47) **Lemma. BP HTC decomposition.** If $G_1 <^{\text{htc.bp.C}} G_2$, then there is a sequence of relations of the form $G_1 \mathcal{R} G_2$, $G_2 \mathcal{R} G_3$, ..., $G_{n-1} \mathcal{R} G_n$, where each $\mathcal{R}$ is either $<^{\text{bp.C}}$ or $\sim^{\text{bp.C}}$ and at least one of the $\mathcal{R}$ is $<^{\text{bp.C}}$. Conversely, if such a sequence exists, then $G_1 <^{\text{htc.bp.C}} G_2$.

Proof. This follows directly from repeated application of the definition. □

The hypertransitively closed relation $<^{\text{htc.bp.C}}$ is well-behaved with respect to numerical $<$.

(48) **Lemma. Universal instantiation of the BP HTC.** For every $U \in \mathcal{U}(T)$, the relation $<^{\text{htc.bp.C}}$ is instantiated as $<$ by the function $C \circ g_U$.

Proof. By Lemma (47), the relation $<^{\text{htc.bp.C}}$ can be rewritten as an overlapping sequence of $<^{\text{bp.C}}$ and $\sim^{\text{bp.C}}$ relations, at least one of which is $<^{\text{bp.C}}$. Each of these may be further rewritten as overlapping sequences of base relations $\prec^{\text{bp.C}}$ and $\equiv^{\text{bp.C}}$, respectively. From the Universal Instantiation Lemma (25), these base relations are simultaneously instantiable by $f = C \circ g_U$ as $<$ and $=$ respectively, for any $U \in \mathcal{U}(T)$. Thus, if $G_1 <^{\text{htc.bp.C}} G_2$, it follows that $f(G_1) < f(G_2)$, establishing that f instantiates $<^{\text{htc.bp.C}}$ as $<$ in every $U \in \mathcal{U}(T)$. □

(49) **Lemma. The HTC relation $<^{\text{htc.bp.C}}$ is a strict partial order.**
Proof. It is transitive by definition. It is asymmetric because it is instantiable as $<$, by Lemma (20). Asymmetry implies irreflexivity. Thus, it is a strict partial order. □

With the hypertransitive closure $<^{\text{htc.bp.C}}$ of $<^{\text{bp.C}}$ in hand, we have completed the construction of all the order relations derived from border point pairs that are at play in the theory of typologies. These formally explicate the privileged and non-privileged relations represented in the bigraph construction. To conclude, we generalize the notion of hypertransitivity to the EPO itself.

(50) **Definition. Hypertransitive closure of EPO(C).** Given a typology T and C ∈ T.Con, we have $\text{EPO}_T(\text{C}) = \langle \text{T}, <^{\text{bp.C}}, \sim^{\text{bp.C}} \rangle$. The hypertransitive closure of $\text{EPO}_T(\text{C})$, which we denote $\text{htcEPO}_T(\text{C})$, is defined to be $\langle \text{T}, <^{\text{htc.bp.C}}, \sim^{\text{bp.C}} \rangle$.

We will often drop the subscript T when is clear from context. We will also refer to the collection of every htcEPO as htcMOAT.

(51) **Definition. Hypertransitive closure of MOAT(T).** Given a typology T, the hypertransitive closure of MOAT(T), denoted htcMOAT(T), is $\{\text{htcEPO}_T(\text{C}) \mid \text{C} \in \text{T.Con}\}$.

The htcMOAT, with its collection of htcEPO(C) for all C in T.Con, will play a crucial role in relating the MOAT proper to a parallel but not quite identical structure, the filtration-based PMOAT, introduced in §4.5, which will allow us to establish one of our major targets: that typologies with the same MOAT are the same typology.

4.3.6 Summary of §4.3 and prospectus

Starting from the border point pairs locally connecting adjacent grammars, we have advanced to the relations $<^{\text{bp.C}}$ and $\sim^{\text{bp.C}}$ defined over all grammars of a typology, adjacent or not. We've established that these are partial orders and equivalence relations, respectively, instantiated in the integers by the function $\text{C} \circ \text{g}_\text{U}$ which maps a grammar G_k to an integer value in the UVT U, via mapping G_k by $\text{g}_\text{U}: \text{T} \to \text{U}$ to the row u_k of U that G_k selects. This allows us to assemble the MOAT as an algebraic structure. From these two relations, we are able to construct the hypertransitive relation $<^{\text{htc.bp.C}}$, which combines with $\sim^{\text{bp.C}}$ in the way that $<$ combines with $=$ among the integers.

With these concepts in place, it is possible to see the overall shape of the argument, which pursues two formal initiatives. In the first of these, the notion of hypertransitivity allows us to relate the MOAT to another parallel but not quite identical order and equivalence structure: the PMOAT (§4.5–6), which is based on a new notion of direct filtration of *grammars*, circumventing once again the multiplicity of UVTs. An intermediate goal is to show that the hypertransitive closure of the MOAT order relation is identical to the hypertransitive closure of the PMOAT order relation. This allows us to understand in some depth how the abstract orders and equivalences of the MOAT characterize a typology, by following a chain of inferences involving the instantiation of the PMOAT and its hypertransitive closure. In particular, we will establish that the relations of the MOAT are not only instantiated in every UVT, but that they completely determine how any UVT is filtered, even though they derive from local relations between a subset of legs, those at the borders of grammars, and even though they abstract away from the details of those legs. The goal of this line of reasoning is to establish that two typologies with the same MOAT are the same typology.

To provide overall guidance, we sketch here the exact line we will follow in Theorem (152), which establishes that if V is a UVT that *instantiates* MOAT(T), then the typology of V is exactly T.

> V instantiates MOAT of T ⇒ V instantiates htcMOAT ⇒
> V instantiates htcPMOAT ⇒ V instantiates PMOAT ⇒
> V is a UVT for T.

Two typologies with relationally isomorphic MOATs will therefore share all instantiatiating UVTs, and it follows that they must be the same typology, as is shown in Theorem (155), §4.7.

The second initiative resolves the relation between typologies and general partitions of Ord(*S*.Con), of which they form a special subtype. The blocks of a general partition give rise to border point pairs in exactly the same way as the grammars of a typology. Consequently, the method of constructing relations from border point pairs developed above is viable on general partitions of Ord(*S*.Con) and not just on typologies. The principal difference is that equivalence carries over to the general context, but the base ≺-relation is no longer guaranteed to lead to a partial order through transitive closure. The utility of this move is that it allows us to reason about arbitrary partitions, which may or may not themselves be typologies, using the general versions of these relations.[6] Development will parallel that of the EPO relations to the extent possible, leading to the GEPO (generalized EPO) and the GMOAT. The ultimate goal is Theorem (183), which establishes that a partition π of Ord(S.CON) is a typology if and only if its GMOAT is acyclic and therefore a MOAT, with its relation $<^{\pi.\text{htc.bp.C}}$ a partial order.

Because of the straightforward parallelism between the GMOAT and the MOAT, we take up its construction (§4.4) before developing the notion of grammar filtration (§4.5–6).

4.4 General partitions: GEPO, GMOAT

Section contents

The base relations just introduced require nothing beyond a partition π of Ord(T.CON), the set of all the orders on some set of constraints T.CON.[7] In themselves, they make no reference to numbers or filtration. They develop from border point pairs, which are definable on any pair of blocks $\text{B}_i, \text{B}_j \in \pi$ which are adjacent in the sense that there exist $\text{P}\underline{\text{XY}}\text{Q} \in \text{B}_i$ and $\text{P}\underline{\text{YX}}\text{Q} \in \text{B}_j$. We can therefore define on any partition a pair of relations that are definitionally identical to those in the EPO. This will allow us to ask, and answer in §4.8 below, the fundamental typological question: which partitions of Ord(T.CON) are typologies?

---

[6] As a side note, observe that every partition of Ord(*S*.CON), typological or not, can be derived from the 'discrete typology' by unioning its grammars, each of which contains but a single leg – 'coarsening' it, in the lingo.

[7] Recall that a partition of a nonempty set Σ is a collection of nonempty subsets $\text{B}_k \subseteq \Sigma$ which (1) are pairwise disjoint, so that $\text{B}_i \cap \text{B}_j = \emptyset$, and (2) together include all of S, so that $\cup\text{B}_k = \Sigma$.

We repeat the relevant definitions here *mutatis mutandis*, noting explicitly that they apply to general partitions of Ord(T.CON), which of course include typologies as a special case. In notating them, we prefix the usual identifying labels with 'π' to signal that they live on a general partition rather than within the narrower confines of a typology. Thus, we develop relations $\prec^{\pi.\mathrm{bp.C}}$, $<^{\pi.\mathrm{bp.C}}$, $<^{\pi.\mathrm{htc.bp.C}}$, $\equiv^{\pi.\mathrm{bp.C}}$, $\sim^{\pi.\mathrm{bp.C}}$, paralleling the relations just defined on typological partitions. When it is desired to limit π to typological partitions, we will write $<^{\mathrm{T.bp.C}}$ and so on. Although $\sim^{\pi.\mathrm{bp.C}}$ is an equivalence relation even in the general case, the relation $<^{\pi.\mathrm{bp.C}}$ is by no means guaranteed to be an order. We will find in Theorem (183) that the hypertransitive closure $<^{\pi.\mathrm{htc.bp.C}}$ of $<^{\pi.\mathrm{bp.C}}$ is an order if and only if π is a typology, settling the typological question.

The relations $<^{\pi.\mathrm{bp.C}}$ and $\sim^{\pi.\mathrm{bp.C}}$ are defined in a way that parallels the definition of $<^{\mathrm{T.bp.C}}$ and $\sim^{\mathrm{T.bp.C}}$, merely dropping the restriction that π be a typology. For each C, these relations are collected into a Generalized EPO, or *GEPO*, and the GEPOs are collected into a Generalized MOAT, or *GMOAT*, paralleling the definitions of EPO and MOAT.

(52) **Definition. Border point pair.** Let $\pi = \{B_1, \ldots, B_n\}$ be a partition of Ord(S), where S is an arbitrary non-empty finite set. Let $\lambda_1 = \mathrm{P}\underline{\mathrm{XY}}\mathrm{Q}$ and $\lambda_2 = \mathrm{P}\underline{\mathrm{YX}}\mathrm{Q}$ be linear orders in Ord(S), with P,Q sequences of elements of S and X, Y ∈ S. Let $B_j, B_k \in \pi$, $B_j \neq B_k$. Then $\{\lambda_1, \lambda_2\}$ is a *border point pair* for B_j, B_k iff $\lambda_1 \in B_j$ and $\lambda_2 \in B_k$.

(53) **Definition. Base relation $\prec^{\pi.\mathrm{bp.C}}$.** Given a partition $\pi = \{B_1, \ldots, B_n\}$ of Ord(S), we say for C ∈ S, $B_j \prec^{\pi.\mathrm{bp.C}} B_k$ iff there is a border point pair (P$\underline{\mathrm{CY}}$Q, P$\underline{\mathrm{YC}}$Q), with P$\underline{\mathrm{CY}}$Q $\in B_j$ and P$\underline{\mathrm{YC}}$Q $\in B_k$.

(54) **Definition. Base relation $\equiv^{\pi.\mathrm{bp.C}}$.** Given a partition $\pi = \{B_1, \ldots, B_n\}$ of Ord(S), with S any nonempty finite set, for each C ∈ S we say $B_j \equiv^{\pi.\mathrm{bp.C}} B_k$ iff there is a border point pair (P$\underline{\mathrm{XY}}$Q, P$\underline{\mathrm{YX}}$Q) with P$\underline{\mathrm{XY}}$Q $\in B_j$ and P$\underline{\mathrm{YX}}$Q $\in B_k$, with C in the prefix P.

(55) **Definition.** The GEPO relation $<^{\pi.\mathrm{bp.C}}$ is the transitive closure of $\prec^{\pi.\mathrm{bp.C}}$.

(56) **Definition.** The GEPO equivalence relation $\sim^{\pi.\mathrm{bp.C}}$ is the transitive closure of the reflexive closure of $\equiv^{\pi.\mathrm{bp.C}}$.

The general relation $\sim^{\pi.\mathrm{bp.C}}$ is always an equivalence relation. It is clearly symmetric, and it is reflexive and transitive by construction. But the relation $<^{\pi.\mathrm{bp.C}}$ isn't necessarily a partial order, because it needn't be asymmetric.

Consider the graphical object based on $S = \{X, Y, Z\}$, the permutohedron whose vertices correspond to the linear orders on three constraints, linked by adjacency. Below we display a 2-block partition of Ord(S), $\pi = \{O, B\}$, indicating the block O by oval encirclement and the block B by rectangular boxing. It is clear that this partition is non-typological, because its blocks are not connected regions (Riggle 2010 and §7 below, Lemma (40)).

(57) A partition $\pi = \{O, B\}$ of Ord(S), with $O = \{YXZ, XZY, ZYX\}$, $B = \{XYZ, ZXY, YZX\}$

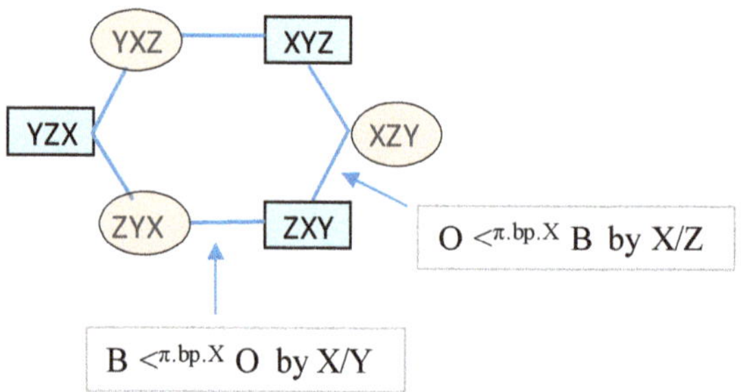

From this we obtain the following relations, noted in the diagram, where the border point pairs are arranged so that the O points are listed first.

$\{\underline{XZ}Y, \underline{ZX}Y\} \Rightarrow O <^{\pi.bp.X} B$

$\{Z\underline{YX}, Z\underline{XY}\} \Rightarrow B <^{\pi.bp.X} O$

The symmetrical relation $<^{\pi.bp.X}$ is clearly not a strict order. It is also clear that it cannot be instantiated as $<$, and therefore cannot represent a typology generated by the violation calculus of OT.

By contrast, consider the following typological partition $T = \{G_O, G_B\}$, where G_B is boxed on the right and G_O is oval-enclosed on the left.

(58) Partition T = {G_B, G_O}, with G_B = {XYZ, XZY, ZXY}, G_O = {YXZ, YZX, ZYX}

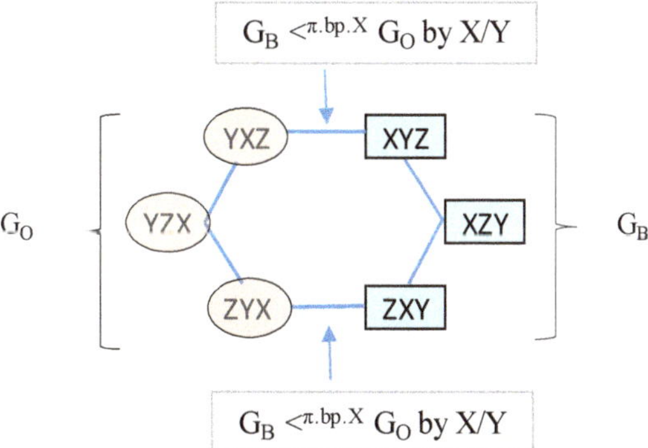

Here, the relation $<^{\pi.bp.X}$ *is* an order, as we can see from its border point base, listed exhaustively here, with the G_B point listed first in each pair.

{<u>XY</u>Z, <u>YX</u>Z} ⇒ $G_B <^{\pi.bp.X} G_O$

{Z<u>XY</u>, Z<u>YX</u>} ⇒ $G_B <^{\pi.bp.X} G_O$

This typology consists of two grammars: G_B, on the right, which consists of all legs in which X ≫ Y, and G_O, on the left, in which all legs satisfy the condition Y ≫ X. It can be associated with this UVT, among of course many others.

(59) A UVT for T of ex. (58)

T	X	Y	Z
G_B	0	1	0
G_O	1	0	0

These two examples give a sense of how the base relations come about in both general and typological partitions. In addition, they go beyond the intuitive cartography of earlier examples and give a concrete glimpse of the actual graphical structures generated by the adjacency data.

With the relations $<^{\pi.bp.C}$ and $\sim^{\pi.bp.C}$ in hand, we generalize the EPO and the MOAT constructions to the GEPO and the GMOAT, definable on any partition of Ord(S).

(60) **Definition. GEPO$_\pi$(C).** For a partition π of Ord(*S*.Con), with C ∈ *S*.Con,

$$\text{GEPO}_\pi(\text{C}) =_{df} \langle \pi, <^{\pi.bp.C}, \sim^{\pi.bp.C} \rangle.$$

When the sponsoring partition is evident from context, we will often write simply GEPO(C). The GMOAT(π) collects the GEPO(C) for every C in *S*.con

(61) **Definition. GMOAT(π).** For a partition π of Ord(*S*.CON),
GMOAT(π) $=_{df}$ {GEPO$_π$(C) | C ∈ *S*.con}.

To complete the parallel with the MOAT proper, we define the hypertransitive closure of GEPO and GMOAT, written htcGEPO and htcGMOAT, respectively. As noted at the introduction of the hypertransitive relation $<^{htc.bp.C}$ (45), there is no dependence in the definition of the (very general notion of) hypertransitive closure on the distinction between *typology* and *partition*, and we will simply take (45), with the replacement of *typology* by *partition* along with the correlated notational changes, as the definition of $<^{\pi.htc.bp.C}$.

(62) **Definition. Hypertransitive closure of GEPO$_π$(C).** Given a partition π of Ord(*S*.Con), the hypertransitive closure of GEPO$_π$(C), denoted htcGEPO$_π$(C), is given by
htcGEPO$_π$(C) $=_{df}$ ⟨π, $<^{\pi.htc.bp.C}$, $\sim^{bp.C}$⟩.

(63) **Definition. Hypertransitive closure of the GMOAT.** Given a partition π of Ord(*S*.Con), the hypertransitive closure of GMOAT(π), denoted htcGMOAT(π), is given by
htcGMOAT(π) $=_{df}$ {htcGEPO$_π$(C) | C ∈ *S*.CON}.

When the partition is a typology, MOAT = GMOAT. In §4.8, we establish the general condition under which this equality holds: all that's required is that the GEPOs of the GMOAT be acyclic, taking account of both equivalence and order. Cycles become obvious in bigraph representations like those in ex. (40) of §1.3.3, ex. (35) of §3.3, ex. (23) of §6.2.1, and ex. (29) of §6.2.2. As defined algebraically in (170) below, the requirement is that the hypertransitive closure of the relation $<^{\pi.bp.C}$ be a partial order.

4.5 Prefix sharing, No Dead Man Walking, and Filtration Uniformity

Section contents

Standing in the way of progress is the brute fact that each typology has many UVTs, which agree in the number of rows and columns but differ in their numerical content. Given a UVT, each grammar corresponds to a single row in it, and vice versa. But the plethora of UVTs means that each grammar has many numerically distinct corresponding rows appearing in different UVTs. This ineradicable multiplicity calls into question the uniqueness of any object defined by filtration of individual UVTs. But contrary to worst-case pessimism, filtration proceeds identically in every UVT. The UVTs for a typology agree not just in corresponding optima, but in every step of the procedure that leads to them.

To obtain this result, we re-create the notion of filtration in the domain of grammars. Since a grammar consists of a single, unique set of linear orders – its legs – when filtration is defined to work on grammars, problems of multiplicity do not arise. Given the correspondence between grammars and UVT rows, this gives us a powerful tool for establishing uniqueness properties in the UVT domain. Furthermore, grammar filtration calls on the manifest content of individual legs rather than on a comparative numerical process, and is therefore much easier to deal with. Our principal results are Filtration Uniformity (84), which establishes that filtration patterns are identical in every UVT for a given typology, and the Converse of Filtration Uniformity (85), which establishes that if two UVTs over the same constraint set have identical filtration patterns, they deliver the same typology.

4.5.1 Filtration of candidates: No Dead Man Walking

I have a plan...a plan that cannot possibly fail.
– Clouseau

The recursive definition of candidate filtration from ex. (1), §4.1, runs like this. Recall that we assume the natural convention that P[K] = K when P = ∅.

(64) **Definition. Candidate filtration.** Let K be any nonempty set of candidates. Let C be any constraint, and P any sequence of one or more constraints.

i. $C[K] = \{k \in K \mid C(k) \leq C(x) \text{ for all } x \in K\}$
ii. $CP[K] = P[C[K]]$

An element k ∈ K is minimal in K with respect to C ('take the best'), in the sense that C(k) is the minimal value assigned by C, i.e. that ∀x ∈ K, C(k) ≤ C(x). Crucially, C[K] ≠ ∅, because C(k) is a non-negative integer and there is always an element k ∈ K, and possibly more than one, such that C(k) is minimal ('forced choice' in the terminology used in Prince 2002:iv). It follows that P[K] ≠ ∅ for any sequence of constraints.

Spelled out, filtration by a linear (ranking) order on the constraints $C_1 \gg \cdots \gg C_n$ plays out as a composition of the constraint functions: $C_n \circ \cdots \circ C_1[K]$. We refer to each function application as a 'step' of filtration. In addition, we regard the first (or zeroth) step as applying to the empty sequence.

OT filtration has a somewhat surprising property that plays a central role in the analysis of typologies. Consider the set of *possible optima*, namely those candidates that are optimal under some linear order of the constraints in the system. If any such candidate survives filtration by a partial sequence of constraints, a 'prefix', then that partial sequence can be completed to a sequence of all the constraints that selects that candidate as optimal.

Symbolically, suppose candidate q ∈ K is a possible optimum. From this commitment, we only know that there is *some* linear order among the set Ord(*S*.Con) that selects q from K. But, because of the way OT filtration works, we will find a much more specific guarantee: if q is among the survivors of filtration by P, formally q ∈ P[K], then there is a total order λ = PQ extending P such that q is selected by PQ; that is, there is a Q such that q ∈ PQ[K].

We call this property 'No Dead Man Walking,' because, among possible optima, partial success on any given sequence of constraints ensures total success under *some* continuation of it. In life, generally, partial success carries no such guarantee.

As background, we recall the definition of possible optimum, which is usefully understood through the notion of harmonic bounding (see P&S 1993/2004, Samek-Lodovici & Prince 1999, 2005, Prince 2002a for detailed study of this notion).

If z ∈ K is *harmonically bounded*, there can be no leg λ ∈ Ord(*S*.CON) for which z ∈ λ[K]. Put in terms of filtration, this means that for every ranking, there's at least one candidate q that beats it in head-to-head competition: i.e., that is selected instead of z from {q, z}.[8] Recall that such a bounding element q need not be optimal over the entire candidate set, only *better* than z in its contest with q, blocking z from optimality.

Put in terms of ranking logic, harmonic bounding means that the set of ERCs [z ~ q] for all candidates q, derived from asserting z as optimal, contains an inconsistent subset, which is not satisfiable by any linear order because it imposes contradictory ordering demands on the constraints.

A candidate is a *possible optimum* iff it is not *harmonically bounded.*[9] Establishing the possible optimality of a candidate z require full knowledge of its entire candidate set, to ensure that there is no lurking q that bounds it. Ascriptions of harmonic bounding require knowledge of the entire constraint set, to ensure that there is no unacknowledged C that crucially favors it. Thus a candidate is possibly optimal or harmonically bounded *with respect to* an explicit candidate set, constraint set pair ⟨K, S⟩.

We now establish the crucial No Dead Man Walking property, offering three proofs, with an eye to facilitating insight into this fundamental if perhaps not entirely expected property of OT. The first two work by contradiction, using the same idea from different perspectives, and the third makes constructive use of the idea.

---

[8] This is sometimes misunderstood, getting the quantifier order wrong, as requiring that there be a single bounder that works for all rankings. See Samek-Lodovic & Prince (1999) for the correct formulation.

[9] We also like Riggle's 'contender' for 'possible optimum', but prefer to retain the explicit reference to optimality. *A man hears what he wants to hear and disregards the rest.*

(65) **Theorem. No Dead Man Walking.** Let *S* be an OT system, possibly abstract, and let K be a set of candidates and *S*.CON a set of constraints. If q ∈ K is a possible optimum for ⟨K, *S*.CON⟩ and q ∈ P[K], for P a sequence of constraints from *S*.CON, then there is a sequence of constraints Q exhausting *S*.CON such that q ∈ PQ[K].

Proof #1. Let P be a sequence of constraints drawn from *S*.CON, not including all the constraints. Say q ∈ P[K] is a possible optimum for K, so that for some λ ∈ Ord(*S*.CON), we have q ∈ λ[K]. Assume for purposes of contradiction that there is no Q such that q ∈ PQ[K], where Q is a sequence of all the constraints not in P. Under this assumption, q would be optimal for some leg not beginning with the sequence P, but not for any leg beginning with P even though q ∈ P[K].

Let B = P[K] \ {q}, consisting of all the survivors of P except for q. It must be that B is nonempty, because by the forced choice property of OT filtration, something other than q wins on each Q; that is, for every such Q, there is some z ≠ q, such that z ∈ PQ[K], and z ∈ B = P[K] by the telescoping property. We make one additional observation: the members of B ∪ {q} must all be equal on each constraint in P ('survivor sameness', §4.1, p. 2). But these facts entail that q is bounded by the members of B, contradicting the assumption that it is a possible optimum.

To spell this out: no constraint of P distinguishes the candidates in P[K] = B ∪ {q}. Therefore, wherever it sits in an arbitrary leg λ, a constraint from P will have no effect on the filtration of B ∪ {q} by λ. All decisions among the members of P[K] are made by the constraints not in P, namely those in Q, which, whatever their ranking in λ, will by assumption eject q in favor of some member of B. Since any arbitrary leg consists of the constraints making up P and Q, no ranking selects q, contradicting the assumption that q is a possible optimum. □

Proof #2. Notation. To keep things concise and clear, we write Ψ* for the set of constraints in the sequence Ψ. We write [q ~ z] for the ERC comparing q and z over the constraint set S. C[q ~ z] is the value from {W, L, *e*} assigned by the constraint C to the comparison of q with z, with q asserted optimal.

Let q ∈ K be a possible optimum over ⟨K, *S*.CON⟩. In terms of ERC logic, this means that every subset of the ERC set **E** = $\{[q \sim z]_{S.\text{Con}} \mid z \in K\}$ is consistent. Assume that q ∈ P[K] and, for purposes of contradiction, that q ∉ PQ[K] for any Q containing all the constraints not in P.

Consider first the behavior of just the constraints in Q* over just the survivor set of candidates P[K]. Since q ∈ P[K] but q ∉ Q[P[K]] for *any* Q, it must be that q is harmonically bounded over ⟨P[K], Q*⟩, where P[K] ⊆ K and $Q^* \subsetneq S.\text{Con}$. In terms of ERC logic, this means that the ERC set $\mathbf{E}_{Q^*} = \{[q \sim z]_{Q^*} \mid z \in P[K]\}$ is inconsistent.

Observe now that $C[q \sim z] = e$ for every $z \in P[K]$ and every $C \in P^*$ because $q \in P[K]$. This means that it is not possible to alleviate the inconsistency of $\mathbf{E}_{Q^*}$ by enlarging the constraint set over which the ERCs are constructed to include P^*. That $\mathbf{E}_{Q^*}$ is inconsistent means that it contains a subset $\mathbf{F}$ that fuses to L^+. This means, in terms of a comparative tableau representation, that every column either contains an L or consists entirely of *e*'s, with at least one column containing an L. Construct a set of ERCs $\mathbf{F}'$ which evaluates $[q \sim z]$ over $P^* \cup Q^* = S.\text{Con}$. Despite the enlargement, $\mathbf{F}'$ must also fuse to L^+, because augmenting the constraint set with constraints that supply only *e* will not remove the fusion from L^+, since it still consists only of *e* and L values. Therefore, $\mathbf{E} = \{[q \sim z]_{S.\text{Con}} \mid z \in K\}$ is inconsistent, since $\mathbf{F}' \subseteq \mathbf{E}$ is inconsistent. From this it follows that q cannot be a possible optimum, contradicting the assumption that it is. Therefore q is not bounded over $\langle P[K], Q^* \rangle$ and there exists some Q such that $Q[P[K]] = q$, equivalently $PQ[K] = q$. □

Proof #3. We now adopt a constructive perspective that yields a leg shaped PQ delivering q as optimal over ⟨K, *S*.Con⟩, given only that q is a possible optimum over ⟨K, *S*.Con⟩ and $q \in P[K]$.

Let $\lambda \in \text{Ord}[S.\text{Con}]$ be such that $\lambda[K] = q$. The existence of such a λ is guaranteed because q is a possible optimum. Now construct a leg $\lambda' = PQ$ by moving all the constraints in P^* to the front of λ, assembling them in the order P. We claim that $\lambda'[K] = q$.

Consider first the filtration of the set of candidates $P[K] \subseteq K$ by λ. In Proof #2, it was noted that $C[q \sim z] = e$ for every $z \in P[K]$ and every $C \in P^*$ because $q \in P[K]$. Thus, the constraints in P^* do not distinguish among the candidates in P[K], and they play no role in the filtration of P[K] by λ, wherever they sit in λ. If we remove them from λ to produce a sequence Q of the constraints not in P, we will still have $Q[P[K]] = q$. It follows from the definition of filtration (64) that $Q[P[K]] = PQ[K]$. Since $\lambda' = PQ$, we have $\lambda'[K] = q$, as claimed. □

4.5.2 Prefix sharing as grammar/block filtration

Filtration of candidate sets proceeds by repeated function application and its basic mode of action is familiar to all practitioners, if not all critics, of OT. We now re-create the process entirely within the realm of grammars.

The rows of a UVT correspond 1:1 to the grammars of its typology, enabling our transparent labeling scheme, which links the kth grammar to the

k^{th} row of the UVT. By this $G_k \in T_U$ corresponds uniquely to $u_k \in U$, and vice versa. Filtration is by a leg, and therefore *every* leg of a grammar G_k selects the grammar's corresponding row u_k in the UVT U. But since u_k corresponds to G_k, a leg may be understood as selecting the grammar that it belongs to.

Filtering a UVT to select a row thus corresponds to filtering a typology to select a grammar. The definition of a grammar as the totality of its language's optima, taken with the definition of UVT, gives us the following dual views of the action of a leg, which depend on what it applies to. We distinguish these related but different functions orthographically by their bracketing style.

(66) **Selection of rows / grammars by a leg**

$$\lambda[U] \;= u_k \quad \text{iff } \lambda \in G_k$$
$$\lambda\langle T_U\rangle = G_k \quad \text{iff } \lambda[U] = u_k$$

The parallelism becomes interesting, and valuable, when we use it to define a step-by-step notion of *grammar* filtration that parallels the familiar step-by-step notion of row filtration. All that's needed is to generalize from filtering grammars by λ, an entire leg, as in (66), to filtering by P, any sequence of constraints, as in the definition of filtration (64).

Consider the progress of grammar filtration under this perspective. All legs that begin with the same constraint C will select the same set of *grammars* at the first step of filtration. Generalizing, all legs beginning with the same prefix P will filter the typology down to the same set of grammars after filtration by P, regardless of what comes next in any of those legs. This pattern of prefix sharing gives a way of selecting grammars on the basis of the legs they contain: all those grammars that contain a leg with prefix P are grouped, reflecting the fact that their corresponding rows survive candidate filtration by P.

This suggests defining *grammar filtration* directly in terms of shared prefixes. The usefulness of this approach, as we will see, is that it proceeds from a single UVT to its unique typology, and then from that typology to the properties of the entire set of UVTs giving rise to it. Filtration by prefix also embodies an important simplification, which makes it much easier to argue from. Candidate filtration requires a calculation over numerical values which depends at every step after the first on the result of a prior such calculation, and therefore has a processual flavor, but grammar filtration requires only monitoring the structure of legs, which they display openly. This shift in perspective on filtration leads to a new set of relations between grammars that parallels those arising form border point pairs, developed below in §4.6.4.

In addition, because it depends only on the structure of the set of linear orders, this notion generalizes to arbitrary partitions of Ord(S), which need not have UVTs. We therefore define the relevant notion of filtration with reference to general partitions. Let $\mathbb{B} \subseteq \pi$ denote a set of blocks $\mathbb{B}$ belonging to a partition π. For a block $B \in \mathbb{B}$ to belong to $P\langle\mathbb{B}\rangle$ requires only that B contain *some* linear order beginning with P. Of course, it may contain others that do not.

(67) **Definition. Block filtration by prefix sharing.** Given a partition π of Ord(S) and a prefix P of $\lambda \in$ Ord(S), we define filtration by P of a set of blocks $\mathbb{B} \subseteq \pi$ as

$$P\langle\mathbb{B}\rangle = \{B \in \mathbb{B} \mid \exists\lambda \in B \text{ such that } \lambda = P...\}.$$

Two special cases are worth noting. When $P = \emptyset$, $P\langle\mathbb{B}\rangle = \mathbb{B}$. When $P = \lambda \in$ Ord(S), then $\lambda\langle\pi\rangle$ is the unique block containing λ.

When a partition is a typology T, where blocks are grammars, this generalized notion yields *grammar filtration* P⟨T⟩. As an example, consider the '3 Bots,' a typology given by, among others, the following UVT.

(68) A UVT for the 3 Bots

3 Bots	X	Y	Z
X-bot	1	0	0
Y-bot	0	1	0
Z-bot	0	0	1

Observe first that the grammars of the 3 Bots are these, where the bottommost name-defining constraint is underlined.

(69) The 3 Bots as a typological partition of Ord{X, Y, Z}

X-bot = {YZ$\underline{\text{X}}$, ZY$\underline{\text{X}}$}
Y-bot = {XZ$\underline{\text{Y}}$, ZX$\underline{\text{Y}}$}
Z-bot = {XY$\underline{\text{Z}}$, YX$\underline{\text{Z}}$}

From this, we obtain these filtrations by the nonempty prefixes of λ = XYZ.

X⟨T⟩ = {Y-bot, Z-bot} 'All grammars containing a leg X...'
XY⟨T⟩ = {Z-bot} 'All grammars containing a leg XY...'
XYZ⟨T⟩ = {Z-Bot} 'All grammars containing a leg XYZ'

To exemplify the general case, let us leave the realm of typologies by a shift in the membership of the blocks. Let $\pi = \{B_1, B_2, B_3\}$ be as follows:

(70) A non-typological partition of Ord{X, Y, Z}

B_1 = {XYZ, ZYX}
B_2 = {YXZ, ZXY}
B_3 = {XZY, YZX}

Here within each block the linear orders are mirror-image reversals and share no common sub-rankings at all. There is no ERC or ERC set that yields the contents of B_1, for example, without also yielding every other linear order. In B_1, we have both X ≫ Y and Y ≫ X, both Y ≫ Z and Z ≫ Y, both X ≫ Z and Z ≫ X. Anything goes, ERC-wise.

Nevertheless, filtration by prefix sharing proceeds unexceptionably.

X⟨π⟩	=	{B_1, B_3}	'All blocks containing a linear order X ...'
XY⟨π⟩	=	{B_1}	'All blocks containing a linear order XY...'
XYZ⟨π⟩	=	{B_1}	'All blocks containing a linear order XYZ'

These two filtration sequences follow similar-looking courses, even though in the second case the blocks of the partition are not grammars and cannot correspond to the coherent OT filtration of a candidate set.

It is instructive to glimpse the geometry associated with these patterns. Here is the 3 Bots typology again, represented on the three-constraint permutohedron, where each grammar is distinguished by its graphical enclosures, and solid lines mark grammar-internal connections.

(71) The 3 Bots

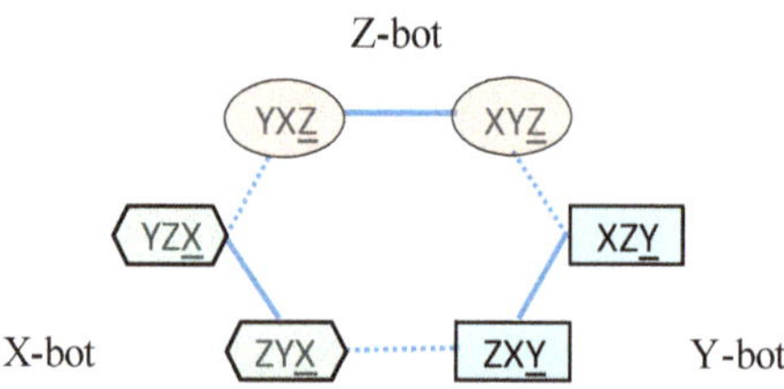

Observe that filtration by X selects those grammars – Z-bot (ovals) and Y-bot (rectangles) – which contain a leg sitting on 'X-top', the grammar (not in the 3 Bots, but a grammar nonetheless) defined by having constraint X at the top of every leg (dotted northeast side of hexagon). Geometrically, then, filtration pursues the membership of a nested sequence of 'tops', in this case running from X-top to XY-top to XYZ-top. It is important to keep in mind that surviving filtration by P requires only that *some* leg of the grammar be present on the top denoted by P. For example Z-bot has just one leg on X-Top (XY$\underline{\text{Z}}$, upper right vertex).

By contrast, the non-typological partition of ex. (70) looks like this. Because regional contiguity is absent, no attempt is made to represent it by line style.

(72) A non-typological partition

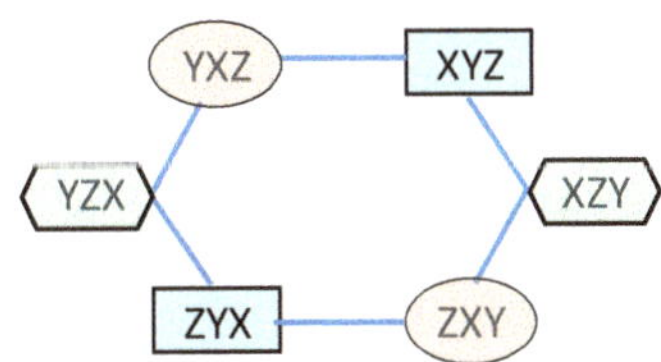

Each block is disconnected. Nevertheless, we can still ask which blocks have representation on X-Top, XY-Top, and so forth, supporting a prefix-sharing filtration.

4.5.3 Prefix-sharing filtration parallels candidate filtration

With the idea of prefix-based grammar filtration in hand, we establish that its basic properties closely parallel those of the more familiar VT-based filtration of candidates.

(73) **Fact. Telescoping property of candidate filtration.** $PQ[K] \subseteq P[K]$

Proof. See proof above, Lemma (2). In essence, candidate filtration is defined as yielding a subset. Thus, $Q[P[K]] \subseteq P[K] \subseteq K$. □

(74) **Fact. Telescoping property of block filtration.** Let $\mathbb{B} \subseteq \pi$ be a set of blocks of a partition π of Ord(S). Then $PQ\langle\mathbb{B}\rangle \subseteq P\langle\mathbb{B}\rangle$for any P and any Q.

Proof. For every $B \in PQ\langle\mathbb{B}\rangle$, by definition (67), there is a linear order $\rho \in B$ such that $\rho = PQ...$. But, for each of these, $\rho = P...$ as well. By the same definition $P\langle\mathbb{B}\rangle = \{B \subseteq \mathbb{B} \mid \exists\lambda \in B \text{ such that } \lambda = P... \}$. Each ρ is such a λ. Therefore $B \in PQ\langle\mathbb{B}\rangle$ implies $B \in P\langle\mathbb{B}\rangle$. □

As an interesting side note, we observe that block filtration is *not* guaranteed to have the forced choice property; that is, for an arbitrary set of blocks $\mathbb{B}$, it can happen that $P\langle\mathbb{B}\rangle$ is empty. If no block in $\mathbb{B}$ contains an element with prefix P, then $P\langle\mathbb{B}\rangle = \emptyset$. However, this will play no role in our discussion, since filtration will always start out from a partition of Ord(S), which is sure to have a block containing P.

Our immediate goal is to establish the equivalence of Grammar Filtration and Row Filtration, which we will denote by 'RF $\Leftrightarrow$ GF'. By this equivalence, if a UVT row is among those selected by a prefix, then its corresponding grammar contains a leg with that prefix (RF $\Rightarrow$ GF); and conversely (GF $\Rightarrow$ RF). To show this, we put No Dead Man Walking (65) to immediate use.

(75) **Lemma. Row to grammar. RF $\Rightarrow$ GF.** Let $U \in \mathcal{U}(T)$ and let P be any sequence of constraints in T.CON. If $u_k \in P[U]$, then $G_k \in P\langle T\rangle$.

Proof. By the definition of UVT (8), §1.2, every $u \in U$ is a possible optimum. Let $u_k \in P[U]$. By No Dead Man Walking (65), there is a leg PQ such that $PQ[U] = u_k$. Therefore $PQ \in G_k$, since by the definition of grammar (5), $G_k = \{\lambda \mid \lambda[U] = u_k\}$. By the definition of block filtration (67), $G_k \in P\langle T\rangle$. □

Note that NDMW (65) is framed in terms of a P-surviving *candidate*, here identified with a UVT row, which consists of a violation profile.

The contrapositive of RF $\Rightarrow$ GF, schematically $\neg$GF $\Rightarrow$ $\neg$RF, will prove to be particularly useful. It states that if no leg of a grammar begins with prefix P, then the row corresponding to that grammar is not selected by P.

We have established one subset relation: $P[U] \subseteq g_U(P\langle T\rangle)$, namely that P selects from U a subset of the set of rows corresponding to grammars that have a leg beginning with P. We proceed to the logical converse: GF $\Rightarrow$ RF. If a grammar contains a leg with a certain prefix, then the grammar's corresponding row in any UVT is among those selected by that prefix.

(76) **Lemma. Grammar to row. GF $\Rightarrow$ RF.** Let $U \in \mathcal{U}(T)$ and let P be any sequence of constraints in T.CON. If $G_k \in P\langle T\rangle$, then $u_k \in P[U]$.

Proof. By the definition of block filtration, $G_k \in P\langle T\rangle$ iff there is a leg $PQ \in G_k$. From the definition of grammar (5), we have that every leg $\lambda \in G_k$ selects u_k. This means that $u_k = PQ[U]$. But then, from telescoping (74), it follows that $u_k \in P[U]$. □

This establishes the subset relation $g_U(P\langle T\rangle) \subseteq P[U]$, namely that the set of rows corresponding to grammars that have a leg beginning with P is a subset of the rows selected by P. Putting the two lemmas together, we have for any UVT a 1:1 relation between filtration of the rows of the UVT by a prefix P and prefixal filtration of the grammars in the UVT's typology. We codify this fact in Theorem (77).

(77) **Theorem. GF $\Leftrightarrow$ RF.** Let $U \in \mathcal{U}(T)$ and let P be any sequence of constraints in T.CON. $u_k \in P[U]$ if and only if $G_k \in P\langle T\rangle$.

Proof. Taking RF $\Rightarrow$ GF (75) with GF $\Rightarrow$ RF (76), we have GF $\Leftrightarrow$ RF.□

Equivalently put, the theorem states that P[U] = g_U(P⟨T_U⟩), asserting that P[U] consists of exactly those rows of U whose associated grammars contain a leg with prefix P. Rephrased, we also have P⟨T_U⟩ = g_U^{-1}(P[U], asserting that P⟨T_U⟩ consists exactly of those grammars whose associated rows in U are selected by legs that begin with P.

A typology has many UVTs, a grammar but one set of legs. The theorem **GF ⇔ RF** (77) leads to the conclusion, which we now derive, that despite the multiplicity of UVTs for a given typology, they all filter identically.

4.5.4 Filtration uniformity across UVTs

An important structure developing from step-by-step filtration is the *filtration pattern*: the entire telescoping sequence of filtered sets that leads to the final result. Because we have two notions of filtration, we have two notions of filtration pattern at play.

(78) **Definition. Candidate filtration pattern.** The *candidate filtration pattern* of a total order λ = C_1...C_n, given a candidate set K, is a sequence of subsets K, C_1[K], C_1C_2[K],..., C_1...C_n[K], starting with K and proceeding through each step of filtration as defined in (64).

(79) **Definition. Prefix-sharing block filtration pattern.** The *prefix-sharing block filtration pattern* of a total order λ = C_1...C_n, given a partition π of Ord(*S*.CON), is a sequence of subsets π, C_1⟨π⟩, C_1C_2⟨π⟩,..., C_1...C_n⟨π⟩, starting with π and proceeding in order of length through each prefix P = C_1...C_k of λ, where each subset in the sequence consists of all orders in π sharing the prefix P, as defined in (67).

When π is a typology T, where each block is a grammar, we refer to the prefix-sharing filtration pattern of T as its *grammar filtration pattern*. In the 3 Bots of example (68), for example, we have a grammar filtration pattern that lines up with prefixes as follows:

(80) Filtration of the 3 Bots by XYZ

Prefixes of XYZ	P⟨XYZ⟩
P = ∅	{X-bot, Y-bot, Z-bot}
P = X	{Y-bot, Z-bot}
P = XY	{Z-bot}
P = XYZ	{Z-bot}

By contrast, the multiplicity of UVTs obscures the relation between candidate filtration patterns holding across $\mathcal{U}$(T). Consider these two UVTs for the 3 Bots:

U	X	Y	Z
u_1	1	0	0
u_2	0	1	0
u_3	0	0	1

V	X	Y	Z
v_1	3	3	3
v_2	2	4	3
v_3	2	3	5

The rows are very different, but the tight relation between their filtration patterns can be seen by following filtration by XYZ.

(81) Candidate and grammar filtration for XYZ in the 3 Bots

Prefixes of XYZ	P[U]	P[V]	P⟨T⟩
P = ∅	{u_1, u_2, u_3}	{v_1, v_2, v_3}	{X-bot, Y-bot, Z-bot}
P = X	{u_2, u_3}	{v_2, v_3}	{Y-bot, Z-bot}
P = XY	{u_3}	{v_3}	{Z-bot}
P = XYZ	{u_3}	{v_3}	{Z-bot}

In this case, as indeed in all others, correctly identifying the corresponding rows of different UVTs allows the parallels in their filtration patterns to be tracked. Observe that just as u_3 and v_3 are the optima for Z-bot, so u_1 and v_1 are optima for X-bot, while u_2 and v_2 are optima for Y-bot.

These considerations lead to the notion of different UVTs having *identical filtration patterns* by virtue of a 1:1 correspondence between their rows.

(82) **Definition. Identical candidate filtration patterns.** Two UVTs U, V ∈ $\mathcal{U}$(T) with columns labeled by T.Con, are said to have *identical filtration patterns* if there is a bijection f: U → V between the rows of U and the rows of V, such that for every prefix P, u_i ∈ P[U] if and only if f(u_i) = v_j ∈ P[V].

The definition is cast in general terms ('if there is a bijection'), but a moment's thought shows that for any U, V ∈ $\mathcal{U}$(T), there can only be one bijection that even has a chance of meeting the tight restriction placed on it, which requires that for *every* prefix P, f(P[U]) = P[V]. The fact that a leg is also a prefix completely determines the correspondence. Thus, for every leg λ, we must have f(λ[U]) = λ[V]. But λ[U] is a unique row of U and λ[V] is a unique row of V. And every row is chosen by some leg.

In our example, XYZ[U] = u_3 and XYZ[V] = v_3. Consequently, $f(u_3) = v_3$. Similar considerations yield $f(u_2) = v_2$ and $f(u_1) = v_1$, determining f.

Since every leg of a grammar selects the same row of a given UVT, the leg-determined bijection is equivalently definable in terms of entire grammars.

The natural bijection between a typology and a UVT, introduced above in (11) as $g_U : T \rightarrow U$ such that $g_U(G_k) = u_k$, puts a grammar in correspondence with the row that its legs select. Its inverse $g_U^{-1} : U \rightarrow T$ such that $g_U^{-1}(u_k) = G_k$ is also bijective; it is arbitrary which of these maps is taken to be basic and which is taken to be the notated inverse of the other. Indeed, the coindexing scheme gives a more natural rendition of the symmetry of the situation.

Writing u_{kj} for the kth row of $U_j \in \mathcal{U}(T)$, which corresponds to grammar G_k via g_{Uj}, the following picture emerges.

(83) G_k mediates row-to-row correspondence in $\mathcal{U}(T)$

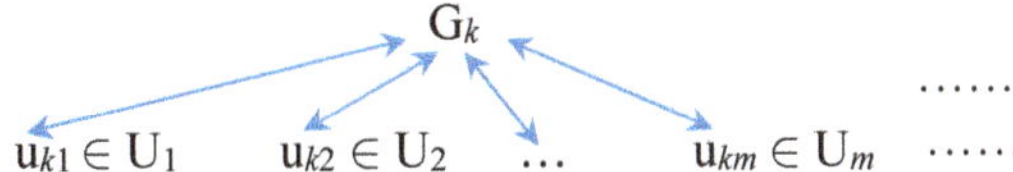

From this, a bijection between candidate filtration patterns of distinct UVTs can be easily constructed. We can bijectively associate rows across UVTs that correspond to the same grammar, where $g_{Ui}^{-1}(u_{ki}) = g_{Uj}^{-1}(u_{kj}) = G_k$. This easily lifts to sets of rows, which correspond bijectively to sets of grammars, allowing for correspondence between filtration patterns.

Given U, V $\in \mathcal{U}(T)$, the bijections $g_U^{-1} : U \rightarrow T$ and $g_V : T \rightarrow V$ compose as $g_V \circ g_U^{-1} : U \rightarrow T \rightarrow V$ to yield a bijection between the rows of U and the rows of V. Now we use this bijection to establish the broader conclusion: that all UVTs for a given typology have identical filtration patterns.

(84) **Theorem. Filtration uniformity (rows).** For any U, V $\in \mathcal{U}(T)$, the filtration patterns of U and V are identical.

Proof. Let U, V $\in \mathcal{U}(T)$. By the definition (82) of 'identical filtration patterns', we must show that there is a bijection $f : U \rightarrow V$ such that for every prefix P, f(P[U]) = P[V].

Enumerate the rows, without loss of generality, so that G_k is associated with $u_k \in U$ and $v_k \in V$. We claim that the desired bijection is $u_k \mapsto v_k$. Formally, since $g_U(G_k) = u_k$ and $g_V(G_k) = v_k$, this amounts to $f = g_V \circ g_U^{-1} : U \rightarrow V$.

A filtration pattern consists of a sequence of sets of rows, with each element of the sequence selected by a prefix of a given leg. Consider any prefix

P. Suppose $u_k \in P[U]$. Then by RF ⇒ GF (75), we have $G_k \in P\langle T\rangle$. By GF ⇒ RF (76), we also have $v_k \in P[V]$. This establishes that $u_k \in P[U] \Rightarrow v_k \in P[V]$, i.e. $f(P[U]) \subseteq P[V]$.

The same argument works from V to U, using the same indexing, where formally the bijection is $f^{-1} = g_U \circ g_V^{-1}$, establishing that $v_k \in P[V] \Rightarrow u_k \in P[U]$. That is, $f^{-1}(P[V]) \subseteq P[U]$, so that $P[V] \subseteq f[P(U)]$. Therefore, $f(P[U]) = P[V]$, as claimed. □

At least as significant is the converse. If we have two UVTs that are comparable in that they share T.Con and thus have the same constraint labels on their columns, we can conclude that they yield the same typology – the same partition of Ord(T.Con) – if they have identical filtration patterns. This is the first of three 'characterization' theorems in which some representation of typologies has a property that entails typological uniqueness. (For the other two, see §4.7, Theorem (150) 'Prefixal Characterization' and Theorem (155) 'Our MOATish Mother'.)

(85) **Theorem. Characterization: Converse of Filtration Uniformity.** (CoFU). Let U, V be two UVTs over the same constraint set T.Con, associated respectively with typologies T_U and T_V. If their filtration patterns are identical, then $T_U = T_V$.

Proof. Since the filtration patterns of U and V are assumed identical, we have by definition (82) a bijection $f: U \rightarrow V$ with $f(P[U]) = P[V]$ for all prefixes P. Without loss of generality, assume an enumeration of the rows of U and V such that for each $u_k \in U$, $f(u_k) = v_k \in V$, so that $f(u_1) = v_1$, $f(u_2) = v_2$, and so on.

The grammar associated with row $u_k \in U$, which we will denote as $G_k^U \in T_U$, contains all and only the legs selecting u_k. Now consider any $\lambda \in G_k^U$. Since λ is itself a prefix, $f(\lambda[U]) = \lambda[V]$. Since $\lambda[U] = u_k$, we have: $\lambda[V] = f(\lambda[U]) = f(u_k) = v_k$.

Since $\lambda[V] = v_k$, we have $\lambda \in G_k^V$, the grammar whose legs select row v_k in V. Therefore $G_k^U \subseteq G_k^V$, and more generally $G_i^U \subseteq G_i^V$ for all i.

The subset relationship also holds in the other direction, so that $G_i^V \subseteq G_i^U$ for all i. In the interests of perspicuity, rather than merely observing the arbitrariness of the designations 'U' and 'V', we offer a distinct proof of this fact. Let $\delta \in G_k^V$ for any k. Assume for purposes of contradiction that $\delta \notin G_k^U$. But $\delta \in G_j^U$ for some $j \neq k$, because every leg belongs to some grammar. By the argument just given, this means that $\delta \in G_j^V$. This is a contradiction since $G_k^V \neq G_j^V$ and each total order is in exactly one grammar. Therefore, $G_i^V \subseteq G_i^U$ for all i. It follows that $G_i^U = G_i^V$ for all i, so that $T_U = T_V$. □

Observe that although the theorem assumes identical filtration patterns, we only use the fact that the prefix-respecting bijection f respects entire legs.

4.5.5 Summary

Each typology has many UVTs, but only one set of grammars. Numbers, however, have a simple order structure, which we would like to be able to make use of. The realm where grammars are defined as leg sets has the considerable virtue of uniqueness, though the relevant notions of order are somewhat harder to get at. Defining a new notion of filtration directly on grammars yields a unique set of *grammar filtration patterns* for a typology. This contrasts with having to manage bijectively-corresponding filtration patterns between UVTs for the same typology.

By relating a UVT's row filtration patterns to the unique grammar filtration patterns, we have established that all UVTs for a given typology have identical filtration patterns, regardless of numerical differences among them. This result has the considerable virtue of allowing us to construct arguments about grammar filtration patterns using a single UVT's filtration patterns, as in Lemma (146) 'Columnar interchange', §4.7.1 below.

4.6 Prefixal relations and the EPO relations

Section contents

WITH GRAMMAR FILTRATION IN HAND, we develop new relations $\sim^{\text{pr.C}}$ and $<^{\text{pr.C}}$ based on prefixal structure, which parallel the EPO relations arising from border point pairs. The goal is to show that, with the exercise of suitable care, identical structure can be found in both domains, in the sense that grammars deemed *equivalent* on one are also equivalent on the other; and that grammars *ordered by the hypertransitive closure* of the one are ordered in the same way by the hypertransitive closure of the other.

The differences are, however, important. Only with the EPO relation $<^{\text{bp.C}}$ can the notion of 'privilege' – crucial for determining the typological status of coarsenings – be recognized. But the identity of $\sim^{\text{pr.C}}$ and $\sim^{\text{bp.C}}$, along with that of $<^{\text{htc.bp.C}}$ and $<^{\text{htc.pr.C}}$, will allow for clean and conceptually simple proofs of the main results characterizing typologies.

We have found that the MOAT relations are instantiable in the integers, by Lemmas (27) and (31). We will demonstrate that the prefixal grammar filtration relations are also instantiable, and so have a shared connection to the UVTs. This will allow us to show that the relations just mentioned – the equivalences, and the hypertransitive closure of the orders – are identical over the set of grammars of a typology. In the next section (§4.7), we use these results to accomplish one of our main goals: establishing that MOAT relations for a typology distinguish one typology from another.

As with the EPO relations, we aim to define an equivalence relation as well as an order relation which we will extend to its hypertransitive closure. Following a path that parallels the course of §4.3 above, we start off with base relations, which are developed into the relations we seek. Among those, we first construct and explore the equivalence relation, then turn to the order relation.

4.6.1 Equivalence

We define a base relation between arbitrary grammars, call them G_1 and G_2, where each contains at least one leg beginning with the same prefix. If a constraint C occurs in such a prefix, the grammars stand in a relation that we denote as $G_1 \equiv^{\text{pr.C}} G_2$, writing 'pr' to signal that it is prefix-based. This relation will lead to an equivalence relation $\sim^{\text{pr.C}}$ on the grammars of the typology. Because this construction relies only on the sequential structure of total orders and not on UVTs or their numerics, it applies as well to general partitions of Ord(S). The base relation is defined as follows in terms of filtration by a prefix.

(86) **Definition. The base relation $\equiv^{pr.C}$.** Let B_1, $B_2 \in \pi$, a partition of Ord(S).

$B_1 \equiv^{pr.C} B_2$ iff there is a prefix P, with C in P, such that B_1, $B_2 \in P\langle\pi\rangle$.

Note that since there's always an initial segment of the prefix running up to C, as we let prefixes be empty, we may equivalently regard C as the last element of a prefix, and speak of PC in place of 'C in P.'

To see this at work, let's look at the '4 Bots' typology on Ord{X, Y, Z, W}. Each grammar contains 6 legs meeting the condition that a certain constraint is dominated by the other three. See table (68) ff. for discussion of the analogous 3 Bots; see table (17), §6.2.1, ff., for more on the 4 Bots.

Consider the filtration of the 4 Bots by the leg XYZW, and the correlated relations.

(87) Filtration of the 4 Bots by XYZW

Step	Prefixes of XYZW	P⟨XYZ⟩
0	P = ∅	{X-bot, Y-bot, Z-bot, W-bot}
1	P = X	{Y-bot, Z-bot, W-bot}
2	P = XY	{Z-bot,W-bot}
3	P = XYZ	{W-bot}
4	P = XYZW	{W-bot}

The Y-bot grammar contains legs beginning with X, as do the grammars of Z-bot and W-bot. See step 1 of table (87) above. This establishes, according to definition (86), the following relations:

Y-bot $\equiv^{pr.X}$ Z-bot

Y-bot $\equiv^{pr.X}$ W-bot

Z-bot $\equiv^{pr.X}$ W-bot

In support of these claimed relations, note that we find the following X-prefixed legs, among others, in the various grammars, where the shared prefix is double-underlined for ease of identification:

$\underline{\underline{\text{X}}}$ZWY ∈ Y-bot

$\underline{\underline{\text{X}}}$WYZ ∈ Z-bot

$\underline{\underline{\text{X}}}$YZW ∈ W-bot

It is the presence of legs like these that drives the filtration shown in table (87) step 1, which therefore leads to pairwise relations $\equiv^{pr.X}$ among the survivors. Continuing along these lines, we also have Z-bot $\equiv^{\text{pr.Y}}$ W-bot from the filtration by prefix XY in step 2.

There's an important definitional distinction between prefixal relations and relations based on border point pairs: the witnessing legs cited here for the prefixal relation *are not adjacent.* All that matters is that they share a prefix containing X, belonging to different grammars. Since the members of a border point pair share a prefix in addition to meeting further conditions, it follows that any grammars that stand in the EPO relation $\equiv^{\text{bp.X}}$ also stand in the prefixal relation $\equiv^{\text{pr.X}}$. But the converse is not true in the general case. From the discussion of EST in §3, we can determine that the adjacency-based equivalences in EPO(**m.Ons**) are the following, drawn from ex. (25), §3.2.

(88) Adjacency-based equivalences in EPO(**m.Ons**)

1 $\equiv^{\text{bp.Ons}}$ **3**	OR.CP.del $\equiv^{\text{bp.Ons}}$ OR.CP.ins
5 $\equiv^{\text{bp.Ons}}$ **7**	OR.CA.del $\equiv^{\text{bp.Ons}}$ OR.CA.ins
3 $\equiv^{\text{bp.Ons}}$ **7**	OR.CP.ins $\equiv^{\text{bp.Ons}}$ OR.CA.ins
1 $\equiv^{\text{bp.Ons}}$ **5**	OR.CP.del $\equiv^{\text{bp.Ons}}$ OR.CA.del

The adjacency structure of the grammars looks like this. See diagram (7), §7.2, for more details.

(89) Adjacencies among the OR in EST

1 — **3**
| |
5 — **7**

The distal relations **1** $\sim^{\text{bp.Ons}}$ **7** and **3** $\sim^{\text{bp.Ons}}$ **5** are secured only by transitivity. But all OR grammars have a leg with **m.Ons** at the top, since **m.Ons** is the constraint that requires onsets and is, concretely, unchallenged by any optima in OR languages.[10] Therefore each contains a leg prefixed with **m.Ons** and every pair, adjacent or not, is directly related by the prefixal relation $\equiv^{\text{pr.X}}$. Nevertheless, we shall find shortly (Theorem (96)) that once the prefixal base relation is augmented to equivalence, the two relations $\sim^{\text{pr.C}}$ and $\sim^{\text{bp.C}}$ are identical.

To advance from the base relation $\equiv^{\text{pr.C}}$ to the equivalence relation $\sim^{\text{pr.C}}$, we note that $\equiv^{\text{pr.C}}$ is reflexive and symmetric: reflexive because in definition (86), B_1 and B_2 don't have to be distinct; and symmetric because B_1 and

[10] For a complete list of the legs, see Appendix I, p. 329.

B_2 are arbitrary. Transitivity is not guaranteed, so we create a new relation $\sim^{pr.C}$ that is the transitive closure of the base relation $\equiv^{pr.C}$. Transitive closure preserves reflexivity and symmetry, and therefore $\sim^{pr.C}$ is an equivalence relation, as desired.

(90) **Definition. Prefixal $\sim^{pr.C}$.** The relation $\sim^{pr.C}$ is the transitive closure of $\equiv^{pr.C}$.

(91) **Lemma. Prefixal equivalence $\sim^{pr.C}$.** The relation $\sim^{pr.C}$ is an equivalence relation.

Proof. Prefixal equivalence $\sim^{pr.C}$ inherits reflexivity and symmetry from $\equiv^{pr.C}$ and is clearly transitive as it's the transitive closure of $\equiv^{pr.C}$. □

(92) **Lemma. Universal instantiation of $\equiv^{pr.C}$ as =.** For every $U \in \mathcal{U}(T)$, the relation $\equiv^{pr.C}$ is instantiated by the function $C \circ g_U$ as =.

Proof: Let G_1, G_2 be arbitrary grammars of T, and let $U \in \mathcal{U}(T)$. Assume $G_1 \equiv^{pr.C} G_2$, with $u_1, u_2 \in U$ as their corresponding rows under g_U. We show that $C(u_1) = C(u_2)$, so that $C \circ g_U$ instantiates $\equiv^{pr.C}$ as =.

By definition of $\equiv^{pr.C}$, there is a P such that $G_1, G_2 \in P\langle T\rangle$. Thus there is a leg $PQ_1 \in G_1$ and a leg $PQ_2 \in G_2$, with C in P. We must have, then, since U generates the typology,

$$PQ_1[u_1, u_2] = u_1$$
$$PQ_2[u_1, u_2] = u_2$$

Clearly, $P[u_1, u_2] = \{u_1, u_2\}$. Because both u_1 and u_2 survive filtration by P, we have that since C is in P, $C \circ g_U(G_1) = C(u_1) = C(u_2) = C \circ g_U(G_2)$. Since U is arbitrary, except for the fact that it generates T, this must hold for all $U \in \mathcal{U}(T)$. □

(93) **Lemma. Universal instantiation of $\sim^{pr.C}$ as =.** For every $U \in \mathcal{U}(T)$, the relation $\sim^{pr.C}$ is instantiated by the function $C \circ g_U$ as =.

Proof: If $G_1 \sim^{pr.C} G_2$, G_1 and G_2 are related through a chain $G_1 = A_1, \ldots, A_m = G_2$, where $A_i \equiv^{pr.C} A_{i+1}$, $1 \leq i < m$. Each such related pair must be assigned equal values in all UVTs by $C \circ g_U$, as per Lemma (92), so $C \circ g_U(G_1) = C(u_1) = C(u_2) = C \circ g_U(G_2)$ in every UVT by transitivity of equality among the integers. □

Thus far we've established relations between prefix sharing and numerical equality. We now show that the equivalence relations $\sim^{pr.C}$ and $\sim^{bp.C}$ are the same, even though they are defined differently. This means that exactly the same pairs of grammars are treated as equivalent by the relations.

As a preliminary, we note the fact, known since the 19th century, that the set Ord(S) is *connected*, in the sense that any two elements $\sigma, \tau \in$ Ord(S) are linked by a sequence of elements $\sigma_k \in$ Ord(S), such that $\sigma = \sigma_1, \ldots, \sigma_n = \tau$, where elements σ_i, σ_{i+1} differ only by a single transposition. Such a sequence will be termed a *path* between σ and τ.

(94) **Fact (Cayley).** Ord(*S*.Con) is connected.

Proof. Easily seen by the 'recursive constraint promotion' reasoning of §7.3, which we sketch here. (See definition (39) and Lemma (40), §7.3.3). Consider any $\sigma, \tau \in$ Ord(S). Identify the first element $x \in$ S in σ on which they disagree; find x in τ and generate a sequence of pairwise-connected elements of Ord(S) by adjacently flipping x up to the position of x in σ, creating $\tau^{(1)}$. This is a path between τ and $\tau^{(1)}$. If $\tau^{(1)} = \sigma$, we are done. If not, reapply the flipping technique until on the nth iteration $\tau^{(n)} = \sigma$. □

(95) **Corollary to the Cayley fact.** Any two elements $PQ_1, PQ_2 \in$ Ord(S) are connected by a path that consists of a sequence of pairwise-adjacent orders, all with prefix P.

Proof. Let $P^* = \{C \in S \mid P = \ldots C \ldots\}$. Consider S\P*. We have $Q_1, Q_2 \in$ Ord(S\P*). By Fact (94), any two elements of Ord(S\P*) are connected by some path. The very same sequence of flips that connects Q_1 and Q_2 in Ord(S\P*) also connects PQ_1 and PQ_2 in Ord(S). □

(96) **Theorem. Equality of equivalences.** Let T be a typology and let $G_1, G_2 \in T$. Then, for any $C \in$ T.Con, $G_1 \sim^{\text{pr.C}} G_2 \Leftrightarrow G_1 \sim^{\text{bp.C}} G_2$.

Proof. RL. Assume that for arbitrary $G_1, G_2 \in T$, we have the border-point-based EPO relation $G_1 \sim^{\text{bp.C}} G_2$. By definition of EPO equivalence (29), the relation $\sim^{\text{bp.C}}$ is the transitive closure of (the reflexive closure of) $\equiv^{\text{bp.C}}$, and thus $G_1 \sim^{\text{bp.C}} G_2$ guarantees the existence of a sequence $G_1 = A_1, \ldots, A_m = G_2$, where $A_i \equiv^{\text{bp.C}} A_{i+1}$, $1 \leq i < m$, with $A_i \in T$.

Now we use the fact that $\equiv^{\text{pr.C}}$ subsumes $\equiv^{\text{bp.C}}$. For each expression $A_i \equiv^{\text{bp.C}} A_{i+1}$, we have a nonempty prefix P_i of some border point pair $\{P_i\underline{XY}Q, P_i\underline{YX}Q\}$ such that C is in P_i, by definition (14) of $A_i \equiv^{\text{bp.C}} A_{i+1}$. Therefore by the definition (86) of $\equiv^{\text{pr.C}}$, we also have the prefixal base relation $A_i \equiv^{\text{pr.C}} A_{i+1}$, which follows from the existence of the prefix P_i containing C which accepts both A_i and A_{i+1} without further conditions on what follows P_i. This yields a sequence of *prefixal* base relations $\equiv^{\text{pr.C}}$ between G_1 and G_2, made up of pairs A_i, A_{i+1} with $A_i \equiv^{\text{pr.C}} A_{i+1}$. Since $\sim^{\text{pr.C}}$ is the transitive closure of $\equiv^{\text{pr.C}}$, we have $G_1 \sim^{\text{pr.C}} G_2$, as claimed.

LR. Assume the prefixal equivalence $G_1 \sim^{\text{pr.C}} G_2$. Consider first the case $G_1 \equiv^{\text{pr.C}} G_2$. (Any relation is a subset of its transitive closure.) We have $PQ_1 \in G_1$

and $PQ_2 \in G_2$ with C in P. By the Corollary (95) to Fact (94), there is a sequence of total orders $PQ_1 = PR_1, ..., PR_n = PQ_2$, where adjacent orders in the sequence differ only in an adjacent transposition of constraints not in P. Each of these total orders is in some grammar. The sequence that runs from PQ_1 to PQ_2 thus passes through a series of adjacent grammars and at each transition from one grammar to the next there is a border point pair with prefix P with C in P. Each pair of adjacent grammars is therefore related by the border-point-based relation $\equiv^{bp.C}$, and all the grammars in the series are equivalent under its transitive closure $\sim^{bp.C}$. In particular, $G_1 \sim^{bp.C} G_2$.

Now assume the prefixal equivalence $G_1 \sim^{pr.C} G_2$ without restriction. In this case, we have no guarantee that there is a single prefix witnessing the relation. But since $\sim^{pr.C}$ is the transitive closure of $\equiv^{pr.C}$, the relation $G_1 \sim^{pr.C} G_2$ entails the existence of a sequence of grammars, $G_1 = A_1, ..., A_n = G_2$ such that $A_i \equiv^{pr.C} A_{i+1}$ for each i, $1 \leq i < n$, where the relevant C-containing prefix may differ from pair to pair. Each adjacent pair in the sequence is $\sim^{bp.C}$ related, by the previous paragraph. Because $\sim^{bp.C}$ is transitive, we have $G_1 \sim^{bp.C} G_2$. □

This line of reasoning can be appreciated as geometry in the setting of the permutohedron, a graphical object that represents the adjacency structure of Ord(S), seen above in exx. (57) and (71), and explored in more detail in §7.

The set of total orders that begin with P is a connected *region* 'P-top' of the permutohedron on Ord(S). Crucially, P-top itself has the form of a permutohedron on the set of orders of all the constraints *not* in P, namely Ord(S\P*). Algebraically, two distinct grammars G_1 and G_2 stand in the base prefixal relation $\equiv^{pr.C}$ just in case each contains a leg with a prefix P. Graphically, this means that the region occupied by each grammar lies (at least) partly on P-top. Co-occupancy of P-top is the geometrical correlate of standing in the algebraic relation $\equiv^{pr.C}$, and vice versa.

The grammars G_1 and G_2 need not be adjacent on P-top; however, it is clear that even if they are not, there is a sequence of adjacent grammars with presence on P-top that connects them, just as (for example) New Jersey and Florida lie nonadjacently on the East Coast of the United States but are connected through a sequence of adjacent coastal states. Consider any path from some point in G_1 to a point in G_2. Any such path crosses a sequence of intermediaries giving rise to a collection of border crossing points between pairs of adjacent grammars. From P-top co-occupancy, we are thus assured of a collection of border point pairs located at crossings from grammar to grammar *within* P-top. This means that from prefixal $G_1 \equiv^{pr.C} G_2$ we may deduce the EPO equivalence $G_1 \sim^{bp.C} G_2$ even when G_1 and G_2 are not adjacent. This is the key fact which may be leveraged to achieve the desired general result. The reader might wish to continue with the geometrization of the argument along these lines.

Nothing in this proof requires that T be a typology rather than a general partition. The 'Generalized MOAT' or GMOAT of §4.4 is constructed like the MOAT from border point pairs, without assuming that the underlying partition is a typology. Theorem (96) thus applies to equivalence relations in the GMOAT as well. We conclude that defining GEPO equivalence on border point pairs is the same as defining GEPO equivalence on prefixes, just as for the EPO.

(97) **Theorem. Equality of equivalences (general).** Let π be a partition of Ord(S.Con), with $B_1, B_2 \in \pi$. Then $B_1 \sim^{\pi.\text{pr.C}} B_2 \Leftrightarrow B_1 \sim^{\pi.\text{bp.C}} B_2$.

Proof. As noted in the text, nothing in the proof of Theorem (96) requires that the partition be a typology. So that proof establishes this theorem as well. □

4.6.2 Separation & order: Base relation to hypertransitive closure

We now know that the equivalence relations arising from border point pairs and from prefix sharing are identical. Continuing with the parallelism, we construct a prefixal order relation $<^{\text{pr.C}}$ and relate it to its border point analog $<^{\text{bp.C}}$.

The EPO order relation $<^{\text{bp.C}}$ transitively closes a base relation $\prec^{\text{bp.C}}$ derived from a border point pair {P$\underline{\text{CY}}$Q, P$\underline{\text{YC}}$Q}. The analogous prefixal order $<^{\text{pr.C}}$ transitively closes a base relation derived from a prefix PC via its effects on block filtration of the survivors of P by C. As with equivalence, the base prefixal relations subsume the base border point relations, since $\prec^{\text{bp.C}}$ requires everything that $\prec^{\text{pr.C}}$ requires and more, namely the other member of the border point pair and the accompanying post-prefixal structure. Unlike equivalence, however, transitive closure to $<^{\text{bp.C}}$ and $<^{\text{pr.C}}$ does not lead to identical orders. The ultimate finding is that although the two order relations may differ in various respects, they become identical only with hypertransitive closure.

When a prefix PC confronts a set of blocks P⟨π⟩, where π may or may not be a typology, prefix sharing distinguishes those blocks containing a total order with prefix PC from those containing a total order with prefix P followed by some constraint other than C. The post-prefixal constraint C distinguishes among the blocks P⟨π⟩, accepting some, ejecting others. This phenomenon we call 'separation'.

(98) **Definition. Separation of blocks.** A Prefix PC *separates* block B_i from block B_j iff $B_i, B_j \in P\langle\pi\rangle$ and $B_i \in PC\langle\pi\rangle$ while $B_j \notin PC\langle\pi\rangle$.

Note that P may be empty. We say that the block B_i is *accepted* by PC (or *survives* PC) and the block B_j is *ejected* by PC. In this case, the ejected block B_j contains no leg $\lambda = PC...$.

When π is a typology, the blocks are grammars and we speak of the *separation of grammars.* A prefix PC might separate multiple pairs of blocks, so the notion of separation generalizes naturally to sets of blocks/grammars.

(99) **Definition. Separation of block sets.** Prefix PC is said to *separate* the set $\mathbb{B}_1 = \{B_i\}$ from the set $\mathbb{B}_2 = \{B_j\}$ iff PC separates each $B_i \in \mathbb{B}_1$ from each $B_j \in \mathbb{B}_2$.

We say that the blocks of $\mathbb{B}_1$ are *accepted* by PC and those of $\mathbb{B}_2$ are *ejected* by PC. Note that the members of the ejected block set $\mathbb{B}_2$ contain no leg $\lambda = PC...$.

Separation immediately gives rise to a base relation. Those blocks accepted by a prefix PC are all related en masse to those ejected by PC. We construct an order from this base following the now-familiar path of development.

(100) **Definition. Base separation relation $\prec^{pr.C}$.** Let $B_1, B_2 \in \pi$, a partition of Ord(S).

$$B_i \prec^{pr.C} B_j \text{ if there is a prefix P such that PC separates } B_i \text{ from } B_j.$$

(101) **Definition. Separation relation $<^{pr.C}$.** The relation $<^{pr.C}$ is the transitive closure of $\prec^{pr.C}$.

When the partition is a typology, so that its blocks are grammars, the relation $<^{pr.C}$ turns out to be a partial order. To show this, we follow a path similar to that just followed with the equivalence $\sim^{pr.C}$ in Lemma (92), first showing how the prefixally-defined relation plays out concretely among the integers and from that behavior deducing that it must be a partial order.

(102) **Lemma. Universal instantiation of the prefixal base relation $\prec^{pr.C}$ as $<$.** For every $U \in \mathcal{U}(T)$, the relation $\prec^{pr.C}$ is instantiated by the function $C \circ g_U$ as $<$.

Proof. Let $U \in \mathcal{U}(T)$ and $G_i, G_j \in T$ with corresponding rows $u_i, u_j \in U$ given by $u_k = g_U(G_k)$. Suppose $G_i \prec^{pr.C} G_j$. Then by definition there exists prefix PC that separates G_i from G_j. Furthermore, in the realm of candidate filtration, by GF $\Leftrightarrow$ RF (77), the rows u_i, u_j corresponding to G_i, G_j survive filtration by P, so that $P[u_i, u_j] = \{u_i, u_j\}$. Further, $PC[u_i, u_j] = u_i$. For this to happen, it must be that $C(u_i) < C(u_j)$. Thus, the function $C \circ G_U : T \to \mathbb{N}$ instantiates $\prec^{pr.C}$ as $<$. □

With the base relation in hand, we move on to its transitive closure.

(103) **Lemma. Universal instantiation of $<^{pr.C}$ as $<$.** For every $U \in \mathcal{U}(T)$, the separation relation $<^{pr.C}$ is instantiated by the function $C \circ g_U$ as $<$.

Proof. The relation $<^{pr.C}$ is the transitive closure of $\prec^{pr.C}$. By Lemma (23), the transitive closure R^+ of an instantiable relation R is instantiable by the same function that instantiates R. Here, R is $\prec^{pr.C}$ and by Lemma (102), $C \circ g_U$ instantiates $\prec^{pr.C}$ in each $U \in \mathcal{U}(T)$. □

From this, we may immediately deduce that $<^{pr.C}$ is a partial order.

(104) **Lemma. $<^{pr.C}$ is a strict partial order on a typology $T = \{G_k\}$.**

Proof. The relation $<^{pr.C}$ is the transitive closure of $\prec^{pr.C}$ and therefore transitive. We need, then, only asymmetry, which implies irreflexivity. Suppose $G_1 <^{pr.C} G_2$ for arbitrary $G_1, G_2 \in T$. This means that there's an overlapping transitive chain of pairwise $\prec^{pr.C}$ relations running from G_1 to G_2. Suppose, for purposes of contradiction, that asymmetry does not hold for this pair, with $G_2 <^{pr.C} G_1$ as well. Under this assumption, there is another sequence of pairwise $\prec^{pr.C}$ relations running from G_2 to G_1 . These two sequences are each instantiable in the integers as $<$ by Lemma (102), a clear contradiction. Therefore, $<^{pr.C}$ is asymmetric. □

This lemma holds of typologies but not of arbitrary partitions, since it depends on the instantiability of the base relation $\prec^{pr.C}$ as the strict partial order $<$.

At this point, with an eye on the fact the equivalences $\sim^{pr.C}$ and $\sim^{bp.C}$ are identical, as shown in the Theorem 'Equality of Equivalences' (97), we might entertain the hope that we are done. But the relations $<^{bp.C}$ and $<^{pr.C}$ are not guaranteed to be equal. The lack of an adjacency requirement allows prefixal $<^{pr.C}$ to see farther, as it were, than border-point-based $<^{bp.C}$, so that the prefixal relation may include some structure that is accessible in the border point system only through hypertransitivity.

A simple example is provided by m.Ons in EST. Recall that its border-point-derived EPO look like this, repeated from diagram (27), §3.3.

(105) EPO(m.Ons) of EST

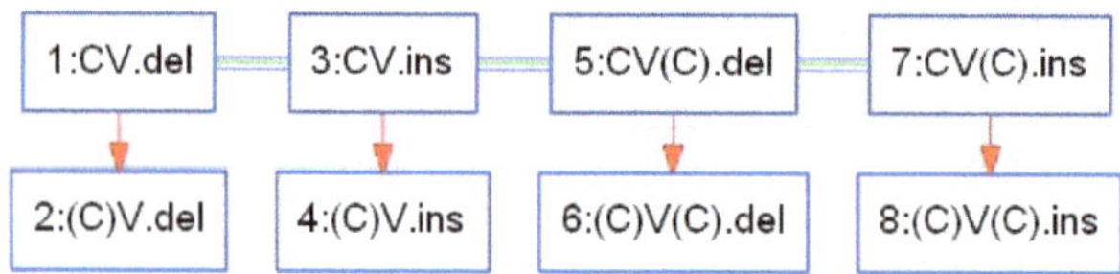

However, as noted above, every member of the OR class $\{\mathbf{1}, \mathbf{3}, \mathbf{5}, \mathbf{7}\}$ has a leg beginning with m.Ons. No member of the OLA class $\{\mathbf{2}, \mathbf{4}, \mathbf{6}, \mathbf{8}\}$ has any such leg.[11] It follows that prefixally every member of OR stands in the relation $<^{\text{pr.Ons}}$ with every member of OLA. The bigraph representing this state of affairs looks like this, where local privileged order information is lost:

(106) Bigraph representing $<^{\text{pr.Ons}}$

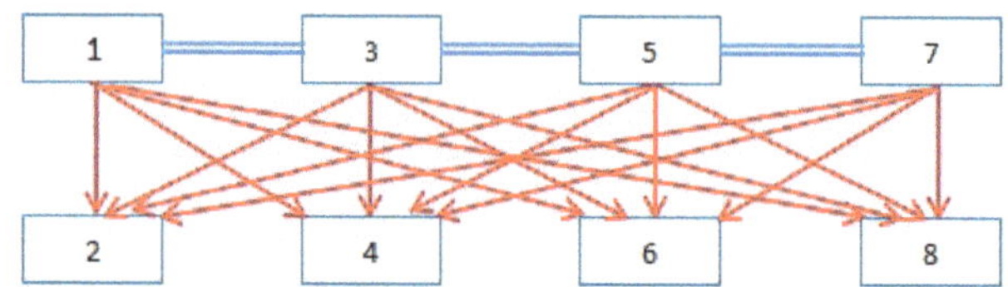

Here prefixal $<^{\text{pr.C}}$ turns out to be the same as $<^{\text{htc.bp.C}}$, the hypertransitive closure of the EPO relation $<^{\text{bp.C}}$. To go beyond this example to the full range of cases, a final step must be taken in the prefixal domain: construction of the hypertransitive closure $<^{\text{htc.pr.C}}$ of $<^{\text{pr.C}}$. We follow the same course of development as with the hypertransitive closure $<^{\text{htc.bp.C}}$ of the EPO relation $<^{\text{bp.C}}$, presented in (45)–(49). We begin by defining and characterizing the hypertransitive closure for prefixal order, paralleling (45).

(107) **Definition. Hypertransitive closure (htc.pr).** Given a typology T and a constraint C, we define the hypertransitively closed relation $<^{\text{htc.pr.C}}$ on T as follows. For all $G_1, H, G_2 \in T$,

i. $G_1 <^{\text{pr.C}} G_2 \Rightarrow G_1 <^{\text{htc.pr.C}} G_2$ '$<^{\text{pr.C}}$ is in $<^{\text{htc.pr.C}}$'

ii. $G_1 <^{\text{htc.pr.C}} H \;\&\; H <^{\text{htc.pr.C}} G_2 \Rightarrow G_1 <^{\text{htc.pr.C}} G_2$ '$<^{\text{htc.pr.C}}$ is transitive'

iii.a $G_1 \sim^{\text{pr.C}} H \;\&\; H <^{\text{htc.pr.C}} G_2 \Rightarrow G_1 <^{\text{htc.pr.C}} G_2$ '~ combines at the left'

---

[11] To confirm this by inspection, consult the leg list in Appendix I, p.260.

iii.b $G_1 <^{htc.pr.C} H$ & $H \sim^{pr.C} G_2 \quad \Rightarrow G_1 <^{htc.pr.C} G_2$. '~ combines at the right'

(108) **Lemma. Hypertransitivity.** The relation $<^{htc.pr.C}$ supports hypertransitive inference, as defined in (38), with respect to the equivalence relation $\sim^{pr.C}$.

Proof. This follows directly from definition (38). Clauses (iii.a) and (iii.b) license the conflation of a sequence of adjacent equivalence relations $\sim^{pr.C}$ with a preceding or following order relation $<^{htc.pr.C}$. This leaves an overlapping chain of relations $<^{htc.pr.C}$. This relation is transitive by construction.□

(109) **Lemma. Prefixal HTC Decomposition.** If $G_1 <^{htc.pr.C} G_2$, then there is a sequence of relations of the form $G_1\mathcal{R}G_2$, $G_2\mathcal{R}G_3$, ..., $G_{n-1}\mathcal{R}G_n$, where each $\mathcal{R}$ is either $<^{pr.C}$ or $\sim^{pr.C}$ and at least one of the $\mathcal{R}$ is $<^{pr.C}$.

Proof. This follows directly from repeated application of the definition.□

(110) **Corollary. Universal instantiation of prefixal HTC.** For every $U \in \mathcal{U}(T)$, the relation $<^{htc.pr.C}$ is instantiated by the function $C \circ g_U$ as $<$.

Proof. Let $U \in \mathcal{U}(T)$. The bijection $f = C \circ g_U$ instantiates $<^{htc.pr.C}$ as $<$, exactly as in the proof of the instantiability of $<^{htc.bp.C}$ (48), where the details may be found. □

(111) **Lemma.** The relation $<^{htc.pr.C}$ is a strict partial order.

Proof. As in Lemma (49) concerning $<^{htc.bp.C}$, we observe that the relation $<^{htc.pr.C}$ is asymmetric because instantiable as $<$, and therefore irreflexive. The relation $<^{htc.pr.C}$ is by definition (107) transitive. □

4.6.3 Main order result: Equality of relations

We now have two distinct order relations defined on the grammars of a typology, each created by hypertransitive closure: $<^{htc.bp.C}$ and $<^{htc.pr.C}$. Our goal is to show that they are identical.

This will allow us to reason about one in terms of the other, and in particular to connect filtration with the EPO relations. A major point of interest, noted at the outset of the discussion, is that the base prefixal relations properly subsume the base border point relations. If we have $G_1 \equiv^{bp.C} G_2$, then there is a witnessing border point pair whose members share a prefix containing C, leading directly to $G_1 \equiv^{pr.C} G_2$. But merely having legs with the same prefix, supporting $G_1 \equiv^{pr.C} G_2$, does not guarantee adjacency of G_1 and G_2 or the existence of a border point pair sufficient to yield $G_1 \equiv^{bp.C} G_2$.

Similarly in the realm of order, if $G_1 \prec^{bp.X} G_2$, then there exists a witnessing border point pair {P<u>XY</u>Q, P<u>YX</u>Q} which contains a leg beginning PX separating G_1 from G_2, yielding $G_1 \prec^{pr.X} G_2$. But the existence of a separating prefix PX provides no guarantee that there is a border point pair embodying the separation. In particular, the prefixal relation orders *every* grammar in PX⟨T⟩, all of them prefixally equivalent on X, with respect to every other grammar in P⟨T⟩, those ejected by PX. Thus, the prefixal order relation can incorporate equivalence information in a way that the EPO relation does not, as may be seen directly in the contrast between $<^{bp.Ons}$ and $<^{pr.Ons}$ bi-graphically portrayed in exx. (105) and (106) above.

Hypertransitive closure of both relations eliminates all disparities. We show that if two grammars are related by one of $<^{htc.bp.C}$ or $<^{htc.pr.C}$, then they are related by the other, establishing equality. We begin by going from prefixal relations to border point relations. We systematically go through the hierarchy of relevant prefixal relations, from $\prec^{pr.C}$ to $<^{pr.C}$ to $<^{htc.pr.C}$, basing each argument on the previous, showing that each relation is included in the hypertransitive closure of the border point order relation $<^{htc.bp.C}$.

Illuminating examples are examined in §4.6.5, providing an appendix to the formal discussion.

(112) **Theorem. Prefixal base to border point HTC.** Let $G_a, G_b \in T$. Then

$$G_a \prec^{pr.C} G_b \Rightarrow G_a <^{htc.bp.C} G_b.$$

Proof. The plan: First, we first chase down a sequence of $<^{bp.C}$ relations following from the $\prec^{pr.C}$ assumption, showing that there's a bridging grammar H_0 such that $H_0 <^{bp.C} G_b$, where the grammar H_0 contains a leg of the form PC. Second, from $G_a \sim^{bp.C} H_0$, we obtain $G_a <^{htc.bp.C} G_b$.

Suppose $G_a \prec^{pr.C} G_b$. Then there's a prefix PC that separates G_a from G_b, so that there is a leg PC... $\in G_a$ but no leg PC... $\in G_b$. From this, it follows that G_b contains a leg $\lambda_k = PX_1...X_kC...$, $k \geq 1$. Now consider the sequence of k legs produced by starting out from $\lambda_k \in G_b$ and swapping C successively with each X_i, $k \geq i \geq 1$, up to the position immediately after P, yielding a leg $\lambda_0 = PCX_1...X_k...$, where λ_0 belongs to some grammar H_0. The grammar H_0 is clearly distinct from G_b, which contains no leg with a prefix PC..., and may be distinct from G_a . At least one of these swaps therefore produces a border point pair transposing some X_i with C. Any such swap orders the involved grammars with respect to $<^{bp.C}$. Note that in this case the grammar containing $...CX_i...$ stands in the relation $<^{bp.C}$ to the grammar containing $...X_iC...$. The upward progress of C therefore yields a nonempty sequence of grammars $H_0,\ldots,H_n$, with $\lambda_0 \in H_0$, $\lambda_k \in H_n = G_b$, and $H_0 <^{bp.C} \cdots <^{bp.C} H_n = G_b$.

Now, the grammar H_0 contains a leg beginning with PC, by construction. All grammars containing a leg prefixed PC are equivalent on C under $\sim^{pr.C}$. By Lemma (96) 'Equality of Equivalences', they are also equivalent under the EPO relation $\sim^{bp.C}$. Thus, $G_a \sim^{bp.C} H_0$ and $H_0 <^{bp.C} G_b$. Since $H_0 <^{bp.C} G_b$ implies $H_0 <^{htc.bp.C} G_b$, we have by hypertransitive inference $G_a <^{htc.bp.C} G_b$. □

(113) **Corollary. PR to HTC.BP.** $G_a <^{pr.C} G_b \Rightarrow G_a <^{htc.bp.C} G_b$.

Proof. The relation $<^{pr.C}$ is the transitive closure of $\prec^{pr.C}$. Suppose $G_a <^{pr.C} G_b$. Then there is an overlapping transitive chain $G_a = H_1,\ldots,H_n = G_b$ where $H_k \prec^{pr.C} H_{k+1}$, $1 \leq k < n$. But $H_k \prec^{pr.C} H_{k+1}$ implies $H_k <^{htc.bp.C} H_{k+1}$, by Theorem (112). Since $<^{htc.bp.C}$ is transitively closed, $G_a <^{htc.bp.C} G_b$. □

The proofs of Theorem (112) and its Corollary (113) do not require that the partition be a typology. Recall that $<^{pr.C}$ is definable on a general partition, as is $<^{bp.C}$, even though in the general case they will not be partial orders. Nevertheless, the implications between the relations established in (113) still hold.

(114) **Corollary. General PR to HTC.BP.** Let π be a partition of Ord(*S*.Con) and let $B_1, B_2 \in \pi$. Then $B_1 <^{\pi.pr.C} B_2 \Rightarrow B_1 <^{\pi.htc.bp.C} B_2$

Proof. Identical to that of (112) and (113), neither of which depend on the distinction between a general partition and a typology. □

(115) **Theorem. HTC.PR to HTC.BP.** $G_a <^{htc.pr.C} G_b \Rightarrow G_a <^{htc.bp.C} G_b$

Proof. If $G_a <^{htc.pr.C} G_b$, then by Lemma (109) 'Prefixal HTC Composition', there is a sequence of relations $<^{pr.C}$ and $\sim^{pr.C}$ between pairs of grammars leading from G_a to G_b, containing at least one instance of $<^{pr.C}$. Each of the pairwise order relations $<^{pr.C}$ is in $<^{htc.bp.C}$ by Corollary (113). Each of the pairwise equivalence relations $\sim^{pr.C}$ is also in $\sim^{bp.C}$ by Lemma (96). By hypertransitive inference, we have $G_a <^{htc.bp.C} G_b$. □

This establishes one direction of the desired equality of the htc relations, schematically pr⇒bp. We now turn to the other direction, which states $G_i <^{htc.bp.C} G_j \Rightarrow G_i <^{htc.pr.C} G_j$, that is: bp ⇒ pr. This is going to be easy, because border point pairs share prefixes. We state the proofs concisely.

(116) **Lemma. BP to PR.** $G_a <^{bp.C} G_b \Rightarrow G_a <^{pr.C} G_b$.

Proof. Each pairwise order relation in $<^{bp.C}$ is representable as an overlapping chain of pairwise $\prec^{bp.C}$ relations, each of which is also a relation in $<^{pr.C}$, beginning with G_a and ending with G_b. Therefore since $<^{pr.C}$ is transitive, we have $G_a <^{pr.C} G_b$. □

(117) **Theorem. HTC.BP to HTC.PR.** $G_a <^{htc.bp.C} G_b \Rightarrow G_a <^{htc.pr.C} G_b$.

Proof. Hypertransitivity is built from the equivalence relations and the order relations in both cases. The equivalence relations $\sim^{bp.C}$ and $\sim^{pr.C}$ are identical, by Theorem (96). The order relation $G_a <^{bp.C} G_b \Rightarrow G_a <^{pr.C} G_b$ by Lemma (116). Therefore $<^{htc.bp.C}$ is a subset of $<^{htc.pr.C}$. □

(118) **Theorem. HTC.BP = HTC.PR.** $G_a <^{htc.bp.C} G_b \Leftrightarrow G_a <^{htc.pr.C} G_b$.

Proof. Follows directly from Theorems (115) and (117). □

We have now built up a full system of OT relations from the notion of prefixal separation. These parallel the border-point-based EPO relations closely, but not exactly. The equivalences are the same, but there is divergence in the order system, where $<^{bp.C}$ implies $<^{pr.C}$, but not vice versa. The two type of order relations come together under hypertransitive closure, as shown in Theorem (118).

4.6.4 Gathering the relations

To complete the parallel with the objects derived from border-point relations, we gather the prefixal relations into an EPO-like and a MOAT-like structure. To mark both the similarities and the differences, we name these the PEO and the PMOAT. 'PEO(C)' abbreviates 'Prefixal Equivalence and Order' structure for C. Note that we must omit the medial 'P' of EPO because it abbreviates 'privileged', a term that refers specifically to the border-point-derived relation $<^{bp.C}$, which is represented in the MOAT, where it determines typological coarsening possibilities, distinguishing it from $<^{htc.bp.C}$.

As with the EPO defined in (33), the PEO rests on a typology T and, for a given C ∈ T.Con, collects the grammars of the typology T and the two relations $<^{pr.C}$ and $\sim^{pr.C}$.

(119) **Definition. $\mathbf{PEO_T(C)}$.** For a typology $T = \{G_i\}$, and C ∈ T.Con

$$PEO_T(C) = \langle T, <^{pr.C}, \sim^{pr.C} \rangle$$

When the sponsoring typology is evident from context, we will write simply PEO(C). The PMOAT(T) collects the $PEO_T(C)$ for every C in T.Con.

(120) **Definition. PMOAT(T).** For a typology $T = \{G_i\}$,
$\text{PMOAT}(T) = \{\text{PEO}_T(C) \mid C \in T.\text{Con}\}$

The most important structure in the family will be the hypertransitive closure of the PMOAT, which we will show to be equal to the hypertransitive closure of the MOAT, defined in (51) above.

(121) **Definition. Hypertransitive closure of PEO(C).** For a typology $T = \{G_i\}$ and $C \in T.\text{Con}$, the hypertransitive closure of PEO(C), which we denote (C), is defined to be $\langle T, <^{\text{htc.pr.C}}, \sim^{\text{pr.C}} \rangle$.

(122) **Definition. Hypertransitive closure of PMOAT(T).** Given a typology T, the hypertransitive closure of PMOAT(T), written htcPMOAT(T), is$\{\text{htcPEO}(C) \mid C \in T.\text{Con}\}$.

As with the other homologous structures, we will permit extended use of 'instantiation' with reference to these, so that a UVT U will be said to *instantiate* a PEO, PMOAT, or htcPMOAT for T if the set of functions $C \circ g_U$ appropriately instantiates both of the relations in integer values present in the columns of U.

This completes the formal development of the relational structures relevant to the argument. We add two appendices that give further insight into to the character and uses of the prefixal relations.

4.6.5 Building on the base relations: Appendix I to §4.6

By way of motivation, we've noted that the prefixal base relations are *not guaranteed* to be transitive or hypertransitive, and thus have proceeded to go through the entire course of development that was manifestly needed for the border point relations. We exhibit here four simple examples showing that the base prefixal relations indubitably *require* the expansions we have submitted them to.

To set up the arena in which the key examples will play out, we consider the relation $<^{\text{pr.X}}$ in the Discrete Typology 'DT3' on Ord{X, Y, Z}, with its 6 grammars, each containing a single leg.

Two grammars will be ordered in DT3 by $<^{\text{pr.X}}$ if they share a prefix P and one contains a leg PX... where the other contains *no* leg PX..., i.e. contains only legs beginning PY... or PZ... . In the Discrete Typology, 'contains' narrows to 'consists of'.

Let $P = \emptyset$, the prefix that contains no constraints. The grammar $\{XYZ\}$ therefore stands in the relation $<^{pr.X}$ to every other grammar except $\{XZY\}$, to which it is equivalent by virtue of sharing the prefix X. But it is related border-point-wise by $<^{bp.X}$ to only two of those four. To see why this is so, consider the following 'curtain' diagram of the typology, which modifies the hexagonal permutohedron on three constraints, as seen in exx. (57)–(58) and (71)–(72) above.

(123) Discrete Typology DT3 on $\mathrm{Ord}\{X, Y, Z\}$: the view from X.

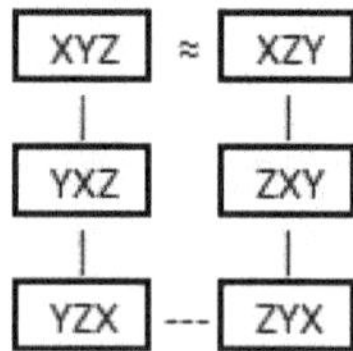

The diagram runs from X-initial legs at the top to X-final legs at the bottom. Each grammar of DT3 is boxed, and the edges connecting adjacent grammars have been modified to show relationship status with respect to X.

i. The double tilde connects those that are equivalent on X.
ii. Vertical lines follow the downward flipping of X, yielding local relations $\prec^{bp.X}$.
iii. The triple hyphen connects those grammars which are adjacent by virtue of a transposition not involving X and which are not related by X-based relations.

Observe that grammar XYZ, upper left, is border-point related to three other grammars:

i. $\mathrm{X\underline{YZ}} \sim^{bp.X} \mathrm{X\underline{ZY}}$, with which it shares X-top in the permutohedron
ii. $\mathrm{\underline{XY}Z} <^{bp.X} \mathrm{\underline{YX}Z}$, with which it stands in the relation $\prec^{bp.X}$.
iii. $\mathrm{XYZ} <^{bp.X} \mathrm{YZX}$, through transitivity via ii.,

These considerations give us EPO(X), diagrammed below. The relations $<^{bp.X}$ derived from base relations $\prec^{bp.X}$ by transitivity are drawn in as well.

(124) EPO(X) of the Discrete Typology on 3 Cs

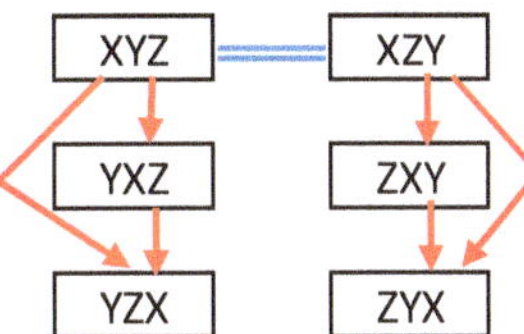

From diagram (124), it is clear that XYZ (upper left) is related border-point-wise to ZXY and ZYX on the right-hand side by neither $\prec^{\text{pr.X}}$ (local) nor $<^{\text{bp.X}}$ (transitive), but only by $<^{\text{htc.bp.X}}$, i.e. hypertransitively.

Nevertheless, XYZ is immediately related to these *prefix*-wise by $<^{\text{pr.X}}$, and indeed by $\prec^{\text{pr.X}}$, because, to repeat the definition, there is a prefix P they share and a prefix PC that separates them, with P the empty prefix.

We have X⟨DT3⟩ = {XYZ, XZY} and therefore

i. XYZ $\prec^{\text{pr.X}}$ ZXY separated by PC, for P = ∅, C = X
ii. XYZ $\prec^{\text{pr.X}}$ ZYX separated by PC, for P = ∅, C = X

Just as with **m.Ons** in EST, as seen in exx. (105) and (106) above, the prefixal $<^{\text{pr.C}}$ relation incorporates what appears in the border-point perspective as equivalence information. Once we take into account that XYZ $\sim^{\text{bp.X}}$ XZY on X-top, we obtain XYZ $<^{\text{htc.bp.X}}$ ZXY and XYZ $<^{\text{htc.bp.X}}$ ZYX, by hypertransitive inference. As guaranteed by Theorem (118), the relations $<^{\text{htc.bp.C}}$ and $<^{\text{htc.pr.C}}$ are identical.

An immediate question arises: since the prefixal relation $<^{\text{pr.C}}$ has *some* equivalence information in it, do we actually need to take it all the way to hypertransitive closure? Indeed, it also contains some transitivity information, because *everything* ejected by PC enters into a prefixal relation with the PC survivors. Thus, in the example, on the border point side, we must combine $\underline{\text{XY}}$Z $<^{\text{bp.X}}$ $\underline{\text{YX}}$Z and Y$\underline{\text{XZ}}$ $<^{\text{bp.X}}$ Y$\underline{\text{ZX}}$ to obtain XYZ $<^{\text{bp.X}}$ YZX, but the analogous long-distance relation can be obtained prefixally by PX alone. Therefore, we can reasonably ask whether the prefixal $\prec^{\text{pr.X}}$ even needs to be transitively closed.

The answer is, reassuringly, that the entire sequence of constructions is necessary. These long-distance effects are limited to the survivors of P, while both transitivity and hypertransitivity expand the prefixal relations beyond this circumscribed domain. To see this, one need only lay permuted copies of the three-constraint structure side-by-side, as occurs in a four-constraint setting, and examine telling examples of subtypologies.

We consider three cases, showing successively by example that

i. $\equiv^{\text{pr.C}}$ must be transitively closed.
ii. $\prec^{\text{pr.C}}$ must be transitively closed.
iii. $<^{\text{pr.C}}$ must be hypertransitively closed.

The field of play is the substructure of Ord{X, Y, Z, W} excluding the legs of X-top. Note that 'C-top' is a structural copy of the entire three-constraint permutohedron. In the four-constraint setting, additional adjacency relations appear, holding across tops, for example the border point pair {YWXZ, WYXZ} connects Y-top and W-top (see 1st and 2nd rows from the bottom).

(125) DT4

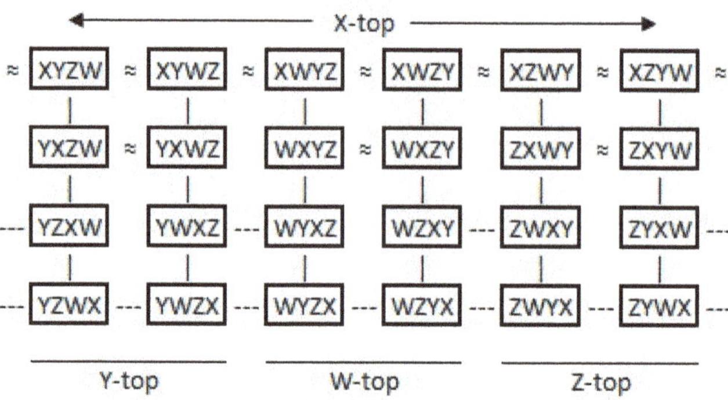

Case (i). To see that $\equiv^{\text{pr.C}}$ must be transitively closed, consider the following typology T_1 on {X, Y, Z, W}, portrayed with the same conventions as the 3-constraint Discrete Typology in (123).

There are five grammars, of which we can name four after their coloration: B(lue), O(range), G(reen), Ye(llow). X-top completes the typology.

(126) T_1. Prefixal $\equiv^{\text{pr.C}}$ must be transitively closed

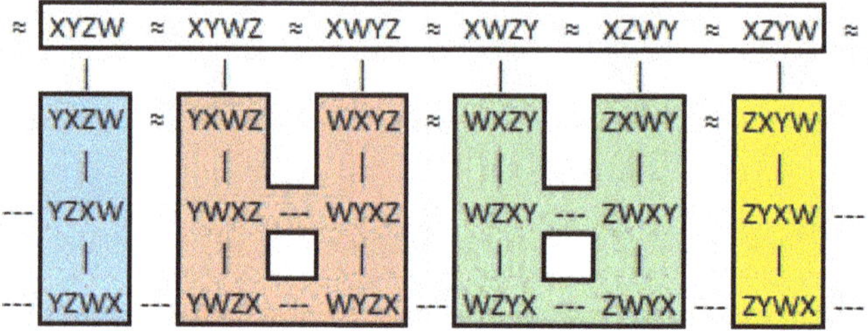

Observe the following prefixal relations.

B $\equiv^{pr.X}$ O	YX⟨T_1⟩ = {B, O}	P = YX, C= X
O $\equiv^{pr.X}$ G	WX⟨T_1⟩ = {O, G}	P = WX, C =X
G $\equiv^{pr.X}$ Ye	ZX ⟨T_1⟩ = {G, Ye}	P = ZX, C= X

Crucially, B and G share no prefix at all. Nor do O and Ye. But if the relation $\equiv^{pr.X}$ is to sit within an equivalence relation $\sim^{pr.X}$, it must be transitively closed, so that B $\sim^{pr.X}$ G and so on.

For the argument to be sound, the subpartition indicated in (126) must belong to a valid typology. The following UVT will generate it, as the reader may confirm.

(127) UVT for T_1

T_1	**X**	**Y**	**Z**	**W**
X-top	0	1	1	1
B	1	0	1	1
O	1	0	2	0
G	1	2	0	0
Ye	1	1	0	1

Case (ii). The relation $\prec^{pr.C}$ must be transitively closed. Consider the following typology T_2.

(128) T_2. Prefixal $\prec^{pr.C}$ must be transitively closed

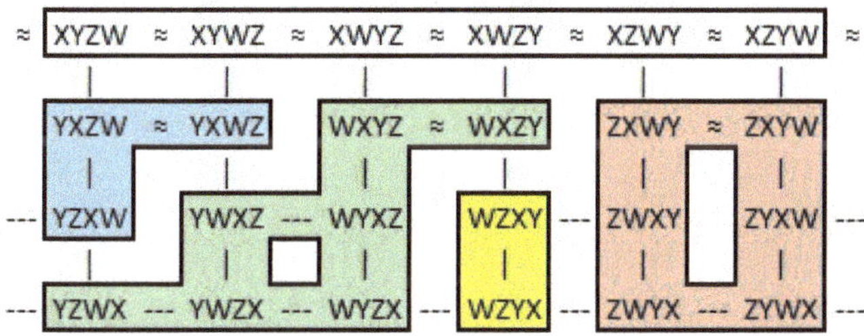

Here B and G share relevant leg substructure, because both have legs on Y-top. Similarly with G and Y, which are both co-resident on W-top, partially in the case of G.

We find the following base prefixal relations $\prec^{pr.X}$, each arising from two different prefixes.

B $\prec^{pr.X}$ G	Y⟨T_2⟩ = {B, G}	YX⟨T_2⟩ = {B}	PC = YX,	C = X
	YZ⟨T_2⟩ = {B, G}	YZX⟨T_2⟩ = {B}	PC = YZX,	C = X
G $\prec^{pr.X}$ Ye	W⟨T_2⟩ = {G, Y}	WX⟨T_2⟩ = {G}	PC = WX,	C = X

If $\prec^{pr.X}$ is to sit inside a partial order $<^{pr.X}$, it must be transitively closed to obtain B $<^{pr.X}$ Ye, since B and Ye are not separated by X.

A UVT witnessing the typological status of T_2 is the following.

(129) UVT for T_2

T_2	**X**	**Y**	**Z**	**W**
X-top	0	1	1	1
Z-top	1	1	0	1
B	1	0	2	1
G	2	0	2	0
Ye	3	1	1	0

Case (iii). The relation $<^{pr.C}$ must be hypertransitively closed if it is to equal $<^{htc.bp.C}$.

(130) T_3

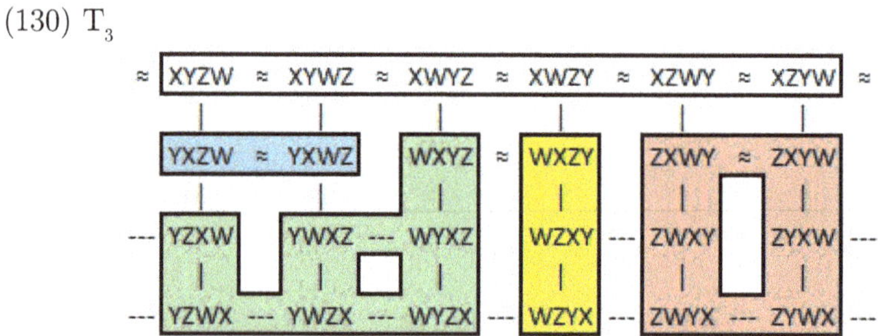

Observe the following:

B $\prec^{pr.X}$ G	Y⟨T_3⟩ = {B, G}	YX⟨T_3⟩ = {B}	P = Y, C = X
G $\sim^{pr.X}$ Ye	WX⟨T_3⟩ = {G, Ye}	—	PC = WX, C = X

With respect to the border point relations we also have B $<^{bp.X}$ G and G $\sim^{bp.X}$ Ye, so that B $<^{htc.bp.X}$ Ye. However, just as there is no adjacency between B and Ye, there is no direct prefixal filtration-based relation between B and Ye either. Therefore, we cannot depend on mere prefixal $<^{pr.X}$ to give us that relation, and we must hypertransitively close $<^{pr.X}$ to $<^{htc.pr.X}$ for a prefixal relation that equals the border-point-based relation $<^{htc.bp.X}$, obtaining B$<^{htc.pr.X}$ Ye.

The typology T_3 (130) is given by this UVT, among of course many others.

(131) UVT for T_3

T_3	X	Y	Z	W
X-top	0	1	1	1
Z-top	1	1	0	1
B	1	0	3	1
G	2	0	2	0
Y	2	1	1	0

4.6.6 Two applications of prefixal filtration: Appendix II to §4.6

We conclude the discussion of the prefixal filtration system by using the theory of prefixal relations to provide new proofs of two important facts holding across all UVTs of a given typology. We then go on to introduce a notion of prefixal filtration of EPOs and a notion of 'rootedness' that explicates the resulting filtration patterns.

When two grammars are equivalent under $\sim^{bp.C}$, then their corresponding numerical entries in column C are equal in every UVT, by Lemma (25). Thus, if $G_1 \sim^{bp.C} G_2$, then for any $U \in \mathcal{U}(T)$, $C(u_1) = C(u_2)$. Secondly, when two grammars are ordered under $<^{bp.C}$, then their corresponding entries in column C are ordered in every UVT, by Lemma (24). Thus, if $G_1 <^{bp.C} G_2$, then for every $U \in \mathcal{U}(T)$, $C(u_1) < C(u_2)$.

(132) **Lemma. Universal instantiation of $\sim^{bp.C}$ as =.** (Prefixal proof). For every $U \in \mathcal{U}(T)$, the EPO relation $\sim^{bp.C}$ is instantiated by $C \circ g_U$ as =.

Proof. Let $G, H \in T$, a typology. Assume $G \sim^{bp.C} H$, and let $U \in \mathcal{U}(T)$ with u_g and u_h being the corresponding rows of G and H in U, respectively, under g_U. Since $G \sim^{bp.C} H$, by 'Equality of Equivalences', Theorem (96), $G \sim^{pr.C} H$. To establish the lemma we need to consider the two cases that figure in the definition of $G \sim^{pr.C} H$.

Case (i). $G \equiv^{pr.C} H$, so that G and H share a prefix containing C. There exist total orders $\lambda = PQ$ and $\delta = PQ'$ with $C \in P$ where $\lambda \in G$ and $\delta \in H$. By Filtration Uniformity, Theorem (84), given any $U \in \mathcal{U}(T)$, u_g and u_h pass through C together under filtration by the prefix P. But this only can occur if $C(u_g) = C(u_h)$ in every $U \in \mathcal{U}(T)$.

Case (ii). $G \sim^{bp.C} H$, but G and H do not share a prefix containing C. Then there is an overlapping transitive chain of grammars $G = G_1 \equiv^{pr.C} G_2 \equiv^{pr.C} \ldots \equiv^{pr.C} G_n = H$, where each successive G_i and G_{i+1} share a prefix containing C. By case (i), the corresponding rows of these grammars, u_i and u_{i+1}, are equal in column C in every UVT of $U \in \mathcal{U}(T)$. By transitivity of equality, $C(u_g) = C(u_h)$ in every $U \in \mathcal{U}(T)$. □

(133) **Lemma. Universal instantiation of $<^{bp.C}$ as $<$.** (Prefixal proof). For every $U \in \mathcal{U}(T)$, the EPO relation $<^{bp.C}$ is instantiated by $C \circ g_U$ as $<$.

Proof. Let $G, H \in T$, a typology, and assume $G <^{bp.C} H$ for $U \in \mathcal{U}(T)$ with u_g and u_h being the corresponding rows in U of G and H, respectively, under g_U. If $G <^{bp.C} H$, then by Lemma (116), $G <^{pr.C} H$. This latter order relation can arise in two ways.

Case (i). $G \prec^{pr.C} H$, so that G and H are separated by a prefix PC. Given $U \in \mathcal{U}(T)$ and u_g and u_h, the corresponding rows of G and H in U, by Filtration Uniformity, Theorem (84), u_g and u_h pass through P together and u_g passes through C, but u_h is ejected by C. For this to happen, $C(u_g) < C(u_h)$.

Case (ii). $G <^{bp.C} H$, but G and H are not separated by a prefix PC. Then there exists an overlapping transitive chain of grammars $G = G_1 \prec^{pr.C} G_2 \prec^{pr.C} \cdots \prec^{pr.C} G_n$. By case (i), each pair of rows u_i, u_{i+1} is ordered numerically on C, with $C(u_i) < C(u_{i+1})$. By transitivity of $<$, $C(u_g) < C(u_h)$. This establishes the lemma. □

Observe that the converse is not true for the order relations. The numerical inequality $C(u_j) < C(u_k)$ may be present in every UVT U through hypertransitivity, even though the relation is not the correlate of a $G_j <^{bp.C} G_k$ relation between the corresponding grammars. To pluck the simplest possible example from the discussion of nGX.IL in §1.3, consider EPO(lamb), repeated from diagram (27), §1.3.1: by the results just re-proved we must have $\mathsf{lamb} \circ g_U(\mathsf{sp}) < \mathsf{lamb} \circ g_U(\mathsf{SD})$ in every U instantiating the typology, even though the grammars sp and SD are not related by $<^{bp.Iamb}$.

(134) EPO(lamb) in nGX.IL

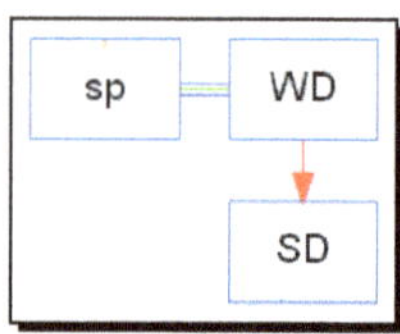

We conclude this section by establishing a connection between filtration and the overall relational structure of EPOs. A key aspect of OT filtration is what we will call 'rootedness', with Hasse-like graphical imagery in mind. Any filtering function C will identify within its input a set of survivors, the input to any further filtration, distinguished from the ejectees. When the survivors are all equivalent under a relation relevant to filtration, and when the ejectees are ordered by another filtration-relevant relation with respect to survivors, we will call the survivor set the 'root' of the input set with respect to C, and speak of the input set as being 'rooted'. In the realm of VTs, those elements in the input to C that receive the unique minimal value on C constitute the 'root' in this sense: they are selected by virtue of numerical minimality, which establishes order with respect to the ejectees. Such a minimal set is always present, so filtration is always well-defined and can always be continued on the members of the root.

In constructing the prefixal relations, we moved filtration from the sea of multitudinous UVTs into the singular realm of grammars, where each grammar is composed of a unique set of legs. The force of this move comes from the fact that all UVTs – despite numerical differences – have the same filtration patterns, shown in Theorem (84), which exactly mirror the pattern of prefixal filtration, as shown in Theorem (77) RF $\Leftrightarrow$ GF.

A similar structure of rootedness is at work in prefixal filtration. A constraint C, given an input set P⟨T⟩, where $C \notin P$, will select the set of grammars PC⟨T⟩, which constitute the 'root' of P⟨T⟩ with respect to C, containing grammars in P⟨T⟩ that are equivalent under $\sim^{pr.C}$. Those grammars in the root are ordered with respect to the ejectees by $<^{pr.C}$. In addition, the set PC⟨T⟩ is suitable for further filtration by any constraint D not in PC, in the sense that the set PC⟨T⟩ is guaranteed to be nonempty and rooted itself with respect to D. The grammars in PCD⟨T⟩ are equivalent under the relation $\sim^{pr.D}$ by virtue of each containing a leg with prefix PCD, and they are ordered by $<^{pr.D}$ with respect to the ejectees under filtration of PC⟨T⟩ by D. And so on.

These observations shed light on the structure of the EPOs of a MOAT when we consider the behavior of successive EPOs under grammar filtration. To proceed, we need a notion of 'sub-EPO', so that we can reason about the structures that result when grammars are ejected in the course of filtration. A sub-EPO is a subset of the typology equipped with the EPO relations as restricted to that subset. For a relation R on a set S, the expression '$R\restriction A$' denotes the subset of R involving only the elements of $A \subseteq S$.

(135) **Definition. Sub-EPO.** A sub-EPO E(C, Γ) is the object
$\langle \Gamma \subseteq T, \sim^{bp.C}\restriction\Gamma, <^{bp.C}\restriction\Gamma \rangle$.

Observe that the EPO(C) itself is E(C, Γ) for Γ = T. The general sub-EPO for arbitrary Γ ⊆ T is not guaranteed to have interesting properties, as its character depends on the choice of its domain Γ. When the domain Γ is the result of grammar filtration, however, the structure that emerges is that of rootedness. To see this, we need to be clear about two further concepts.

First, the 'prefix-filtered EPO', E(C, Γ) for Γ = P⟨T⟩, which is the sub-EPO where the domain Γ is a prefix-filtered subset of the typology. Second, the notion of rootedness as it applies to the sub-EPO.

(136) **Definition. Prefix-filtered EPO.** Given an EPO(C) = ⟨T, $<^{\text{bp.C}}$, $\sim^{\text{bp.C}}$⟩, and prefix P where C ∉ P, we say that the sub-EPO(C, Γ) is *prefix-filtered by* P, if Γ = P⟨T⟩. A prefix-filtered EPO is the object ⟨P⟨T⟩, $<^{\text{bp.C}}$↾P⟨T⟩, $\sim^{\text{bp.C}}$↾P⟨T⟩⟩, where P⟨T⟩ are grammars of T having a leg with prefix P as defined in (67) and the relations $<^{\text{bp.C}}$↾P⟨T⟩, $\sim^{\text{bp.C}}$↾P⟨T⟩ are the respective relations of EPO(C) restricted to P⟨T⟩.

(137) **Definition. Rooted sub-EPO.** A sub-EPO E(C, Γ) is *rooted* if there exists an equivalence class M ⊆ Γ under $\sim^{\text{bp.C}}$, such that each grammar H ∈ P⟨T⟩ is either in M or there is some G ∈ M such that G $<^{\text{bp.C}}$ H. The set M is said to be the 'root' of E(C, Γ).

The designation 'M' is chosen to suggest the word 'minimal'. We now establish that a prefix-filtered sub-EPO is rooted.

(138) **Theorem. Rootedness and EPO filtration.** Let C ∈ T.Con for a typology T. Let P be a prefix not containing C. The prefix-filtered sub-EPO E(C, P⟨T⟩) is rooted.

Proof. Consider a prefix P that does not contain C. We wish to show that E(C, P⟨T⟩) = ⟨P⟨T⟩, $<^{\text{bp.C}}$↾P⟨T⟩, $\sim^{\text{bp.C}}$↾P⟨T⟩⟩ is rooted. Let M = PC⟨T⟩, the set of grammars of T having a leg with prefix PC. Claim: M is the root of E(C, P⟨T⟩).

M is clearly non-empty. Note that for all G_i, G_j ∈ M, we have $G_i \sim^{\text{pr.C}} G_j$ and therefore, crucially, $G_i \sim^{\text{bp.C}} G_j$ by Equality of Equivalences (96). Thus, M is an equivalence class under $\sim^{\text{bp.C}}$, as required by the definition of rootedness (137).

Let H ∈ P⟨T⟩ be a grammar not in M. To fulfill the remaining definitional requirement, we will show that there is some G ∈ M such that G $<^{\text{bp.C}}$ H. Because H ∈ P⟨T⟩, and H ∉ M = PC⟨T|⟩, H contains a leg, λ = PQCR, where Q and R are sequences of constraints and Q is non-empty, though R may be empty.

Through a series of adjacent transpositions, we can move the C in λ stepwise through Q to immediately follow the P, producing λ′ = PCQR ∈ PC⟨T⟩ = M and a path between λ and λ′. At least one of the transpositions along the path yields a border point pair between grammars of EPO(C, P⟨T⟩), producing a non-empty sequence of ordered grammars: G = $H_k <^{\text{bp.C}} \dots <^{\text{bp.C}} H_1$ = H. The grammar H = H_1 contains the leg λ′ = PCQR and the final grammar G $= H_k$ contains $\lambda =$ PQCR. But this means that G $= H_k <^{bp.C} H_1$ $=$ H, where G $\in$ M, as desired. □

The argument may also be conducted in terms of the hypertransitive order relation. Let G $\in$ M $=$ PC⟨T⟩. Suppose for purposes of contradiction that there is some H $\in \Gamma$ $=$ P⟨T⟩ such that H $<^{bp.C}$ G. Observe that H cannot contain a leg PC..., lest G $\sim^{pr.C}$ H and thus G $\sim^{bp.C}$ H by Equality of Equivalences (96). But two grammars may not be simultaneously equivalent to each other and ordered with respect to each other by the EPO relations, a simple consequence of their instantiability.

Therefore, H contains no leg PC..., only legs PD..., D $\neq$ C and C $\notin$ P. Prefixally, then, G $<^{pr.C}$ H. This, however, is impossible. From definition (107) of $<^{htc.pr.C}$, we have G $<^{pr.C}$ H $\Rightarrow$ G $<^{htc.pr.C}$ H. But the hypertransitive order relations are identical by (118), so that we also have border-point-wise G $<^{htc.bp.C}$ H. But we assumed for contradiction that H $<^{bp.C}$ G, which implies H $<^{htc.bp.C}$ G, by the definition of hypertransitive closure (45). We cannot have both G $<^{htc.bp.C}$ H and H $<^{htc.bp.C}$ G because $<^{htc.bp.C}$ is a strict order by (49), so no such H exists. □

We close by noting that the same rootedness result may be obtained from a notion of filtration that is more akin to that used on VTs, as in the definition of candidate filtration in ex. (1), §4.5. There, at each C in a sequence of filtration, those candidates with the minimal numerical value on C are accepted and the others are ejected. The essence of the idea is repeatedly selecting minima on some order. EPO(C) supplies us with the components from which we have already built the relevant order: $<^{htc.bp.C}$. If we tranform the definition of UVT filtration into EPO filtration by referring to grammars minimal on $<^{htc.bp.C}$ rather than to rows minimal numerically on C, we will define a filtration pattern consisting of a sequence of sub-EPOs, each taking its domain from the survivors of the previous step of filtration. We will find that each successive sub-EPO in a filtration pattern is rooted in the same sense as given in definition (137), with the roots identical to those that emerge under prefixal filtration (136).

4.7 Typological equivalence

Section contents

Border points delimit the grammars of a typology and therefore distinguish different typologies on the same constraint set.[12] The relations of §4.3 are built from border point data, but in abstracting from them provide both more and less information about the grammars than the border points do

[12] It's clear that if T_1 and T_2, two typologies over the same set of constraints, have *different* border points, then they must be different typologies. Suppose $\{\lambda_1, \lambda_2\}$ is a border point pair in T_1, so that λ_1 is a border point in T_1 belonging to a different grammar than λ_2. Suppose that λ_1 is *not* a border point in T_2. Then the (adjacent) leg λ_2 must belong to the same grammar in T_2 as λ_1. Thus $T_1 \neq T_2$. If some such T_1 and T_2 have the *same* set of border points, then it follows from Theorem (155) of §4.7.2 that they must be the same typology.

in themselves. All such relations lose information about the details of the border point pairs they are ultimately based on. In addition, the EPO relations go beyond the base relations via transitive closure, which is long-range rather than local, and therefore imposes structure on the grammars that is not explicit in the border point data. Hypertransitive closure takes the relations even farther from their ultimate sources.

A border point pair linking grammars G and H supports a set of order and equivalence relations in concert with the other border point pairs. A pair of the form $\{\mathrm{P}\underline{\mathrm{XY}}\mathrm{Q}, \mathrm{P}\underline{\mathrm{YX}}\mathrm{Q}\}$ directly delivers relations G $<^{\text{bp.X}}$ H and H $<^{\text{bp.Y}}$ G, but from the relations alone we cannot conclude that G is adjacent to H, because the relations $<^{\text{bp.X}}$ and $<^{\text{bp.Y}}$ are the transitive closures of the border point base relations and thus may be mediated by chains of local grammar-to-adjacent-grammar relations. Similarly, although we have G $\sim^{\text{bp.C}}$ H for every C in the prefix P of the cited border point pair, we cannot conclude from the relation itself that C lies in the prefix of a single border point pair linking G and H. Furthermore, details about the position of the other constraints in a given witnessing border point pair are irrecoverably lost. These gains and losses are, we shall see, the strength of the EPO relations: they identify relevant information, eliminate the irrelevant, and contain key implications that are not overt in the raw data they are based on.

Absent proof, however, there is a legitimate worry that the information loss from the abstraction and from transitive closure is so severe that it could obscure the identity of the underlying typology: specifically, that the border point pair relations from two distinct typologies on the same constraint set could be the same or might transitively close to the same relational structure. If this were the case, the MOAT would fail to uniquely characterize a typology.

To see more deeply into the issue, it's useful to consider how a MOAT connects with a typology. The MOAT is a structure in which grammars are opaque objects bearing relations to each other. A typology *per se* is a certain partition of the set of linear orders on a constraint set, in which grammars are understood as blocks of the partition, as sets. These are very different formal entities. The progression from a given UVT to its unique typology and from there to *its* unique MOAT is straightforward, and rests on the now-familiar tools of filtration and border point analysis (§4.1–§4.3.3). Fixing some key terminology, let's say that a UVT *produces* its typology. Starting from a MOAT rather than a UVT to arrive at a typology requires a different route, but the UVT provides the key link. Every typology is produced by a UVT, which is generically just a VT of the appropriate size that lacks redundant or harmonically bounded rows. The abstract relations of a particular MOAT must therefore be numerically instantiated in a UVT and from that, a typology derived.

This strategy is not going to run smoothly if, as worried above, distinct typologies give rise to the same MOAT (or to relationally equivalent MOATs that instantiate in the same way). Instantiating a MOAT in a UVT can only produce a single typology, because a UVT produces exactly one. Therefore, if two typologies could converge on a single MOAT, we'd only get one of them back through instantiation.

A second concern emerges on the instantiation side. A given typology pairs with only one MOAT via border point analysis. But suppose a given UVT could *instantiate* two (or more) relationally distinct MOATs, which necessarily come from distinct typologies. Here again, the instantiation route would falter, since that relationally-ambiguous UVT could reproduce only one of the typologies whose MOATs it would instantiate.[13]

Both worries are dispelled by the major results of this section. Theorem (152) 'Instantiating the MOAT' guarantees that every UVT instantiating MOAT(T) will produce T. This means *only* T, as noted, because a UVT produces a unique typology. Thus, no UVT can instantiate the MOATs from two distinct typologies, eliminating the second concern.

From this, it follows rapidly in Theorem (155) that if two MOATs have the same relational structure, they come from identical typologies. Contraposing, this result ensures that distinct typologies have relationally distinct MOATs. Thus, the abstraction of leaving border point details behind in favor of relations $\prec^{bp.C}$ and $\equiv^{bp.C}$ in fact never loses typology-distinguishing information, nor does transitively closing these to $<^{bp.C}$ and $\sim^{bp.C}$, nor does hypertransitively closing $<^{bp.C}$ to $<^{htc.bp.C}$, so the first worry may be confidently set aside. A typology's MOAT is not only unique but *characterizing*, in that MOAT(T) distinguishes T from all other typologies on the same constraint set. The move from border point data to abstract relations, exactly as hoped, is revelatory rather than obscuring, and uncovers essential information about typological structure.

---

[13] This situation is identical to one in which two typologically inequivalent UVTs each instantiate the same MOAT. From Lemma (37), we know that $U \in \mathcal{U}(T_1)$ implies that U instantiates MOAT(T_1). Now suppose U also instantiates some other MOAT, call it MOAT(T_2), where $T_1 \neq T_2$. But any $V \in \mathcal{U}(T_2)$ also instantiates MOAT(T_2) by Lemma (37). Thus MOAT(T_2) is instantiated in both U and V, which produce distinct typologies. This formulation brings out the parallelism between the two cases. In the first, distinct typologies give rise to the same MOAT. In the second, typologically inequivalent UVTs instantiate the same MOAT. The shared concern is that the MOAT may be too weak to distinguish typologies (in the first case) and inequivalent UVTs (in the second).

Among the families of relations on grammars developed in §4.2 and §4.3, the major conceptual split lies between those derived from the border point pairs and those derived from prefixal considerations. The prefixal relations closely track the way that filtration proceeds on UVTs, and at the same time correspond in determinate ways with their border point analogs. Prefixal relations, incorporated in the 'PMOAT', thus serve as a bridge on the route between the border-point-derived MOAT(T) and T itself, which derives from filtration.

The key relations-between-relations may be summarized as follows:

☐ Among the equivalence relations, Theorem (97) 'Equality of Equivalences' establishes that $\sim^{\text{bp.C}}$ and $\sim^{\text{pr.C}}$ are entirely identical.

☐ The relation $<^{\text{bp.C}}$ is a subset of $<^{\text{pr.C}}$, typically proper. Among the orders, equality of relations is reached at the level of hypertransitive closure; see Theorem (118) 'HTC.BP = HTC.PR'. Thus, $\sim^{\text{htc.bp.C}}$ and $\sim^{\text{htc.pr.C}}$ are identical.

These findings undergird Theorem (152), which establishes that any UVT instantiating a MOAT will also produce its typology. The course of reasoning runs like this:

V instantiates MOAT(T) ⇒
V instantiates htcMOAT(T) ⇒ V instantiates htc**P**MOAT(T) ⇒
V instantiates **P**MOAT(T) ⇒
$V \in \mathcal{U}(T)$.

The crucial last step, the validity of which is established below in Lemma (146) and Theorem (147), relies on the relative ease of connecting instantiatiability of prefixal relations in a UVT with the process of row filtration that produces its typology.

Since everything turns on the properties of instantiation, we examine those first in §7.1, then turn to establishing the characterization theorem (155) 'Our Moatish Mother' in §7.2, which confirms the centrality of the MOAT in the theory of typologies. Having seen how MOAT(T) delimits the UVTs that produce T, we turn in §4.7.3 to show how the MOAT determines the structure of VTs in the general case of concrete OT, where a typology derives from a set of VTs based on diverse inputs.

4.7.1 Instantiation in UVTs

We begin with the properties of instantiation. To instantiate, we require relational homomorphisms between a typology T and ℕ, functions $f_C:T \rightarrow \mathbb{N}$

that respect the relevant relations on T. For each C, we need one function that simultaneously respects a relation of the equivalence family, such as $\sim^{bp.C}$, and a relation of the order family, such as $<^{bp.C}$. As defined in (17), this requires for each C a function f_C:T → ℕ which has the property

$$x\, R_T\, y \Rightarrow f_C(x) < f_C(y)$$
$$x\, E_T\, y \Rightarrow f_C(x) = f_C(y)$$

where we write R_T for the order-type relation and E_T for the equivalence-type relation. Of use to us is a version of the function f_C that is keyed to a specific UVT U. The function we seek is this:

$$C \circ g_U : T \rightarrow U \rightarrow \mathbb{N}$$

which associates each grammar $G_k \in T$ with its unique corresponding row u_k in U, via g_U, and then retrieves the value that the constraint C assigns in that row. This composite function associates grammars to integers according to the following scheme, which notates the pairs associated by g_U with subscripts:

$$G_k \mapsto C(u_k)$$

We have extended the terminology of instantiation from its primary sense, in which a function *instantiates*, to include a usage in which a UVT U *instantiates*. In particular, U instantiates relations R_T and E_T, when for every C and every G_k, the function $G_k \mapsto C(u_k)$ instantiates both relations.

Because this usage is central to the current argument, we introduce a notation to represent it, borrowing the 'double turnstile' ⊨ used to express the modeling relation, and writing $U \models R_T$ and $U \models E_T$ to indicate that U instantiates R_T and that U instantiates E_T, respectively. When the relations belong to the (P)MOAT structure for T, we also write U ⊨ MOAT(T) and U ⊨ PMOAT(T).

A UVT is a VT with no redundant or harmonically bounded rows. Any such VT qualifies as a UVT, and, when filtered by all orders of its columns, produces a unique typology. To instantiate a given MOAT, a UVT must meet certain minimal specifications: its columns must match 1:1 with the set of constraints represented as the EPOs of the MOAT, and its rows with the grammars that are related by $<^{bp.C}$ and $\sim^{bp.C}$ in EPO(C). Given these dimensions and identifications, the functions $C \circ g_U$ are well-defined, and it can be ascertained whether they are relational homomorphisms in the desired sense.

In the course of building up the relational systems, we have attended closely to instantiation and found that each relation is appropriately instantiated in every UVT of the typology from which it derives. All such results have the following logical form: if U is a UVT for T, then U instantiates the relation $\mathcal{R}$ under discussion. Symbolically put, we have this, over and over again:

$$U \in \mathcal{U}(T) \Rightarrow U \vDash \mathcal{R}$$

These results may summarized as follows, organized by relation type:

(139) Instantiating all relations

Relation Type		Symbols	$U \in \mathcal{U}(T) \Rightarrow$	Established
bp	Base	$\prec^{bp.C}, \equiv^{bp.C}$	$U \vDash \{ \prec^{bp.C}, \equiv^{bp.C} \}$	(25)
	Order, equivalence	$<^{bp.C}, \sim^{bp.C}$	$U \vDash \{ <^{bp.C}, \sim^{bp.C} \}$	(27), (31)
	HTC	$<^{htc.bp.C}$	$U \vDash \{ <^{htc.bp.C} \}$	(48)
pr	Base	$\prec^{pr.C}, \equiv^{pr.C}$	$U \vDash \{ \prec^{pr.C}, \equiv^{pr.C} \}$	(92), (102)
	Order, equivalence	$<^{pr.C}, \sim^{pr.C}$	$U \vDash \{ <^{pr.C}, \sim^{pr.C} \}$	(103), (93)
	HTC	$<^{htc.pr.C}$	$U \vDash \{ <^{htc.pr.C} \}$	(110)

Recall that $\sim^{bp.C}$ and $\sim^{pr.C}$ name identical relations, as shown in Theorem (96) 'Equality of Equivalences. Similarly, $<^{htc.bp.C}$ and $<^{htc.pr.C}$ are identical, as shown in Theorem (118).

It's striking that instantiability does not distinguish among UVTs: there's no such thing as a UVT that instantiates the base relations but not the EPO relations, and so on. The role of the relational distinctions is thus not to discriminate among UVTs, but to provide a structure within which we may reason about their properties.

This perspective assumes that we have in hand T and $U \in \mathcal{U}(T)$ and ask which relations the UVT U must instantiate. Suppose instead that we have only the information that a certain non-redundant VT instantiates one or more of the relations. For example, suppose we know that V instantiates $\prec^{bp.C}$. What other relations are we guaranteed that it also instantiates? Along the same lines, suppose we know that in addition, V instantiates $\equiv^{bp.C}$. What then of the others?

The most useful form of the question deals with instantiations of the MOAT, the PMOAT, and the htcMOAT. Each case requires a function, always in fact $C \circ g_U$, which instantiates both of the relations involved in the MOAT-type structure. We lay out the relations in four quick lemmas. In each case, assume that V is a VT lacking redundant and harmonically bounded rows, of the appropriate dimensions to host relations based on T.

(140) **Lemma. htcMOAT and htcPMOAT.** $V \vDash$ htcMOAT(T) $\Leftrightarrow$ $V \vDash$ htcPMOAT(T).

Proof. These structures are identical, so the biconditional is trivial. By Theorem (96) 'Equality of Equivalences', the relations $\sim^{bp.C}$ and $\sim^{pr.C}$ are the same. By Theorem (118) 'HTC.BP = HTC.PR', the relations $<^{\text{htc.bp.C}}$ and $<^{\text{htc.pr.C}}$ are the same. But htcMOAT and htcPMOAT contain exactly these, so that, unsurprisingly, instantiation of the one implies instantiation of the other. □

(141) **Lemma. htcMOAT to MOAT.** V ⊨ htcMOAT(T) ⇒ V ⊨ MOAT(T).

Proof. The relation $<^{\text{bp.C}}$ is a subset of the relation $<^{\text{htc.bp.C}}$. Therefore any function that instantiates $<^{\text{htc.bp.C}}$ also instantiates $<^{\text{bp.C}}$. The relation $\sim^{\text{bp.C}}$ is common to both htcMOAT and MOAT. □

(142) **Lemma. htcPMOAT to PMOAT.** V ⊨ htcPMOAT(T) ⇒ V ⊨ PMOAT(T).

Proof. Same argument as for Lemma (141), using the .pr version of the relations. □

The following is slightly less trivial, since the crucial implication runs from the subset relation $<^{\text{bp.C}}$ to the superset $<^{\text{htc.bp.C}}$ which includes it.

(143) **Lemma. MOAT to htcMOAT.** V ⊨ MOAT(T) ⇒ V ⊨ htcMOAT(T).

Proof. Suppose V ⊨ MOAT(T). Then, by definition of instantiation, for every C ∈ T.Con we have $C \circ g_V$ as a function instantiating EPO(C) in column C of V. Thus, $C \circ g_V$ instantiates both $\sim^{\text{bp.C}}$ and $<^{\text{bp.C}}$. Since the equivalence relation $\sim^{\text{bp.C}}$ is common to both MOAT(T) and htcMOAT(T), it is also instantiated by $C \circ g_V$ in htcMOAT(T).

Now suppose $G_j <^{\text{htc.bp.C}} G_k$, for grammars $G_j, G_k \in T$. Decompose this relation into a overlapping chain $G_j = H_1 \mathcal{R}\, H_2\, \mathcal{R} \cdots \mathcal{R}\, H_n = G_k$, where $\mathcal{R}$ is either $<^{\text{bp.C}}$ or $\sim^{\text{bp.C}}$, with at least one of the former, as per Lemma (47). These relations are instantiated by $C \circ g_V$ as $<$ and $=$ respectively, by Lemmas (27) and (31). Thus $C(u_j)<C(u_k)$. It follows that the relation $<^{\text{htc.bp.C}}$ is appropriately instantiated by $C \circ g_V$ as $<$. Thus, V ⊨ htcMOAT(T). □

(144) **Lemma. PMOAT to htcPMOAT.** V ⊨ MOAT(T) ⇒ V ⊨ htcMOAT(T).

Proof. Same argument as in Lemma (143), using the .pr version of the relations. □

Putting these results together: a UVT which instantiates any one of the MOAT-type structures is guaranteed to instantiate all of them

$$\begin{array}{lcl} \mathrm{V} \vDash \mathrm{MOAT(T)} & \Leftrightarrow & \mathrm{V} \vDash \mathrm{htcMOAT(T)} \\ \mathrm{V} \vDash \mathrm{htcMOAT(T)} & \Leftrightarrow & \mathrm{V} \vDash \mathrm{htcPMOAT(T)} \\ \mathrm{V} \vDash \mathrm{htcPMOAT(T)} & \Leftrightarrow & \mathrm{V} \vDash \mathrm{PMOAT(T)} \end{array}$$

Of particular interest to the argument is the implication established by this chain of inferences between instantiation of the MOAT and instantiation of the PMOAT:

$$\mathrm{V} \vDash \mathrm{MOAT(T)} \Leftrightarrow \mathrm{V} \vDash \mathrm{PMOAT(T)}$$

Reading left to right, this tells us that if we assume V ⊨ MOAT(T), in the realm of the border point-based relations, we are guaranteed V ⊨ PMOAT(T), so that we can move into the realm where filtration is easily accessed. This is exactly the implicational link we will use in Theorem (152) to show that V ⊨ MOAT(T) ⇒ V ∈ $\mathcal{U}$(T). Taken with its converse in Lemma (37), this establishes that the MOAT(T) contains exactly the information that delimits T.

4.7.2 Isomorphism of MOATs = identity of typologies

We begin by establishing that the PMOAT(T) has two major properties. First, if a UVT V instantiates the PMOAT(T), then V produces T. Then, from this, if two PMOATs are relationally equivalent in the sense defined below, they must come from the same typology. We complete the argument by carrying these results over to MOAT(T).

As background, recall that all UVTs producing a given typology have identical filtration patterns. This fact characterizes a typology in terms of an invariant shared by all UVT representations of that typology. It is proved in Theorem (85) 'Converse of Filtration Uniformity (CoFU)', repeated here for convencience.

(145) **Theorem (85). Characterization: Converse of Filtration Uniformity (CoFU).** For any two UVTs U, V over the same constraint set T.Con, if their filtration patterns are identical, then $T_U = T_V$.

Proof. See (85) for details. Sketch: a leg is also a prefix, so assuming identical filtration patterns identifies corresponding rows of different UVTs with the same grammar. □

We now use this result to establish that any VT instantiating the relations of PMOAT(T) is necessarily a UVT for T. The strategy is to advance from numerical filtration in an arbitrary U ∈ $\mathcal{U}$(T) to prefixal relations that hold over the grammars of T, and then to examine a VT V which instantiates those prefixal relations, showing that they force the same filtration pattern in V as obtains in U. Since having the same filtration patterns implies producing the same typology by Theorem (85) 'CoFU', it follows that V yields T, as claimed.

First, we take a small preliminary step: if a VT V differs in just one column from a known UVT for T, where that one column instantiates PMOAT relations, then V must also be a UVT for T. Then we transit easily to the desired broader conclusion.

(146) **Lemma. Columnar Interchange.** Let $U \in \mathcal{U}(T)$. Let V be identical to U except for one column C which instantiates the PEO(C) from PMOAT(T). Then $V \in \mathcal{U}(T)$.

Proof. Let $U \in \mathcal{U}(T)$ and let V be identical to U except for one column C which instantiates the relations $\sim^{pr.C}$ and $<^{pr.C}$ of PEO(C). Each row $u_k \in U$ corresponds bijectively to the row $v_k \in V$ which is identical to u_k except possibly for the entry in column C. Let P be a prefix that doesn't contain C. Since U and V are identical on the constraints in P, we have $u_k \in P[U]$ iff $v_k \in P[V]$ for all $u_k \in U$, $v_k \in V$. Now consider arbitrary u_1, $u_2 \in U$.

(*) Suppose u_1, $u_2 \in PC[U]$. By No Dead Men Walking (65), G_1 and G_2 both contain legs beginning with the prefix PC. Thus in T, $G_1 \sim^{pr.C} G_2$. Now since by assumption column C in V instantiates PEO(C), we have that $C(v_1) = C(v_2)$.

(**) Now suppose that PC separates u_1 from u_2, so that $u_1, u_2 \in P[U]$ while $u_1 \in PC[U]$ and $u_2 \notin PC[U]$. (Since indexation is arbitrary, there is no loss of generality.) This gives us $G_1 <^{pr.C} G_2$ in PEO(C) because row filtration implies grammar filtration by Theorem 'RF ⇔ GF' (77). Since V instantiates PEO(C), we have $C(v_1) < C(v_2)$.

These two considerations go from filtration in U to numerical equality and order in V. We need filtration in V. Suppose $u_1 \in PC[U]$. We want $v_1 \in PC[V]$. First, note that $C(v_1) = C(v_k)$ for all v_k with a corresponding u_k that passes through PC in U, by (*). Second, note that $C(v_1) < C(v_j)$ for all v_j with corresponding u_j that are ejected by C from PC[U], by (**). This exhausts the competitors in P[V] and therefore v_1 is minimal on C in P[V]. Therefore, the filtration steps at PC[U] and at PC[V] select corresponding rows. Since C is the only place where U and V differ, they have identical filtration patterns. By CoFU (85), repeated above as (145), UVTs with identical filtration patterns sponsor the same typology, and we have $V \in \mathcal{U}(T)$.□

(147) **Theorem. *R.E.S.P.E.C.T.* Instantiating the PMOAT.** If V is a UVT that instantiates PMOAT(T), then V produces T. Concisely, $V \models PMOAT(T) \Rightarrow V \in \mathcal{U}(T)$.

Proof. We simply interchange the columns of V with those of any UVT in $\mathcal{U}$(T). Specifically, define the sequence $U_0,..., U_n$ where U_0 is any UVT in $\mathcal{U}$(T) and $U_n = V$, and for $1 \le i \le n$, U_i is the UVT that is identical to U_{i-1} except that the values in the ith column of U_i are those of the ith column of V. By Columnar Interchange (146), each $U_i \in \mathcal{U}$(T). □

We now approach our second characterization theorem, based on prefixally-defined relations rather than directly on row filtration as in CoFU (85).

The goal is to show that each PMOAT defines a unique typology. To make this precise, we need to say what it means for two PMOATs to have the same structure in the relevant sense: that is, to be relationally equivalent. We do not want to trivialize the result by presupposing that the typologies at issue consist of the same grammars-as-leg-sets, but we will assume that they are comparable to the extent that they share the same constraint set, which functions as a shared set of labels for the relevant relations. We therefore need a relation-respecting bijection between the underlying typologies, which renders relational equivalence as isomorphism.

(148) **Definition. Isomorphism of PMOATs.** Let T_1 and T_2 be typologies over the same set of constraints T.Con. We say PMOAT(T_1) is isomorphic to PMOAT(T_2), and we write PMOAT(T_1) ≅ PMOAT(T_2), if there exists a bijection f : $T_1 \rightarrow T_2$ such that for every C ∈ T.Con, and for every G, H ∈ T_1, the following biconditionals hold:

$$G <^{T1.pr.C} H \Leftrightarrow f(G) <^{T2.pr.C} f(H)$$
$$G \sim^{T1.pr.C} H \Leftrightarrow f(G) \sim^{T2.pr.C} f(H).$$

In such a case, the bijection f is said to be an isomorphism between PMOAT(T_1) and PMOAT(T_2). Its existence establishes that the two PMOATs have the same relational structure. Intuitively, if a phenomenon responds purely to relational structure, it should treat isomorphic PMOATs alike. Thus, we want to show that if a UVT U instantiates PMOAT(T_1), it also instantiates the isomorphic PMOAT(T_2).

(149) **Lemma. Instantiation of isomorphic PMOATs.** Suppose PMOAT(T_1) is isomorphic to PMOAT(T_2). Let U be a UVT. If U instantiates PMOAT(T_1), then U instantiates PMOAT(T_2). Concisely put: If PMOAT(T_1) ≅ PMOAT(T_2), then U ⊨ PMOAT(T_1) ⇒ U ⊨ PMOAT(T_2).

Proof. Assume PMOAT(T_1) ≅ PMOAT(T_2) by virtue of a bijection f : $T_1 \rightarrow T_2$, and suppose that U, a UVT, instantiates PMOAT(T_1). This means that there are instantiating functions $C \circ g_U : T_1 \rightarrow U \rightarrow \mathbb{N}$ for PMOAT(T_1), where we can set up the enumeration of grammars and rows of U so that

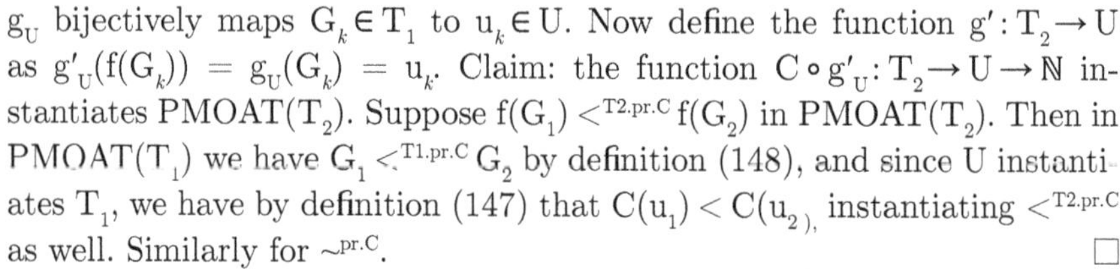
g_U bijectively maps $G_k \in T_1$ to $u_k \in U$. Now define the function $g' : T_2 \rightarrow U$ as $g'_U(f(G_k)) = g_U(G_k) = u_k$. Claim: the function $C \circ g'_U : T_2 \rightarrow U \rightarrow \mathbb{N}$ instantiates PMOAT(T_2). Suppose $f(G_1) <^{T2.pr.C} f(G_2)$ in PMOAT(T_2). Then in PMOAT(T_1) we have $G_1 <^{T1.pr.C} G_2$ by definition (148), and since U instantiates T_1, we have by definition (147) that $C(u_1) < C(u_2)$, instantiating $<^{T2.pr.C}$ as well. Similarly for $\sim^{pr.C}$. □

(150) **Theorem. Prefixal characterization.** Let T_1, T_2 be typologies over the same set of constraints. If PMOAT(T_1) ≅ PMOAT(T_2), then $T_1 = T_2$.

Proof. Let U instantiate PMOAT(T_1). Then by Theorem (147) '*R.E.S.P.E.C.T.*', we have $U \in \mathcal{U}(T_1)$. But U also instantiates PMOAT(T_2) by Lemma (149), because PMOAT(T_1) and PMOAT(T_2) are assumed isomorphic. Thus $U \in \mathcal{U}(T_2)$, also by (147) '*R.E.S.P.E.C.T.*'. But U produces only one typology, so $T_1 = T_2$. □

We now move from prefixal relations to border point relations, from PMOAT to MOAT.

The argument relies on the fact that, although $<^{pr.C}$ and $<^{bp.C}$ differ in that the first may properly contain the second, the two relations $<^{htc.pr.C}$ and $<^{htc.bp.C}$ are identical, as shown in (118). Consequently, the htcMOAT(T) and htcPMOAT(T) are also identical, since their equivalence relations are identical, a fact recorded in the following Lemma.

(151) **Lemma. htcMOAT = htcPMOAT.** For every typology T, htcMOAT(T) is identical to htcPMOAT(T).

Proof. See Theorem (118) 'Equality of HTC Order Relations' for $<^{htc.bp.C} = <^{htc.pr.C}$ and Theorem (96) 'Equality of Equivalences' for $\sim^{bp.C} = \sim^{pr.C}$. Thus the relations of htcMOAT(T) and htcPMOAT(T) are the same. □

Recall that although htcMOAT contains in $<^{htc.bp.C}$ a superset relation of $<^{bp.C}$, any UVT that instantiates the MOAT(T) will also instantiate htcMOAT(T), shown in Lemma (143). With this in hand, we now show that any UVT instantiating a MOAT will also produce the typology that the MOAT comes from.

(152) **Theorem. Instantiating the MOAT.** If V is a UVT that instantiates MOAT(T), then V produces T. Concisely put: $V \vDash$ MOAT(T) $\Rightarrow V \in \mathcal{U}$(T)

Proof. Assume $V \vDash$ MOAT(T). Then by Lemma (143), we have $V \vDash$ htcMOAT(T). Because htcMOAT(T) = htcPMOAT(T), as in Lemma (151), it follows that $V \vDash$ htcPMOAT(T). We have transitioned from border-point-based relations to prefixally based relations.

Since V ⊨ htcPMOAT(T), we also have V ⊨ PMOAT(T), since the relations of the PMOAT(T) are a subset of the relations of the htcPMOAT(T), as noted in Lemma (142). Finally, by the Theorem (147) '*R.E.S.P.E.C.T.*', because V ⊨ PMOAT(T), it follows that $V \in \mathcal{U}(T)$. □

Our third and final characterization theorem, based on EPO relations rather than prefixal relations, as in Theorem (150), or row filtration, as in Theorem (85), is now within reach. The goal here is to show that the relational structure of a MOAT defines a unique typology. Just as with the PMOAT, to make this precise we need to say what it means for two MOATs to have the same structure: we need a relation-respecting bijection between the underlying typologies.

(153) **Definition. Isomorphism of MOATs.** Let T_1 and T_2 be typologies over the same set of constraints T.Con. We say MOAT(T_1) is isomorphic to MOAT(T_2), and we write MOAT(T_1) ≅ MOAT(T_2), if there exists a bijection $f : T_1 \rightarrow T_2$ such that for every C ∈ T.Con, and for every G, H ∈ T_1, the following biconditionals hold:

$$G <^{T1.bp.C} H \Leftrightarrow f(G) <^{T2.bp.C} f(H)$$
$$G \sim^{T1.bp.C} H \Leftrightarrow f(G) \sim^{T2.bp.C} f(H) .$$

When MOAT(T_1) ≅ MOAT(T_2) holds, f is said to be an isomorphism between MOAT(T_1) and MOAT(T_2). As with isomorphic PMOATs, if a UVT U instantiates T_1, it also instantiates isomorphic T_2. The instantiating function $C \circ g_U$ for T_1 gives rise to an instantiating function $C \circ g'_U$ for T_2, where $g'_U(f(G_k)) = g_U(G_k)$.

(154) **Lemma. Instantiation of Isomorphic MOATs.** Suppose MOAT(T_1) ≅ MOAT(T_2). Let U be a UVT. If U ⊨ MOAT(T_1), then U ⊨ MOAT(T_2).

Proof. Exactly as in Lemma (149), with 'PMOAT' replaced by 'MOAT'. □

We have now arrived at one of our principal destinations.

(155) **Theorem. Our MOATish mother.** Let T_1, T_2 be typologies over the same set of constraints. Then MOAT(T_1) ≅ MOAT(T_2) ⇒ $T_1 = T_2$.

Proof. Let U be a UVT such that U ⊨ MOAT(T_1). By Theorem (152), $U \in \mathcal{U}(T_1)$. But by Lemma (154), we also have U ⊨ MOAT(T_2), because MOAT(T_1) and MOAT(T_2) are isomorphic. Thus $U \in \mathcal{U}(T_2)$, also by (152). But U produces only one typology, so $T_1 = T_2$. □

Looked at contrapositively, this tells us that two distinct typologies cannot have isomorphic MOATs. Although the MOAT construction rests ultimately only on the border point structure of adjacent grammars and loses information about its particularities, this relatively impoverished source of information is sufficient to identify the leg content of every grammar in the typology.

4.7.3 VTs in their multitudes

MOAT(T) determines the structure of any UVT that yields T. It is ecologically typical, however, for a concrete OT system to sponsor many csets, each with its own VT, often an unbounded number, though of course every minimal universal support for T is finite. With the UVT results in hand, we now show that the MOAT also determines the behavior of the constraints within each of these VTs, though in the case of the order relation, not quite as strictly as in the single UVT.

□ Equivalence in EPO(C) entails that within every cset the constraint C will assign equal numerical values to the candidates belonging to the languages associated with C-equivalent grammars.

□ Order between two grammars in EPO(C) entails that within every cset the values assigned by constraint C will respect the non-strict version of the order between the candidates belonging to the languages associated with the C-ordered grammars. In short, the EPO relation $<^{\text{bp.C}}$ leads to numerical ≤ within individual csets, with the caveat that in any universal support – any collection of csets from which the typology may be derived – there must be at least one cset in which the order is strict.

□ From these results, it follows that the same may be said of the hypertransitive closure of the EPO order $<^{\text{htc.bp.C}}$. It must be respected in every VT as ≤, and within a universal support, some VT must instantiate it as < holding between optima belonging to the htc-related grammars.

To see why these properties hold, consider a set of VTs $\mathbb{V} = \{V_1,..., V_n\}$, each with columns indexed by the same set of constraints *S*.CON, which contains a universal support for some typology T. Every VT $V_i \in \mathbb{V}$ has concretely a set of candidates K_i which we take to be simply the rows of the VT. Thus, a VT V_i is regarded as a set of candidate violation profiles, or vectors with entries from $\mathbb{N}$. A sample from a *language* L of the typology T is a collection (or, for ease of book-keeping, a sequence) of candidates, in particular an element $(\mathbf{k}_1,...,\mathbf{k}_n) \in V_1 \times \cdots \times V_n$ which is such that there is a grammar G over *S*.CON which selects each candidate vector $\mathbf{k}_i \in V_i$ as optimal in V_i.

We can derive a UVT U from $\mathbb{V} = \{V_1,..., V_n\}$ by taking its Minkowski sum $\bigoplus\mathbb{V}$ and plucking out the harmonically bounded candidates. Recall that the sum of two vectors $\mathbf{x} + \mathbf{y}$ is a vector in which the ith component is the sum of the ith components of $\mathbf{x}$ and $\mathbf{y}$.

(156) **Vector sum**

$$(\mathbf{x} + \mathbf{y})[i] = \mathbf{x}[i] + \mathbf{y}[i]$$

The Minkowski sum of two *sets* of vectors A, X builds on this: it is a set of vectors that contains the vector sum of every vector in A with every vector in X.

(157) **Minkowski sum**

$$A \oplus X = \{\mathbf{a} + \mathbf{x} \mid \mathbf{a} \in A, \mathbf{x} \in X\}$$

In both cases, the higher-order notion of 'sum' inherits the basal properties of numerical addition, and thus immediately extends beyond pairs to arbitrary finite collections, so we can write e.g. $\bigoplus\mathbb{V} = V_1 \oplus \cdots \oplus V_n$ without fear of ambiguity.

Let's consider two UVT rows $\mathbf{a}^{\oplus}$, $\mathbf{x}^{\oplus} \in U$, where U is derived from $\bigoplus\mathbb{V}$, which we notate as follows, subscripting the summing VT rows (bolded) to indicate the VT they belong to.

$$\mathbf{a}^{\oplus} = \mathbf{a}_1 + \cdots + \mathbf{a}_n \qquad \mathbf{a}_i \in V_i$$
$$\mathbf{x}^{\oplus} = \mathbf{x}_1 + \cdots + \mathbf{x}_n \qquad \mathbf{x}_i \in V_i$$

The row $\mathbf{a}^{\oplus} \in U$ corresponds to the language in which rows (candidates) $\mathbf{a}_1,.., \mathbf{a}_n$ are optimal in each of their VTs $V_1,..., V_n$, and similarly for $\mathbf{x}^{\oplus}$. A constraint C assigns a value to each candidate, so that $C(\mathbf{a}_i)$, $C(\mathbf{x}_i)$ are the values assigned to candidates $\mathbf{a}_i$, $\mathbf{x}_i \in V_i$, appearing in the Cth column of the VT V_i. Put another way, the constraint function $C(\mathbf{a}_k)$ projects the Cth component of vector $\mathbf{a}_k$.

We first establish a key fact: any strict order on a given constraint C between two candidates inside a single V_i can be magnified so as to determine the UVT order relation on C between the entire languages they belong to, without affecting the grammatical structure of the typology.

(158) **Lemma. Inflation.** Let T be a typology over *S*.CON, and let $\mathbb{V} = \{V_1,..., V_n\}$ be a set of VTs over *S*.CON which contains a universal support for T. Let U be $\bigoplus V_i$ with all harmonically bounded rows removed, therefore a UVT for T. Let $u_a = \mathbf{a}^{\oplus}$, $u_x = \mathbf{x}^{\oplus}$ be rows of U, corresponding to G_a,

$G_x \in T$. Suppose for some $C \in S.\textsc{Con}$, $C(\mathbf{a}_1) > C(\mathbf{x}_1)$. Then there is a UVT U* for T such that $C(u^*_a) > C(u^*_x)$, where optimal u^*_a yields G_a and optimal u^*_x yields G_x.

Proof. Suppose that $C(\mathbf{a}_1) > C(\mathbf{x}_1)$ but $C(\mathbf{a}_1) + \cdots + C(\mathbf{a}_n) \leq C(\mathbf{x}_1) + \cdots + C(\mathbf{x}_n)$, so that in U, we have $C(\mathbf{a}^{\oplus}) \leq C(\mathbf{x}^{\oplus})$. We manipulate this expression to isolate the terms from V_1.

$$(C(\mathbf{a}_1) + \cdots + C(\mathbf{a}_n)) - ((C(\mathbf{x}_1) + \cdots + C(\mathbf{x}_n)) \leq 0$$
$$C(\mathbf{a}_1) - C(\mathbf{x}_1) + \cdots + C(\mathbf{a}_n) - C(\mathbf{x}_n) \leq 0$$
$$C(\mathbf{a}_1) - C(\mathbf{x}_1) \leq C(\mathbf{x}_2) - C(\mathbf{a}_2) + \cdots + C(\mathbf{x}_n) - C(\mathbf{a}_n)$$

Observe that the expression on the left-hand side of the last inequality is positive, because by assumption $C(\mathbf{a}_1) > C(\mathbf{x}_1)$. The Archimedean property of the integers ensure that there exists $n > 0$ such that

$$n{\cdot}(C(\mathbf{a}_1) - C(\mathbf{x}_1)) > C(\mathbf{x}_2) - C(\mathbf{a}_2) + \cdots + C(\mathbf{x}_n) - C(\mathbf{a}_n)$$

Running through the manipulations in reverse, we arrive at the following:

$$(*)\ n{\cdot}C(\mathbf{a}_1) + \cdots + C(\mathbf{a}_n) > n{\cdot}C(\mathbf{x}_1) + \cdots + C(\mathbf{x}_n)$$

Now consider the typology T* derived from the collection of VTs $\mathbb{V}^*$ obtained by replacing V_1 in $\mathbb{V}$ by $n{\cdot}V_1$, the matrix in which all values of $\mathbb{V}$ are multiplied by n. (Equivalently, one may think of $\mathbb{V}^*$ as expanding $\mathbb{V}$ by adding $n - 1$ copies of V_1 to it, which clearly does not affect the typology.) In either case, the set of grammars is clearly unchanged, so that $T = T^*$.

Now construct a UVT U* from the Minkowski sum $\bigoplus\mathbb{V}^*$ by removing all harmonically bounded rows. Because $T = T^*$, we have $G_a, G_x \in T^*$, and the candidates from $\mathbb{V}^*$ that belong to the associated languages are exactly the same except in the case of the replacement for V_1, where their values have been multiplied by n. The relevant sums that appear in the UVT U* are as in (*) above, from which it is clear that $C(u^*_a) > C(u^*_x)$, as desired. □

From this lemma, we may immediately derive the effects of EPO relations on the individual VTs that are derived from an OT system.

First, we are guaranteed that EPO equivalence $\sim^{bp.C}$ forces numerical equality on C in every VT of the system. This follows because the only way we can achieve equality in all the UVTs of the typology is to have equality in all the VTs.

(159) **Theorem. Equivalence respected.** Let $T = \{G_k\}$ be a typology over $S.\textsc{Con}$. Suppose that in EPO(C) for some $C \in S.\textsc{Con}$, we have $G_i \sim^{bp.C} G_j$ for some $G_i, G_j \in T$. Let V be any VT allowed by S, where **a** is a candidate of V that is optimal under G_i and **x** is a candidate of V that is optimal under G_j. Then $C(\mathbf{a}) = C(\mathbf{x})$.

Proof. Because by assumption $G_i \sim^{bp.C} G_j$, we have by Lemma (132) that $C(u_i) = C(u_j)$ in every $U \in \mathcal{U}(T)$. Now consider a VT V in which the candidate $\mathbf{a} \in$ V is optimal under G_i and the candidate $\mathbf{x} \in$ V is optimal under G_j. Suppose for purposes of contradiction that $C(\mathbf{a}) \neq C(\mathbf{x})$. We may also suppose without loss of generality that $C(\mathbf{a}) > C(\mathbf{x})$. By the Inflation Lemma (158), we are assured of a $U^* \in \mathcal{U}(T)$ in which $C(u^*_i) > C(u^*_j)$, a contradiction. □

Second, we are guaranteed that the EPO order $<^{bp.C}$ requires numerical ≤ on C in every VT of the system. The only way to achieve a strict order in all UVTs of the typology is for it never to be reversed in any VT of the system.

(160) **Theorem. EPO order weakly respected.** Let T = $\{G_k\}$ be a typology over *S*.CON. Suppose that in EPO(C) for some C ∈ *S*.CON, we have $G_i <^{bp.C} G_j$ for some G_i, $G_j \in$ T. Let V be any VT allowed by S, where $\mathbf{a} \in$ V is a candidate of V that is optimal under G_i and $\mathbf{x} \in$ V is a candidate of V that is optimal under G_j. Then $C(\mathbf{a}) \leq C(\mathbf{x})$.

Proof. Because by assumption $G_i <^{bp.C} G_j$ in EPO(C), we have by Lemma (133) that $C(u_i) < C(u_j)$ in every $U \in \mathcal{U}(T)$. Now consider a VT V allowed by the system in which the candidate **a** is optimal under G_i and the candidate **x** is optimal under G_j. Suppose for purposes of contradiction that $C(\mathbf{a}) > C(\mathbf{x})$. By the Inflation Lemma (158), we have a $U^* \in \mathcal{U}(T)$ in which $C(u^*_i) > C(u^*_j)$, a contradiction. □

We can go one step further: if $G_i <^{bp.C} G_j$, then there is at least one VT in every universal support for T in which this inequality is instantiated as <, with C assigning to the candidate optimal under G_i a value strictly less than the value it assigns to the candidate optimal under G_j.

(161) **Corollary. Inevitability of the strict.** Let $\mathbb{V} = \{V_m\}$ be any set of VTs providing a universal support for a typology T = $\{G_k\}$ over a constraint set *S*.Con. Suppose that in EPO(C) for some C ∈ *S*.CON, $G_i <^{bp.C} G_j$. Then there is a $V \in \mathbb{V}$ in which there are rows v_i, v_j, rendered optimal by G_i and G_j respectively, such that $C(v_i) < C(v_j)$.

Proof. Let U be a UVT derived from $\bigoplus\mathbb{V}$ by removal of harmonically bounded rows. Suppose $G_i <^{bp.C} G_j$ for some G_i, $G_j \in$ T. From Theorem (160) 'EPO order weakly respected' we have in every $V \in \mathbb{V}$ that $C(\mathbf{v}_i) \leq C(\mathbf{v}_j)$, for $\mathbf{v}_i$, $\mathbf{v}_j$ optimal under G_i, G_j respectively. Since $G_i <^{bp.C} G_j$ is instantiated in U as $C(u_i) < C(u_j)$, and since $C(u_i)$ is the sum of the C-values of all optima in $\mathbb{V}$ belonging to G_i, and similarly *mutatis mutandis* for $C(u_j)$, it cannot be that the relation ≤ on C-values is everywhere realized as equality. □

(162) **Theorem. HTC order respected.** Suppose G $<^{\text{htc.bp.C}}$ H. Then in any VT V, for $v_g \in G$, $v_h \in H$, $C(v_g) \leq C(v_h)$ and in some VT V, $C(v_g) < C(v_h)$.

Proof. If G $<^{\text{htc.bp.C}}$ H, there is an overlapping transitive chain between G and H of the form $G = G_1\ \mathcal{R}\ G_2, \ldots, G_{n-1}\ \mathcal{R}\ G_n = H$, consisting of grammars G_i, G_{i+1} related pairwise by either $\sim^{\text{bp.C}}$ or $<^{\text{bp.C}}$, where at least one relation $\mathcal{R}$ is $<^{\text{bp.C}}$, as guaranteed by Lemma (47). Now consider any VT V under T. The grammars in the chain all have optima in V. Apply Theorems (159) 'Equivalence Respected', (160) 'EPO order weakly respected' and Corollary (161) 'Inevitability of the strict' to these and note that inequality and equality are transitive among the integers. □

We have focused on relations that derive ultimately from border point pairs. It is natural to ask whether the analogous prefixal relations are manifested among the VTs of a concrete typology in the same way. And indeed they are. Note first that by Theorem (118), the order relation $<^{\text{htc.pr.C}}$ is identical to $<^{\text{htc.bp.C}}$, and by Theorem (96) the equivalence relation $\sim^{\text{pr.C}}$ is identical to $\sim^{\text{bp.C}}$. Thus everything true of the one is true of the other. We may immediately conclude that $\sim^{\text{pr.C}}$ is realized as numerical equality in every VT, and that $<^{\text{htc.pr.C}}$ is weakly respected as numerical ≤ everywhere and strictly respected as < somewhere.

What, then, of $<^{\text{pr.C}}$? The first observation to make is that any relation G$<^{\text{pr.C}}$H implies the existence of a hypertransitive overlapping chain of relations relating G and H via $<^{\text{bp.C}}$ and $\sim^{\text{bp.C}}$.

(163) **Lemma. PR order to BP order and equivalence.** Suppose G $<^{\text{pr.C}}$ H. Then there is a sequence $G = G_1\ \mathcal{R}\ G_2, \ldots\ G_{n-1}\ \mathcal{R}\ G_n = H$, where $\mathcal{R}$ is either $<^{\text{bp.C}}$ or $\sim^{\text{bp.C}}$ and at least one $\mathcal{R}$ is $<^{\text{bp.C}}$.

Proof. Suppose G $<^{\text{pr.C}}$ H. Then G $<^{\text{htc.pr.C}}$ H, by the definition (107) of $<^{\text{htc.pr.C}}$. But the relation $<^{\text{htc.pr.C}}$ is identical to the border-point-derived relation $<^{\text{htc.bp.C}}$. Therefore G $<^{\text{htc.bp.C}}$ H. But this means that there is an overlapping chain $G = G_1\ \mathcal{R}\ G_2, \ldots, G_{n-1}\ \mathcal{R}\ G_n = H$, where $\mathcal{R}$ is either $<^{\text{bp.C}}$ or $\sim^{\text{bp.C}}$ and at least one $\mathcal{R}$ is $<^{\text{bp.C}}$. □

We may now conclude that $<^{\text{pr.C}}$ is realized among VTs in exactly the same way as $<^{\text{bp.C}}$.

(164) **Theorem. PR order respected.** Suppose G $<^{\text{pr.C}}$ H. In any VT V under T, for $v_g \in G$, $v_h \in H$, optima respectively under G and H, $C(v_g) \leq C(v_h)$ and in some VT V, $C(v_g) < C(v_h)$.

Proof. Suppose G $<^{\text{pr.C}}$ H. By Lemma (163), there is an overlapping chain $G = G_1\ \mathcal{R}\ G_2, \ldots, G_{n-1}\ \mathcal{R}\ G_n = H$, where $\mathcal{R}$ is either $<^{\text{bp.C}}$ or $\sim^{\text{bp.C}}$ and at least one $\mathcal{R}$ is $<^{bp.C}$. Now consider numerical relations in any VT V among the candidates $v_i \in V$ optimal under the various $G_i \in T$. Each $\mathcal{R}$ in the chain requires either numerical equality if $\mathcal{R}$ is $\sim^{bp.C}$, by Theorem (159), or numerical $\leq$ if $\mathcal{R}$ is $<^{bp.C}$, by Theorem (160). Clearly, by hypertransitive inference among the integers, $v_g \leq v_h$ for v_g optimal under G and v_h optimal under H. Further, by Corollary (161), for some pair G_j, G_{j+1} in the chain, there must be some VT V in which $v_j < v_{j+1}$, and in that VT, the chain of bp relations sustains the inequality, leading to $v_g < v_h$. □

Let's look at an EST example that makes the force of these results clear. Recall the m.Ons EPO, repeated here from (27), §3.2.

(165) EPO(m.Ons) of EST

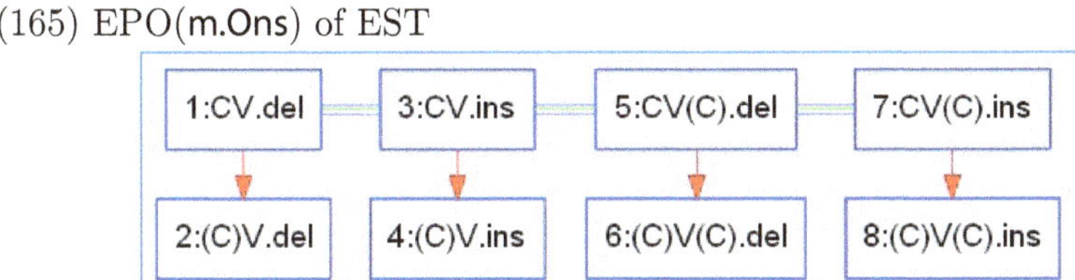

From Theorem (159) 'Equivalence Respected', we know that in every EST candidate set, no matter how complex the input, the optima belonging to the languages of the OR grammars 1-3-5-7 (top row) must have equal values assigned by m.Ons, because those grammars are all equivalent under $\sim^{bp.Ons}$ (and of course, therefore, $\sim^{pr.Ons}$).

The behavior of the CV (OR) optima from 1-3-5-7 with respect to the (C)V (OLA) optima from grammars 2-4-6-8 is somewhat more subtle. Consider the EPO order relation 3:CV.ins $<^{bp.Ons}$ 4:(C)V.ins (left of center). It is emphatically *not* the case that the optimal 3:CV.ins candidate in a given candidate set must always receive from m.Ons a value strictly less than the optimal 4:(C)V.del candidate.

For example, every language must contend with the input /C/. It has only two optimal outputs, [CV] in the insertional regime, and ε (the empty string) when deletion is optimal. Since 3:CV.ins and 4:(C)V.ins are both insertional, they share the output [CV] and thus, rather trivially, their optima (i.e. shared optimum) in the /C/ candidate set will be evaluated identically, in particular by m.Ons. By Theorem (160) 'EPO order weakly respected', the optimum from OR.ins must be *less than or equal to* that from OLA. del on m.Ons in every candidate set. From input /C/, we have equality. Theorem (160) also establishes that in some candidate set the OR.del optimum will be strictly less than the OLA.del optimum on m.Ons. The input /V/ supplies an example. In any OR grammar, the optimal output is [CV], earning a perfect score on m.Ons, while its more faithful but onsetless OLA competitor [V] trails strictly behind at 1.

The EPO relations do not, of course, tell the whole ordering story without further construction. The grammars **3:CV.ins** and **2:(C)V.del** are noncomparable on $<^{\text{bp.Ons}}$. Therefore respecting the EPO order, as per Theorem (160), does not constrain the numerics associated with their optima. In particular, noncomparability on $<^{\text{bp.Ons}}$, taken in isolation, allows the avatars of **3:CV.ins** and **2:(C)V.del** to stand in any numerical relation whatever. But hypertransitive inference, as enabled by $<^{\text{htc.bp.Ons}}$, taken together with Theorem (162) 'HTC order respected', ensures that because **3:CV.ins** $<^{\text{htc.bp.Ons}}$ **2:(C)V.del**, we will in fact always find, in every VT associated with EST, that the optimum in the language of **3:CV.ins** receives from m.Ons a value less than or equal to that of the **2:(C)V.del** optimum, and in some VT a value strictly less. More generally, with respect to m.Ons, Theorem (162) guarantees that VT by VT, *every* OR grammar (first row of the EPO diagram) will be associated with an optimum that m.Ons evaluates as less than or equal to, and in some VT strictly less than, the optimum from any OLA grammar (second row).

A final observation about order and equivalence among the concrete. Let's turn the focus from relations between grammars to relations between entire languages. Represent a language as a list of optima $\mathbf{L}_i \in V_1 \times \cdots \times V_i \times \cdots$, where the V_i are VTs thought of as sets of labeled violation profiles. The EPO/PEO equivalence and the htcEPO/htcPEO hypertransitive closure of the order relation on grammars are directly related to the familiar *componentwise* order and equality relations[14] on their associated languages.

Relations between vectors can be defined through relations on their corresponding components. To make it clear that these vectorial relations are different from ordinary numerical = and <, we write $=_{\text{comp}}$ and $<_{\text{comp}}$. We are interested in two such relations, writing x_i for the ith component of $\mathbf{x} = (x_1, \ldots)$.

i. Equality. $\mathbf{x} =_{\text{comp}} \mathbf{y}$ iff for all i, $x_i = y_i$.
ii. Componentwise Order. $\mathbf{x} <_{\text{comp}} \mathbf{y}$ iff for all i, $x_i \leq y_i$ and for some j, $x_j < y_j$.

In the case of EPO relations with respect to some constraint C, we will be dealing with the values assigned by C to each of the optima in the language

[14] The componentwise order is also known as the product order or coordinatewise order. See Product order, Wikipedia.

and comparing those, VT by VT, with the values assigned by C to the optimum from a different language.

A language $\mathbf{L}_j$ consists of a list of candidates ($\mathbf{q}_1$,...), each from its own candidate set, each optimal under $G_j \in T$, so that we may write $\mathbf{q}_1 = G_j(V_1)$, the result of filtering V_1 by any leg of G_j, and so on for the other VTs sponsored by the inputs allowed by *S*.GEN.

A candidate $\mathbf{q}_i$ is a row in V_i, a vector of non-negative integers, with one component for each constraint in *S*.CON. In comparing two languages with respect to C, we are interested in the values that C assigns in each VT to each optimum in the languages. For a candidate $\mathbf{q}_i$, we may write this value as $C(\mathbf{q}_i)$, that is, the Cth component of the vector $\mathbf{q}_i$, that is $C(G_j(V_i))$. From this point of view, given a language $\mathbf{L}_j = (\mathbf{q}_1,...)$, to ascertain its order relations with respect to constraint C, we are concerned with the vector $C(\mathbf{L}_j) = (C(\mathbf{q}_1), C(\mathbf{q}_2),...)$. Given a competing language $\mathbf{L}_k = (\mathbf{z}_1, ...)$, its behavior on C is given by $C(\mathbf{L}_k) = (C(\mathbf{z}_1), C(\mathbf{z}_2),...)$. The componentwise relations we seek are just $=_{comp}$ and $<_{comp}$ between the vectors $C(\mathbf{L}_j)$ and $C(\mathbf{L}_k)$, which depend on the numerical relations between $C(\mathbf{q}_i)$ and $C(\mathbf{z}_i)$, for all *i*.

In this discussion, since $\sim^{bp.C}$ and $\sim^{pr.C}$ are identical, we emphasize their identity by writing $\sim^{C}$, omitting the prefix that distinguishes the indistinguishable. Similarly, since $<^{htc.bp.C}$ and $<^{htc.pr.C}$ are identical, we write $<^{htc.C}$ for the one relation that they both denote.

With the notation in place, we may see how the componentwise relations follow from the EPO and PEO relations, and their hypertransitive closures.

Equality & Equivalence. For $G_j, G_k \in T$, if $G_j \sim^C G_k$, then Theorem (159) 'Equivalence Respected' guarantees that in every VT associated with T, the optima associated with G_j and G_k will have equal values on C. At the whole language level, this is the content of $C(\mathbf{L}_j) =_{comp} C(\mathbf{L}_k)$, namely that in every VT V_m under T, $C(\mathbf{q}_m) =_{comp} C(\mathbf{z}_m)$.

Order. If $G_j <^{htc.C} G_k$, then by Theorem (162) 'HTC order respected', in every VT V_m under T, $C(\mathbf{q}_m) \leq C(\mathbf{z}_m)$ and in some VT V_n, we must have $C(\mathbf{q}_n) < C(\mathbf{z}_n)$. At the language level, this is exactly the meaning of $C(\mathbf{L}_j) <_{comp} C(\mathbf{L}_k)$. Similar remarks may be made about $<^{bp.C}$ and $<^{pr.C}$.

It is natural to think of going in the opposite direction, arguing from equality and componentwise order on languages in some system *S* to EPO and PEO relations on grammars, but the potential idiosyncrasies of concrete *S*.GEN stand in the way. Consider the observation, evident in the m.Ons EPO, that the *OLA* languages (bottom row) are noncomparable to each other in the m.Ons order $<^{bp.Ons}$, and notice that this is also true for its hypertransitive closure $<^{\text{htc.bp.Ons}}$. Nevertheless, it can be shown that in any VT of EST, the optima associated with the OLA languages all receive exactly the same value on m.Ons.[15] By contrast, the optima of the OR languages also receive exactly the same value, namely 0. So both show equality across all VTs. Yet, in the case of the OR languages, this reflects equivalence of grammars on m.Ons, while in the OLA case it reflects only the restrictions on EST.GEN and the way they interact with the definition of m.Ons.

Contrast this concrete situation with the behavior of the UVT. Because a UVT for T owes nothing to T.GEN and is responsible only to the grammars of T, it can be shown that noncomparability always entails that the full range of numerical relations will show up in somewhere in $\mathcal{U}$(T).[16] The summative character of the UVT, which compresses the information in a universal support into a single VT, supports the strong instantiation theorems that go in every UVT from strict orders $<^{\text{bp.C}}$, $<^{\text{pr.C}}$, $<^{\text{htc.C}}$ to the numerical strict order $<$, crucial to the large-scale argument developed here.

We conclude by observing that, for a given typology T comprised of k grammars, if any collection of csets both gives rise to k grammars and obeys the order and equivalence restrictions of theorems in this section, then it will also produce T, and is thus guaranteed to be a universal support for T. This is because, as is easy to show, the Minkowski sum of these csets instantiates MOAT(T), and therefore, by the Theorem 'Instantiating the MOAT' (152), yields T.

4.7.4 Summary

We have now found three objects that uniquely characterize a typology: the set of filtration patterns of a UVT; the PMOAT, which is built from the prefixal relations; and the MOAT, which is built from relations derived from border point pairs.

According to Theorem (85) 'Converse of Filtration Uniformity,' for U, V two UVTs over the same constraint set T.CON, if their filtration patterns are identical, then $T_U = T_V$.

Theorem (150) 'Prefixal Characterization' deals with isomorphic PMOATs. The PMOATs of two typologies are isomorphic, written using the symbol ≅, if there is a bijection identifying the grammars of the typologies

---

[15] This is the number of 'problematic' vowels in the input, those V which are either string-initial or stand after V. In an OLA language, each of these appears in an onsetless syllable in the output, because faithfulness breach is banned.

[16] See the discussion of the m.Ons in EST in §3.1 for an example of this effect.

which respects the relations of the PMOAT in both directions. For two such typologies T_1, T_2, if PMOAT(T_1) ≅ PMOAT(T_2), then $T_1 = T_2$.

Theorem (155) deals with MOATs that are isomorphic in the same sense. For any T_1, T_2 which are typologies over the same set of constraints. If MOAT(T_1) ≅ MOAT(T_2), then $T_1 = T_2$.

Of these, perhaps the last is most intriguing because of its localistic character. A UVT expresses the relationship of every grammar in a typology to every other. The PMOAT relations are defined from a perspective in which all legs of the grammars are available for inspection. The MOAT, by contrast, is built from the information derived only from the border where one grammar meets an adjacent neighbor.

Precisely because of its localism, the MOAT alone determines licit coarsenings of the underlying typology. In the next section, we show that this property of the MOAT leads to the exact conditions under which a partition is a typology.

4.8 Acyclicity and general partitions of Ord(*S*.Con)

'I was lucky in the order...'
– Will Munny

Section contents

We now shift to a broader perspective, starting from general partitions of Ord(*S*.Con) rather than the partitions that derive from UVTs. This allows us ask, with border-point-based relations in mind, which of these general partitions are *typologies*. Crucial to the answer is the fact that the notion 'border point pair' has exactly the same definition in the general case as in the special typological subcase: thus the entire apparatus of border-point-based relations carries over to general partitions. For details, see §4.4.

Given a partition π of Ord(*S*.Con), we have base relations $\prec^{\pi.bp.C}$ and $\equiv^{\pi.bp.C}$, with their transitive (and in the case of $\equiv^{\pi.bp.C}$, reflexive) closures $<^{\pi.bp.C}$ and $\sim^{\pi.bp.C}$, from which may be defined the hypertransitive relation $<^{\pi.htc.bp.C}$. We use the same symbols here, and the $\sim^{\pi.bp.C}$ relation is indeed an equivalence, but crucially there is no guarantee that the general relations denoted $<^{\pi.bp.C}$ and $<^{\pi.htc.bp.C}$ have any desirable properties, in particular those of order.

These border-point-based relations are gathered into structures that parallel the EPO and the MOAT. For convenience, we repeat the definitions.

(166) **Definition (60). GEPO$_\pi$(C).** For a partition π of Ord(S.Con), with C ∈ *S*.Con,

$$\text{GEPO}_\pi(\text{C}) =_{\text{df}} \langle \pi, <^{\pi.bp.C}, \sim^{\pi.bp.C} \rangle.$$

(167) **Definition (61). GMOAT(π).** For a partition π of Ord(*S*.Con),

$$\text{GMOAT}(\pi) =_{\text{df}} \{\text{GEPO}_\pi(\text{C}) | \text{ C} \in S.\text{Con}\}.$$

The hypertransitively closed versions of these structures are defined as follows.

(168) **Definition (62). Hypertransitive closure of GEPO$_\pi$(C).** Given a partition π of Ord(*S*.Con), the hypertransitive closure of GEPO$_\pi$(C), denoted htcGEPO$_\pi$(C) is given by

$$\text{htcGEPO}_\pi(\text{C}) =_{\text{df}} \langle \pi, <^{\pi.htc.bp.C}, \sim^{bp.C} \rangle.$$

(169) **Definition (63). Hypertransitive closure of the GMOAT.** Given a partition π of Ord(*S*.Con), the hypertransitive closure of GMOAT(π), denoted htcGMOAT(π) is given by

$$\text{htcGMOAT}(\pi) =_{\text{df}} \{\text{htcGEPO}_\pi(\text{C}) \mid \text{C} \in S.\text{Con}\}.$$

With these in hand, we define the key notion 'acyclic GEPO'.

(170) **Definition. Acyclic GEPO.** GEPO(C) is *acyclic* if the htcGEPO(C) relation $<^{\pi.htc.bp.C}$ is a partial order.

Behind this usage is the graphical notion of a cycle, as seen in the discussion of bigraph representation of the EPO and GEPO, as in ex. (40), §1.3.3 above, or in ex. (23), §6.2.1, and ex. (29), §6.2.2 below. A cycle is a sequence of relations running from any arbitrary G_1 back to itself, namely $G_1 \mathcal{R} G_2$, $G_2 \mathcal{R} \cdots \mathcal{R} G_1$, where each $\mathcal{R}$ is either $<^{\pi.htc.bp.C}$ or $\sim^{\pi.bp.C}$ and at least one is $<^{\pi.htc.bp.C}$. Because the hypertransitive relation $<^{\pi.htc.bp.C}$ is based on relations $<^{bp.C}$ and $\sim^{bp.C}$ in the way it is, any such cycle may be expanded to a chain of relations involving $\sim^{bp.C}$ and the basic GEPO/EPO relation $<^{bp.C}$, as shown in Lemma (47). Thus, any hypertransitive cycle containing $<^{\pi.htc.bp.C}$ and $\sim^{\pi.bp.C}$ will correspond to a similar, perhaps longer cycle containing $<^{\pi.bp.C}$ and $\sim^{\pi.bp.C}$, and therefore appear in the bigraph representation as a graphical cycle, a sequence of nodes starting out from a node and returning to it, where the nodes are connected by edges that are either undirected (represented as =) or directed (→), with at least one directed edge in the sequence.

The partial order requirement rules out cycles because $<$ is asymmetric.[17] Observe that the acyclicity of htcGEPO(C) implies that the GEPO relation $<^{\pi.bp.C}$ is itself a partial order, since it is transitive by definition and contained in the $<^{\pi.htc.bp.C}$ order, therefore asymmetric.

We will say that a GMOAT is acyclic if all of its GEPOs are acyclic.

(171) **Definition. Acyclic GMOAT.** GMOAT(π) is acylic if for every C, $GEPO_\pi(C)$ is acyclic.

These notions allow us to state the thesis we will establish.

(172) **Thesis. Acyclicity is all.** For a partition π, if GMOAT(π) is acyclic, then π is a typology and GMOAT(π) is its MOAT.

While the occurrence of cycles in GMOAT(π) is obviously a fatal obstruction to a connection with OT filtration, which crucially uses the asymmetry of $<$, it is somewhat remarkable that nothing more is required than the absence of cycles: that acyclicity of GMOAT(π) is sufficient for π to be a typology and for GMOAT(π) to be its MOAT.

Crucial to the argument is the *instantiation* of each $GEPO_\pi(C)$, and therefore of GMOAT(π) and htcGMOAT(π). As with the EPO in (35), and similarly for other similar structures, we will say that an acyclic $GEPO_\pi(C)$ is instantiated by a certain function when that function instantiates *both*

---

[17] In the non-strict version $\leq$ of a partial order, $A \leq B$ and $B \leq A$ implies $A = B$, ruling out a (non-trivial) cycle.

of its relations appropriately: $\sim^{\pi.\text{bp.C}}$ as $=$ and $<^{\pi.\text{bp.C}}$ as $<$. When working with a general partition π, we have no UVT U to call on to generate π, and therefore no function $\text{C} \circ \text{g}_\text{U}$ to provide instantiation. But acyclicity allows us to re-create instantiation in a VT in this more general context, and from that we will proceed in the usual way from an instantiating VT V to the typology T_V it produces, showing then that the partition of T_V is exactly the same as the π we started from.

Recall that any finite strict partial order can be instantiated as $<$, as noted in Remark (21), because any such order may be linearly extended to a strict total order. Since in any acyclic GEPO(C), $<^{\pi.\text{bp.C}}$ is a finite strict partial order, it can be instantiated as $<$. We now show how both GEPO relations can be instantiated by a single function, thereby instantiating the GEPO.

(173) **Lemma. Instantiability of GEPO.** Let π be a partition of Ord(*S*.Con). Let $\text{C} \in$ *S*.Con. If $\text{GEPO}_\pi(\text{C})$ is acyclic, it can be instantiated.

Proof. Let π be a partition of Ord(*S*.Con) and assume that $\text{GEPO}_\pi(\text{C})$ is acyclic, so that, by definition (170), the hypertransitively closed relation $<^{\pi.\text{htc.bp.C}}$ is a strict, finite partial order. By Remark (21), every strict finite partial order can be instantiated as $<$. Let $\text{h}_\text{C} : \pi \rightarrow \mathbb{N}$ be a function that instantiates the order relation $<^{\pi.\text{htc.bp.C}}$ of $\text{htcGEPO}_\pi(\text{C})$ as $<$. The function h_C also instantiates $<^{\pi.\text{bp.C}}$, a subset of $<^{\pi.\text{htc.bp.C}}$, but there's no guarantee that h_C instantiates the equivalence relation $\sim^{\pi.\text{bp.C}}$ as $=$, and h_C could very well give different values to blocks that are equivalent under the relation $\sim^{\pi.\text{bp.C}}$. Therefore we construct a new function f_C based on h_C that instantiates both relations.

For each equivalence class $[\text{B}] \subseteq \pi = \{\text{X} \in \pi \mid \text{X} \sim^{\pi.\text{bp.C}} \text{B}\}$, choose a representative element $\text{B} \in [\text{B}]$ and define $\text{f}_\text{C} : \pi \rightarrow \mathbb{N}$ by $\text{f}_\text{C}(\text{A}_i) = \text{h}_\text{C}(\text{B})$ for all $\text{A}_i \in [\text{B}]$. Claim: f_C instantiates both relations of the GEPO(C).

First, it is clear that the function f_C instantiates $\sim^{\pi.\text{bp.C}}$ as $=$.

Now, for some blocks $\text{A}_1, \text{A}_2 \in \pi$, suppose $\text{A}_1 <^{\pi.\text{bp.C}} \text{A}_2$. We want to show $\text{f}_\text{C}(\text{A}_1) < \text{f}_\text{C}(\text{A}_2)$. The block A_1 sits in some equivalence class $[\text{B}_1]$ and, using B_1 as the representative of the class, $\text{f}_\text{C}(\text{A}_1) = \text{h}_\text{C}(\text{B}_1)$. Similarly, for $\text{A}_2 \in [\text{B}_2]$, we have $\text{f}_\text{C}(\text{A}_2) = \text{h}_\text{C}(\text{B}_2)$, using B_2 as the representative of $[\text{B}_2]$. We want to establish the inequality in the expression

$$(*)\ \text{f}_\text{C}(\text{A}_1) = \text{h}_\text{C}(\text{B}_1) < \text{h}_\text{C}(\text{B}_2) = \text{f}_\text{C}(\text{A}_2).$$

By construction, $\text{B}_1 \sim^{\pi.\text{bp.C}} \text{A}_1$ and $\text{A}_2 \sim^{\pi.\text{bp.C}} \text{B}_2$. Therefore by hypertransitive inference from $\text{A}_1 <^{\pi.\text{htc.bp.C}} \text{A}_2$, which follows from the assumed $\text{A}_1 <^{\pi.\text{bp.C}} \text{A}_2$, we are licensed to conclude $\text{B}_1 <^{\pi.\text{htc.bp.C}} \text{B}_2$. But this means that $\text{h}_\text{C}(\text{B}_1) < \text{h}_\text{C}(\text{B}_2)$ because h_C was chosen to instantiate $<^{\text{htc.bp.C}}$. Therefore $\text{f}_\text{C}(\text{A}_1) < \text{f}_\text{C}(\text{A}_2)$ from (*), establishing that f_C instantiates $<^{\pi.\text{htc.bp.C}}$ as $<$ and therefore $<^{\pi.\text{bp.C}}$ as $<$.

Thus f_C instantiates both $\sim^{\pi.bp.C}$ and $<^{\pi.bp.C}$, and therefore instantiates $GEPO_\pi(C)$. □

Instantiation of an acyclic GMOAT(π), we will now show, supports standard OT filtration of a VT in a way that mirrors the prefixal filtration of π. The key concept behind filtration is *minimality*: at each step, accept the minimal, eject all others. Prefixal separation takes as input only the blocks that contain an order with a prefix P and, within those, distinguishes those blocks containing an order with a prefix PC from those lacking any such order. We will establish that this corresponds under instantiation to separating the numerically minimal from the nonminimal.

We repeat here the definitions relevant to prefixal separation, and then state the relevant notion of minimality, which narrows the familiar general concept of minimality on a function to the current context.

(174) **Definition (98). Separation of blocks.** A Prefix PC *separates* block B_i from block B_j iff $B_i, B_j \in P\langle\pi\rangle$ and $B_i \in PC\langle\pi\rangle$ while $B_j \notin PC\langle\pi\rangle$.

(175) **Definition (99). Separation of block sets.** Prefix PC *separates* the set $\mathbb{B}_1 = \{B_i\}$ from the set $\mathbb{B}_2 = \{B_j\}$ iff PC separates each $B_i \in \mathbb{B}_1$ from each $B_j \in \mathbb{B}_2$.

Now the relevant notion of minimality may be easily stated.

(176) **Definition. Minimal on f_C with respect to P.** Given a function $f_C: \pi \rightarrow \mathbb{N}$ that instantiates GEPO(C) and a prefix P, $A \in P\langle\pi\rangle$ is *minimal* on f_C with respect to P if and only if for all $B \in P\langle\pi\rangle$, $f_C(A) \leq f_C(B)$.

Under this definition, minimality and nonminimality have the following expected properties.

i. If blocks $A, B \in P\langle\pi\rangle$ are both minimal on f_C with respect to P, then $f_C(A) = f_C(B)$, because by the definition $f_C(A) \leq f_C(B)$ and $f_C(B) \leq f_C(A)$.
ii. If $A \in P\langle\pi\rangle$ is minimal and $B \in P\langle\pi\rangle$ is *not* minimal with respect to P, then $f_C(A) < f_C(B)$.

In this case, we can't have $f_C(A) = f_C(B)$ because then B would also be minimal, and we can't have $f_C(B) < f_C(A)$, because then A wouldn't be minimal.

As a preliminary step, we first establish the useful fact that instantiation of both $<^{\pi.bp.C}$ and $\sim^{\pi.bp.C}$ by a given function implies instantiation of $<^{\pi.htc.bp.C}$

by that same function. (Compare the argument in Lemma (143), made in the context of typological partitions.)

(177) **Lemma. Instantiation: GEPO ⇒ htcGEPO.** If f : $\pi \rightarrow \mathbb{N}$ instantiates $GEPO_\pi(C)$, then f instantiates $htcGEPO_\pi(C)$.

Proof. If f *instantiates* $GEPO_\pi(C)$, then f simultaneously instantiates $\sim^{\pi.bp.C}$ as $=$ and $<^{\pi.bp.C}$ as $<$. The equivalence relations in $htcGEPO_\pi(C)$ are the same as those in $GEPO_\pi(C)$, so f instantiates them as $=$.

Suppose $B_1 <^{\pi.htc.bp.C} B_2$ for some $B_1, B_2 \in \pi$. From the definition of hypertransitive closure, it is guaranteed by Lemma (47) that there is an overlapping chain of relations $B_1 = B_i\mathcal{R}...\mathcal{R}B_k = B_2$ where each $\mathcal{R}$ is either $<^{\pi.bp.C}$ or $\sim^{\pi.bp.C}$ and at least one is $<^{\pi.bp.C}$. Each $\mathcal{R}$ is instantiated by f as either $<$ or $=$, with at least one as $<$, so $f(B_1) < f(B_2)$, establishing that f instantiates $<^{\pi.htc.bp.C}$ as $<$. □

We now establish the crucial relation between prefixal filtration and numerical minimality in the instantiations of a GEPO.

The proof uses prefixal relations on the partition π, namely $<^{\pi.pr.C}$ and $<^{\pi.htc.pr.C}$, defined in (101) and (107) as the transitive and hypertransitive closures, respectively, of the base relation $\prec^{\pi.pr.C}$. When introduced, this relation was specifically defined on general rather than typological partitions.

(178) **Definition (100). Base separation relation $\prec^{pr.C}$.** Let $B_1, B_2 \in \pi$, a partition of Ord(S).

$B_i \prec^{pr.C} B_j$ if there a prefix P such that PC separates B_i from B_j.

The crucial connection with the border point relations of the GMOAT is at the level of hypertransitive closure, because $<^{\pi.htc.pr.C}$ and $<^{\pi.htc.bp.C}$ are identical, as shown in Theorem (118) 'HTC.BP = HTC.PR'. Nothing in the lemmas and theorems leading up to (118) depends on the partitions being typological, and therefore we may use them in the present context without qualification. Similarly, the equivalence relation $\sim^{\pi.pr.C}$ defined in (90) does not depend on any special properties of π, and thus is identical to the equivalence relation $\sim^{\pi.bp.C}$ by Theorem (97), which is explicitly stated in terms of general partitions.

(179) **Lemma. Acyclic GEPO: Separation Instantiation Minimality (SIM).** Let $GEPO_\pi(C)$ be acyclic and let $f_C : \pi \rightarrow \mathbb{N}$ be a function instantiating $GEPO_\pi(C)$. Given a prefix P and sets of blocks $\mathbb{A}, \mathbb{B} \subseteq \pi$ such that $\mathbb{A} \cup \mathbb{B} = P\langle\pi\rangle$, if PC separates the set $\mathbb{A}$ from the set $\mathbb{B}$, then each $A \in \mathbb{A}$ is minimal on f_C with respect to P and each $B \in \mathbb{B}$ is not minimal.

Proof. By the definition of minimality (176), this means that we must show that $f_C(A) < f_C(B)$ for $A \in \mathbb{A}$ and $B \in \mathbb{B}$, and that $f_C(A_i) = f_C(A_k)$ for all $A_i, A_k \in \mathbb{A}$.

Let $\mathbb{A} \cup \mathbb{B} = P\langle\pi\rangle$, and suppose PC separates $\mathbb{A}$ from $\mathbb{B}$, so that $\mathbb{A} = PC\langle\pi\rangle$ and $\mathbb{A} \cap \mathbb{B} = \emptyset$. Let f_C be an instantiating function for $GEPO_\pi(C)$, the existence of which is guaranteed by Lemma (173).

Suppose $A \in \mathbb{A}$ and $B \in \mathbb{B}$. Since PC separates A from B, we have prefixally $A <^{\pi.pr.C} B$ and thus $A <^{\pi.htc.pr.C} B$. From Theorem (115) 'HTC.PR to HTC.BP', we have therefore, among the border point-based relations, $A <^{\pi.htc.bp.C} B$. By Lemma (177) 'Instantiation: GEPO ⇒ htcGEPO', if a function instantiates GEPO(C), then it instantiates htcGEPO(C). Thus f_C instantiates $<^{\pi.htc.bp.C}$, and therefore $f_C(A) < f_C(B)$. This shows that B is not minimal.

Now consider any $A_i, A_j \in \mathbb{A}$. Since $A_i, A_j \in PC\langle\pi\rangle$, we have $A_i \sim^{\pi.pr.C} A_j$. By Theorem (97) 'Equality of Equivalences (General)', it follows that $A_i \sim^{\pi.bp.C} A_j$ and thus $f_C(A_i) = f_C(A_j)$.

Thus, for all $X \in P\langle\pi\rangle$, $f_C(A) \leq f_C(X)$, and therefore, by definition (176), A is minimal with respect to P. □

We note, but leave for the reader to pursue, that SIM (179) allows us to conclude, with a little further effort, that if f_C instantiates the GEPO relations $<^{\pi.bp.C}$ and $\sim^{\pi.bp.C}$, then it also instantiates the prefixal relations $<^{\pi.pr.C}$ and $\sim^{\pi.pr.C}$.

At this point, we have assembled all we need to make the transit from instantiation to filtration. First, we architect an appropriate instantiating VT from GMOAT(π), assuming acyclicity, then we show that its native typology is exactly the partition π.

The construction runs as follows. Suppose we have a partition $\pi = \{B_1,\ldots, B_m\}$ with an acyclic GMOAT and a set of instantiating functions $f_C : \pi \rightarrow \mathbb{N}$ as in Lemma (173), one for each $C \in S$.CON.

Let V have the same number of rows m as there are blocks in π, and the same number of columns as there are constraints in S.CON. The columns of V are labeled with the elements of S.CON, and the rows correspond 1:1 with the blocks of π. This gives us a bijection $b_V : \pi \rightarrow V$, paralleling the bijection $g_U : T \rightarrow U$ for $U \in \mathcal{U}(T)$. We notate the bijection by the same indexing scheme used for g_U, associating B_k with v_k, $1 \leq k \leq m$.

Now we define the entries in V. For each $C \in S$.Con and for each $B_k \in \pi$, let the entry of row $v_k = b_V(B_k)$ at column C be the numerical value $f_C(B_k) \in \mathbb{N}$. That is, $C(v_k) = f_C(B_k) = C \circ b_V(B_k)$. When we assert that a VT V *instantiates* the acyclic GMOAT(π), we are thus able to point to the function $C \circ b_V : \pi \rightarrow V \rightarrow \mathbb{N}$ just defined for each C, associating each block B_k with $C(v_k)$, as the instantiating function that licenses the usage.

At this point we have no assurance that a VT V instantiating GMOAT(π) has any special properties. For example, we don't even know whether it contains harmonically bounded rows. But independent of any relation with π, like any other VT, V produces a typology T_V generated from OT candidate filtration (64) by the members of Ord(*S*.CON) as applied to its rows.

The first step is to show that prefixal filtration of blocks (BF) is related to row filtration (RF) in much the same way that grammar filtration is related to row filtration in the realm of typologies. Recall that in Theorem (77) it is established that

GF ⇔ RF for $G_k \in T$, $u_k \in U$, $G_k \in P\langle T\rangle \Leftrightarrow u_k \in P[U]$

whereas here we need

BF ⇔ RF for $B_k \in \pi$, $v_k \in V$, $B_k \in P\langle \pi\rangle \Leftrightarrow v_k \in P[V]$.

The argument is somewhat simpler in the GF ⇔ RF case because we start out with $U \in \mathcal{U}(T)$, which ensures that 'No Dead Man Walking' (65) will allow us to proceed immediately from P to a full leg PQ. Here we only have instantiation to guide us, and we must proceed incrementally through filtration, one C at a time.

(180) **Lemma. Acyclic GMOAT: BF ⇔ RF.** Let $\pi = \{B_k\}$, $1 \le k \le m$, be a partition of *S*.CON with an acyclic GMOAT. Let V be a VT instantiating GMOAT(π). Let P be any sequence of distinct constraints in *S*.CON. For all $B_k \in \pi$, $B_k \in P\langle\pi\rangle$ if and only if $v_k \in P[V]$.

Proof. For each C ∈ *S*.CON, let $f_C : \pi \rightarrow \mathbb{N}$ be an instantiating function for C. Such a set of functions exists by Lemma 'Instantiability of GEPO' (173), since each GEPO(C) is acyclic. Let V be a VT with exactly one row v_k for each block $B_k \in \pi$, and one column C, for each C ∈ *S*.CON. Let the bijection $b_V : \pi \rightarrow V$ be given by $b_V(B_k) = v_k$. The entry of V at row v_k and column C is defined to be $f_C(B_k)$, so that $C(v_k) = C \circ b_V(B_k) = f_C(B_k)$.

We prove the theorem by induction on the length |P| of the prefix P.

Base step. |P| = 0.

LR. For some arbitrary C ∈ *S*.CON, consider any $B_k \in C\langle\pi\rangle$. Now, C separates a set of blocks $\mathbb{B} = C\langle\pi\rangle$ from $\pi\backslash\mathbb{B}$. Since $B_k \in \mathbb{B}$, by Lemma (179) 'Separation Instantiation Minimality' (SIM), B_k is numerically minimal on the instantiating function of C, namely $f_C = C \circ b_V$. Therefore, by the definition of candidate filtration (1), $v_k \in C[V]$.

RL. We prove the contrapositive: if, for any $B_k \in \pi$, $B_k \notin C\langle\pi\rangle$, then $v_k \notin C[V]$. Assume $B_k \notin C\langle\pi\rangle$. There is some block $B_i \in \pi$, $B_i \neq B_k$, such that $B_i \in C\langle\pi\rangle$, because some total order starts with C and must reside in some block of π. Then by SIM (179), B_i is minimal on f_C and B_k is not.

Putting it together, $C(v_i) = C \circ b_V(B_i) = f_C(B_i) < f_C(B_k) = C \circ b_V(B_k) = C(v_k)$. Therefore $v_k \notin C[V]$.

Induction step. For P with $|P| < n$, assume that $B_i \in P\langle\pi\rangle \Leftrightarrow v_i \in P[V]$ for all i, $1 \leq i \leq m$.

Let P be a prefix of length $n-1$ and C be an arbitrary constraint not in P. We show that the theorem holds for any prefix PC of length n.

LR. Consider any $B_k \in PC\langle\pi\rangle$. Observe that $B_k \in P\langle\pi\rangle$ by the telescoping property of prefixal filtration (74). By thc induction hypothesis, we have $v_k \in P[V]$, since for each block $B_i \in P\langle\pi\rangle$, we have $v_i \in P[V]$. Because $B_k \in PC\langle\pi\rangle$, it follows from SIM (179) that B_k is minimal on the instantiating function f_C among the $B_i \in P\langle\pi\rangle$. This means $C(v_k) = f_C(B_k) \leq f_C(B_i) = C(v_i)$ for all rows $v_i \in P[V]$. Thus, v_k is guaranteed to be minimal on C in P[V] if there are no other rows in P[V] besides those corresponding to blocks in $P\langle\pi\rangle$. By the induction hypothesis $v_i \in P[V] \Rightarrow B_i \in P\langle\pi\rangle$ for all v_i so that, as needed, every row in P[V] has its (unique) correspondent in $P\langle\pi\rangle$. Therefore, $v_k \in PC[V]$.

RL. We prove the contrapositive, $B_k \notin PC\langle\pi\rangle \Rightarrow v_k \notin PC[V]$. Consider any $B_k \notin PC\langle\pi\rangle$. There are two cases. i. If $B_k \notin P\langle\pi\rangle$, then by the induction hypothesis, $v_k \notin P[V]$, and so $v_k \notin PC[V]$ by telescoping. ii. Now assume that $B_k \in P\langle\pi\rangle$. Then PC separates $PC\langle\pi\rangle$ from B_k because $B_k \notin PC\langle\pi\rangle$. By SIM (179), each block $B_i \in PC\langle\pi\rangle$ has the property that $f_C(B_i) < f_C(B_k)$. Therefore $C(v_i) < C(v_k)$. By the induction hypothesis, each $v_i \in P[V]$ and so $v_k \notin PC[V]$ because in filtration by PC it loses on C to each such v_i. □

As a side note, observe that the V constructed for this theorem has no harmonically bounded rows, and is therefore a UVT. Since a leg is a prefix, we have it directly that $B_k = \lambda\langle\pi\rangle \Rightarrow v_k = \lambda[V]$. But by definition of prefixal filtration, $B_k = \lambda\langle\pi\rangle$ iff $\lambda \in B_k$, because, $\lambda\langle\pi\rangle$ is the set of blocks containing λ, i.e. the one block of the partition π that contains λ. Thus $\lambda \in B_k \Rightarrow v_k = \lambda[V]$, and each row of V is selected as optimal by some leg of *S*.Con.

(181) **Theorem. GMOAT(π) acyclic ⇒ π is a typology.** Let π be a partition of Ord(*S*.Con). If GMOAT(π) is acyclic, then π is a typology.

Proof. Let V be a VT that instantiates GMOAT(π) in the way defined in Lemma (180). Let $T_V = \{G_j\}$ be the typology associated with V. Then we argue as follows:

1. $\lambda \in G_k \Leftrightarrow \lambda[V] = v_k$	Definition of grammar (5)
2. $v_k = \lambda[V] \Leftrightarrow B_k = \lambda\langle\pi\rangle$	Lemma 'Acyclic GMOAT: BF ⇔ RF' (180)
3. $B_k = \lambda\langle\pi\rangle \Leftrightarrow \lambda \in B_k$	Definition of prefixal filtration (67)
4. $\therefore \lambda \in G_k \Leftrightarrow \lambda \in B_k$.	[1], [2], [3]

Thus, $G_k = B_k$ for all k, and $\pi = T_V$. Since T_V is a typology, so is π. □

From this, we may conclude that an acyclic GMOAT is a MOAT.

(182) **Corollary. GMOAT to MOAT.** If GMOAT(π) is acyclic, then GMOAT(π) is MOAT(π).

Proof. Assume that GMOAT(π) is acyclic. By Theorem (181), π is a typology. Its GMOAT is therefore a MOAT. □

The main result follows immediately.

(183) **Theorema Egregium. Acyclic GMOAT ⇔ typology.** A partition π of Ord(*S*.Con) is a typology iff GMOAT(π) is acyclic.

Proof.

LR. If π is a typology, its GMOAT is a MOAT. Every MOAT is acyclic because the order relation of each htcEPO(C) is a partial order, as noted in Lemma (49). Therefore every EPO(C) in the MOAT is acyclic according to definition (170), and consequently the MOAT itself is acyclic, according to definition (171).

RL. If GMOAT(π) is acyclic, then π is a typology, as shown in Theorem (181). □

Worthy of note is the contrapositive formulation of the LR direction: if GMOAT(π) is *not* acyclic, then π is *not* a typology. Coarsening of a typology through union of grammars is faithfully represented by node merger in EPO bigraphs. From Theorem (183), it follows that when node merger induces cycles, the resulting coarsened partition has lost typological status.

4.9 Grammar at the edge: The ERC and the ERCoid

Section contents

The border point pairs of a typology determine its MOAT, and therefore all of its grammars indirectly through any instantiating UVT. But each individual grammar has its own border, independent of whatever typologies it sits in. A border point of a grammar G is a leg λ ∈ G such that some adjacent transposition within λ produces a leg $\lambda' \notin G$. An interior point is a leg $\mu \in G$ such that every such transposition within μ produces a leg in G. We explore here how the border points of a grammar determine the entire contents of the grammar without reference to its interior.

Border points, we propose, participate in an extended version of ERC representation, which in addition to the familiar values $\{W, L, e\}$ deploys a fourth value 'u' indicating lack of information. Fusion of ERCs, central to their logic, can be extended formally to the 4-valued 'ERCoid' by taking u to be the identity, displacing e from this role but retaining the rules for combining $\{W, L, e\}$ with each other. Under this assumption, the natural conjecture is that the Fusional Reduction Algorithm (FRed: Brasovenau & Prince 2005/11) can operate without modification on border point data, with the goal of yielding ERC grammars from sets of ERCoids. Proof of general efficacy is not extant as of this writing, but the approach is sufficiently promising to warrant discussion here.

4.9.1 Grammars from border points

Returning to our touchstone example, let's consider two different grammars from EST, which indicate how ERCoids emerge and combine.

First, consider 1:CV.del, extensionally describable as onset required, coda prohibited, and all faithfulness breaches by deletion, concisely OR.CP.del.

(184) 1:CV.del

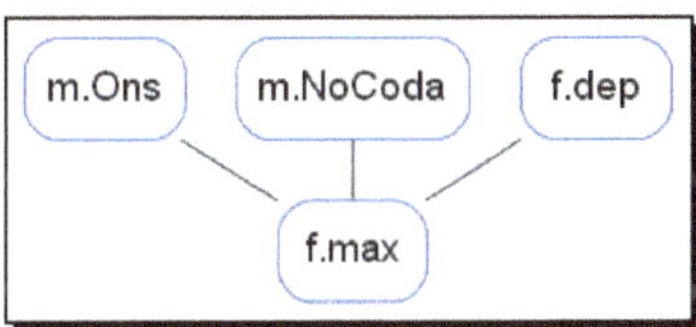

(185) ERC grammar of 1:CV.del in MIB/SKB form

m.Ons	m.NoCoda	f.dep	f.max
W			L
	W		L
		W	L

This grammar – like all the grammars of EST, see diagram (7), §7.2 – is adjacent to three other grammars. These are:

2:(C)V.del	OLA.CP.del
3:CV.ins	OR.CP.ins
5:CV(C).del	OR.CA.del

Each of these differs from 1:CV.del (OR.CP.del) along one extensional dimension.

For convenience, we give them all here as Hasse diagrams.

(186) Grammars adjacent to 1:CV.del (Hasse)

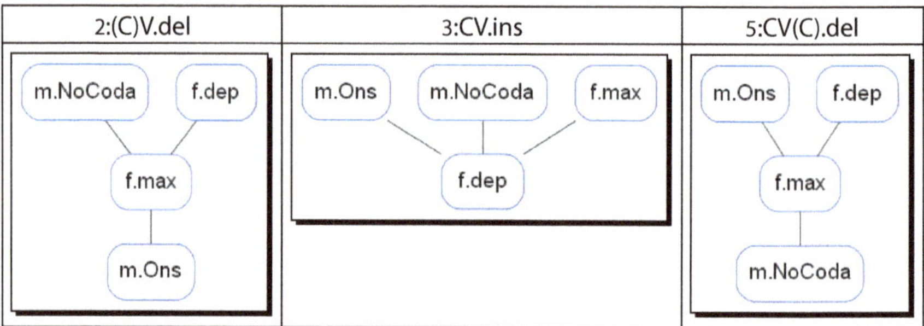

Anticipating the full geometric development of §7, we portray the adjacencies of 1:CV.del in a simple diagram, annotated to show the relevant transposition at the border. The transpositions involve f.max flipping with each of the other constraints in EST.Con, which are ranked above it in 1:CV.del, as may be seen in (185) and (186).

(187) A corner of EST

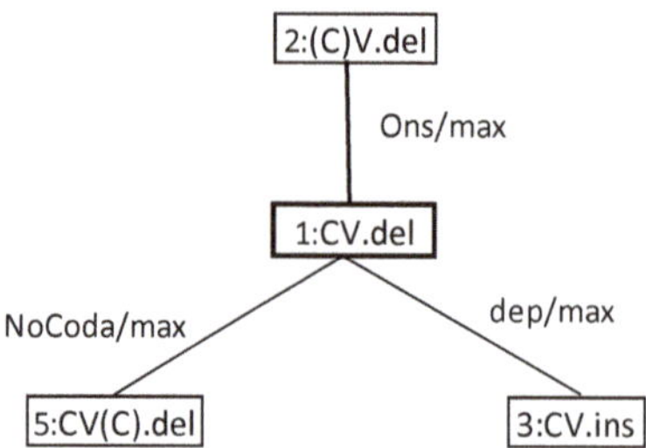

Each grammar adjacent to 1:CV.del (center) shares two border point pairs with it. Since the two differ only in the ordering of constraints in the prefix, they provide exactly the same information, and we show just one border point pair for each neighbor.

(188) Border point pairs of 1:CV.del

Grammar	P	X/Y		**Transposition**
1:CV.del	m.NoCoda ≫ f.dep ≫	*m.Ons*	≫ **f.max**	m.Ons / f.max
2:(C)V.del	m.NoCoda ≫ f.dep ≫	**f.max**	≫ *m.Ons*	
1:CV.del	m.Ons ≫ m.NoCoda ≫	*f.dep*	≫ **f.max**	f.dep / f.max
3:CV.ins	m.Ons ≫ m.NoCoda ≫	**f.max**	≫ *f.dep*	
1:CV.del	f.dep ≫ m.Ons ≫	*m.NoCoda*	≫ **f.max**	m.NoCoda / f.max
5:CV(C).del	f.dep ≫ m.Ons ≫	**f.max**	≫ *m.NoCoda*	

From the transposition in the pair (**1**, **2**), we obtain

$\mathbf{1} <^{\text{bp.Ons}} \mathbf{2}$

$\mathbf{2} <^{\text{bp.max}} \mathbf{1}$.

From its prefix, we obtain

$\mathbf{1} \sim^{\text{bp.NoCoda}} \mathbf{2}$

$\mathbf{1} \sim^{\text{bp.dep}} \mathbf{2}$.

All constraints are covered, so these facts translate directly into an ERC.

(189) BP-derived ERC: [**1**~**2**]

	m.Ons	m.NoCoda	f.dep	f.max
1:CV.del ~ 2:(C)V.del	W	*e*	*e*	L

Continuing in this vein, we derive two more ERCs from the other border pairs in (188). Putting everything together, we get the full grammar of 1:CV.del, which is exactly as in (185) above.

(190) BPP-derived grammar of 1:CV.del

	m.Ons	m.NoCoda	f.dep	f.max
1 ~ 2	W	*e*	*e*	L
1 ~ 5	*e*	W	*e*	L
1 ~ 3	*e*	*e*	W	L

In the case of 1:CV.del, the grammar emerges directly from border point analysis. In cases like that of 2:(C)V.del, by contrast, a subtlety arises and further interpretation is required. In particular, the constraint m.Ons ends up in the suffix of two of the three border point pairs, and suffixes provide no information.

The grammar 2:(C)V.del (OLA.CP.del) is adjacent to the following three grammars:

1:CV.del	OR.CP.del
4:(C)V.ins	OLA.CP.ins
6:(C)V(C).del	OLA.CA.del

For convenience of comparison, here are the relevant Hasse diagrams.

(191) Grammar of 2:(C)V.del (Hasse)

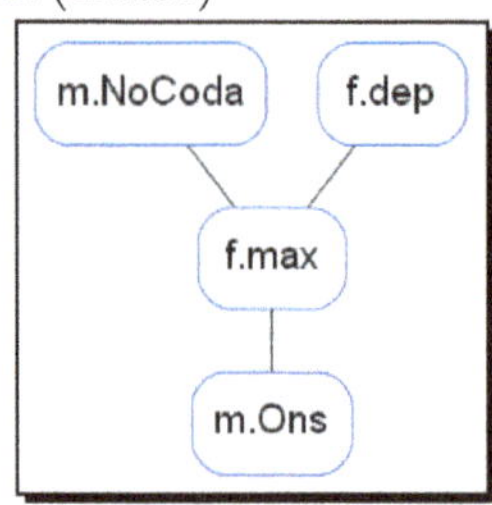

(192) Grammars adjacent to 2:(C)V.del (Hasse)

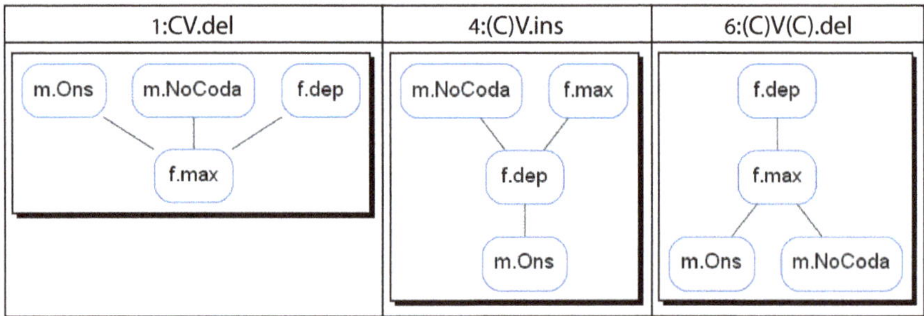

These are the adjacencies of 2:(C)V.del, with the associated transpositions.

(193) Another corner of EST

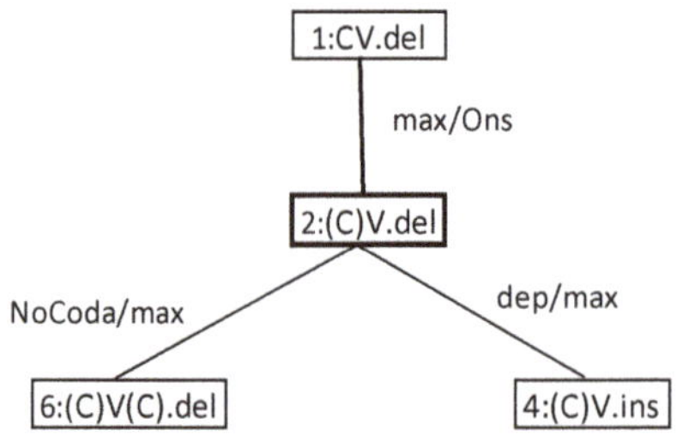

Grammars **2** and **1** meet at two border point pairs, differing only on the order of constraints within the prefix, so we show just one of them.

(194) Border point pair **2**/**1**

Grammar	P	X/Y	Transposition
2:(C)V.del	m.NoCoda ≫ f.dep ≫	*f.max* ≫ **m.Ons**	f.max / m.Ons
1:CV.del	m.NoCoda ≫ f.dep ≫	**m.Ons** ≫ *f.max*	

From this, we derive the ERC [**2** ~ **1**], the negation of [**1** ~ **2**].

(195) BP-derived ERC: [2 ~ 1]

	m.Ons	m.NoCoda	f.dep	f.max
2:(C)V.del ~ 1:CV.del	L	*e*	e	W

Grammars **4** and **6** share one border pair each with grammar **2**. In both cases, m.Ons falls in the suffix.

(196) BPPs {**2**, **4**}, {**2**, **6**}

Grammar	P	X/Y	Q	Transposition
2:(C)V.del	m.NoCoda ≫	*f.dep* ≫ **f.max**	≫ m.Ons	f.dep / f.max
4:(C)V.ins	m.NoCoda ≫	**f.max** ≫ *f.dep*	≫ m.Ons	
2:(C)V.del	f.dep	≫ *m.NoCoda*≫ **f.max**	≫ m.Ons	m.NoCoda / f.max
6:(C)V(C).del	f.dep	≫ **f.max** ≫ *m.NoCoda*	≫ m.Ons	

These two pairs yield only partial information: in particular, none about the relational structure associated with m.Ons. The pair {**2**, **4**}, for example, submits to the following interpretation:

i. The prefix consists solely of m.NoCoda, establishing $\mathbf{2} \sim^{\text{bp.NoCoda}} \mathbf{4}$.
ii. The transposition yields $\mathbf{2} <^{\text{bp.dep}} \mathbf{4}$ and $\mathbf{4} <^{\text{bp.max}} \mathbf{2}$.
iii. The suffix, where m.Ons resides, supplies no information.

To represent this state of affairs, we expand the vocabulary of comparison to include the fourth value 'u', which denotes the 'no information' case. The border point analysis of {**2**, **4**} yields the following 'ERCoid':

(197) ERCoid derived from border point pair {**2**, **4**}

	m.Ons	m.NoCoda	f.dep	f.max
2:(C)V.del ~ 4:(C)V.ins	u	*e*	W	L

The same mode of analysis, applied to {**2**, **6**}, produces the following:

(198) ERCoid derived from border points of **2** and **6**

	m.Ons	m.NoCoda	f.dep	f.max
2:(C)V.del ~ 6:(C)V(C).del	u	W	*e*	L

The entirety of the information in the border point relations of **2** is included in the following tableau:

(199) ERCoid tableau for 2:(C)V.del

BPPs	m.Ons	m.NoCoda	f.dep	f.max
2 ~ **1**	L	*e*	*e*	W
2 ~ **4**	u	*e*	W	L
2 ~ **6**	u	W	*e*	L

Locally, within the last two ERCoids, there is indeterminacy in the role of m.Ons, but globally no information is missing. The value u in the m.Ons column is accompanied by the ERC value L, which takes over. Here, because of the L, the two u's in m.Ons may be realized as *any* value from $\{W, L, e\}$. Whatever the choice, logical combination with [**2**~**1**] will always yield L.

It is not the case, however, that u can simply be replaced *salva veritate* by anything anywhere. It is specifically the L in the m.Ons column of (199) that liberates it. To see this, consider a 2-grammar typology T $=\{G, H\}$ of the Top/coTop form, based on the 3 constraints $\{A, B, C\}$. Let the grammar G be defined by the single ERC WWL (co-C-top), and H by the ERC LLW (C-top). G meets H in two border point pairs, (a) and (b).

(200) Border point pairs of T

Grammar	**X/Y**	**Q**	**Transposition**
G(a)	*A* ≫ **C**	≫ B	A/C
H(a)	**C** ≫ *A*	≫ B	
G(b)	*B* ≫ **C**	≫ A	B/C
H(b)	**C** ≫ *B*	≫ A	

These give rise to the following two ERCoids. Note that B is in the suffix of border point pair (a) and A is in the suffix of border point pair (b).

(201) BP-derived ERCoids

T	A	B	C
G(a) ~ H(a)	W	u	L
G(b) ~ H(b)	u	W	L

These must combine to give the ERC WWL, which characterizes G. Combination of W with u is the only source of disjunction in the transit from ERCoids to ERCs; an individual ERCoid has but one W. Observe that free replacement of u with values drawn from {W, L, *e*} does not give the desired result. If, for example, the u in constraint B were L, the resulting grammar would be A≫B≫C rather than G. If both u's were L, we'd have no grammar at all. If both were *e*, we'd have a *conjunction* of two ERCs, leading to 'A≫C *and* B≫C', instead of G = WWL = 'A≫C *or* B≫C'.

To integrate border point information correctly, we propose that ERCoids must be combined by fusion, just as ERCs are in the FRed algorithm (Brasoveanu & Prince 2005/2011). To do so, we need to take account of the behavior of u. Recall that the fusion of ERC values {W, L, *e*} works as follows (Prince 2002ab). (The symbol ∘ is borrowed from the standard representation of the logic RM3, which ERC logic sits within, and has nothing to do with the ∘ of function composition.)

(202) Fusion of ERC-logic values, $x \in \{\mathrm{W}, \mathrm{L}, e\}$

i. $\mathrm{L} \circ x = \mathrm{L}$ – L is dominant
ii. $x \circ x = x$ – fusion is idempotent (like *and* and *or*)
iii. $e \circ x = x$ – *e* is the identity

Fusion is symmetric, so that the order of fusands doesn't matter.

To bring u into the fold, we posit that u is the identity, displacing *e*. Note that $e \circ \mathrm{u} = e \neq \mathrm{u}$.

(203) Fusion of ERCoid values

iv. $\mathrm{L} \circ x = \mathrm{L}$ – L is dominant
v. $x \circ x = x$ – fusion is idempotent
vi. $e \circ x = x$ for $x \in \{\mathrm{W}, \mathrm{L}, \mathrm{e}\}$ – *e* is an identity for ERC values
vii. $\mathrm{u} \circ x = x$ – u is the identity for all values

If we think of fusion as delivering the maximal element of the fusing pair, as determined by an auxiliary scale of values, then standard ERC fusion operates on the scale $e < \mathrm{W} < \mathrm{L}$. In the ERCoid extension of this mode of combination, we merely append u to the bottom, so that the augmented fusion scale is u < e < W < L. This allows for a concise definition: $x \circ y = y$ iff $x \leq y$.

We hypothesize that with these extensions, FRed runs in its familiar way. For this to work properly, it must be the case that the fusions produced by FRed never contain u: every u must be absorbed into some ERC value {W, L, e}, a phenomenon we will refer to as 'ERCoid confinement'. In the end, nothing compares to 'u'. Of course, the success of FRed over ERCoids requires proof, yet to be obtained.

If this is right, the definition of FRed persists unchanged. In particular, an 'Info Loss Configuration' in FRed is still defined to be a column fusing to W which contains e as well as W. This definition is retained without modification. Thus, a column containing u and W without e is *not* an Info Loss Configuration, as is shown in ex. (201). Qualitatively speaking, fusion of u and W does not lose information about a constraint, since there is no information in u to be lost.

To see this in action, let's apply FRed to the complete set of BP-derived ERCoids associated with the border of 2:(C)V.del. Recall that an Info Loss Configuration brings with it an 'Info Loss Residue', the set of rows within it bearing e, which must be further scrutinized.

FRed

Step 1: Fuse all.

Result: LWWL. Status of fusion: entailed by ILRs {a, b, c}, {a, b, d}.

ERC		m.Ons	m.NoCoda	f.dep	f.max
a	**2 ~ 1** (a)	L	*e*	*e*	W
b	**2 ~ 1** (b)	L	*e*	*e*	W
c	**2 ~ 4**	u	*e*	W	L
d	**2 ~ 6**	u	W	*e*	L
a ∘ b ∘ c ∘ d		**L**	**W**	**W**	**L**

We have two Info Loss Configurations, the columns of m.NoCoda and f.dep. Associated with them are two *Info Loss Residues* (ILRs), sets of ERCs whose content not preserved in the fusion of the whole:

ILR_1 = {a, b, c}, with e in m.NoCoda,

ILR_2 = {a, b, d}, with e in f.dep.

Since these collectively include every ERCoid {a, b, c, d}, their fusion $f\{\text{ILR}_1 \cup \text{ILR}_2\}$ = a ∘ b ∘ c ∘ d entails the fusional result of the first step, by virtue of being identical to it. We therefore dismiss the first step's uninformative (entailed) fusion and proceed to examine each ILR separately.

Step 2a. ILR_1 {a, b, c}

ERC		m.Ons	m.NoCoda	f.dep	f.max
a	**2 ~ 1** (a)	L	*e*	*e*	W
b	**2 ~ 1** (b)	L	*e*	*e*	W
c	**2 ~ 4**	u	*e*	W	L
a ∘ b ∘ c		**L**	***e***	**W**	**L**

The new $ILR_{1.1}$ here is {a, b}, which consists of identical ERCs. Thus $f(ILR_{1.1})$ = a ∘ b = a = b = L*ee*W, which doesn't entail $f(ILR_1)$ = a ∘ b ∘ c = L*e*WL. We therefore enter a ∘ b ∘ c into the MIB.

Step 2b. ILR_2 {a, b, d}

ERC		m.Ons	m.NoCoda	f.dep	f.max
a	**2 ~ 1** (a)	L	*e*	*e*	W
b	**2 ~ 1** (b)	L	*e*	*e*	W
d	**2 ~ 6**	u	W	*e*	L
a ∘ b ∘ d		**L**	**W**	***e***	**L**

The new $ILR_{2.1}$ here is also {a, b}, which does not entail the fusion $f(ILR_2)$ = a ∘ b ∘ d = LW*e*L. Therefore we also enter $f(ILR_2)$ = a ∘ b ∘ d = LW*e*L into the MIB.

Step 3. $ILR_{1.1}$ = $ILR_{2.1}$ = {a, b}. This is the ILR from both preceding steps, and as noted, is just L*ee*W, which itself has no ILR. We therefore enter this into the MIB and we're done. The MIB (204) derives the Hasse diagram (191), repeated below as (205).

(204) ERC grammar of 2:(C)V.del in MIB form

MIB	m.Ons	m.NoCoda	f.dep	f.max
a ∘ b ∘ d	L	W		L
a ∘ b ∘ c	L		W	L
a ∘ b	L			W

For convenience we repeat the Hasse diagram representing (204):

(205) Grammar of 2:(C)V.del (Hasse)

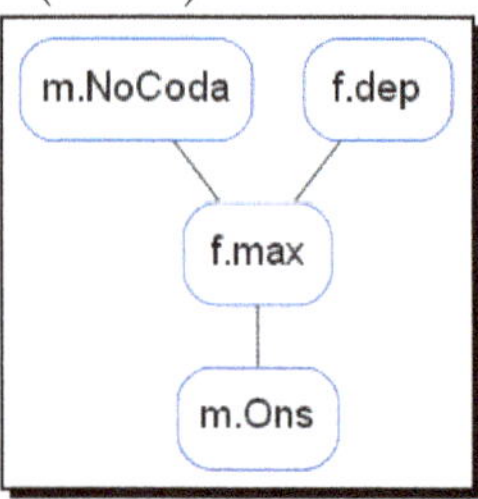

This analysis shows that to apply FRed to ERCoids, we must set u ∘ L = L. See the m.Ons column in steps 1, 2a, and 2b above. To show the utility of u ∘ W = W, let's examine the grammar G = WWL on {A, B, C} from ex. (201) above. It has two border point pairs: a = $\{\underline{AB}C, \underline{BA}C\}$, and b = $\{\underline{BC}A, \underline{CB}A\}$. The associated ERCoids and what must be their fusion are given below. This is the first (and in this case, only) step of FRed.

(206) BP-derived ERCoids

	A	B	C
G(a) ~ H(a)	W	u	L
G(b) ~ H(b)	u	W	L
fu(all)	**W**	**W**	**L**

There are *no* Info Loss Configurations. We are done and the MIB is WWL, as promised.

A final simple example motivates u ∘ *e* = *e*. Consider the grammar J = {WL*e*} on {X,Y,Z}. Its two border point pairs are a = $\{\underline{XY}Z, \underline{YX}Z\}$ and b = $(Z\underline{XY}, Z\underline{YX})$. The associated ERCoids and their fusion are given below.

(207) BP-derived ERCoids

	X	Y	Z
J(a) ~ J′(a)	W	L	u
J(b) ~ J″(b)	W	L	*e*
fu(all)	W	L	*e*

Here too there can be no Info Loss Configurations. To arrive at WL*e*, we must have u ∘ *e* = *e*.

4.9.2 ERCoid confinement

It is natural to hope that u can be incorporated into a 4-valued logical system, some kind of extension of ERC logic, but it is not immediately clear how this is to be done. An ERCoid containing u is 'open' in the sense that, unlike an ERC, it does not denote a set of legs; replacement of u with an ERC value from {W, L, *e*} 'closes' it. It appears that ERCoids form a kind of pre-logic: they can combine to give the elements of ERC logic but do not themselves obviously support the basic operations and relations expected in a logic.

The mode of combination on which FRed depends is fusion, and we have seen how it can transform a set of ERCoids into a set of ERCs. Fusion is aggressive in that it allows for change of ERC values, which carry information. In the interests of allowing only the specification of what is unspecified, it is natural to suspend this possibility and allow only u to be replaced. This leads to a notion of 'weak combination' of ERCoids that are 'compatible' in the sense that at each component they are either identical or one of the components contains u. Weak combination, we shall see, plays an important role in constructing ERCoid representations from border point pairs.

(208) **Definition. Compatible.** Two ERCoids are *compatible* if they are identical in every constraint where neither has the value u.

(209) **Definition. Weak composition.** The *weak composition* $\alpha\star\beta$ of two compatible ERCoids α, β is defined componentwise as follows:

i. Combination of values. $x\star x = \mathrm{u}\star x = x\star \mathrm{u} = x$ for $x \in \{\mathrm{W}, \mathrm{L}, e, \mathrm{u}\}$
ii. Combination of ERCoids. $(\alpha\star\beta)[i] = \alpha[i] \star \beta[i]$

Note that weak combination is trivially commutative and only slightly less trivially associative, as may verified by calculations such as $(x\star\mathrm{u})\star x = x\star x = x\star(x\star\mathrm{u})$. Let's consider now the set of ERCoids along the border of two adjacent grammars: we will find that they are pairwise compatible and can therefore be weakly composed into a single ERCoid.

(210) **Definition. Shared border.** The shared border of G,H $\in$ T, notated ∂(G,H) is the set of border point pairs $\{\lambda, \mu\}$ where $\lambda \in$ G, $\mu \in$ H.

ERCoids derived from border point pairs along a shared border are mutually compatible. Each ERCoid component with a value drawn from {W, L, *e*} determines a relation in the EPO of the corresponding constraint, and there can be only one such.

(211) **Lemma. Compatibility at the shared border.** Let G, H $\in$ T be grammars on n constraints in typology T and let $\partial(\mathrm{G}, \mathrm{H}) = \{\mathrm{b}_1,\ldots, \mathrm{b}_m\}$ be their shared border. Let $\mathcal{B} = \{\beta_1,\ldots,\beta_m\}$ be the set of ERCoids derived from the border point pairs in ∂(G, H), oriented with respect to W,L so that G is the asserted optimum of the ERCoids. Every pair of ERCoids β_i, $\beta_j \in \mathcal{B}$ is compatible.

Proof. Enumerate the constraints of T.Con as C_j, $1 \le j \le n$, and let the components of the ERCoids follow that order. Suppose for some constraint

C_k that $\beta_i[k] = x \in \{W, L, e\}$. Since T is a typology, it has a MOAT. Consider the EPO of constraint C_k. The border point pair b_i giving rise to ERCoid β_i imposes a base relation between G and H that appears in EPO(C_k) and is determined by the value x. If $x = W$, then G $\prec^{bp.Ck}$ H. If $x = L$, then H $\prec^{bp.Ck}$ G. If $x = e$, then G $\equiv^{bp.Ck}$ H. If there is another ERCoid $\beta_j \in \mathcal{B}$ such that $\beta_j[k] = \bar{x} \in \{W, L, e\}$ for $\bar{x} \neq x$, then EPO(C_k) is cyclic, an impossibility. Therefore, any other ERCoid in $\mathcal{B}$ either has the value x for constraint C_k, or the value u. □

The immediate consequence is that the ERCoids along a shared border can be weakly composed to yield a single 'Unified Border ERCoid', which exhaustively characterizes the local information about the relations between the bordering grammars.

(212) **Theorem. Unified Border ERCoid (UBE).** Let G, H, $\mathcal{B}$ be as in Lemma (211). The ERCoids in $\mathcal{B}$ may be weakly composed to form a single ERCoid.

Proof. Take the first two ERCoids from $\mathcal{B} = \{\beta_1, \beta_2, ..., \beta_n\}$. At every component, they have either the same value from {W, L, e} or the value u, by Lemma (211). These are precisely the compatibility preconditions for weak composition (209), therefore we may construct $\mathcal{B}^{(1)} = \{\beta_1 \star \beta_2, ..., \beta_n\}$. If $n > 2$, observe $\beta_1 \star \beta_2$ also meets the preconditions for weak composition with any other ERCoid in $\mathcal{B}^{(1)}$. We may therefore repeat the construction to obtain $\mathcal{B}^{(2)}$. Continue in this fashion until we reach $\mathcal{B}^{\star} = \{\beta_1 \star \beta_2 \star \cdots \star \beta_n\}$. Since weak combination is commutative and associative, the order of combination here is immaterial, and it is legitimate to disregard it. □

Weak combination appears harmless at the level of individual values, since combinations $x \star x$ and u $\star x$ neither add nor remove information. In the context of an ERCoid, however, weak combination makes substantive claims about how information is nontrivially amalgamated. Thus, in combining {WuL, uWL}, we obtain WuL $\star$uWL = WWL, an ERC that asserts that *either* the first *or* the second constraint dominates the third. This contrasts with {WeL, eWL}, whose members do not weakly combine, where the content of the set is that *both* the first *and* the second constraint dominate the third.

To see that weak combination leads to the correct interpretation of the ranking information implicit in border point pairs, observe that the values {W, L, e} in the UBE record grammar-to-grammar relations that show up in the EPOs and are thus realized numerically in every UVT. From any UVT, we may construct standard ERCs, which can be seen to reproduce the values we started with. To pursue our example, imagine a typology on constraints {X, Y, Z} and a UVT U. Suppose we compare two grammars G, H corresponding to rows u_g and u_h in U, and obtain the ERCoid WuL. Then we have

$$G <^{bp.X} H \Rightarrow X(u_g) < X(u_h)$$
$$H <^{bp.Z} G \Rightarrow Z(u_h) < Z(u_h)$$

In the standard ERC $[u_g \sim u_h]$, the constraint X takes the value W, and the constraint Z takes the value L, exactly as in the ERCoid WuL. A similar argument may be constructed for the *c* value. This establishes that the relational information encoded in border ERCoids leads to ranking information that is always transmitted *in propia persona* to ERCs derived from any UVT.

Focus on the UBE derived from the border between two grammars may suggest, misleadlingly, that weak combination is informationally harmless in general sets of ERCoids. It's worth our while to see that this is not true. Different patterns of weak combination may produce different results.

For example, given an ERCoid set {a, b, c, d} with suitable compatibilities, it may happen that {a ⋆ b, c ⋆ *d*} is not the logical equivalent of {a ⋆ *d*, b ⋆ c}. Consider the following collection of ERCoids, which do not (and cannot) arise from a single shared border, per Lemma (212).

(213) A general ERCoid set with non-equivalent weak combinations

a	W	L	u	L
b	W	L	*e*	u
c	W	L	W	u
d	W	L	*u*	W

Here are two non-equivalent patterns of weak combination, both of which produce ERCs.

(214) Weak composition in {a, b, c, d}

i. {a ⋆ b, c ⋆ d} = {WLuL ⋆ WL*e*u, WLWu ⋆ WLuW}
= {WL*e*L, WLWW} ⇔ {WL*e*L}

ii. { a ⋆ c, b ⋆ d} = {WLuL ⋆ WLWu, WL*e*u ⋆ WLuW}
= {WLWL, WL*e*W}

ERC sets (i) and (ii) are maximally reduced on the end of each chain; they do not converge. In the end, this is perhaps not too shocking. A u-containing ERCoid can compose (weakly) to give either conjunction or disjunction, which does not suggest that weak combination is logically harmless. In particular, this property undermines the hopes of defining entailment on ERCoids.

A set of ERCoids, then, does not have the status of a set of ERCs. Any consistent ERC set unambiguously defines a grammar. But not so any set of ERCoids. The viability of an ERCoid set is tied to its origin as a representation of a set of border point pairs; therefore, it is closely tied to particularities of the structure of the border points of a grammar. Thus, we do not know, right off, whether the kind of ambiguous situation constructed above ever arises ecologically.

If FRed unmodified is to succeed on the collection ERCoids gathered from the entire border of a grammar, it must handle the u value properly. It cannot stumble on weak combination effects; it must work correctly on the full assembly of border point ERCoids, without regard to their provenance.

Even more fundamentally, the fusions produced by FRed must all be free of u. Were this false, the algorithm simply would not run, because of the Entailment Check Step, in which the fusion is tested for entailment against the collection of Info Loss Residues. General ERCoids do not appear to support a notion of entailment. And, ultimately, the result of FRed must be an ERC set: a grammar.

We want the output of integrating ERCoids over the entire border of the target grammar G via FRed to be an ERC set, devoid of u and identical to the unique MIB of G. But if we have a column that consists entirely of u's, we can only get u out of it. To resolve this matter, we'd have to show that no column containing only u shows up in an ILR at any step of FRed. We will not complete this task here, but we will begin it, showing that for the entire ensemble of border points of G, it cannot be the case that a constraint evaluates everywhere to u.

Observe that if a constraint C has u in every ERCoid associated with G's border, then u must be in the suffix of all of G's border points. This cannot happen.

(215) **Theorem. Not all u.** No constraint evaluates to u in every ERCoid derived from the border points of a grammar.

Proof. Let G be a grammar. Let $\mathcal{B}_G$ be the set of its border points and $\mathcal{E}_G$ the set of ERCoids associated with them. If $\mathcal{B}_G = \emptyset$, then $\mathcal{E}_G = \emptyset$. G is borderless and alone in its typology, and the theorem is vacuously true.

Now consider the case where $\mathcal{B}_G \neq \emptyset$. Suppose for purposes of contradiction that there is a constraint C ∈ T.Con, such that C evaluates to u in every ERCoid in $\mathcal{E}_G$. Every border point in $\mathcal{B}_G$ must therefore have a nonempty suffix and C must lie within it.

Now consider EPO(C). All base relations of equivalence and order on C derive from border points in which C is either prefixal or in the transposition; thus G stands in no base relations with any other grammars and consequently no EPO relations of equivalence or order on C. Thus, EPO(C) is unrooted, an impossibility because all EPOs are rooted, as shown in (138). From this contradiction, it follows that no such constraint exists. □

It is also of interest that no constraint can be entirely *prefixal* in the border points of a grammar. This does not exclude the possibility of a constraint's values fusing to *e* over the border ERCoid set, though it does ensure that any such fusion will contain both *e* and u.

(216) **Theorem. Not all prefixal.** No constraint can be entirely prefixal in the border points of a grammar.

Proof. For a grammar G, let $\mathcal{B}_G$ be the collection of its border points. If $\mathcal{B}_G = \emptyset$, the theorem is vacuously true, since there are no border points in which C is nonprefixal.

Now suppose $\mathcal{B}_G \neq \emptyset$. Let T be any typology that G belongs to. Assume for purposes of contradiction that there is a constraint C ∈ T.Con that is entirely prefixal in the border points of G. Consider any leg PCQ ∈ G.

(*) Observe first that CPQ ∈ G. To see this, start with PCQ and repeatedly transpose C leftward over any immediately preceding constraint to create a path between PCQ and CPQ. This path cannot exit G, since by assumption C is never part of a border point pair transposition.

(**) Similarly, PQC ∈ G. To see this, start with PCQ and repeatedly transpose C rightward over any immediately following constraint to create a path between PCQ and CPQ. This path cannot exit G either, for the same reason as in (*).

We now claim that all legs terminating in C belong to G. Suppose to the contrary that there is a leg RC ∉ G. From the algebra of permutations, using the same form of reasoning as in Lemma (95), we are guaranteed a path between PQC and RC in which every member of the path terminates in C. Somewhere in this path is a border point of G in which C is suffixal, contradicting the assumption that it is always prefixal. So RC ∈ G for every R.

Now consider any arbitrary leg RC. From (*), we know that CR ∈ G. Transpose C rightward to create a path to RC ∈ G. This path must never exit G. But because R is arbitrary, the set of all such paths includes every order on the constraint set of G. Therefore $\mathcal{B}_G = \emptyset$, contrary to our initial assumption. Thus no such entirely prefixal C can exist. □

It follows then, that the distribution of border points is such that, for each grammar a constraint C either participates in a border transposition, evaluating to W and L, or appears both prefixally and suffixally, generating both *e* and u values in the border point ERCoids. This is a crucial part of the workings of OT that confines, as it were, the u value to situations in which the information it lacks will be supplied from elsewhere. Theorem (215) guarantees that as we run FRed on the set of border ERCoids for a grammar, the first step, which constructs the fusion of the entire set, will produce an ERC. It remains to be shown that further steps, which operate Info Loss Residues, will maintain this pattern of eliminating u in favor of ERC values {W, L, *e*}.

4.9.3 Remark: ERCoids from the MOAT

The extension of ERCs to ERCoids allows us to represent a grammar's position in each EPO with an ERCoid. Given any two grammars G,H in a typology, the ERCoid [G ~ H] has component values from {W, L, *e*, u} which express the following relations in the Cth component:

[G ~ H](C) = W $G <^{bp.C} H$

[G ~ H](C) = L $H <^{bp.C} G$

[G ~ H](C) = *e* $G \sim^{bp.C} H$

[G ~ H](C) = u $G \,||^{bp.C}\, H$ Verbose: 'G is noncomparable to H on C'

The u value arises when G and H do not stand in either of the two relations $<^{bp.C}$ or $\sim^{bp.C}$, and is notated by ||. If we compare each grammar with every other in this way, we arrive at an unambiguous algebraic representation of EPO(C) which consists entirely of ERCoids.

What is the relationship of these MOAT ERCoids to the Unitary Border ERCoids (UBEs) of the grammars? Recall that the UBE of G with respect to H is the weak composition of all the border point ERCoids arising from the border of G and H. We can deduce the answer by examining the way the information in the MOAT differs from that in the border points.

Only adjacent grammars have border point ERCoids. The MOAT, by contrast, provides ERCoids relating every pair of grammars. We might wish to disregard MOAT ERCoids between non-adjacent grammars by fiat. Nevertheless, those that remain may still differ from border point ERCoids in the relations they represent.

The base relations $\prec^{bp.C}$ and $\equiv^{bp.C}$ are transitively closed to produce the EPO relation $<^{bp.C}$ and $\sim^{bp.C}$. An EPO relation may therefore be a proper superset of the base relation from which it is derived. In ERCoid terms, this means that some of the u's in a UBE $[G \sim H]_{BP}$ can be matched to W's, L's, or *e*'s in the MOAT ERCoid $[G \sim H]_M$. In terms of weak composition, we may write $[G \sim H]_{BP} \star [G \sim H]_M = [G \sim H]_M$.

Any attempt to reach the base relations from the MOAT by transitive reduction cannot, of course, succeed in the general case. Suppose $G_1 \prec^{bp.C} G_2$ and $G_2 \prec^{bp.C} G_3$ in $EPO_T(C)$ for some T. This gives us $G_1 <^{bp.C} G_3$, but whether or not a particular relation $G_1 \prec^{bp.C} G_3$ is present among the base relations depends entirely on the leg structure of T, the fine structure of which does not survive into the MOAT. Similarly for $=^{bp.C}$ and [illegible]$^{bp.C}$.

4.10 Retrospect and overview

THE GOAL OF THIS SECTION is to provide a relatively full account of the argument just made, emphasizing motivation, conceptual structure, and logical flow. For the interested reader, it may serve as a companion and guide to §4 as much as a summary of its content.

The UVT lets us define the OT notion of 'typology' in a way that reflects the content of intuitive practice, while liberating us from having to deal with collections of VTs of various sizes and contents. Each row of a UVT corresponds to one and only one grammar in its typology, allowing a simple coindexing system that represents the grammar-row bijection. Because of its simplicity and conciseness, the UVT opens up avenues of advance into the intrinsic structure of the typology object. To pursue them, we must however go beyond the UVT itself, using it as a starting point and place to stand rather than as a final destination.

The obvious weaknesses of the UVT as a representation of typologies are two-fold: plethora and process. Many, many UVTs yield the same typology, and they may differ nontrivially in the numerical relations within them. In addition, the consequences of the numerics are revealed only through filtration, the basic mechanism that chooses optima. But to filter a VT requires grinding through a stepwise sequential process that attends only to certain properties of the array of values – order and equality – and even to these only in certain circumstances. We need to know, in answer to the problem we have deemed 'typological equivalence', what the essential features shared by a typology's UVTs are, those that select and organize the typology it generates.

These complications fade when we shift focus from UVTs to the grammars they produce. A grammar is a unique set of legs, and we may uncover the relevant typological structure directly in terms of relations between grammars. Although a first encounter with this line of analysis might trigger the sense that one complicated apparatus has been exchanged for another, further reflection reveals that the relational system is surprisingly simple at its core and only involves straightforward generalization of familiar notions of numerical order (<) and equality (=). The useful, somewhat more abstract notions of grammar order and grammar equivalence are constructed from patterns manifest in leg sets.

There are two natural ways to approach these relations, broadly paralleling the way that grammars can be arrived at through mass filtration of entire candidate sets on the one hand and through pairwise comparison on the other.

4.10.1 Relations from border point pairs

Let's first consider the pairwise approach. If we focus on a grammar and an immediate neighbor, we arrive at the system of relations based on the *border point pair*. This arises from the key notion of *adjacency between legs* originating in the theory of permutations and introduced to the linguistic literature by Riggle (2010). Two legs are *adjacent* if they differ only in a single transposition of two constraints adjacent in their orders. Schematically, we have adjacency for a pair of legs $\{\lambda_1, \lambda_2\}$ if for sequences P, Q (possibly empty) and constraints X, Y, we have

$$\lambda_1 = \mathrm{P\underline{XY}Q}$$
$$\lambda_2 = \mathrm{P\underline{YX}Q}.$$

The notion transfers to entire grammars if we define leg sets G_1 and G_2 to be *adjacent* when G_1 contains a leg adjacent to a leg in G_2. In that case, G_1 contains a leg shaped like λ_1 while G_2 contains a leg like λ_2 and we call $\{\lambda_1, \lambda_2\}$ a *border point pair.*

Grammars are *connected regions* under this notion of adjacency (Riggle 2010; see §7.3.3 below for discussion and proof). Between every pair of legs in a grammar, there is a path of legs that stays inside the grammar and in which each step along the way runs from a leg to an adjacent leg. A border point is one for which there is a transposition that creates a leg outside the grammar. It turns out that a grammar's border points define it completely and determine not only its relations to immediate neighbors but to every other grammar in the typology. Each border point pair $\{\lambda_1, \lambda_2\}$, with $\lambda_1 \in G_1$ and $\lambda_2 \in G_2$, gives rise to the *base relations* between G_1 and G_2. Observe that the set of border points of a grammar is well-defined regardless of what typology or typologies it sits in: given a leg of the grammar, if any transposition of a pair of sequential constraints leads to a leg not in the grammar, that leg is a border point.

From legs $\mathrm{P\underline{XY}Q} = \lambda_1 \in G_1$ and $\mathrm{P\underline{YX}Q} = \lambda_2 \in G_2$, we have the following 'base' relations with respect to the constraints in the transposing pair:

$$G_1 \prec^{bp.X} G_2$$
$$G_2 \prec^{bp.Y} G_1$$

To see the background sense of this, consider rows u_1, u_2 in some UVT U which are selected by the legs of adjacent grammars G_1 and G_2, respectively. For convenience, suppose that the leg λ_1 selects the row u_1 corresponding to G_1 and the leg λ_2 selects the row corresponding to G_2. Now consider a competition narrowed to just the pair $\{u_1, u_2\}$. Because of the minimal difference between the legs, we can pin down the exact characteristics that are operative in this selection. The constraint X will be the one that selects u_1 by ejecting u_2, and the constraint Y will do the same service for u_2, ejecting u_1. Intuitively put, we have discerned a crucial quantum of information about how the ranking of constraints discriminates G_1 and G_2. Somewhat remarkably, this kind of limited information, gathered along its entire border, determines the contents of a grammar. In addition, it determines how the grammars of a typology may be unioned together in such a way as to create a new, coarser typology.

These base relations have a close relation with the numerics. In every UVT U for the typology that G_1 and G_2 belong to, the relation

$$G_1 \prec^{bp.X} G_2$$

entails the numerical relation $X(u_1) < X(u_2)$.[18] Along the same lines, for every C in the prefix P shared by λ_1 and λ_2, we define the relation

$$G_1 \equiv^{bp.C} G_2$$

with the background sense that the corresponding rows u_1, u_2 of any UVT for the typology will be treated identically by C. And indeed, we must have $C(u_1) = C(u_2)$.

The relations $\prec^{bp.X}$ and $\equiv^{bp.C}$ are thus tied to numerical $<$ and $=$, as established in Lemma (10). But they lack key properties that the numerical relations have, due to their definitional reliance on the details of border point contact. The most obvious shortcoming is that $\equiv^{bp.C}$ is not reflexive, since no grammar has a border point pair with itself. More significantly, the base relations are not guaranteed to be transitive. From $G_1 \prec^{bp.X} G_2$ and $G_2 \prec^{bp.X} G_3$, we cannot conclude anything about the existence of a base relation $\prec^{bp.X}$ between G_1 and G_3, and similarly for $\equiv^{bp.X}$. Base-related grammars must be adjacent, although the numerical relations $<$ and $=$ are not limited to anything like that, for example to sequentially adjacent integers. The base relations are sensitive to what border point pairs happen to exist in a

---

[18] Recall that we write $C(u_k)$ for the numerical value in u_k assigned by C, the entry of the kth row and C^{th} column of the UVT U.

given typology. In the broader picture, this limitation makes it all the more striking that border point pair data always suffices to determine a typology.

We therefore advance beyond the base relations to new relations that incorporate them.

i. $<^{bp.C}$ is the transitive closure of $\prec^{bp.C}$

ii. $\sim^{bp.C}$ is the transitive closure of the reflexive closure of $\equiv^{bp.C}$

With these moves, $<^{bp.C}$ is a strict partial order, and $\sim^{bp.C}$ is an equivalence relation, proved in Lemmas (28) and (30). Notice that $<^{bp.C}$ fully respects $\prec^{bp.C}$ in that, by definition, $\prec^{bp.C}$ is included in $<^{bp.C}$, so that $G_1 \prec^{bp.X} G_2$ entails $G_1 <^{bp.X} G_2$ and similarly for $\equiv^{bp.X}$ and $\sim^{bp.X}$.

As with the original base relations $\prec^{bp.C}$ and $\equiv^{bp.C}$, the order $<^{bp.C}$ and the equivalence $\sim^{bp.C}$ impose themselves on every UVT as $<$ and $=$, proved as Lemmas (27) and (31).

The relations $<^{bp.C}$ and $\sim^{bp.C}$ give the relational content of $EPO_T(C) = \langle T, <^{bp.C}, \sim^{bp.C} \rangle$. The EPO reconstructs the fundamental OT notion of 'constraint' within the domain of grammars. A constraint is a function that assigns non-negative integers to candidates, which are then used for comparison and selection of candidates based on numerical $<$ and $=$. The EPO relations $<^{bp.C}$ and $\sim^{bp.C}$ associated with a constraint C neither assess nor compare candidates, but hold between entire grammars.

After one further step of formal relation-building, we arrive at an order relation that retains exactly enough of the properties of the number system to complete the set of analytical tools. The EPO relational system has both order and equivalence, independent of each other in principle, but we need an order relation that respects equivalence in the same way that $<$ respects $=$. What's required is the notion of *hypertransitive closure* (45). A relation $<^{htc.bp.C}$ is *hypertransitively closed* with respect to $\sim^{bp.C}$, and therefore allows *hypertransitive inference* (38). Hypertransitive inference may be schematized as follows, using bare $\sim$ and $<$ to represent generic equivalence and order relations.

i. $G_1 \sim G_2 \ \& \ G_2 < G_3 \Rightarrow G_1 < G_3$

ii. $G_1 < G_2 \ \& \ G_2 \sim G_3 \Rightarrow G_1 < G_3$

Among integers, if we are given $a = b$ and $b < c$, we may safely and without astonishment conclude that $a < c$. Hypertransitive closure extends the same guarantee to $<^{htc.bp.C}$.

The hierarchy of relations thus constructed looks like this on the order side:

T	$\mathbb{N}$	Status
$\boldsymbol{<}^{C}$		Base
$<^{C}$		Strict P.O.
$<^{htc.C}$	$<$	Strict P.O. & supports HT inference

This is a hierarchy because each relation is included in the one below it.

i. If two grammars stand in the relation $\boldsymbol{<}^{bp.C}$, then they also stand in the relation $<^{bp.C}$.

ii. If two grammars stand in the relation $<^{bp.C}$, then they also stand in the relation $<^{htc.bp.C}$.

The inclusions are typically proper, and the implications typically go in the one direction.

There is a similar scheme on the equivalence side:

T	$\mathbb{N}$	Status
$\equiv^{C}$		Base
$\sim^{C}$	$=$	Equivalence

In these tables, numerical $<$ and $=$ are listed at the point in the hierarchy where the EPO-related relations have taken on all relevant properties. See §4.3.2 for the base relations, §4.3.4 for the order and equivalence relations, and §4.3.5 for hypertransitive closure.

The EPOs of the constraints in T.Con are collected in the MOAT for the typology, as defined in ex. (34):

$$\text{MOAT(T)} = \{\text{EPO(C)} \mid \text{C} \in \text{T.Con}\}.$$

MOAT(T) is thus intended to represent the grammatically relevant features of each constraint in T.Con. Intuitively, EPO(C) represents the essential relational core of the constraint C, in its typological context. MOAT(T) is thus the analog, or (perhaps better) the *analysis*, of T.Con.

The first target of MOAT development is to *characterize* the typology. A characterizing property is such that if two objects can be shown to have it, then they are isomorphic in some relevant sense or even completely identical. For example, if T_1 and T_2 come from the same UVT, then we can be sure that they are the same typology. Life would indeed be difficult otherwise, but the fact amounts to no more than the observation that filtration is well-defined, and though useful and used, it provides only the starting point for investigation of typological structure. Many distinct UVTs also have the same typology: what shared organization unites all of them? A typology has but one MOAT, and the goal – reached in Theorem (155) – is to show that the MOAT characterizes the typology and therefore embodies that sought-for organization.

Among characterizations, the MOAT stands out because it is built from just the leg data that is relevant to the compatibility of grammars within a typology and thus to delimiting the possibilities of coarsening a typology by joining its grammars into more inclusive grammars that generalize across structural distinctions.

4.10.2 Relations from prefixal filtration of grammars

To cross the notional gap between MOAT and typology, we must deal with the fact that the typology object is defined through filtration of candidates, which in the case of the UVT consist of the totality of its rows. The EPO relations, based on local and pairwise data from grammars, don't give us an immediate handle on mass filtration of candidates. Our approach is to reconstruct the notion of filtration within the realm of grammars, in order to bring the notion of typology into the purview of MOAT-oriented reasoning.

The key observation is that a grammar carries in the *prefixal* structure of its legs a signature that allows row filtration of UVTs to be correlated with grammar filtration. Given a typology T, we understand the result of filtering T by a prefix P, as per definition (67), to be the set of all those grammars that *contain a leg with prefix* P:

$$\mathrm{P}\langle\mathrm{T}\rangle = \{\mathrm{G} \in \mathrm{T} \mid \exists\lambda \in \mathrm{G} \text{ such that } \lambda = \mathrm{P}\ldots\}$$

The analogous entity in candidate filtration is P[K], the set of candidates in the set K that survive filtration by P. When K names the rows of a UVT, then P[K] consists of the rows selected by a grammar in P⟨T⟩, because those grammars are the ones with legs beginning with P. To arrive at P[K] we must work our way through the sequence of constraints in P. By contrast, the grammars in P⟨T⟩ exhibit their membership right in their leg structure.

The match between row filtration and grammar filtration in this sense is perfect. Theorem (77) 'RF ⇔ GF' states it this way: given $\mathrm{U} \in \mathcal{U}(\mathrm{T})$, the set of UVTs for T,

$$\mathrm{u}_k \in \mathrm{P}[\mathrm{U}] \text{ if and only if } \mathrm{G}_k \in \mathrm{P}\langle\mathrm{T}\rangle.$$

This means that we can understand filtration in typologically equivalent UVTs, despite their vast number, by contemplating the leg structure of the grammars in the one typology they all produce.

An immediate result is Filtration Uniformity (84): for any $\mathrm{U}, \mathrm{V} \in \mathcal{U}(\mathrm{T})$, the filtration patterns of U and V are *identical*, a notion defined in (82). This is perhaps slightly surprising, since all that's required is that U, V respond to entire legs in the same way. But, given a leg, every detail of its filtration sequence from first constraint to last must be the same in all UVTs.[19] Qualitatively put, the argument runs as follows: given T, we can go from a prefix-filtered set of rows in any UVT for T to a prefix-filtered set of grammars and from that set of grammars back to the corresponding rows in any other UVT for T.

A key step in the argument is provided by the 'No Dead Man Walking' (NDMW) property (65) of OT filtration. Consider a set of *possible optima* K, such as the rows of a UVT, which are guaranteed to succeed on *some* leg. By NDMW, survival of any candidate $q \in K$ through a particular prefix P guarantees the existence of an entire leg beginning with P that selects q as optimal. This allows us to go immediately from u_k's membership in P[K] to the existence of a full leg PQ choosing u_k, and thence to the grammar G_k containing that leg.

More important for our overall argument is the converse (85) of Filtration Uniformity: if the filtration patterns of two UVTs are identical, then they sponsor the same typology. This characterizes typologies in a way that allows us to move to an even more useful characterization in prefixal terms, leading us along the path toward the MOAT-based characterization.

With prefixal filtration successfully shadowing row filtration, we can now develop prefix-based *relations* between grammars that are immediately responsive to the role of filtration in defining typologies. These parallel the border-point based relations quite closely.

Like its border point-based analog, the prefixal base relation $\equiv^{pr.C}$ requires that related grammars each contain a leg with a shared prefix P to which C belongs. When that base relation is transitively closed, we arrive at an equivalence relation $\sim^{pr.C}$. It's clear that $\sim^{bp.C}$ is contained in $\sim^{pr.C}$, since the base border point relation meets strictly stronger requirements: it demands not only the shared prefix, but adjacency of witnessing legs. Despite the disparity in definitions, the opposite is also true, and the two relations turn out to be identical, as shown in Theorem (96), 'Equality of Equivalences'.

A stepwise filtration effect is obtained in the prefixal domain when a prefix is extended by a single constraint, leading to a binary prefixal order relation. Given grammars $G_1, G_2 \in P\langle T\rangle$, we say that PC *separates* G_1 from G_2 if $G_1 \in PC\langle T\rangle$ and $G_2 \notin PC\langle T\rangle$, so that C ejects G_2 from the set of survivors of P. Both G_1 and G_2 contain legs beginning with P, but only G_1 contains a leg beginning PC. In this case, we say $G_1 \prec^{pr.C} G_2$ and following the previous

[19] The intuitive notion of 'identity' and 'sameness', when made precise, requires a bijective correspondence between rows of different UVTs, which serves to identify those chosen by the same grammar; see definition (82).

pattern of the development, we transitively close the base relation $\prec^{pr.C}$ to obtain the prefixal order relation $<^{pr.C}$. See §4.6 for details.

As with the equivalence family, the border point base relation $\prec^{bp.C}$ between grammars falls under tighter requirements than the prefixal relation $\prec^{pr.C}$, since it requires a border point pair {P<u>XY</u>Q, P<u>YX</u>Q} featuring symmetrical separations. In this case, the consequence is that while $<^{bp.C}$ is included in $<^{pr.C}$, the opposite is not guaranteed, and the general implication goes only one way.

Once again, the order relation must be tweaked so as to comport with the equivalence relation in a way that mirrors the relations between numerical $<$ and $=$. Hypertransitively closing $<^{pr.C}$ to $<^{htc.pr.C}$ gives us what we need in this regard – and more, since with hypertransitive closure the prefixal order becomes identical with the border point-based order, as shown in Theorem (118).

Two families of relations between grammars emerge from these developments. In every case, the border point version is included in the prefixal version. At the grammar-to-grammar level, this means, schematically, that $G_1\ R^{bp}\ G_2$ implies $G_1\ R^{pr}\ G_2$, writing R for relation type and super-scripting to indicate the border point/prefixal distinction. At the base level in both families, there is no guarantee of implication in the other direction, an asymmetry that also recurs at the *order* level. But complete identity is seen between the equivalences, and between the hypertransitively closed orders. This gives us the bridging structure that we need to show that the border-point based MOAT determines the filtration-based typology. We summarize this state of affairs in the following tables, dropping the bp/pr superscript where it makes no material distinction. Observer that in the T columns, there is a left-to-right inclusion relation within rows.

(217) Equivalence family

T		ℕ	Status
$\equiv^{bp.C}$	$\equiv^{pr.C}$		Base
$\sim^{C}$		$=$	Equivalence

(218) Order family

T		ℕ	Status
$\prec^{bp.C}$	$\prec^{pr.C}$		Base
$<^{bp.C}$	$<^{pr.C}$		Strict P.O.
$<^{htc.C}$		$<$	Strict P.O. & HTC wrt $\sim^{C}$ and $=$ respectively

4.10.3 Instantiation

In every case, the abstract relations are appropriately reflected in the numerical structure of UVTs. Given a $U \in \mathcal{U}(T)$, any relation between grammars in T implies a corresponding numerical relation between entries in the corresponding rows of U. Thus, writing $\mathcal{R}$ for members of the order family and $\mathcal{E}$ for members of the equivalence family, with C to index the relevant constraint, we have:

i. $G_1 \mathcal{R}^C G_2 \Rightarrow C(u_1) < C(u_2)$
ii. $G_1 \mathcal{E}^C G_2 \Rightarrow C(u_1) = C(u_2)$

We call this relation-between-relations by the name 'instantiation', and when a UVT U follows this pattern, we write $U \models \mathcal{R}^C$, $U \models \mathcal{E}^C$, and so on. In each case the instantiating function for C maps $G_k \mapsto C(u_k)$, numerically instantiating $\mathcal{R}^C$ as $<$ and $\mathcal{E}^C$ as $=$. For details, see §4.3.3.

This result is laid out in detail in table (139), which we repeat here.

(219) Table (139). Instantiating all relations

Relation Type		Symbols	$U \in \mathcal{U}(T) \Rightarrow$	Established
bp	Base	$\prec^{bp.C}, \equiv^{bp.C}$	$U \models \{\prec^{bp.C}, \equiv^{bp.C}\}$	(25)
	Order, equivalence	$<^{bp.C}, \sim^{bp.C}$	$U \models \{<^{bp.C}, \sim^{bp.C}\}$	(27) , (31)
	HTC	$<^{htc.bp.C}$	$U \models \{<^{htc.bp.C}\}$	(48)
pr	Base	$\prec^{pr.C}, \equiv^{pr.C}$	$U \models \{\prec^{pr.C}, \equiv^{pr.C}\}$	(92) , (102)
	Order, equivalence	$<^{pr.C}, \sim^{pr.C}$	$U \models \{<^{pr.C}, \sim^{pr.C}\}$	(103) , (93)
	HTC	$<^{htc.pr.C}$	$U \models \{<^{htc.pr.C}\}$	(110)

This makes it clear that the relations, though derived from grammars qua leg sets and distant from the numerics, capture important aspects of numerical structure: necessary conditions that UVTs must satisfy if they produce a given typology. The immediate question is then *sufficiency.*

Given that a VT of appropriate dimensions and non-redundancy happens to instantiate these relations, may we then deduce that by the usual filtration-dependent definition it *produces* the typology from which they derive? Establishing this will be the key to providing the MOAT-based characterization of the typology object.

The useful form of instantiation is one in which both relations of a MOAT-like structure are simultaneously instantiated in a VT, which we refer to as instantiating the MOAT, PMOAT, htcMOAT, and so on. The result runs according to the slogan 'instantiate one, instantiate all'. From

Lemmas (140)–(144), we have the following biconditionals, writing V ⊨ M for 'the VT V instantiates the structure M'.

$$\begin{array}{lcl} \text{V} \vDash \text{MOAT(T)} & \Leftrightarrow & \text{V} \vDash \text{htcMOAT(T)} \\ \text{V} \vDash \text{htcMOAT(T)} & \Leftrightarrow & \text{V} \vDash \text{htcPMOAT(T)} \\ \text{V} \vDash \text{htcPMOAT(T)} & \Leftrightarrow & \text{V} \vDash \text{PMOAT(T)} \end{array}$$

Chained, these give us the bridge that crosses from border-point-based relations to prefixal relations:

$$\text{V} \vDash \text{MOAT(T)} \quad \Rightarrow \quad \text{V} \vDash \text{PMOAT(T)}.$$

Thus: a UVT which instantiates the MOAT also instantiates the filtration-friendly PMOAT. What we learn about instantiating the PMOAT will therefore be inherited by a UVT which is only known to instantiate the MOAT itself.

4.10.4 Our MOATish mother

Our target is, formally, to show that typologies with the same MOAT are the same typology; or to view it contrapositively, that distinct typologies have distinct MOATs. Much of the interest of this connection lies in the fact that the MOAT and the typology are very different entitities. The MOAT is an abstract order and equivalence structure, in which grammars are named opaquely and treated as atomic entities that stand in relation. In a typology *per se*, grammars are sets of legs, blocks in a certain kind of partition of Ord(*S*.Con) for some *S*. The MOAT derives by definition from a typology. Crucially, we find that we may also go in the other direction: given only a MOAT, we can reproduce every detail of its underlying typology. A typology rests on a UVT, and only one is required to produce it. The MOAT governs every UVT and thus may be said to contain the essential information that each UVT holds.

The route from an order/equivalence structure to a typology therefore advances through a typology-defining UVT via instantiation. Because producing a typology rests on filtration, the PMOAT is the natural starting point. We first establish in Theorem (147) '*R.E.S.P.E.C.T.*' that instantiating the PMOAT(T) in a VT V entails that V produces T. Concisely,

$$(*)\ \text{V} \vDash \text{PMOAT(T)} \Rightarrow \text{V} \in \mathcal{U}(\text{T})\ .$$

The theorem itself follows from the more narrowly focused Lemma (146) 'Columnar Interchange' which establishes that if we have a $\text{U} \in \mathcal{U}(\text{T})$ in hand and we alter it by exchanging just one column C for a column that merely instantiates both $\sim^{\text{pr.C}}$ and $<^{\text{pr.C}}$, which are the relation content of PEO(C), the prefixal analog of EPO(C), then we still have a UVT for T.

Theorem (147) uses this result to establish the key implication (*). In the proof, repeated application of Columnar Interchange allows us to replace all columns of any $U \in \mathcal{U}$ (T) one by one with columns chosen from a V known only to instantiate PMOAT(T), until we are assured that $V \in \mathcal{U}$ (T) as well. Since we already have the converse of (*) from the study of the relations themselves, this result gives a tight biconditional relation between instantiating the prefixal relations and producing (via VT filtration) the typology they come from.

To broaden the result to embrace just the relational structure of PMOAT(T), we abstract away from the grammar labels that happen to have been used in it, by recognizing a notion of isomorphism between PMOATs. With two PMOATs to examine, if we have a bijection between their grammars that respects the relations $<^{\text{pr.C}}$ and $\sim^{\text{pr.C}}$ in both directions, then we say that they are isomorphic, writing $\text{PMOAT}(T_1) \cong \text{PMOAT}(T_2)$. Lemma (149) shows that instantiability of one PMOAT in any V ensures instantiability of all of its relational equivalents in that same V. Thus, assuming $\text{PMOAT}(T_1) \cong \text{PMOAT}(T_2)$, we have

$$V \vDash \text{PMOAT}(T_1) \Rightarrow V \vDash \text{PMOAT}(T_2).$$

The desired result follows immediately: typologies having relationally equivalent PMOATs are identical, shown in Theorem (150):

$$\text{PMOAT}(T_1) \cong \text{PMOAT}(T_2) \Rightarrow T_1 = T_2\,.$$

From here, it is only a few steps to the desired conclusion, using the instantiation implications between PMOAT and MOAT relations to re-create the PMOAT results in MOAT territory. The first principle finding is thus

$$V \vDash \text{MOAT}(T) \Rightarrow V \in \mathcal{U}(T)$$

indicating that any V *instantiating* the MOAT(T), according to the definition of instantiation, which involves relational homomorphism, is also a V that *produces* T, according to the filtration-dependent definition of typology.

Recognizing relational isomorphism of MOATS in a way that exactly parallels isomorphism of PMOATs then delivers the main result, Theorem (155), 'Our MOATish Mother'

$$\text{MOAT}(T_1) \cong \text{MOAT}(T_2) \Rightarrow T_1 = T_2.$$

This shows, as claimed, that the MOAT characterizes the typology notion. Since we already have the converse, this result gives us the formal content of the intuitive prescription that the MOAT contains the essential content of the typology, which is both contained and disguised in the UVT.

To this point the argument has taken place in context of the UVT. Since every typology comes from a UVT, no generality has been lost and every typology is covered. But life is different in the world of concrete OT. There's no guarantee that a concrete typology, with a nontrivial GEN component, can be derived from a single concrete input. Even when such a thing can be found in principle, there is no guarantee that analytical practice aimed at language data (even carried out correctly) will lead to a Universal Support that provides any such single VT. Nevertheless, every typology has a MOAT. Therefore it is important to ask what the MOAT(T) imposes not just on a single UVT $U \in \mathcal{U}(T)$ but on any assembly of VTs that collectively supports T. Two results obtain.

[1] $\sim^{bp.C}$. Equivalence instantiates as equality always and everywhere, by Theorem (159).

When candidates α and β compete in some VT allowed by T.GEN, and are optimal in grammars G_α and G_β respectively, if $G_\alpha \sim^C G_\beta$, then $C(\alpha) = C(\beta)$. Consider for example, the simple case of m.Ons from EST. In optima, the input /V/ yields outputs .V., ε, and .ℂV., as notated in ex. (5), §2.2.1. In EPO(m.Ons), the grammars which select either the deletional or the insertional candidate are equivalent. It follows, without any more information about the constraint system, that m.Ons must assign equal values to the candidates /V/ → ε and /V/ → .ℂV.

[2] $<^{bp.C}$. Strict order instantiates not as $<$, but as $\leq$ everywhere and $<$ somewhere, established in Theorems (159) and (160).

In sum, the relation may never be reversed, but equality is allowed, though every Universal Support must contain a VT where $<^{bp.C}$ is matched to numerical $<$. More exactly, if $G_1 <^{bp.C} G_2$, then we are assured that there is in every Universal Support a VT where the candidate optimal for G_1 receives a value from C that is strictly less than that accorded to a competitor chosen by any leg of G_2. An example so simple that it's easy to miss is provided by input /CVC/, for which all 3 optimal outputs have onsets and thus all trivially satisfy m.Ons at penalty 0. These are apportioned among the 8 EST grammars, although every *grammar* of the OR type stands in the relation $<^{bp.Ons}$ with the minimally distinct grammar of the OLA type. Thus, we have

1:CV.del $<^{m.Ons}$ 2:(C)V.del

and so on, as in EPO(m.Ons) displayed in (27), §3.2.

Behind these conclusions is the Inflation Lemma (158). If the slightest numerical difference on C shows up between two candidates in any VT, that difference can be blown up to dominate the relevant relation in a Minkowski sum involving an equivalent of that VT, or just copies of it, without changing the typology in any respect. Therefore no difference in the wrong direction can be tolerated.

This effect, whereby a strict order $<$ on a composite structure reflects nonstrict $\leq$ on the components with the caveat that at least one component pair must fall under $<$, is also seen in the componentwise or product order on vectors. It reflects the fact that an order on grammars can also be constructed from a representation of grammars as a list of optima, drawn from a Universal Support, or even from an entire denumerable list of candidates. In this construction, the C-sensitive product order on languages construed as vectors of optima mirrors the hypertransitively closed relation $<^{\text{htc.C}}$ on their corresponding grammars.

4.10.5 Partitions and typologies: Acyclicity

The typology of any OT system *S* must, for obvious and natural reasons, be a partition of Ord(*S*.Con). If filtration always leads from a nonempty input set to a determinate nonempty output that is a subset of the input, then every leg must belong to a grammar, and to only one. This will be true no matter how we define the action of filtration.

We may then ask which *partitions* count as typologies under OT assumptions. The first, definitional answer is this: those produced by a UVT. The EPO relations developed in §4.3 reveal the order and equivalence information implicit in the structure of border point pairs, but the concepts they rest on remain well-defined in the context of general partitions. Two blocks B_1 and B_2 of a partition π are linked by a border point pair in exactly the same way that two grammars are: P$\underline{\text{XY}}$Q $\in B_1$ and P$\underline{\text{YX}}$Q $\in B_2$. Nothing in this definition requires that the partitions be typologies: that is, derivable from a UVT. Thus, the entire relation-defining apparatus may be carried over to the general setting, establishing relations between blocks, as in §4.4. Of course, we are not guaranteed that $\prec^{\text{bp.X}}$, when transitively closed, will give rise to an order relation. It may be transitively closed nonetheless. As it happens, $\equiv^{\text{bp.X}}$ does give rise to an equivalence relation; see Definition (56) and the discussion below it. We collect these relations in the GEPO or generalized EPO, where GEPO(C) = $\langle \pi, <^{\pi.\text{bp.C}}, \sim^{\pi.\text{bp.C}} \rangle$, and the GMOAT, or Generalized MOAT, is the collection of all GEPOs. We may thus re-pose the question: what characteristics of GMOAT(π) ensure that π is a typology?

The answer turns out to be about as simple as one could possibly hope for, thereby illuminating the basal character of OT as a theory of choice. A partition is a typology if (and only if) its GMOAT is *acyclic.* The term *acyclic* alludes to the graphical structure of the bigraph that represents the relations of an EPO or GEPO. Acyclicity is given an algebraic definition in (170) and (171): a GMOAT is acyclic if in each of its constituent GEPOs, the hypertransitive closure of the order and equivalence relations is a partial order. Qualitatively put, this means that the order and equivalence relations combine like numerical $<$ and $=$ do. The consequence is that instantiating these relations allows OT filtration to proceed.

As of §4.3, we already knew that the MOAT derived from a UVT-generated typology is acyclic in this sense, as shown in Lemma (49) of §4.3.5, which relies on the guarantees of MOAT instantiability in UVTs (§4.3.4). To proceed in the other direction, starting from the assumption of GMOAT acyclity with no UVT to rely on, we make use of the full range of constructions developed here: border-point-based relations, prefixal relations, hypertransitive closure, prefixal filtration, instantiation. The path of argument may be schematized as follows:

$$\pi \rightarrow_{\text{bp}} \text{GMOAT}(\pi) \rightarrow_{\text{inst}} \text{V} \rightarrow_{\text{filtr}} \text{T}_{\text{V}}$$

Border point analysis of the partition π leads to GMOAT(π). If it is assumed acyclic, we can *instantiate* it in a VT V. The VT V is subject to standard OT candidate *filtration* to produce the typology that is associated with it. The goal is then to show that $\pi = \text{T}_{\text{V}}$.

This is accomplished through showing that prefixal filtration tracks candidate filtration perfectly. Given a partition π with an acyclic GMOAT, we examine a VT V that instantiates GMOAT(π). This involves a bijection between the rows v_k of V and the block B_k of π. As with the UVT case, we have an instantiation function that maps $\text{B}_k \mapsto \text{C}(\text{v}_k)$. What we want to show is that the native typology produced by such a V, namely T_{V}, is identical to the partition π from which we derived the GMOAT that is instantiated in V.

First, we show in Lemma (179) 'Separation Instantiation Minimality' (SIM) that a single step of prefixal filtration applied to the blocks of π, separating PC⟨π⟩ from its complement in P⟨π⟩, identifies among the corresponding rows of V those that are *numerically minimal* on C. These correspond exactly to the blocks in PC⟨π⟩. This establishes the bridge between numerical filtration and GMOAT instantiation, because filtration accepts minima and ejects non-minima. Echoing the form of the earlier result GF ⇔ RF (77), but starting with a GMOAT-instantiating VT rather than a known UVT for some T, SIM leads to the result that in every case block filtration by prefixes maps to row filtration by numerical values (BF ⇔ RF). See Lemma (180).

From this it follows easily, since a leg is prefix, that the blocks of π contain exactly the legs of the corresponding grammars of T_V, so that $\pi = T_V$. The (acyclic) GMOAT of π is therefore the MOAT of T_V, since both were built from border-point analysis. An acyclic GMOAT is therefore a MOAT, and the partition it comes from is a typology. As claimed, GMOAT acyclicity is all that's needed to ensure that π is a typology.

4.10.6 Across the borderline: The ERCoid and the ERC (184)

The grammar of a UVT row is completely determined by pairwise comparisons of that row with each of the other rows. These produce a set of ERCs, which may be compressed to a minimal canonical form by the use of the central algorithm of OT, Fusional Reduction (FRed: Brasoveanu & Prince 2005/2011), which exploits the logic native to OT (Prince 2002a). The ERC-generating comparisons work on a constraint-by-constraint basis, each resulting in one of three evaluations, marking order and equivalence between a targeted optimum **q** and a candidate **z** compared with it.

W	$C(\mathbf{q}) < C(\mathbf{z})$	– **q** is better than **z** on C
e	$C(\mathbf{q}) = C(\mathbf{z})$	– **q** is equal to **z** on C
L	$C(\mathbf{z}) < C(\mathbf{q})$	– **z** is better than **q** on C

The information assembled from every $C \in S.\text{Con}$ will give the exact conditions under which a leg will select **q** over **z** in a filtration of the set $\{\mathbf{q}, \mathbf{z}\}$. The grammar-as-leg-set consists of all the legs simultaneously satisfying the entirety of such 'elementary ranking conditions', ensuring that **q** is selected over every competitor, attaining optimality. In a related usage, the set of all such conditions, or a logical equivalent, is said to constitute an 'ERC grammar'.

From the results of §4.7, we know that a grammar, regardless of whatever VTs produce it, is determined by its border points. Each border point is involved in at least one border point pair with neighboring grammars in whatever typology or typologies it sits in. These support a relational system pitting grammar against grammar, represented in the base relations $\prec^{bp.C}$ and $\equiv^{bp.C}$ and leading to the developments we have focused on throughout. Like the relations between VT rows recorded in ERCs, the relations inherent in the border point pair may be given symbolic representation as values assigned to grammars. Whereas the numerical entries of a VT admit of just three relations of interest, numbers being what they are – greater than, less than, equal to – the positional structure of the border point pair gives rise to *four*. Those shared with the ERC are determined by the prefix and the transposition. But when a constraint lies in the suffix, no information at all is supplied about how it evaluates grammars. Thus, a fourth value arises, to indicate lack of commitment.

Given a border point pair $\{\lambda_1, \lambda_2\}$, and two distinct grammars G_1, G_2, where $\lambda_1 \in G_1$ and $\lambda_2 \in G_2$, we have, generically, $\lambda_1 = \mathrm{P}\underline{\mathrm{XY}}\mathrm{Q}$ and $\lambda_2 = \mathrm{P}\underline{\mathrm{YX}}\mathrm{Q}$. From this familiar configuration, we obtain the following, orienting the comparison as G_1(W) vs. G_2(L).

e	$C \in P$	$G_1 \equiv^{bp.C} G_2$
W	$C = X$	$G_1 \prec^{bp.C} G_2$
L	$C = Y$	$G_2 \prec^{bp.C} G_1$
u	$C \in Q$	*no information*

These four values, calculated for each constraint in the legs, may be listed in some arbitrary order to provide a list (or 'vector') that we call an ERCoid.

The effect of having u in the system can be seen in the contrast between two languages in the simple typology 'Top/coTop' (TcoT), which consists of two one-ERC languages, one the complement of the other. Rendering TcoT for concreteness on the constraints {X, Y, Z} as {XTop, co-XTop}, we arrive at the following data. The border point pairs are represented here as *ordered* rather than as sets, with the table row's grammar placed in first position.

(220) The typology TcoT

Grammar	ERC Grammar	BPPs	
XTop (XT)	{WLL}	($\underline{\mathrm{XY}}$Z, $\underline{\mathrm{YX}}$Z)	(X$\underline{\mathrm{ZY}}$, $\underline{\mathrm{ZX}}$Y)
co-XTop (coXT)	{LWW}	($\underline{\mathrm{YX}}$Z, $\underline{\mathrm{XY}}$Z)	($\underline{\mathrm{ZX}}$Y, X$\underline{\mathrm{ZY}}$)

From this data, we may construct the ERCoids implied by the border point pairs. Let's first examine the grammar of XTop.

(221) Border ERCoids of XTop

XT~ coXT	X	Y	Z
$\underline{\mathrm{XY}}$Z ~ $\underline{\mathrm{YX}}$Z	W	L	u
$\underline{\mathrm{XZ}}$Y ~ $\underline{\mathrm{YZ}}$X	W	u	L
Grammar	W	L	L

To arrive at the grammar {WLL} by combining its border ERCoids, it must be that $L \star u = u \star L = L$. (We write $\star$ for the appropriate mode of combination.) Idempotency is required as well: namely, $V \star V = V$, for a value V, here exemplified as $L \star L = L$.

The complement grammar co-XTop looks like this:

(222) Border ERCoids of co-XTop

coXT~XT	X	Y	Z
YXZ ~ XYZ	L	W	u
ZXY~ XZY	L	u	W
Grammar	L	W	W

To arrive at the grammar {LWW} from these ERCoids, we must have W ⋆ u = u ⋆ W = W. This example shows the power of the ERCoid. Because u is not restricted as to ERC value, it combines to yield both conjunction, as in WLL = 'X dominates both Y & Z', and disjunction, as LWW = 'Either Y or Z dominates X'.

Call this mode of amalgamating ERCoids 'weak composition', defined in (209). Two ERCoids may 'weakly compose' only when they match up componentwise as same-to-same or u-to-anything, in which case we need nothing more than idempotence and u ⋆ V = V ⋆ u = V to combine them. This gives us our first result: the subset of border ERCoids obtained by comparing a target grammar along its border with just one other neighboring grammar weakly composes to give a single 'Unified Border ERCoid' (UBE). Such a UBE completely characterizes the information obtainable from the border point pairs involving just those two grammars.

To go beyond weak composition, we turn to 'Fusional Reduction' (FRed: Brasoveau & Prince 2005/2011). FRed takes an ERC set and through recursive fusions reduces it to a canonical representation (the MIB or 'Most Informative Basis') that is guaranteed to be logically equivalent to the starting point. We conjecture that the entire set of ERCoids gathered from the border of a grammar, when subjected to FRed, yields the MIB of that grammar. The only modification that's required, on this view, is to extend fusion to the 4th value. The value u displaces *e* from the position of being the identity element for fusion, so that u ∘ V = V ∘ u = V for all V ∈ {W, L, *e*, u}.

Everything else remains the same. FRed itself is untouched. FRed works by fusing sets of ERCs, and omitting subsets entailed by their fusion, while retaining for further recursive processing those subsets that are not entailed, i.e. where information is crucially lost in fusion. The hallmark of information loss is the appearance of *e* in a column that fuses to W. The ERC containing that *e* carries information that must be extracted by further recursive application of the algorithm. What's required to deal with u, then? Our answer is: nothing. Unlike *e*, the presence of u in a column that fuses to W does not induce info loss, as is indeed exemplified in (222).

FRed depends on the properties of entailment between ERCs, as studied in Prince 2002a. In particular, to arrive at a MIB, an entailed fusion must be discarded. But a u-containing ERCoid denotes a set of legs and thus u does not obviously fit into any scheme of entailment relations. The ERCoid proper, containing u, appears to be an entity that can combine to yield expressions which have a logical syntax and semantics, although it does not itself support such constructions. In addition, thc ultimatc output of FRed must be a set of ERCs proper, without u, so that it denotes a determinate set of legs. For FRed to work, then, its fusions must never contain u. At present, we have only the result that the first round of FRed produces a fusion without u. This is a consequence of Theorem (215), which establishes that a constraint cannot be suffixal in every border point pair of grammar. Any such putative constraint would generate u in the ERCoid representation of every border point pair, so that the whole set would fuse to u in that constraint.

Despite this incompleteness in the argument, we offer the ERCoid as an algebraic representation of the information in border point pairs, with the expectation that it offers an algebraic route to deeper understanding of the way that the border structure of a grammar determines its content.

Chapter 5

Working out the MOAT: Jump to the CSys

Chapter contents

SINCE TYPOLOGIES ARE COMPOSITE OBJECTS, it is often illuminating to study restricted subparts in isolation from the whole. For example, we can instructively distinguish in EST between the treatment of underlying C and that of underlying V, since these function independently, as may be seen from the Universal Support (5), §2.2.1, where different csets from different inputs determine their behaviors.

To put it more generally: in examining the typology T of a system S, it will often be valuable to study a coarser typology T^c that amalgamates some of the grammars of T into typological classes. Coarsening T to T^c means abolishing some distinctions that are respected in T. Two roads lead to MOAT(T^c). We may be able to restrict *S*.GEN concretely in such a way that T^c emerges from a Universal Support of candidate sets in a related system S'. Or, more abstractly, we can merge nodes of the MOAT of the finer T in such way that the MOAT of coarser T^c is produced, with no concern about whether it is even possible to achieve the same result within the conception of linguistic structure embodied in the concrete system *S* underlying T. When both approaches are possible, the paths look like this:

(1) To the MOAT of coarsened T^c, concretely and abstractly

$$\begin{array}{rcccl} & & bpa & & \\ & S{:}\mathrm{T} & \longrightarrow & \mathrm{MOAT(T)} & \\ \textit{mod } S.\textsc{Gen} & \downarrow & & \downarrow & \textit{merge nodes} \\ & S'{:}\mathrm{T^c} & \longrightarrow & \mathrm{MOAT(T^c)} & \\ & & bpa & & \end{array}$$

Here we will examine a coarsened version of EST which recognizes distinctions only in the treatment of consonants. We will call it the *C-System* of EST, abbreviated to CSys, or more fully to EST.CSys. To obtain it, we effectively disable the constraint m.Ons by modifying *S*.GEN so that m.Ons makes no distinctions, while retaining it *pro forma* in CSys.CON. Because CSys.CON = EST.CON, we can still directly compare the two typologies because their grammars are built from the same constraints.

We modify EST.GEN so as to disallow all inputs containing 'problematic' V, those that admit unfaithful optima due to the location of V in the input. We retain EST.CON in its entirety. Distinctions in the handling of onsets are thereby lost, because m.Ons is never violated in the admitted candidates. This tactic creates a simplified system in which the handling of consonants is unimpeded by irrelevancies related to vowels.

There are other more abstract ways to construct the CSys. For example, we could hold EST.GEN constant but on the constraint side redefine m.Ons so that it assigns the same value to each candidate, say 0. The constraint $\text{m.Ons}_{\text{CSys}}$ is a different function on EST.GEN than m.Ons and therefore formal steps would have to be taken to identify them, along the lines of how the language labels are identified across typologies in our analysis of the MOAT above (§§3–4). With no distinctions on $\text{m.Ons}_{\text{CSys}}$ allowed, faithfulness breaches due strictly to improvements in the syllabic status of V will not occur in optima. Thus, among the outputs for /V/ that are optimal in EST, namely ∅, $[_\sigma\text{CV}]$, and $[_\sigma\text{V}]$, only the faithful $[_\sigma\text{V}]$ would be optimal in this version of EST.CSys, since all are equal on $\text{m.Ons}_{\text{CSys}}$. Violation of f.max or f.dep results in harmonic bounding by the faithful candidate.

Setting aside whatever virtues this approach may have, we will proceed concretely by limiting EST.GEN. The CSys will therefore be defined in the in the usual way: articulating CSys.GEN and CSys.CON, calculating the typology from a Universal Support, and then determining the MOAT via border point analysis.

But modifying *S*.GEN or *S*.CON or both can be cumbersome. The candidate-centered approach in particular lacks generality and depends on the unusually simple way that the candidate sets of EST are structured. We will therefore also pursue a formally quite distinct second route to the CSys MOAT, one which frees us entirely from the need for such concrete manipulations. We will start from the MOAT of EST and merge nodes within it, focusing on those nodes whose corresponding languages vary only in the way they deal with onset issues. The mergers produce a new MOAT: one that is structurally identical to the MOAT of the concrete EST.CSys. Identical MOAT structure ensures exact grammatical correspondence, allowing us to investigate our system either in the specialized setting of Concrete OT or in the general setting of Abstract OT.

5.1 A universal support for EST.CSys

We are interested in the effect of unioning the pairs of grammars that differ only in the treatment of onsets. The grammars pair up as follows. Recall the abbreviations OR 'Onset Required', OLA 'Onset Lack Allowed', CP 'Coda Prohibited', CA 'Coda Allowed.' The cited output canon identifies the language up to faithfulness breach.

(2) Grammars of EST

Name	Outputs	IO disparities	Output Type
1:CV.del	$[_{\sigma}CV]^*$	deletion	**OR**.CP
2:(C)V.del	$[_{\sigma}(C)V]^*$	deletion	**OLA**.CP
3:CV.ins	$[_{\sigma}CV]^+$	insertion	**OR**.CP
4:(C)V.ins	$[_{\sigma}(C)V]^+$	insertion	**OLA**.CP
5:CV(C).del	$[_{\sigma}CV(C)]^*$	deletion	**OR**.CA
6:(C)V(C).del	$[_{\sigma}(C)V(C)]^*$	deletion	**OLA**.CA
7:CV(C).ins	$[_{\sigma}CV(C)]^+$	insertion	**OR**.CA
8:(C)V(C).ins	$[_{\sigma}(C)V(C)]^+$	insertion	**OLA**.CA

The grammars we're looking for are then **1∪2**, **3∪4**, **5∪6**, **7∪8**. The extensional effect is to eliminate the distinction between syllables with and without onsets, while retaining all the other distinctions. The retained distinctions involve *problematic* C, those which do not sit right before V in the input. At issue is whether to retain problematic C when possible, faithfully as a coda if it is preceded by a vowel; or, unfaithfully, to delete problematic C or insert a V to support it.

In this particular case, we are fortunate in that a concrete version of the system can be obtained by omitting one candidate set from our universal support for EST, given in ex. (5), §2.2.1, which devolves from just three inputs: /V/, /C/, /CVC/. The input /V/ is the only one in which m.Ons is violated in optima. Eliminating it ensures that m.Ons always gives the value 0 for every admitted optimum in the support. To achieve this omission, we set up CSys.Gen so as to not produce /V/ or anything like it in the relevant respect, while retaining the input /C/ and the input /CVC/. These latter two pose no problems for m.Ons, as their optima have onsets consisting of input C. This, then, gives us a universal support for the C-System of EST, shown below:

(3) EST.CSys Universal Support

input	output	m.Ons	m.NoCoda	f.dep	f.max	Type
C_1	ε	0	0	0	1	del
	$[C_1\mathbb{V}]$	0	0	1	0	ins
C_1VC_2	$[C_1VC_2]$	0	1	0	0	F
	$[C_1V_2]$	0	0	0	1	del
	$[C_1V]\ [C_2\mathbb{V}]$	0	0	1	0	ins

The abbreviations in the rightmost 'Type' column specify the character of the IO map from the input to each output: as usual, we write F for faithful, del for deletion, ins for insertion. As before, we distinguish epenthetic V typographically.

To arrive at the CSys, we specify CSys.GEN and CSys.CON.

i. CSys.CON = EST.CON.
ii. CSys.GEN must undergo a modification to exclude problematic V from inputs.

To meet the GEN requirement, we eliminate from the set of inputs produced by CSys.GEN all V not preceded by C. Other than that, the two specifications remain the same, as does every other aspect of admitted structure. The grammars of this new typology can be generated from just the two candidate sets of ex. (3).

(4) CSys.GEN and EST.GEN, input and output sets

$\text{IN}_{\text{EST}} = \{C, V\}^+$

$\text{IN}_{\text{CSys}} = \{C, CV\}^+$

$\text{OUT}_{\text{EST}} = \text{OUT}_{\text{CSys}} = \{\ [_\sigma(C)V(C)]\ \}^*$

Our CSys.GEN disallows *inputs* beginning with V as well as those containing sequences of V. In order to maintain as close a relation as possible to EST.GEN, we set CSys.GEN to allow exactly the same outputs as EST.GEN. This means that deletional maps are allowed to produce onsetless syllables in output candidate sets. However, as in EST, deletion of underlying C occurring before V is harmonically bounded, always losing to an otherwise identical competitor where the C is syllabified with the V, as may be shown by the techniques used in P&S:§6:116–118.

Our newly defined CSys.GEN along with the assumption that CSys.CON = EST.CON yields a factorial typology of four languages. The languages differ along two binary dimensions, each addressed in a separate cset.

i. CA/CP: whether to allow codas (CA) or to prohibit them (CP).
   ☐ choice determined by /CVC/.
ii. del/ins: whether to *delete* to handle all problematic input C , or to *insert* a vowel to support their output correspondents, necessarily as an onset in optima.
   ☐ choice determined by /C/.

We use the following descriptors to identify the languages as CA.del, CA.ins, etc.

(5) Extensional languages of EST.CSys

Grammar	Optimal Outputs	Faithfulness breach
1∪2:CP.del	$[_\sigma \text{CV}]^*$	del
3∪4:CP.ins	$[_\sigma \text{CV}]^+$	ins
5∪6:CA.del	$[_\sigma \text{CV(C)}]^*$	del
7∪8:CA.ins	$[_\sigma \text{CV(C)}]^+$	ins

Because EST.Con = CSys.Con, direct comparison is possible between the grammars of EST and CSys. Each of the four ranking grammars of the CSys is literally the union of two ranking grammars from EST. This alignment is recorded in the naming of the four languages of CSys. The legs of 1∪2:CP.del, for example, combine the legs of 1:CV.del, named OR.CP.del by our conventions, with those of 2:(C)V.del, namable as OLA.CP.ins. See Appendix I for a classified list of all legs of the EST grammars.

(6) 1∪2:CP.del = 1:OR.CP.del ∪ 2:OLA.CP.del

CSys Lg.	EST Lg.	Leg#	Legs						
1∪2:CP.del	1	1	m.Ons	≫	m.NoCoda	≫	f.dep	≫	f.max
	1	2	m.Ons	≫	f.dep	≫	m.NoCoda	≫	f.max
	1	3	m.NoCoda	≫	m.Ons	≫	f.dep	≫	f.max
	1	4	m.NoCoda	≫	f.dep	≫	m.Ons	≫	f.max
	1	5	f.dep	≫	m.Ons	≫	m.NoCoda	≫	f.max
	1	6	f.dep	≫	m.NoCoda	≫	m.Ons	≫	f.max
	2	7	m.NoCoda	≫	f.dep	≫	f.max	≫	m.Ons
	2	8	f.dep	≫	m.NoCoda	≫	f.max	≫	m.Ons

Legs 1–6 are those of 1:OR.CP.del, as can be seen from the fact that f.max sits in bottom position in the rankings. Legs 7 and 8 are those of 2:OLA. CP.del, with m.Ons in bottom position and both m.NoCoda and f.dep dominating f.max.

5.2 A Unitary VT for CSys

Equipped with the Univeral Support for EST.CSys in tableau (3) we perform Minkowski summation over its two csets to get a UVT from which the MOAT may be calculated (Prince 2015b). In this VT, **CP.del** is the constraint-wise sum of the violation profile of **OR.CP.del** with that of **OLA.CP.del**, and so on.

(7) EST.CSys. UVT = /C/ ⊕ /CVC/

EST.CSys	m.Ons	m.NoCoda	f.dep	f.max
1U2:CP.del	0	0	0	2
3U4:CP.ins	0	0	2	0
5U6:CA.del	0	1	0	1
7U8:CA.ins	0	1	1	0

Now we have left Concrete OT with its inputs, outputs, and associated paraphernalia. Once again in the realm of Abstract OT, we turn to construction of the MOAT.

Here is a list of all the grammars of the CSys, as computed from UVT (7):

(8) 1U2:CP.del

m.Ons	m.NoCoda	f.dep	f.max
	W		L
		W	L

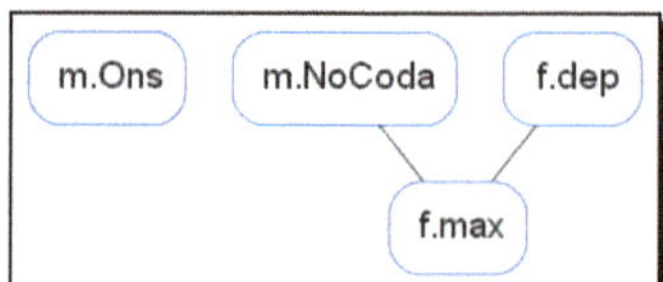

(9) 3U4:CP.ins

m.Ons	m.NoCoda	f.dep	f.max
	W	L	
		L	W

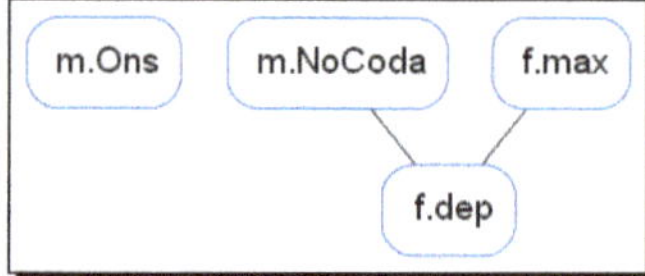

(10) 5∪6:CA.del

m.Ons	m.NoCoda	f.dep	f.max
		W	L
	L		W

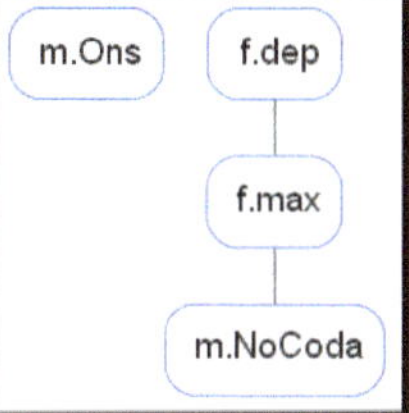

(11) 7∪8:CA.ins

m.Ons	m.NoCoda	f.dep	f.max
		L	W
	L	W	

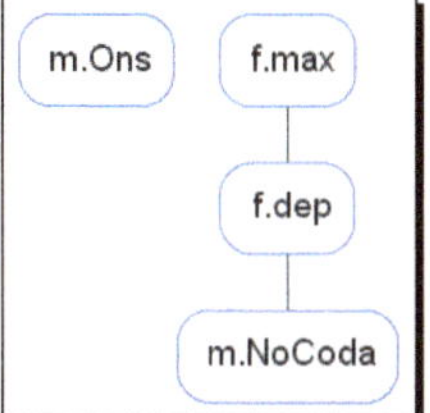

5.3 The CSys MOAT

To collect the EPOs of the MOAT, one for each constraint of the system, we assemble a sufficient collection of border point pairs.

(12) 12 border point pairs of CSys

Grammar	Border Point Pairs	Transposition
1∪2:CP.del	m.Ons ≫ m.NoCoda ≫ *f.dep* ≫ **f.max**	f.dep / f.max
3∪4:CP.ins	m.Ons ≫ m.NoCoda ≫ **f.max** ≫ *f.dep*	
1∪2:CP.del	m.NoCoda ≫ m.Ons ≫ *f.dep* ≫ **f.max**	f.dep / f.max
3∪4:CP.ins	m.NoCoda ≫ m.Ons ≫ **f.max** ≫ *f.dep*	
∪2:CP.del	m.NoCoda ≫ *f.dep* ≫ **f.max** ≫ m.Ons	f.dep / f.max
∪4:CP.ins	m.NoCoda ≫ **f.max** ≫ *f.dep* ≫ m.Ons	
3∪4:CP.ins	m.Ons ≫ f.max ≫ *m.NoCoda* ≫ **f.dep**	m.NoCoda / f.dep
7∪8:CA.ins	m.Ons ≫ f.max ≫ **f.dep** ≫ *m.NoCoda*	
3∪4:CP.ins	f.max ≫ m.Ons ≫ *m.NoCoda* ≫ **f.dep**	m.NoCoda / f.dep
7∪8:CA.ins	f.max ≫ m.Ons ≫ **f.dep** ≫ *m.NoCoda*	
3∪4:CP.ins	f.max ≫ *m.NoCoda* ≫ **f.dep** ≫ m.Ons	m.NoCoda / f.dep
7∪8:CA.ins	f.max ≫ **f.dep** ≫ *m.NoCoda* ≫ m.Ons	
7∪8:CA.ins	m.Ons ≫ *f.max* ≫ **f.dep** ≫ m.NoCoda	f.dep / f.max
5∪6:CA.del	m.Ons ≫ **f.dep** ≫ *f.max* ≫ m.NoCoda	
7∪8:CA.ins	*f.max* ≫ **f.dep** ≫ m.Ons ≫ m.NoCoda	f.dep / f.max
5∪6:CA.del	**f.dep** ≫ *f.max* ≫ m.Ons ≫ m.NoCoda	
7∪8:CA.ins	*f.max* ≫ **f.dep** ≫ m.NoCoda ≫ m.Ons	f.max / f.dep
5∪6:CA.del	**f.dep** ≫ *f.max* ≫ m.NoCoda ≫ m.Ons	
5∪6:CA.del	m.Ons ≫ f.dep ≫ *f.max* ≫ **m.NoCoda**	f.max / m.NoCoda
1∪2:CP.del	m.Ons ≫ f.dep ≫ **m.NoCoda** ≫ *f.max*	
5∪6:CA.del	f.dep ≫ m.Ons ≫ *f.max* ≫ **m.NoCoda**	f.max / m.NoCoda
1∪2:CP.del	f.dep ≫ m.Ons ≫ **m.NoCoda** ≫ *f.max*	
5∪6:CA.del	f.dep ≫ *f.max* ≫ **m.NoCoda** ≫ m.Ons	f.max / m.NoCoda
1∪2:CP.del	f.dep ≫ **m.NoCoda** ≫ *f.max* ≫ m.Ons	

We'll go through the system constraint by constraint, constructing each EPO, explicitly gathering relations between grammars induced by the border point pairs. Above we identify each border point by the grammar it comes from. Note that the cited leg is just one among several from that grammar.

1. m.Ons

No distinctions of order are made, as can be seen in the UVT (3), in which all m.Ons values are the same, by design. This means that m.Ons can go anywhere in a leg without changing the outcome. Consequently, for every adjacent pair of languages there is a border point pair that has m.Ons somewhere in its prefix. Indeed, there will always be such a pair with m.Ons undominated, making for easy collection. To make life easier, m.Ons could be moved to the front of every leg in (12). It follows that all grammars are equivalent on m.Ons.

(13) EPO_{CSys}(m.Ons)

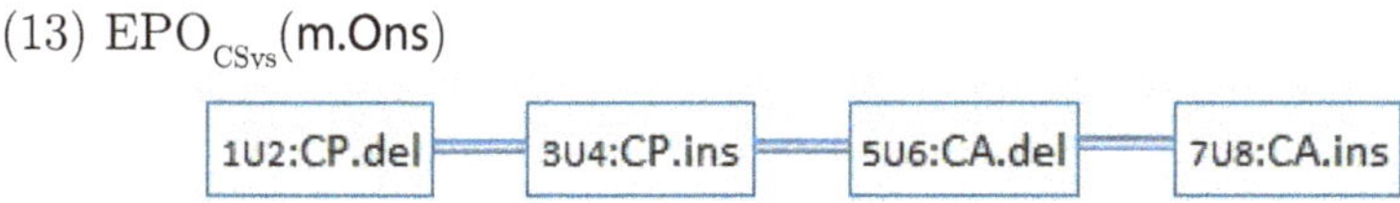

2. m.NoCoda

The crucial information about order and equality need not come from a unique source. For m.NoCoda, several border points provide the same information, sufficient to produce its EPO. We present a minimal set of border point pairs, which yields all the privileged relations for m.NoCoda, namely:

CP.del $<^{\text{bp.NoCoda}}$ CA.del

CP.ins $<^{\text{bp.NoCoda}}$ CA.ins.

No other privileged order relations obtain on m.NoCoda. Each border point gives information about another constraint as well, which we include for completeness.

(14) Privileged orders in Border Point Pairs involving m.NoCoda

Grammars	Border Point Pairs	Privileged Relations
1U2:**CP**.del	m.Ons ≫ f.dep ≫ *m.NoCoda* ≫ **f.max**	**CP**.del $<^{\text{bp.NoCoda}}$ **CA**.del
5U6:**CA**.del	m.Ons ≫ f.dep ≫ **f.max** ≫ *m.NoCoda*	**CA**.del $<^{\text{bp.max}}$ **CP**.del

3U4:**CP**.ins	f.max ≫ m.Ons ≫ *m.NoCoda* ≫ **f.dep**	**CP**.ins $<^{\text{bp.NoCoda}}$ **CA**.ins
7U8:**CA**.ins	f.max ≫ m.Ons ≫ **f.dep** ≫ *m.NoCoda*	**CA**.ins $<^{\text{bp.dep}}$ **CP**.ins

Although we're in the midst of formal calculations, it might be worth a brief pause to notice that the abstract orders in the right-hand column make clear intuitive sense.

CP.del, in which optima *never* have codas, is better on m.NoCoda than the otherwise well-matched grammar CA.del, in which they may.

CA.del is better on f.max than CP.del; it is 'less unfaithful'. CA.del adheres to faithfulness whenever GEN-possible and therefore admits codas given the right input, deleting only input C that cannot be faithfully syllabified, like /C/. By contrast, CP.del agrees that /C/ and the like must be deleted but abandons faithfulness wholesale to avoid the threat of codas.

This order relation is recognizable as the 'componentwise' order on vectors discussed on p. 2 above. Think of a language as a vector (i.e. list) of optimal candidates and apply a targeted constraint C to every one of them. Two optima vectors **u** and **v** stand as $\mathsf{C}(\mathbf{u}) \leq^{\text{coord}} \mathsf{C}(\mathbf{v})$ if at each component i, they are either (numerically) equal or $\mathsf{C}(\mathbf{u}[i]) < \mathsf{C}(\mathbf{v}[i])$, with the strict relation $\mathsf{C}(\mathbf{u}) <^{\text{coord}} \mathsf{C}(\mathbf{v})$ occurring when the numerical relation $<$ holds in at least one component.

Equivalence relations follow from border point pairs in which m.NoCoda lies in the prefix. The following pair meets this description.

(15) Equivalence on m.NoCoda

Grammars	Border Point Pair	EPO Equivalence
1U2:CP.**del**	m.NoCoda ≫ <u>*f.dep* ≫ **f.max**</u> ≫ m.Ons	CP.**del** $\sim^{\text{bp.NoCoda}}$ CP.**ins**
3U4:CP.**ins**	m.NoCoda ≫ <u>**f.max** ≫ *f.dep*</u> ≫ m.Ons	

Here languages CP.del and CP.ins both pass through m.NoCoda in the first position of these two legs. (Concretely, in these languages all syllables are open because no optimum violates m.NoCoda.) Hence CP.del $\sim^{\text{bp.NoCoda}}$ CP.ins. Note that equivalence on a constraint C is necessitated by any single total order in which multiple languages pass through C, sharing a prefix. The cited border point pair gives us two such legs.

Coupling the order relations and equivalence relations produces EPO(m.NoCoda).

(16) EPO_{CSys}(m.NoCoda)

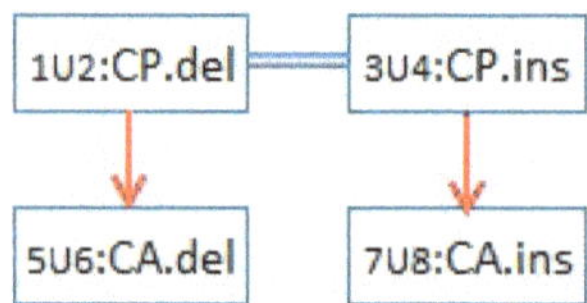

3. **f.dep**

There are three privileged order relations. Observe that from the last two we have a transitively-derived order relation between non-adjacent CA.del and CP.ins, ensuring that f.dep must make a three-way distinction among the languages in any instantiation of CSys.

CP.del $<^{\text{bp.dep}}$ CP.ins
CA.del $<^{\text{bp.dep}}$ CA.ins
CA.ins $<^{\text{bp.dep}}$ CP.Ins.

These emerge from various border point pairs, three of which are shown in (17).

(17) Privileged orders on f.dep

Grammars	Border Point Pairs	Privileged Relations
1U2:CP.**del**	m.NoCoda ≫ m.Ons ≫ *f.dep* ≫ **f.max**	CP.**del** $<^{\text{bp.dep}}$ CP.**ins**
3U4:CP.**ins**	m.NoCoda ≫ m.Ons ≫ **f.max** ≫ *f.dep*	CP.ins $<^{\text{bp.max}}$ CP.del

5U6:CA.**del**	m.Ons ≫ *f.dep* ≫ **f.max** ≫ m.NoCoda	CA.**del** $<^{\text{bp.dep}}$ CA.**ins**
7U8:CA.**ins**	m.Ons ≫ **f.max** ≫ *f.dep* ≫ m.NoCoda	CA.ins $<^{\text{bp.max}}$ CA.del

7U8:**CA**.ins	f.max ≫ *f.dep* ≫ **m.NoCoda** ≫ m.Ons	**CA**.ins $<^{\text{bp.dep}}$ **CP**.ins
3U4:**CP**.ins	f.max ≫ **m.NoCoda** ≫ *f.dep* ≫ m.Ons	CP.ins $<^{\text{bp.NoCoda}}$ CA.ins

Only two languages are equivalent in EPO(f.dep): CA.del and CP.del. Either of the two legs from the border point pair below demonstrates this, as both languages pass together through highest-ranked f.dep in each.

(18) Equivalence on f.dep

Grammars	Border Point Pair	EPO equivalence
5U6:**CA**.del	f.dep ≫ *f.max* ≫ **m.NoCoda** ≫ m.Ons	**CA**.del $\sim^{\text{bp.dep}}$ **CP**.del
1U2:**CP**.del	f.dep ≫ **m.NoCoda** ≫ *f.max* ≫ m.Ons	

The border-point-derived relations are represented in the following bigraph.

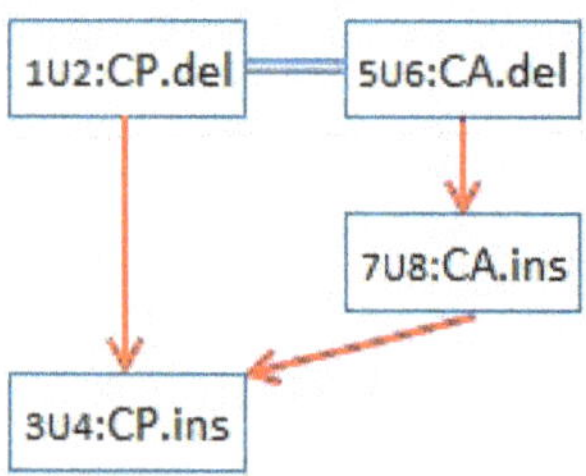

It's worth contemplating the concrete sense of the right-hand downward descent – a cline of componentwise increasing use of f.dep-defying epenthesis. CA.del (upper right) displays no epenthesis at all, relying on deletion only to handle /C/ and like inputs that require a faithfulness breach. One step down, CA.ins is minimally different in that it uses epenthesis rather than deletion with unfaithfulness-requiring input C like /C/, but nowhere else. CP.ins uses epenthesis for the same purpose, but also uses it quite generally to avoid codas altogether.

4. f.max

The structure of the f.max EPO mirrors that of the f.dep EPO: one can be obtained from the other by swapping the *ins* and *del* versions of output-identical languages. As we would expect from this symmetry, there are three privileged order relations in the f.max EPO, with the last again forming a transitive chain.

CP.ins $<^{\text{bp.max}}$ CP.del
CA.ins $<^{\text{bp.max}}$ CA.del
CA.del $<^{\text{bp.max}}$ CP.del.

The following three border point pairs establish these relations.

(20) Privileged relations on f.max

Grammars	Border Point Pairs	Privileged Relations
3U4:CP.**ins**	m.NoCoda ≫ m.Ons ≫ *f.max* ≫ **f.dep**	CP.**ins** $<^{\text{bp.max}}$ CP.**del**
1U2:CP.**del**	m.NoCoda ≫ m.Ons ≫ **f.dep** ≫ *f.max*	CP.del $<^{\text{bp.dep}}$ CP.ins

7U8:CA.**ins**	m.Ons ≫ *f.max* ≫ **f.dep** ≫ m.NoCoda	CA.**ins** $<^{\text{bp.max}}$ CA.**del**
5U6:CA.**del**	m.Ons ≫ **f.dep** ≫ *f.max* ≫ m.NoCoda	CA.del $<^{\text{bp.dep}}$ CA.ins

5U6:**CA**.del	f.dep ≫ *f.max* ≫ **m.NoCoda** ≫ m.Ons	**CA**.del $<^{\text{bp.max}}$ **CP**.del
1U2:**CP**.del	f.dep ≫ **m.NoCoda** ≫ *f.max* ≫ m.Ons	CP.del $<^{\text{bp.NoCoda}}$ CA.del

One equivalence relation holds: CP.ins $\sim^{\text{bp.max}}$ CA.ins. The prefix of either border point in the following pair gives this result:

(21) Equivalence on f.max

Grammars	Border Point Pair	EPO Equivalence
3U4:**CP**.ins	f.max ≫ *m.NoCoda* ≫ **f.dep** ≫ m.Ons	**CP**.ins $\sim^{\text{bp.max}}$ **CA**.ins
7U8:**CA**.ins	f.max ≫ **f.dep** ≫ *m.NoCoda* ≫ m.Ons	

Putting these relations together yields this EPO bigraph.

(22) EPO_{CSys}(f.max)

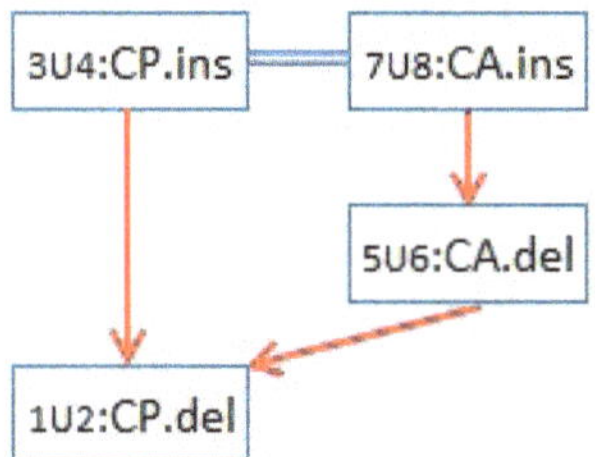

The collection of these four EPOs constitutes the MOAT of CSys, which we have derived by analyzing border point pairs from the concretely-derived Universal Support (3).

Let's now approach the CSys from the fully abstract side, starting from the EST MOAT and merging its nodes in such a way that their associated grammars are typological classes which line up with the grammars of the CSys.

How do we connect the abstract calculation with the concrete results from the CSys? Because EST and CSys share Con, the grammars of one may be matched with the grammars of the other through their ranking content. Our strategy is to merge nodes in the EST MOAT, producing derived EPOs in which the constituent languages have ranking grammars that match those of the CSys leg for leg.

As above, we advance EPO by EPO. We begin with m.Ons in EST.

1. From $\mathrm{EPO}_{\mathrm{EST}}$ (m.Ons)

(23) $\mathrm{EPO}_{\mathrm{EST}}$(m.Ons) with iconic labels

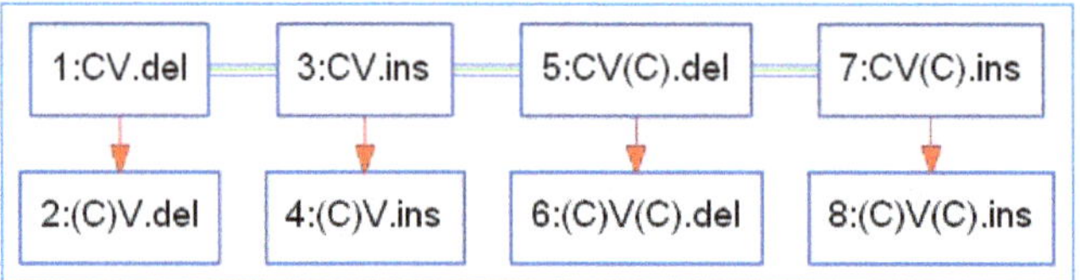

Using the descriptive labels, the m.Ons EPO looks like this:

(24) $\mathrm{EPO}_{\mathrm{EST}}$(m.Ons) with descriptive labels

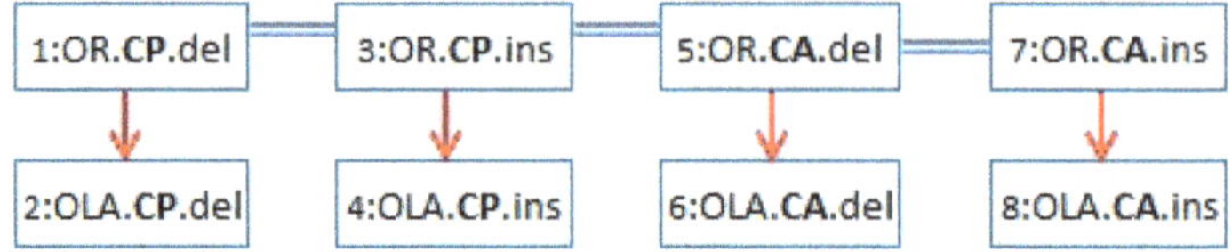

Merging nodes **1** and **2** corresponds to unioning their legs. Since **1** is OR.CP.del and **2** is OLA.CP.del, merging them into a node **1•2** gives us the graphical correlate of CP.del, as desired. Similarly, merging 3:OR.CP.ins with 4:OLA.CP.ins gives 3•4:CP.ins, and so on.

This operation collapses distinctions between the languages on the onset dimension, leaving the four merged nodes equivalent, and consequently induces no cycles. This new EPO is structurally identical to the EPO for m.Ons for CSys (13), reproduced as ex. (26).

(25) $\mathrm{EPO}_{\mathrm{CSys}}$(m.Ons). *Derived by node mergers* on $\mathrm{EPO}_{\mathrm{EST}}$(m.Ons)

(26) $\mathrm{EPO}_{\mathrm{CSys}}$(m.Ons). *Derived by border point analysis* on the CSys.

Node merger in the graph corresponds to union in the ranking grammars, and the CSys is built directly from unions, as illustrated above in ex. (6), §5.1. These EPOs therefore denote identical leg content in the corresponding grammars. The significance is that we are able to construct the EPO of the coarsened typology without analyzing the legs of its grammars: once we have the MOAT, all such calculations can be performed through merger. Two courses of action lead to the same result. We can represent this fact in a diagram.

(27) Two routes to the EPOs of a coarsened typology

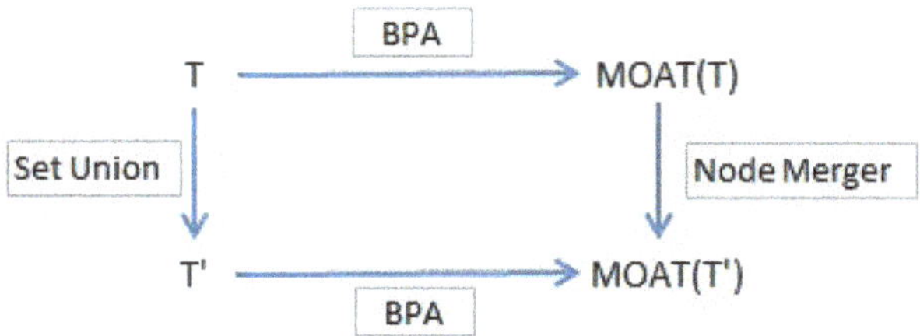

This diagram resembles that of ex. (1), which compares node merger with modifying EST.GEN as modes of coarsening EST. But here the action is more abstract, taking place at the level of grammars and typologies, making no direct contact with the extensional languages. The diagram indicates that the composition of set union (in the typology) with Border Point Analysis (BPA) yields the same result as the composition of BPA with node merger (in the MOAT). For this to work, the set union involved must be typological coarsening and node merger must not introduce cycles. When node merger preserves acyclicity, then it follows from what we've shown in Theorem (183), §4.8, that the corresponding set union is typological coarsening; and vice versa.

2. From EPO$_{\text{EST}}$ (m.NoCoda)

EPO$_{\text{EST}}$(m.NoCoda) mirrors EPO$_{\text{EST}}$(m.Ons), *mutatis mutandis*, overall. In it, the four CP grammars are equivalent (**1** $\sim^{\text{bp.NoCoda}}$ **2** $\sim^{\text{bp.NoCoda}}$ **3** $\sim^{\text{bp.NoCoda}}$ **4**), with each of the four ordered above one grammar from the CA series.

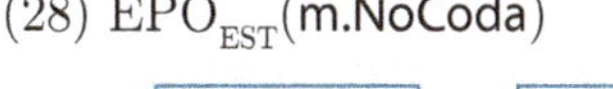
(28) EPO$_{\text{EST}}$(m.NoCoda)

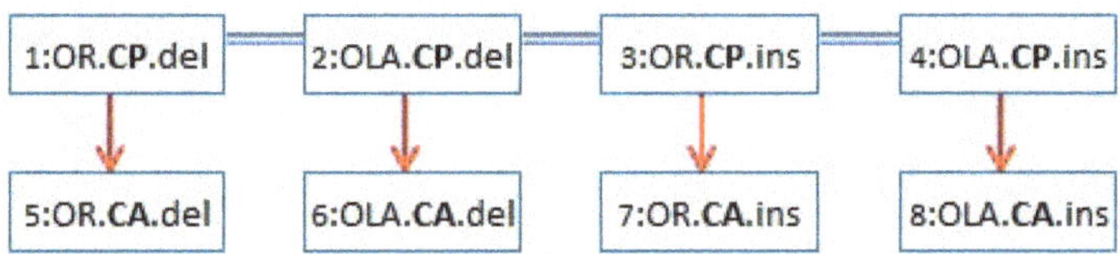

We merge the four pairs of horizontal neighbors (**1**,**2**), (**3**,**4**), (**5**,**6**), (**7**,**8**), leading to a well-formed EPO with no cycles.

(29) EPO_{CSys}(m.NoCoda) from node merger

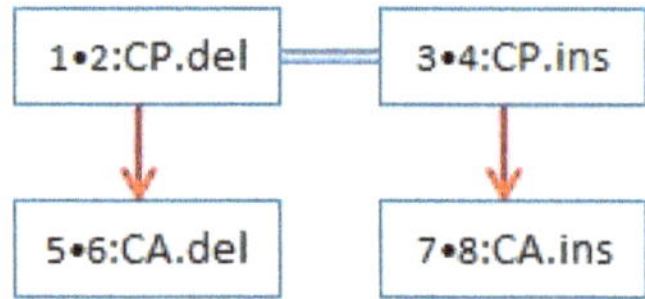

Our direct calculation by border point analysis on the CSys yielded the following result, derived in tables (14) and (15):

(30) $\text{EPO}_{\text{CSsys}}$(m.NoCoda) from border point analysis

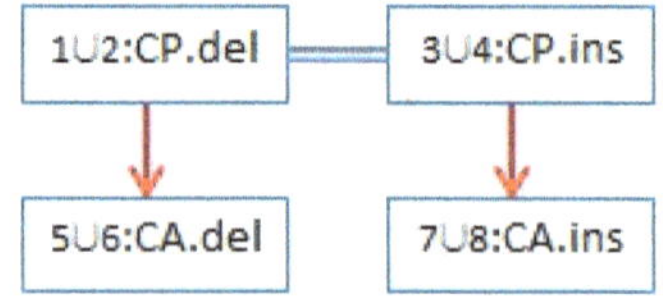

As before, these EPOs are equivalent, denoting the same grammars with the same order and equivalence relations holding among them.

3. From EPO_{EST} (f.dep)
EPO_{EST}(f.dep) is given below, repeated from (29), §3.2.

(31) EPO_{EST}(f.dep)

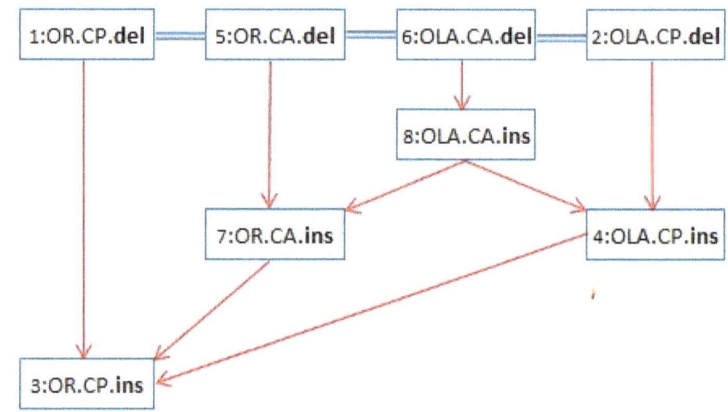

Forming, as always, the mergers **1•2**, **3•4**, **5•6**, **7•8** will derive the following:

(32) EPO_{CSys}(f.dep) via node merger

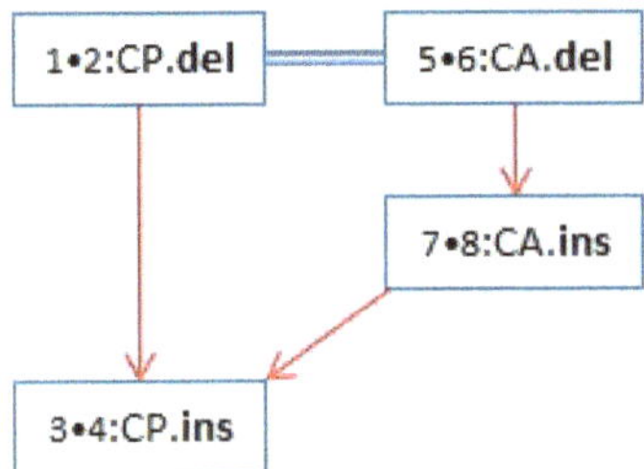

Calculating from border points in the CSys yields the following result, as in (19).

(33) EPO_{CSys}(f.dep) via BPA

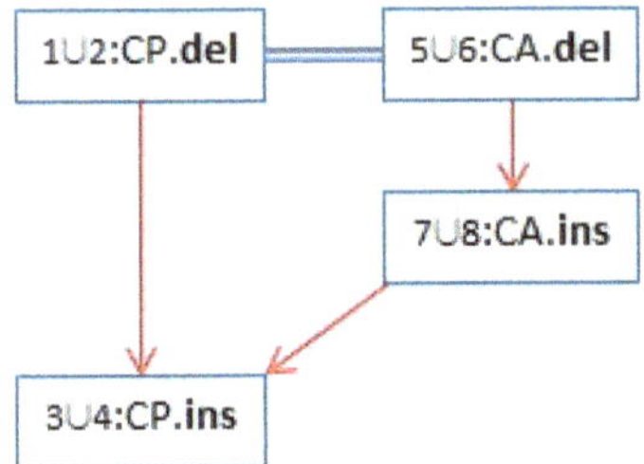

Once again, inevitably, isomorphic results are obtained.

4. From EPO_{EST} (f.max)

We conclude by examining the last remaining EPO in the EST MOAT: f.max, which symmetrically reflects that of f.dep. The EST version of the f.max is repeated from (30), §3.2.

(34) EPO_{EST}(f.max)

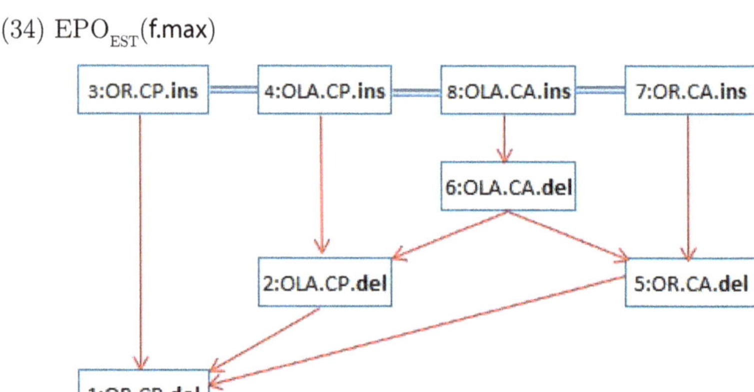

Merging the nodes that differ only in onset specification yields this EPO:

(35) EPO_{CSys}(f.max) via node merger

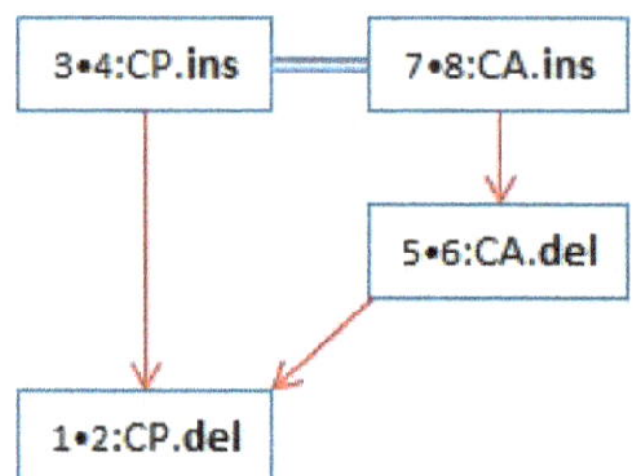

Direct calculation from the concrete CSys yields this EPO, reproduced from (22):

(36) EPO_{CSys}(f.max) via BPA

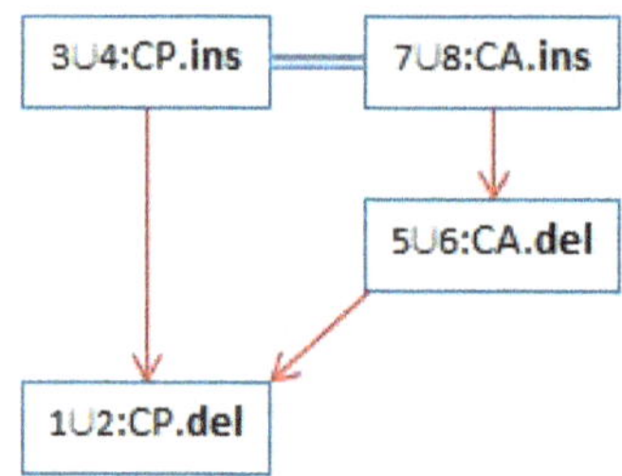

The two paths arrive at the same goal. This concludes the demonstration. □

The merger of nodes in every EPO corresponds, in this case, to grouping together pairs of grammars, and correspondingly, pairs of extensional languages, into empirically meaningful classes. By merging EST grammar 1:OR.del with 2:OLA.del, and 3:OR.ins with 4:OLA.ins, and so on, we obtain a coarser typology whose grammars are classes of EST grammars and whose languages are classes of EST languages. These classes abstract away from the distinctions in treatment of onsets, retaining the EST distinctions in consonant behavior and modes of unfaithfulness. This gives an analysis of one aspect of EST. Similarly, by merging nodes of grammars that differ only in the treatment of consonants, we can achieve a parallel analysis of onset behavior – the VSys.

In this simple case, these abstract maneuvers are reflected exactly in the concrete OT system under analysis. The CSys may be obtained by tailoring CSys.Gen so that an onsetless configuration never arises. From the abstract point of view, however, there is no need to search for a concrete instantiation, which may not exist within the structural strictures of the original typology. In the stress typologies studied by Alber & Prince (2021, in prep.), for example, we can abstractly merge information from forms of different lengths, even though no concrete form can have both an even and an odd number of syllables. The formal system of MOAT manipulation based on node merger provides the entire inventory of possible typological classes, a starting point for principled classification of language types in terms of ranking relations that define structural patterns. This strategy of abstract analysis pushes the Classification Program forward in both practice and theory.

Chapter 6

Compatibility and the join

Chapter contents

CLASSIFYING GRAMMARS TOGETHER IS MIRRORED by merger of their nodes in the EPOs of a MOAT. We have seen in §5 how EST grammars merge to form classes like CP.del and CP.ins in the coarser CSys typology. But merger has its perils: when the result contains cycles, typological status is lost.

There are two sources for this outcome. First, the merger may not be a grammar at all: in this case, it is not ERC-characterizable, not a 'grammatical class' and it has no hope of being hosted in a typology. Second, and more subtly, a set of grammars may merge to a licit abstract grammar but may nonetheless fail to be EPO-orderable with its neighbors, failing to be a 'typological class' of its host typology.

In studying the first case (§6.1), we show how the question of grammatical class status can be resolved in a typology-independent way by the ERC-logic based operation of the *join* (Merchant 2008, 2011). The second case is fleshed out with two examples which show different aspects of MOAT structure at play (§6.2), leading inter alia to the conclusion that a set of grammars may when merged form a typological class even though when unmerged it cannot sit in any typology due to internal cycles.

6.1 To form a more perfect union

All typological classes can be obtained by node merger in the MOAT diagram, but when merger yields a cyclic bigraph, it takes us outside the class of well-formed MOATs altogether. The block of legs denoted by the merged nodes in a cycle does not form a typological class because merger does not derive a typology, and it may not even constitute a grammatical class – an abstract grammar, characterizable by an ERC set. In this section, we examine a method based in ERC logic, the 'join' (Merchant 2008, 2011), which allows us to determine when grammars can union into a grammatical class, regardless of their position in any surrounding typology.

We begin by examining in detail the character of a cycle-inducing merger in the full EST. Let us return to the extensionally-motivated grouping 'Onset Required' (OR), consisting of languages $\{\mathbf{1}, \mathbf{3}, \mathbf{5}, \mathbf{7}\}$, which contrasts with the grouping $\{\mathbf{2}, \mathbf{4}, \mathbf{6}, \mathbf{8}\}$ 'Onset Lack Allowed' (OLA). We'll examine the merger in the $\mathrm{EPO}_{\mathrm{EST}}$(f.max), repeated here in its unmerged form:

(1) $\mathrm{EPO}_{\mathrm{EST}}$(f.max)

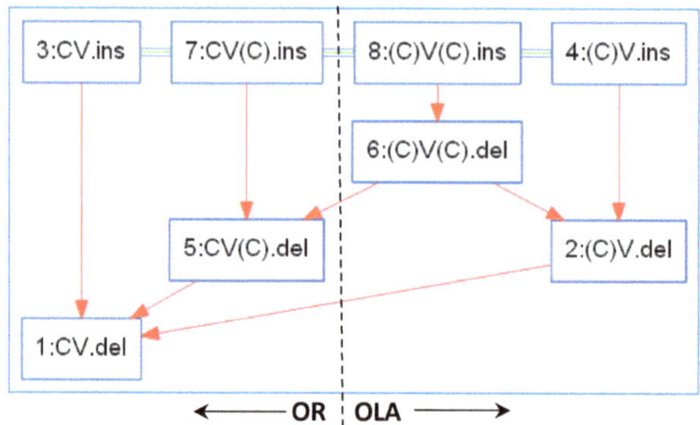

Let's approach the problem incrementally, by first merging languages that only disagree along the (vertical) ins/del axis in diagram (1), such as 3:CV.*ins* and 1:CV.*del* at the far left. These mergers are **1•3**, **2•4**, **5•7**, **6•8**. In terms of the descriptive labels, we have:

(2) EST unions of ins/del pairs

Unions: *X.del* ∪ *X.ins*			Result	Mergers
1:OR.CP.del	∪	3:OR.CP.ins	OR.CP	**1•3**
5:OR.CA.del	∪	7:OR.CA.ins	OR.CA	**5•7**
2:OLA.CP.del	∪	4:OLA.CP.ins	OLA.CP	**2•4**
6:OLA.CA.del	∪	8:OLA.CA.ins	OLA.CA	**6•8**

This serves as an instructive step on the way to merging all nodes $\{\mathbf{1}, \mathbf{3}, \mathbf{5}, \mathbf{7}\}$ on the OR side (left) and all nodes $\{\mathbf{2}, \mathbf{4}, \mathbf{6}, \mathbf{8}\}$ on the OLA side (right).

These four mergers just listed generalize away from faithfulness distinctions and will divide EST into the four familiar Jakobsonian output classes:

(3) Jakobsonian output classes of EST (cf. P&S:ch. 6, p. 105)

CV	OR.CP
CV(C)	OR.CA
(C)V	OLA.CP
(C)V(C)	OLA.CA

The results of merger are shown graphically below.

(4) Bigraph of EPO(**f.max**) with merger of ins/del classes

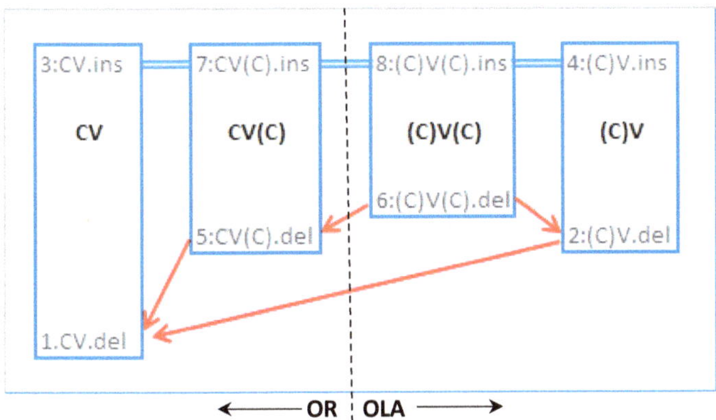

The Jakobsonian bigraph (4) is already cyclic in a way that spells doom for the project of getting the OR/OLA distinction from typological classes. The diagram has been constructed to indicate how prior relations between the components of distinct merged nodes persist into the merger.

Every pair of box-shaped nodes in bigraph (4) is involved in a cycle, which may traverse other nodes. By virtue of their *ins* components, the members of any pair are connected by the double blue line '=', signaling grammar equivalence via $\sim^{\text{bp.max}}$. By virtue of their *del* components, however, all pairs are forced into a $<^{\text{bp.max}}$ relationship, in some cases directly, in some cases by transitivity of the $<^{\text{bp.max}}$ relation denoted by the red arrow '→'. The hypertransitive relation $<^{\text{htc.bp.max}}$, which collates the consequences of $<^{\text{bp.max}}$ and $\sim^{\text{bp.max}}$ taken together, fails to be a partial order because of the cycles.[1]

Some of the cycles are erased in the further mergers that create the OR/OLA distinction. For example, we see in ex. (4) that the inherited, retained relations **3=7** and **5→1** produce a cycle between the left-hand pair of nodes, which comprise the OR half of the typology. This particular cycle will be erased when we merge them further to produce OR = **1•3•5•7**, because the obstructing relation **5→1** is no longer external to the merged node. But the relations between components of OR (left side) and components of OLA (right side) have the same character and will undermine the typological status of the OR and OLA groupings.

To see this, we merge again to produce the OR/OLA bigraph.

(5) OR/OLA bigraph for f.max with all external relations shown

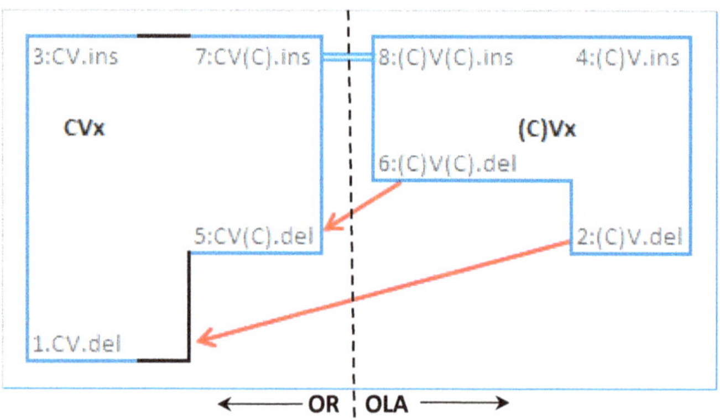

Consolidating the '→' information yields the following concise form.

[1] Recall that relations due to hypertransivity proper, crucially involving equivalence, are *not* represented in the EPO, as they do not obstruct merger (see §3.3). However, an EPO cycle in a bigraph may implicate hypertransitive inference.

(6) OR/OLA bigraph for f.max

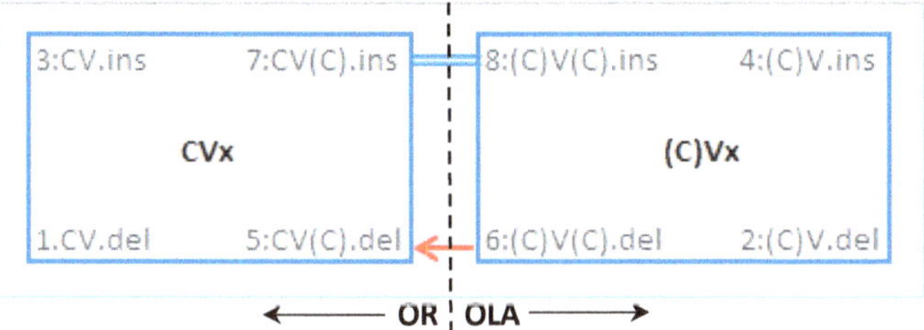

The class OR **1•3•5•7** must be EPO-equivalent and UVT-equal to OLA **2•4•6•8** by virtue of relations involving **3**,**7** (OR.ins) and **4**,**8** (OLA.ins). At the same time **1•3•5•7** must be greater than (i.e. *worse than*) **2•4•6•8** by virtue of relations between **1**,**5** (OR.del) and **2**,**6** (OLA.del). No consistent assignment of numbers is in the offing. Recall that $<^{\text{htc.X}}$, obtained by combining information from $<^{\text{X}}$ and $\sim^{\text{X}}$, must be instantiable as numerical $<$ in any UVT, as shown in Lemma (48) of §4.3.5.

The algebraic details run like this:

(7) Cycle logic

Relations	**Rationale**
OLA $<^{\text{htc.bp.max}}$ OR	because OLA $<^{\text{bp.max}}$ OR, inherited from e.g. **2** ⊆ OLA $<^{\text{bp.max}}$ **1** ⊆ OR
OR $\sim^{\text{bp.max}}$ OLA	inherited from e.g. **7** ⊆ OR $\sim^{\text{bp.max}}$ **8** ⊆ OLA
OLA $<^{\text{htc.bp.max}}$ OLA	by hypertransitivity.

Observe that the project was doomed at the lowest level: the class CV, descriptively OR.CP, tries to amalgamate the grammar of 1:CV.del, in which f.max is dominated by every other constraint, with that of 3:CV.ins, in which f.dep is dominated by every other constraint. But in this collocation, there is no single constraint that is necessarily dominated throughout, and therefore no ERC that expels some legs from the presumed grammar. Thus 1∪3:CV, descriptively OR.CP, is not even a *grammatical* class; and similarly for the others.

There's a further subtlety that can be wrung from the full bigraph of EPO(f.max). The OLA and OR classes cannot coexist, as we've just seen in (6), but the class OLA represented by **2•4•6•8** is perfectly legitimate typologically when accompanied by non-merger among the OR classes along the *ins*/*del* dimension. The join of all the OLA grammars is conservative and embodies the entirely ERCable requirement that *both* f.max and f.dep dominate m.Ons. The complement of that join is the OR class, but de Morgan steps in to tell us that it must require **m.Ons** to dominate *either* **f.max** *or* **f.dep**, expressible by neither ERC nor ERC set, and therefore no grammar. We return to this point below, exploring both the underlying leg set of OR and its join in more detail.

We have arrived at the border of what a grammatical or typological classification system allows. Alber & Prince (*op. cit.*) observe that the issue arises because classes of constraints may be systematically related in ways that requires a generalization of the logic of single ERCs. In the system at hand, **f.dep** and **f.max** behave symmetrically with respect to the grammars of the system, as is readily visible in their EPOs, repeated here for ease of comparison.

(8) EPO_{EST}(f.max)

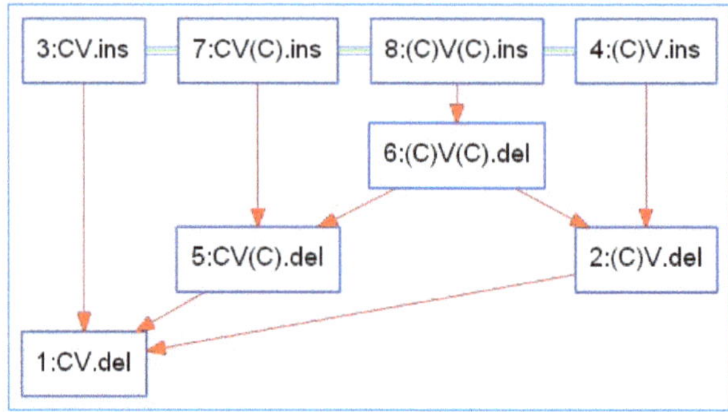

(9) EPO_{EST}(f.dep)

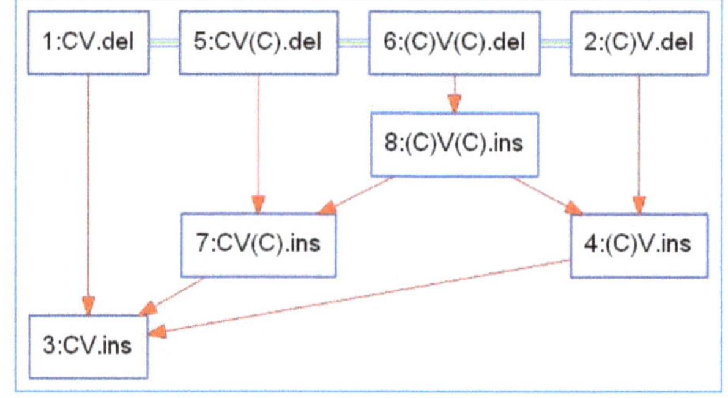

In such cases, the parallelism indicates that constraints form classes to which analysis must refer. The relevant class here is 'Faithfulness', abbreviated as F, with F = {**f.max**, **f.dep**} for EST. The classification theory of Alber & Prince allows reference to the member of that class which is *subordinate* in a leg λ – lowest ranked among its class – as 'F.sub(λ)'. Applying this to the present case, note that every λ ∈ OR meets, in their notation, the condition 'm.Ons(λ) > F.sub(λ)' because in every OR leg, the occurrence of m.Ons dominates *that member of the faithfulness class* which is subordinate to the other. Thus, in a given OR grammar, m.Ons dominates one member *or* the other. But ERCs require conjunction of the dominated; the cited condition imposes a disjunctive requirement.

OLA meets the ranking-wise opposite condition 'F.sub(λ) > m.Ons(λ)'. In this case, since in any leg the F constraints are ordered with respect to each other, when F.sub(λ) dominates m.Ons, it follows from transitivity of domination that *both* faithfulness constraints dominate m.Ons. When the theory is further augmented by the ability to refer to *dominant* member of a constraint class in a leg as e.g. F.dom(λ), ERCs are expressible, and a theory of reference to constraint classes emerges that generalizes the ERC. See Alber & Prince (*op. cit.*) for development. For present purposes, the significant finding is that the theory of typological classification, whose structure we are investigating here, sets the stage for analyzing such further articulations, of which it forms a proper part.

The MOAT allows us to determine, via node merger, whether the union of grammars results in a grammar that belongs to a coarsened version of a reference typology. We may also focus on the grammars and pose the question independent of a typological surround: given two grammars, is their leg-union also a grammar? Taken together, do they form a *grammatical class*? Recall that a grammatical class is a set of grammars whose union is itself a grammar, whereas a typological class within a typology T is a set of grammars within T whose union forms a coarser typology T′.

The MOAT allows us to answer the narrower question – when does a collection of grammars form a *typological* class? – narrower because a typological class is *a fortiori* a grammatical class. The more general question may be answered directly within the realm of ERC grammars without reference to a containing typology. There, the use of the *join*, an operation on grammars introduced by Merchant (2008, 2011), makes use of ERC logic to determine the smallest grammar that contains the legs of the union.

To see how this works in practice, we begin by observing that the class OR has the following leg collection, which includes all the legs of the four grammars of the languages in which all well-formed syllables have onsets. The relationship between m.Ons and faithfulness is highlighted by boxing the relevant constraints.

(10) OR legs

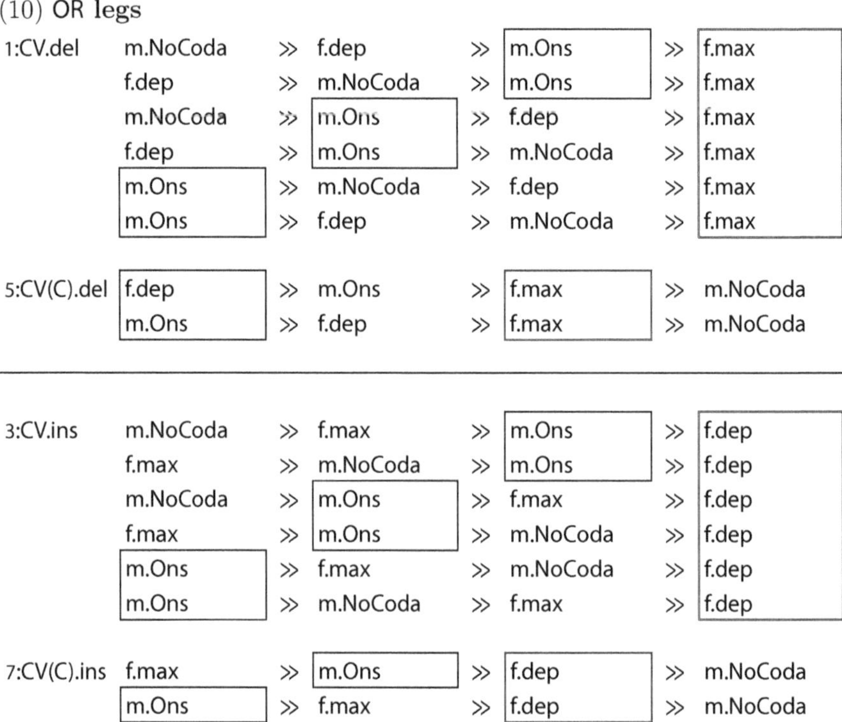

1:CV.del	m.NoCoda	≫	f.dep	≫	m.Ons	≫	f.max
	f.dep	≫	m.NoCoda	≫	m.Ons	≫	f.max
	m.NoCoda	≫	m.Ons	≫	f.dep	≫	f.max
	f.dep	≫	m.Ons	≫	m.NoCoda	≫	f.max
	m.Ons	≫	m.NoCoda	≫	f.dep	≫	f.max
	m.Ons	≫	f.dep	≫	m.NoCoda	≫	f.max
5:CV(C).del	f.dep	≫	m.Ons	≫	f.max	≫	m.NoCoda
	m.Ons	≫	f.dep	≫	f.max	≫	m.NoCoda
3:CV.ins	m.NoCoda	≫	f.max	≫	m.Ons	≫	f.dep
	f.max	≫	m.NoCoda	≫	m.Ons	≫	f.dep
	m.NoCoda	≫	m.Ons	≫	f.max	≫	f.dep
	f.max	≫	m.Ons	≫	m.NoCoda	≫	f.dep
	m.Ons	≫	f.max	≫	m.NoCoda	≫	f.dep
	m.Ons	≫	m.NoCoda	≫	f.max	≫	f.dep
7:CV(C).ins	f.max	≫	m.Ons	≫	f.dep	≫	m.NoCoda
	m.Ons	≫	f.max	≫	f.dep	≫	m.NoCoda

As we've just shown by a MOAT-based argument, the legs of all OR languages, taken together, do not form a grammar in any typology coarsened from EST, indeed in any typology. By inspecting table (10), we can deduce, independent of typological considerations, that there is no ERC set that delimits OR.

The most elementary argument would be to audit the leg table and to note, paralleling the discussion of ex. (6), that each of the four constraints appears in top position in some leg. Since no constraint is crucially dominated, there is no ERC grammar that excludes any leg. A nontrivial ERC grammar, one that denotes less than the entire set of rankings, requires that there be at least one constraint that is everywhere subordinated.

We may also expand on an observation of greater generality, first made in §1.3.3. Admission to the OR leg set requires *either* m.Ons ≫ f.dep *or* m.Ons ≫ f.max. An ERC says that *some* constraint assessing W of the competing pair must dominate *every* constraint assessing L, so that disjunction among the dominated is not ERC-representable. Nor can there be a *set* of ERCs that embodies this disjunction. A set imposes the conjunction of the requirements of each ERC in the set. Every ERC must be satisfied, and there's no general way to say, disjunctively, that some ERC *or* another must hold. This argument establishes that **OR** is not a grammar and applies to any case where a leg set is only describable with disjunction among the dominated. The Alber & Prince classification theory, which refers to classes like **OR** by the operators *dom* and *sub*, generalizes (via *sub*) beyond the descriptive capacity of the ERC and the ERC set.

What this means in the realm of ERC grammars is that the *join* of the four OR grammars, which we represent as $\mathbf{1}+\mathbf{3}+\mathbf{5}+\mathbf{7}$, has more legs in it than $\mathbf{1} \cup \mathbf{3} \cup \mathbf{5} \cup \mathbf{7}$, which is shown in table (10). The join of the four includes every leg in EST. This superfluity means that the simple union of the four is not a grammatical class.

The logic of the join is that of componentwise ERC disjunction. Just as in propositional logic the formula p ∨ q is the 'smallest' formula that is entailed by both p and q individually, so with ERC grammars P and Q, the join P + Q is the 'smallest' grammar containing both P and Q (Merchant 2008, 2011).[2] 'Smallest' means here that P + Q contains the legs of P and the legs of Q, along with possibly more, with the proviso that any ranking grammar R containing the legs of P and the legs of Q also contains those of P + Q.

The join of two ERC grammars is constructed from a suitably full ERC representation of both: each ERC in the first is disjoined in the componentwise ERC logic manner with each ERC in the second. The result is an ERC set – a grammar – shown by Merchant to be the smallest grammar legwise that contains both joining grammars. We sketch the operation here.

ERC logic disjunction is like Boolean disjunction in that it is idempotence ($x \vee x = x$) and commutative ($x \vee y = y \vee x$). The W value behaves like T and L behaves like F; the third value *e* is interpolated between them. See Prince (2002a:51) for the details. The basic recipe runs like this:

(11) ERC logic disjunction (applies to each component). For $x \in \{\mathrm{W}, \mathrm{L}, e\}$,

$\mathrm{W} \vee x = \mathrm{W}$	*cf.* $\mathrm{T} \vee x = \mathrm{T}$
$\mathrm{L} \vee x = x$	*cf.* $\mathrm{F} \vee x = x$
$e \vee e = e$	

Note that $\mathrm{L} \vee e = e$ and $\mathrm{W} \vee e = \mathrm{W}$. We may also think of this as working from a scale $\mathrm{W} > e > \mathrm{L}$. Disjunction of values returns the greatest value among the disjuncts. Boolean logic, from this perspective, operates on the binary scale $\mathrm{T} > \mathrm{F}$.

[2] Details, details: q ∨ p and Q + P also fill the bill as 'smallest'. To be more precise, one must deal with equivalence classes of formulae. See e.g. Lindenbaum–Tarski algebra, Wikipedia.

The join of two grammars $G_1 + G_2$ disjoins every ERC in an ERC grammar of G_1 with every ERC in an ERC grammar of G_2. (Caveat: the operation requires these grammars to be suitably rich in ERC content.[3]) An ERC grammar unique up to logical equivalence results. Because the join, like disjunction itself, is commutative and associative, we may easily extend the definition to arbitrary finite sets of languages.

What, then, is the result of *joining* the grammars of OR, namely $\mathbf{1} + \mathbf{3} + \mathbf{5} + \mathbf{7}$? Equivalently: what is the smallest grammar that contains the legs of all of these? We know already that it is the trivial grammar that includes all legs. Why does the join give us this result?

As Merchant observes, to produce a nontrivial ERC in the join, one that is not true of every ranking, a disjoining pair of ERCs must share an L in some constraint. According to the disjunction table (11), the only way to get L in the output is to disjoin two Ls in the input: $L \vee L = L$. Since **1**, **3**, **5**, and **7** do not share even one dominated constraint, the join is going to be trivial in the sense that it admits all rankings.

By contrast, compare the nontrivial join of 1:CV.del (OR.CP.del) and 2:(C)V.del. (OLA.CP.del). These two grammars disagree on the obligatoriness of onsets, but both ban codas in optima and achieve conformity with the CP requirement by deletion. In the joined grammar 1+2:CP.del the distinction between the onset requirements in the joinards is wiped out. The constraint f.max is crucially dominated in both.

(12) ERC grammars of 1:CV.del and 2:(C)V.del

i. 1:CV.del

ERC	m.Ons	m.NoCoda	f.dep	f.max
a_1	W			L
a_2		W		L
a_3			W	L

[3] In particular, the grammars must be such that for every α with $G \models \alpha$, there must be an ERC $\gamma \in G$ such that $\gamma \models \alpha$. Merchant uses the fusional closure of G to ensure that this condition is met.

ii. 2:(C)V.del

ERC	m.Ons	m.NoCoda	f.dep	f.max
b_1	**L**			**W**
b_2		**W**		**L**
b_3			**W**	**L**

The join, cleared of redundancy, comes out like this:

(13) Join: 1:CV.del + 2:(C)V.del

ERC	m.Ons	m.NoCoda	f.dep	f.max
$a_2 \vee b_2$		**W**		**L**
$a_3 \vee b_3$			**W**	**L**

Here we use the disjunction symbol ∨ to indicate componentwise application of ERC logic disjunction as defined in (11) above.

The join may be formed by combining every ERC of (12)a with every ERC of (12)b, or more economically, by combining those pairs of ERCs, one from each grammar, which share L in some constraint. Those which share no L disjoin to an ERC without L. An ERC with only W and *e* asserts no restrictions on ranking, and is therefore true of every ranking; it may be discarded, or ignored uncomputed, as uninformative.

Further elements of the join are discarded because they are entailed by other elements, and therefore redundant. Here is full display of the results of joining all the elements of (12)a with those of (12)b, arranged to make visible the flow of redundancy.[4]

[4] We depart from Merchant's algorithm in one respect: we do not form the fusional closure of the joinards prior to joining. In this case, the participating ERC sets are already sufficiently rich to guarantee validity.

ERC		m.Ons	m.NoCoda	f.dep	f.max
i	**$a_1 \vee b_1$**	**W**		**W**	
ii	**$a_3 \vee b_1$**			**W**	
iii	**$a_1 \vee b_2$**	**W**	**W**		**L**
iv	**$a_1 \vee b_3$**	**W**		**W**	**L**
v	**$a_2 \vee b_1$**		**W**	**W**	**L**
vi	**$a_2 \vee b_3$**		**W**	**W**	**L**
vii	**$a_3 \vee b_2$**		**W**	**W**	**L**
viii	**$a_2 \vee b_2$**		**W**		**L**
ix	**$a_3 \vee b_3$**			**W**	**L**

Only the bottom-most ERCs (viii) and (ix) are non-redundant. ERCs (i) and (ii) lack L and are thus trivially true and say nothing of interest. The next five, (iii)–(vii), are entailed by ERC (viii) or ERC (ix) or both, by virtue of sharing a W and having one further W than (viii) or (ix).

The join **1** + **2** is nontrivial and *conservative*, in the sense that the leg set of the join is exactly the union of the leg sets of the participating grammars. The smallest language containing both 1:CV.del and 2:(C)V.del thus contains only legs from one or the other. The join **1** + **3** + **5** + **7** of the OR languages, by contrast, is *nonconservative* since it includes every total order on EST.Con.

(14) **Definition. Conservative join.** Let G_1, G_2 be ranking grammars. Let $G_1 + G_2$ denote the ranking grammar of the join of G_1 and G_2. The join of G_1 and G_2 is *conservative* iff $G_1 + G_2 = G_1 \cup G_2$. Otherwise, the $G_1 + G_2$ is *nonconservative.*

The join **1** + **2** is also a typological class of EST. To validate this claim, we show the m.Ons and f.max EPOs with the merger **1** • **2**. The other two EPOs mirror these structurally, *mutatis mutandis*, so we need not examine them. To make it easier to see the relation to EST proper, we also include the unmerged EPOs.

(15) EPO_{EST}(m.Ons), unmerged and merged

i. m.Ons: EST unmerged

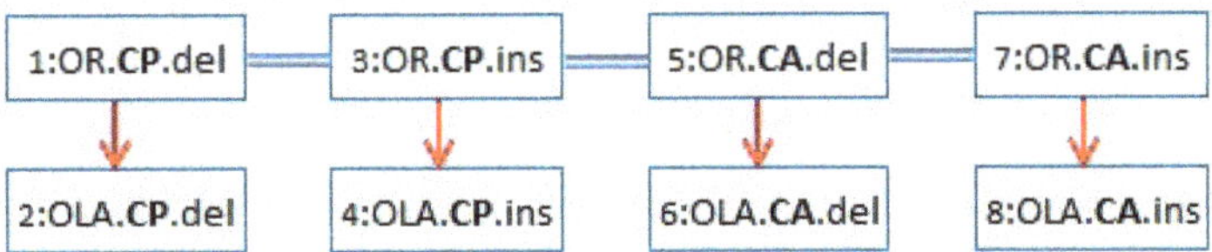

ii. m.Ons with 1•2 merger

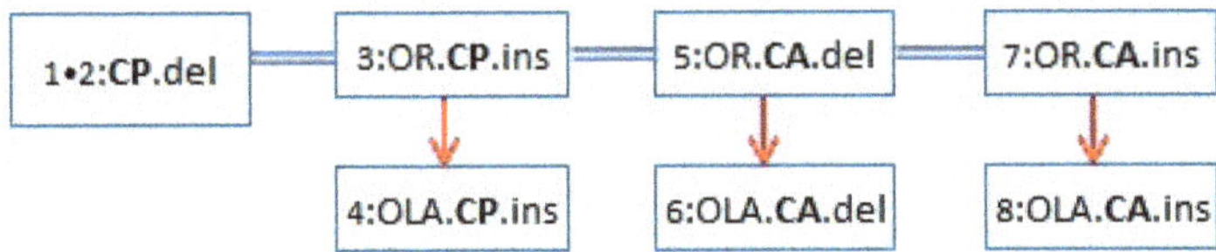

(16) f.max EPOs, unmerged and merged.

i. f.max:EST, unmerged

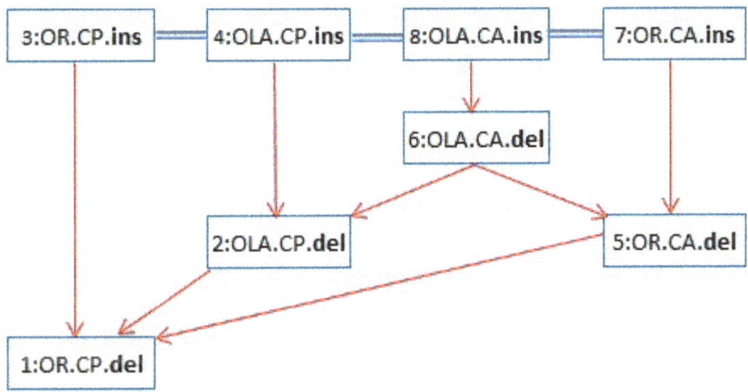

ii. f.max with **1•2** merged

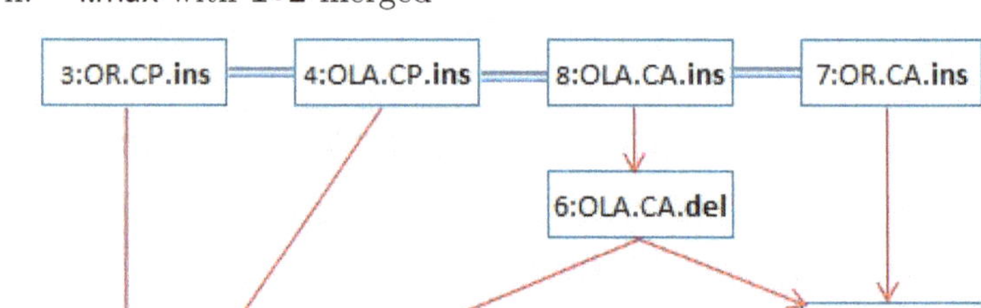

Numerical remark. The contrast between the behavior of **1•2** in the various EPOs shows how the join resists a simple numerical definition within a UVT. In EPO b, **1•2** assumes the ordinal position of grammar **1**. But **1** holds the *minimal* value for m.Ons and the *maximal* value for f.max. Therefore no simple rule of numerical combination – that the join assumes the maximum, or that it assumes the minimum of the joinards – will properly characterize its functioning. Constructing a UVT for the join apparently requires a detour through the MOAT.

6.2 Problem 2: Typological compatibility

In the cases examined so far, the notions 'grammatical class' and 'typological class' track each other perfectly. It is natural to conjecture that whenever grammars are conservatively joinable, they may be joined in any typology that hosts them, coarsening their host typology. This conjecture is false: MOAT structure imposes nontrivial conditions on the coexistence of grammars within a typology. We present two examples where conservatively joinable grammars cannot be merged in a typology without introducing cycles. The first case (§6.2.1) involves hypertransitivity: an ill-fated combination of equivalence and order. The second (§6.2.2) involves only order and also provides the extreme case of a set of pairwise disjoint grammars that are conservatively joinable but cannot be co-resident unjoined in any typology. The notions of grammar class and typological class are therefore distinct. The join retains its singular value in being able to compute the first from the internal content of grammars, regardless of the typology they sit in, while the MOAT stands as the arbiter of typological status.

6.2.1 *The Split Bots*

To find divergences between the notions of typological and grammatical classes, we consider abstract typologies on 4 constraints, named for convenience x, y, z, w. For conciseness, we will relax our scruples and use the same label to refer to a language, its grammar, and the corresponding node in the relevant bigraph.

Our first example derives from a simple typology with four grammars. Each grammar has one constraint ranked at the bottom, beneath the others, with no further order restrictions. For mnemonic purposes, we call this starter typology the 4 Bots, and each 'Bot' grammar is named after its bottom-most constraint: x-Bot is {y, z, w} ≫ x, and so on.[5]

(17) The 4 Bots

Name	Grammar
x-Bot	{y, z, w} ≫ **x**
y-Bot	{x, z, w} ≫ **y**
z-Bot	{x, y, w} ≫ **z**
w-Bot	{x, y, z} ≫ **w**

The following UVT produces the 4 Bots typology:

(18) UVT for the 4 Bots

Name	**x**	**y**	**z**	**w**
x-Bot	**1**	0	0	0
y-Bot	0	**1**	0	0
z-Bot	0	0	**1**	0
w-Bot	0	0	0	**1**

The typology of interest is slightly more articulated. It splits both z-Bot and w-Bot into two grammars each. In one half of the split, x ≫ y; in the other, y ≫ x. Since neither z-Bot nor w-Bot imposes any ranking relation between x and y, we are free to refine the typology by doing so. We also apply the splitting conditions to x-Bot and y-Bot, but their grammars are untouched. They either satisfy or contradict its components; for example, x-Bot entails y ≫ x and contradicts x ≫ y. In the first case x-Bot 'splits' to itself; in the second, no grammar results. The grammars of the Split Bot typology are these:

---

[5] For the sake of conciseness, we write 'y ≫ x & z ≫ x & w ≫ x' as '{y, z, w} ≫ x', and similarly for the others.

(19) The Split Bots

Name	**Grammar**
x-Bot	y, z, w ≫ **x**
y-Bot	x, z, w ≫ **y**
z-Bot-a	x, y, w ≫ z & x≫y
z-Bot-b	x, y, w ≫ z & y≫x
w-Bot-a	x, y, z ≫ w & x≫y
w-Bot-b	x, y, z ≫ w & y≫x

We can create the Split Bots by adjoining an abstract cset to the UVT for the 4 Bots:

(20) The Split Bots

		x	y	z	w
xy-split	x≫y	0	**1**	0	0
	y≫x	**1**	0	0	0
4 Bots	x-Bot	**1**	0	0	0
	y-Bot	0	**1**	0	0
	z-Bot	0	0	**1**	0
	w-Bot	0	0	0	**1**

From this, we derive a UVT for the Split Bots typology by Minkowski summation. The crucial entries differentiating x≫y from y≫x are boxed. In z-Bot-a/b, for example, the original z-Bot profile (0,0,1,0) splits to (1,0,1,0) and (0,1,1,0), introducing the distinction between y ≫x (a) and x≫y (b) while maintaining the status of z as the bottom-ranked constraint.

(21) UVT for Split Bots

Names	x	y	z	w
x-Bot	**2**	0	0	0
y-Bot	0	**2**	0	0
z-Bot-a	**1**	0	**1**	0
z-Bot-b	0	**1**	**1**	0
w-Bot-a	1	0	0	**1**
w-Bot-b	0	1	0	**1**

The key observation is that z-Bot-a and z-Bot-b are conservatively joinable into z-Bot. Their join simply neutralizes the x≫y / y≫x distinction and returns us to z-Bot. We may therefore ask whether we can create a coarsened version of the Split Bots typology, in which *only* z-Bot-a and z-Bot-b are joined. Our target would be a typology with just one pair of Split Bot languages, all the others being full Bots.

The acid test occurs in the node mergers of the Split Bot MOAT. Here is the EPO for x.

(22) EPO(x) in the Split Bots

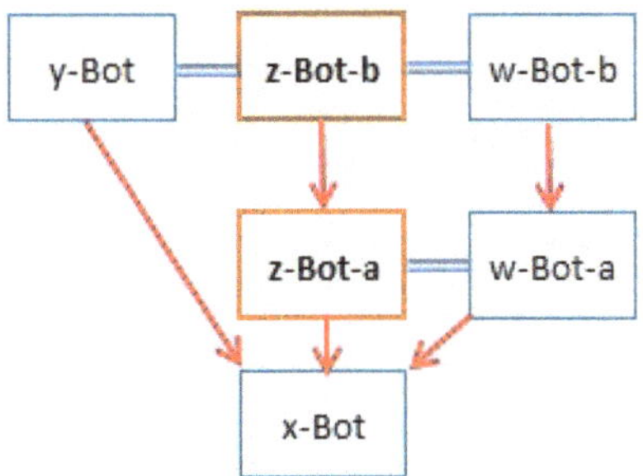

Merging z-Bot-a and z-Bot-b, boxed in red, the two halves of z-Bot, results in a bigraph that is not an EPO, but rather a Generalized EPO or GEPO as in §4.4 (60), because it contains a cycle consisting of two equivalences and a strict order. The cycle, shown on the right side of the following diagram, involves the merged node z-Bot-a • z-Bot-b and the two halves of w-Bot. Because z-Bot-a and z-Bot-b are conservatively joinable, we label this merged node z-Bot-a+b. It is of course equivalent to z-Bot.

(23) GEPO(x) from merger of z-Bot-a and z-Bot-b

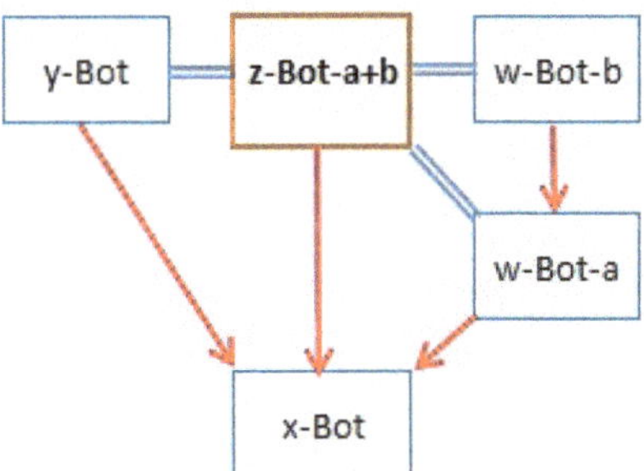

The joined language z-Bot-a+b is, by virtue of its z-Bot-b component, equivalent to w-Bot-b (top row). By virtue of its z-Bot-a component, the node z-Bot-a+b is equivalent to w-Bot-a (second row). But w-Bot-b and w-Bot-a are in a strict order relation with *each other* as per constraint x. Therefore, z-Bot-a+b cannot be equivalent to both of them.

Observe that if we merge w-Bot-a and w-Bot-b as well, we recover w-Bot. This leads us back to the original, entirely healthy EPO(x) in the 4 Bots.

(24) $\text{EPO}_{\text{4Bots}}$(x)

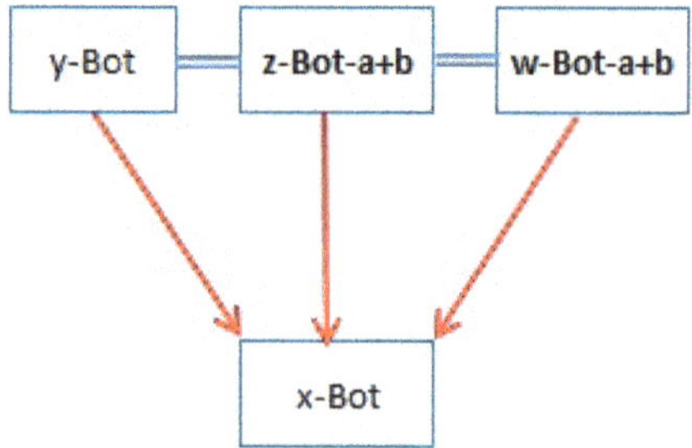

This confirms the observation that z-Bot-a and z-Bot-b are conservatively joinable. But their join in the 4 Bots is typologically valid only when w-Bot-a and w-Bot-b are simultaneously joined to w-Bot so that we recover the 4 Bots. This example shows that membership in a typology imposes restrictions on fellow languages, restrictions which follow from the relations that hold between them in the MOAT.

6.2.2 The Contradictory Snake

The Split Bots example shows a debilitating interaction between equivalence and order. Here we show that contradiction can be achieved with order alone. In addition, we find a conservatively joinable set of pairwise disjoint grammars that cannot sit together in any typology.

Our reference typology with constraint set {x, y, z, w} contains five 5 languages; let's call it the Snake, for reasons that will shortly become apparent. The following UVT derives it.

(25) The Snake

Names	x	y	z	w
x-Top	0	1	1	1
S_1	1	1	0	1
S_2	2	0	0	1
S_3	3	0	1	0
S_4	4	1	0	0

The languages labeled S_1 and S_4 are conservatively joinable, as determined by the Join Explorer of OTWorkplace. We reproduce here ERC grammars of both, along with their join, all in MIB form. The notation 'a ∨ c' refers to the 3-valued *or* of ERC logic (RM3: see Prince 2002a:51). Note that the join requires a sufficiently rich representation of the grammars; here the MIB works, though that is not always the case (Merchant: 2008, 2011).

(26) MIB of S_1

S_1	x	y	z	w
a	**L**	**L**	**W**	**L**
b	**W**	**L**		**L**

(27) MIB of S_4

S_4	x	y	z	w
c	**L**	**L**	**W**	
d	**L**	**L**		**W**

(28) Join(S_1, S_4)

$S_1 + S_4$	x	y	z	w
a ∨ c	**L**	**L**	**W**	
b ∨ d	**W**	**L**		**W**

To show that this is conservative, it suffices to enumerate the legs of each of these, and establish that the third is equal to the union of the first two. The Join Explorer of OTWorkplace automates the check like so: it imposes the ERCs of the join (28) as fixed ranking conditions on the Snake's UVT (25), and determines that no other grammar besides S_1 and S_4 has any legs in this restriction of the typology.

Turning to the MOAT, we derive the Contradictory Snake partition by merging S_1 and S_4, the head and tail of the serpentine substructure of the EPO. The crucial action takes place in the x-bigraph, GEPO(x).

(29) Deriving the Contradictory Snake

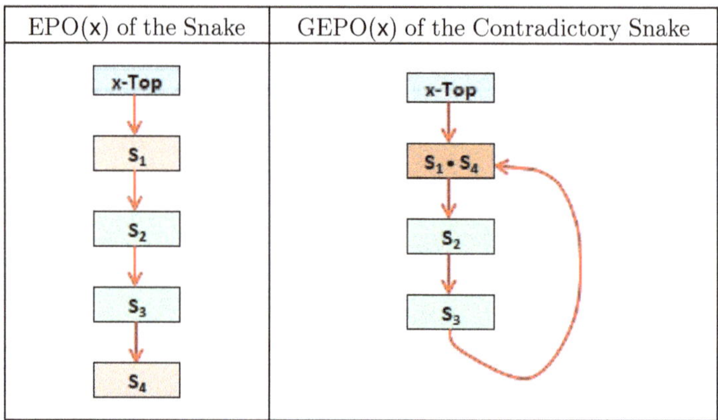

Node merger induces a cycle that is defined purely in terms of order relations. From this it follows that union of grammars S_1 and S_4, though exactly equal to their join, cannot be imposed on the Snake typology to coarsen it. The merger partitions the entire leg set on four constraints into valid grammars, but it is a non-typology nonetheless, because its order relations do not respect the structural logic of OT.

The three grammars in the ouroboros-like cycle, namely $\Sigma = \{S_1 \bullet S_4, S_2, S_3\}$, collectively form a join that is both conservative and typological.

(30) Joining to gain acyclicity

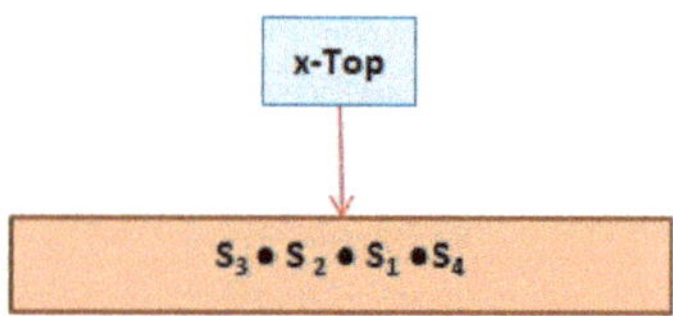

The join is the complement of x-Top, namely co-x-Top = {LWWW}. This illustrates the fact that it is possible for a set of grammars, here Σ, to be typologically joinable, and therefore conservatively joinable, even though the set contains an internal cycle that bars its members from appearing together unjoined in any typology. In the extreme case, if Ord(*S*.CON) is partitioned into grammars with a cyclical tangle anywhere within it, then *all* grammars may be joined to conservatively produce the trivial grammar that contains all legs; the Contradictory Snake provides a subtler example of join as repair.

Chapter 7

Geometry

Chapter contents

THE NOTION OF 'BORDER POINT PAIR' arises from a natural geometry on the set of all total orders, one that has been studied since the early 20th century (Schoute 1911). Each total order is identified as the vertex of a graph, with graphical adjacency holding between points distinguished by a single adjacent transposition. The resulting object is known as the *permutohedron*. It provides a perspective on typological structure that engages a new range of concepts and analytical tools.

We introduce the permutohedron through a series of examples (§7.1). Since grammars are connected regions on the permutohedron, we can define a graphical representation of a typology, the *typohedron*, in which each grammar is shrunk to a single vertex that is connected to another grammar exactly when they share border point pairs (§7.2). Because the typohedron represents the adjacency structure of grammars in a typology, it supports a representation of the order and equivalence relations in any EPO, giving alternative views of the MOAT.

We conclude (§7.3) with an analysis of typologies on the permutohedron, using a notion of distance. Riggle (2012) has announced that OT grammars have a surprising geometric coherence, in that they are not only connected regions but are also convex. We establish that Riggle's notion of distance is a *metric* in the formal sense, which we therefore call the 'Riggle metric'. With this in hand, we introduce a constructive means of producing a shortest path between two points, Recursive Constraint Promotion (RCP), which stays within any grammar containing those points. This allows us to establish that grammars are connected regions, and further, that they are convex, thereby relating geometric and algebraic structures.[1]

7.1 The permutohedron

Behind the geometry of grammars lies a method of generating all permutations of a finite set. Consider all length-3 sequences, XYZ, ZYX, and so on – permutations of letters X, Y, Z. Start out from any one such sequence and flip an adjacent letter pair, continuing on in the same fashion with the resulting permuted sequences. Take, for example, the sequence XYZ as the point of departure, using underlining to draw attention to the transposition. Flipping the first two letters yields XYZ → YXZ. Flipping the last two yields XYZ → XZY. Deal with each of the derived sequences in the same way; so that we get YXZ → YZX and XZY → ZXY. And yet once more, accumulating all 6 permutations. The procedure of repeatedly flipping adjacent pairs always works to assemble the entirety of any finite set of permutations. This fact is familiar from group theory. Although a given permutation is defined over the entire sequence, it can be related to any other through a sequence of local actions – permutations of just two adjacent elements.

A *Cayley graph* represents this process by connecting each permutation with all the others that differ from it in exactly one adjacent flip.[2] The resulting structure can be displayed as a geometrical figure known as a *permutohedron* (originally, *permutoèdre*:[3] coined by Guilbaud & Rosenstiehl 1963, first studied by Schoute 1911), a geometrical figure in which each permutation labels a vertex. The permutohedron on three objects X, Y, Z has $3! = 6$ vertices. Each vertex is adjacent to two others. It looks like this:

[1] Leading us to become, perhaps, as Descartes puts it (1637), masters and possessors of nature.

[2] A Cayley graph is a way of representing the structure of a group, S_n here, the group of permutations of n elements. A Cayley graph of a group G is based on a set of generators S for G. Each $g \in G$ is a vertex; for each generator $s \in S$, g is connected to gs by a directed edge of color C_s. In the present instance, the generators are 'swap adjacent elements at position k' and the $n-1$ different colors are neutralized. Because $s^{-1} = s$, $(gs)s = g$ ensures a returning edge for each outgoing edge, so that the edges are not directed.

[3] 'Le mot *permutoèdre* est barbare, mais il est facile à retenir; soumettons le aux critiques des lecteurs.' References from Wikipedia article 'Permutohedron'.

(1) Permutohedron on sequences of X,Y,Z

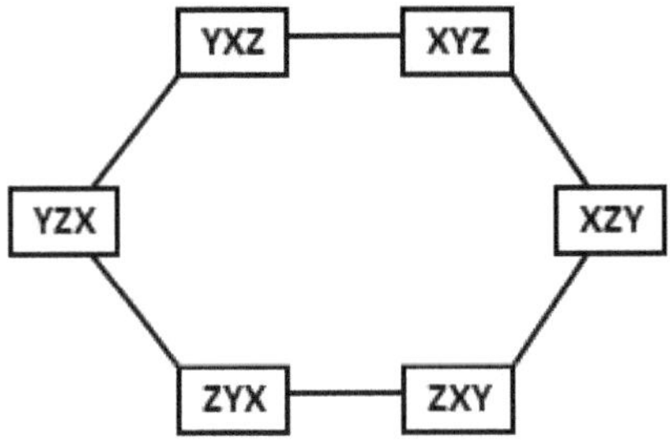

For convenient viewing, we compile the clockwise-moving flips here:

$\text{X}\underline{\text{YZ}} \rightarrow \text{X}\underline{\text{ZY}}$

$\underline{\text{XZ}}\text{Y} \rightarrow \underline{\text{ZX}}\text{Y}$

$\text{Z}\underline{\text{XY}} \rightarrow \text{Z}\underline{\text{YX}}$

$\underline{\text{ZY}}\text{X} \rightarrow \underline{\text{YZ}}\text{X}$

$\text{Y}\underline{\text{ZX}} \rightarrow \text{Y}\underline{\text{XZ}}$

$\underline{\text{YX}}\text{Z} \rightarrow \underline{\text{XY}}\text{Z}$

The $n!$ total orders of an OT system of n constraints can be represented on a permutohedron with $n!$ vertices. Each vertex is labeled with a single linear order, and its neighbors are the $n-1$ legs that differ from it by a single adjacent flip.

The 3-constraint permutohedron is a hexagon, as in ex. (1). The 4-constraint permutohedron is a 3-dimensional object, the truncated octahedron (*a.k.a.* omnitruncated tetrahedron). The general permutohedron that accommodates the permutations of n objects lives in $n-1$ dimensions (the omnitruncated regular simplex). After 4 constraints, it becomes somewhat more challenging to visualize the permutohedron, but its high degree of regularity makes it easier to deal with than one might imagine at first glance.

A grammar, geometrically, is a collection of vertices. It is a remarkable fact, established below as Corollary (41), that the legs of a grammar are *connected*, in the sense that for any two legs of the grammar, there is a trail of legs connected by adjacent flips that leads from one to the other, staying entirely within the grammar. We have not located a source for this observation, which we suspect may be found in the relevant combinatorics literature. A grammar, then, is a *region* of the permutohedron, where by *region* we mean a connected set of vertices. As we will see in §7.3 below, this can be taken one important step further: Riggle (2012) has announced that when *distance* is defined between vertices in the right way, a grammar includes all *shortest* paths between its legs: it is 'spherically convex', a result we establish as Theorem (51) and again in Corollary (62) below. A *typology* of ranking grammars on n constraints is therefore a certain kind of collection of disjoint regions, each of which is connected and convex, entirely covering the permutohedron.

The notion of a *border point pair* in OT, as defined above in ex. (16), §3.2, rests on the same concept of adjacency as in permutation theory. A leg of a grammar is a *border point* if there is an adjacent flip of constraints that produces a leg belonging to another grammar. The members of a *border point pair* are adjacent, and each lies in a different region. All points of the region which are not border points are *interior* points, and will be said to reside in the *interior* of the region.

Here is a view of the order-4 permutohedron. Each vertex has three neighbors.

(2) The 4 element permutohedron with the 4 Tops displayed

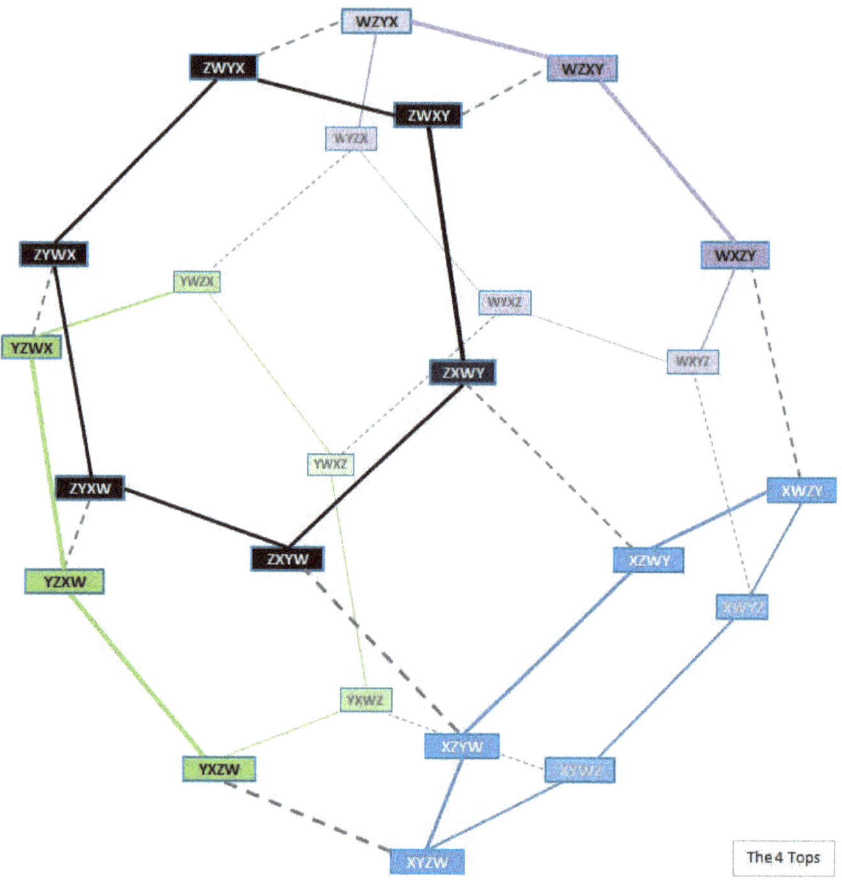

Node and edge colors distinguish the regions that correspond to the grammars of the '4 Tops', a typology comprising four of the 8 hexagonal faces of the permutohedron; each face represents a grammar in which one constraint dominates all the others. The legs of X≫ {Y, Z, W}, which would be called X-Top in the parlance of the preceding section, are shown in blue; those of Y-Top in green, and so on.[4]

The dashed lines in the diagram connect border point pairs. For example, XYZW (bottom-most) is adjacent to YXZW (to its northwest) and they belong to different languages, X-top and Y-top respectively. Every point is a border point; a grammar that is a top has no interior. To see this, note that a generalized top, P-top, consists of every leg having prefix P. But for any such leg, a transposition involving a constraint within P leads off the top. Therefore, every leg of a top grammar is adjacent to another grammar, i.e. participates in a border point pair.

Consider, by contrast, the simple 2-grammar typology that splits the permutohedron into two symmetrical halves: G = {legs such that X≫ Y} and H = {legs such that Y≫ X}.

[4] X-Top has 6 six legs because its defining condition allows Y, Z, W to occur in any order, so long as they are all dominated by X. Similarly, *mutatis mutandis*, for X-Bot. The square faces have the form X&Y≫ Z&W, etc. Each 'top' is thus an image of the order-3 permutohedron. The order-4 permutohedron can be obtained by arranging 4 copies of the order-3 permutohedron as the 4 tops, stepping up one dimension to get enough room. The n-element permutohedron is built from n copies of the order $n-1$ permutohedron in the same way, just as $n!$ is defined by the equation $n! = n \times (n-1)!$. This extreme simplicity of construction provides a way to grasp what's going on even as complexity increases.

(3) Half & Half (X, Y)

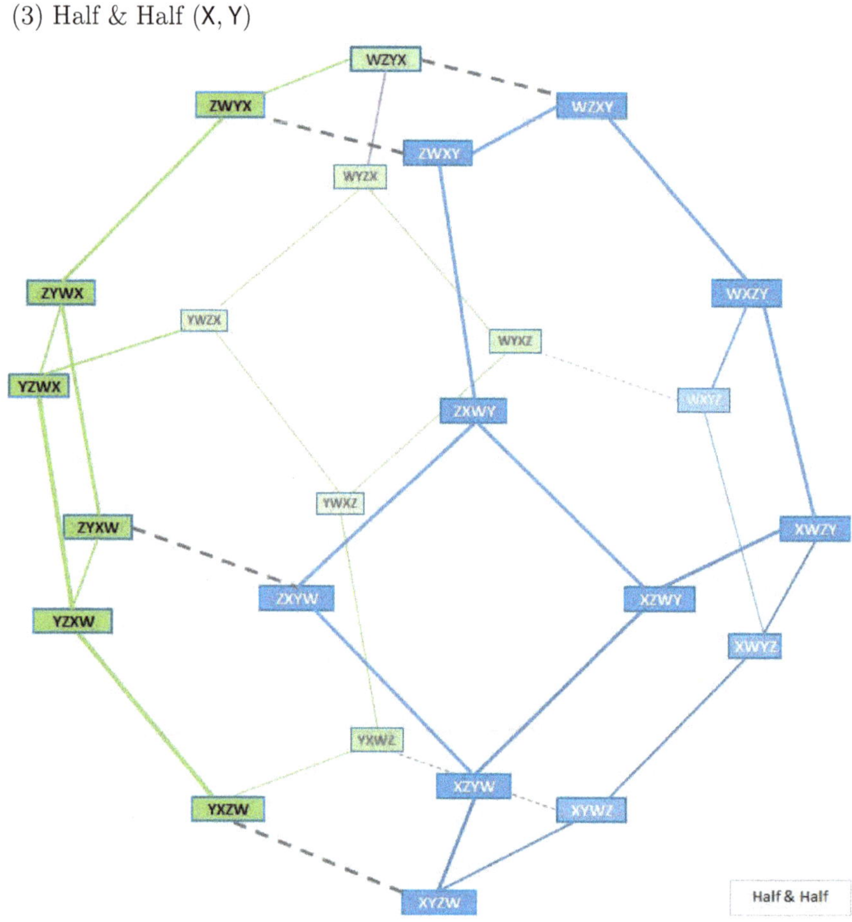

Twelve of the 24 vertices lie in the interior of one or the other half: these are the vertices with only solid lines connecting them to their three neighbors.

Each grammar visibly occupies a *region.* In the 4 Tops, a grammar circumscribes a hexagonal face of the permutohedron. In Half & Half, each grammar embraces two hexagonal faces, a top and a bot joined along an edge, along with two more points subtending two square faces.

The metaphor of the 'border point' is now concrete: border points reside where one region of the typology abuts another. They come in pairs, with one in one grammar, the other in its neighbor; thus graphically they correspond to special edges, shown dashed here. Regions may have interiors, consisting of legs adjacent only to other legs of the same grammar, or no interiors at all.

Remarkably, the entire contents of a grammar as well as the significant relations between grammars are both completely determined at the borders. This follows because the MOAT is constructed entirely from border point pairs (§4.3), and the MOAT determines all order and equivalence relations between the grammars in the typology (§4.7).

7.2 The typohedron

As we've seen, two legs are adjacent in the order-based sense when they differ only by a single flip of sequentially adjacent constraints. On the permutohedron, they are geometrically adjacent. Going up a level, two regions of the permutohedron may be said to be *adjacent* when they are connected by adjacent vertices: a border point pair.

Grammars partition the permutohedron, and from the partitioned permutohedron we may construct a simpler object by shrinking each region to a point while retaining its external connections. In this condensed representation, each vertex now represents an entire grammar. Simplifying yet further, we connect vertices with a single edge when their associated regions are adjacent, perhaps at many points in the permutohedron.[5] The resulting object we call a *typohedron*. The vertices in the typohedron inherit their adjacencies from the regions they represent.

Applying this construction to the 4 Tops, we see that its adjacency structure is that of the tetrahedron.

(4) 4 Tops typohedron

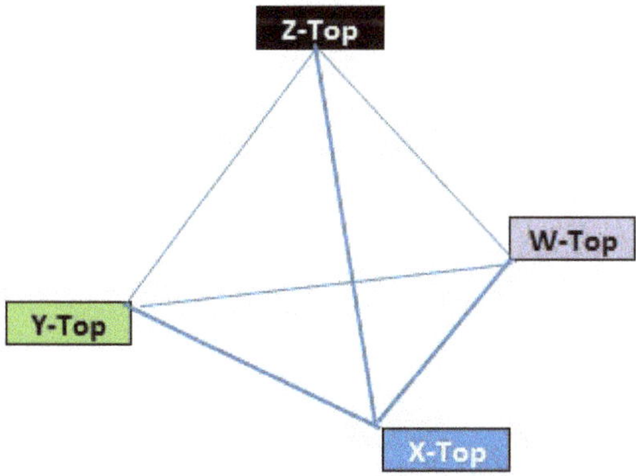

[5] This is the usual way that (geographical) maps are transformed into graphs so that certain of their properties can be studied, like how many colors it takes to distinguish their regions.

The Half & Half typohedron poses no challenges to visualization, in any dimension:

(5) Half & Half typohedron

Returning to the main theme of our analysis, we first portray the EST typology as a partition of the permutohedron, using again the convention that solid lines connect the vertices within a region and dashed lines connect regions across border points.

(6) EST partition of the permutohedron

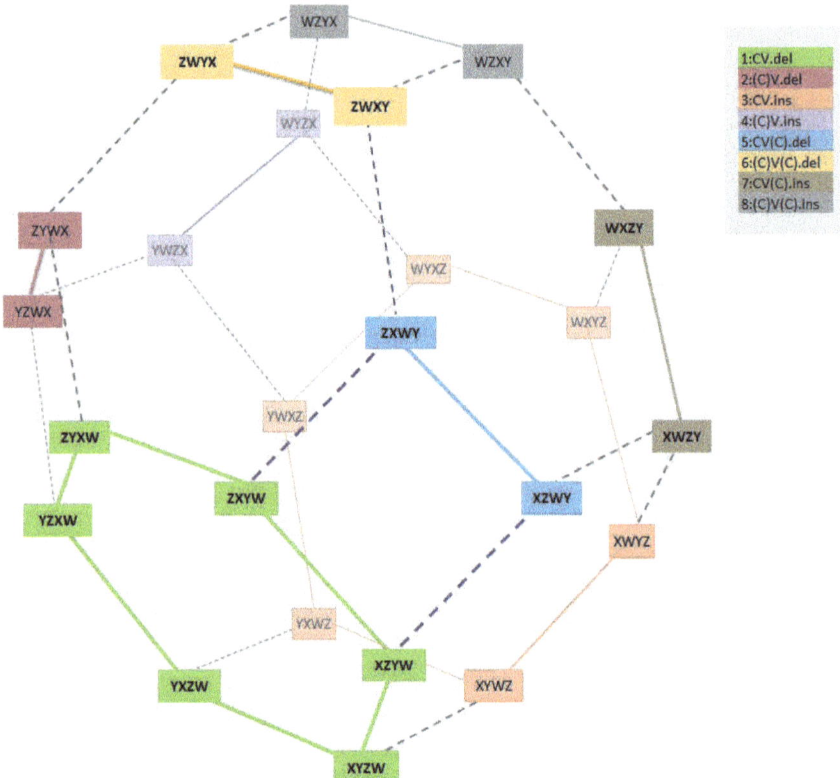

Key: X = m.Ons
Y = m.NoCoda
Z = f.dep
W = f.max

Reduced to the typohedron, the EST typology takes the form of a cube.

(7) EST typohedron

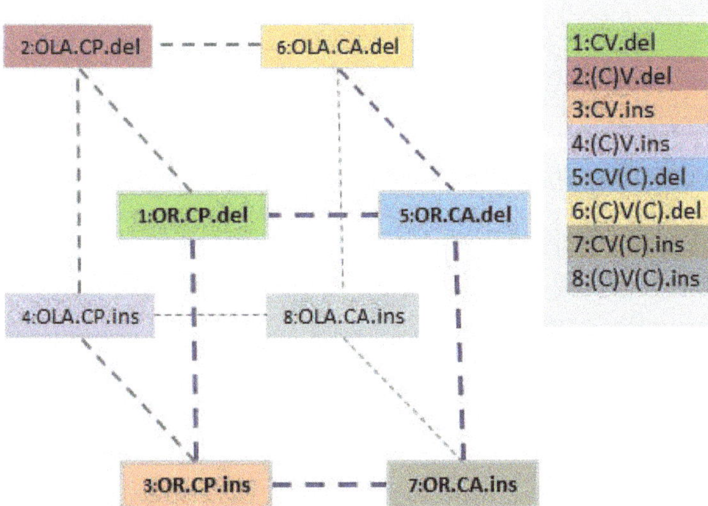

The front-face nodes correspond to the OR languages with syllables CVx; the rear face, the OLA languages with syllables (C)Vx, where x is restricted at the language level. The top face contains the deleters; the bottom face, the inserters. The left face has all those that disallow codas (CP), with syllables xV; the right face, those that permit codas (CA), with syllables xV(C).

The typohedron for the CSys shows the effect of merging each vertex on the front face (OR) of diagram (7) with its neighboring vertex on the rear face (OLA), collapsing the cube to a square. Here we arbitrarily retain front-face colorations.

(8) CSys typohedron

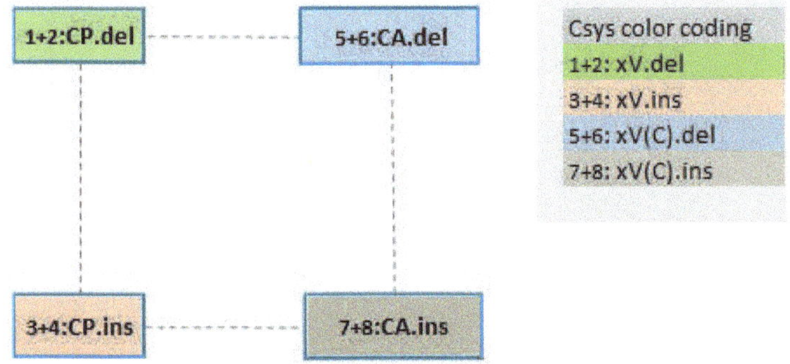

The connectivity of the typohedron is reflected in the base orders that underlie its EPO orders (§4.1). Border point analysis examines every border point pair and returns the concomitant base relations $\equiv^{bp.C}$ and $\prec^{bp.C}$ on which the equivalences $\sim^{bp.C}$ and privileged order relations $\lessdot^{bp.C}$ are built. If any two grammars stand in the base order $\prec^{bp.C}$ with respect to any constraint C, they are adjacent in the typohedron. In terms of our graphical conventions, the typohedron may be assembled from the MOAT by marking as adjacent any two nodes connected by a red arrow in some EPO. This algorithm is used in OTWorkplace to produce the typohedron.

The typohedron represents adjacency of grammars, which is relevant to typological coarsening. We're never going to be able to join **1:CV.del** and **6:(C)V(C).del** conservatively, regardless of what other relations hold between them, because they are separated by other nodes. Typohedral adjacency provides a necessary but not sufficient condition for joinability, both conservative and typological.

In EST, for example, as shown in ex. (6), §6.1, it is not typologically valid to merge along the vertical dimension (faithfulness) of typohedron (7), thereby generalizing away from the distinction between ***del*** and ***ins***. This is true despite the fact that the would-be joinards are neighbors. To see the cause of the failure in terms of typohedral structure, we deploy EPO-style annotations, where edges are rendered as blue double lines if the connected vertices are equivalent in the EPO and as red arrows if an order relation exists between them.

Consider the **f.dep** EPO, mapped out on the EST typohedron.

(9) $\mathrm{EPO}_{\mathrm{EST}}$(**f.dep**) mapped on the typohedron

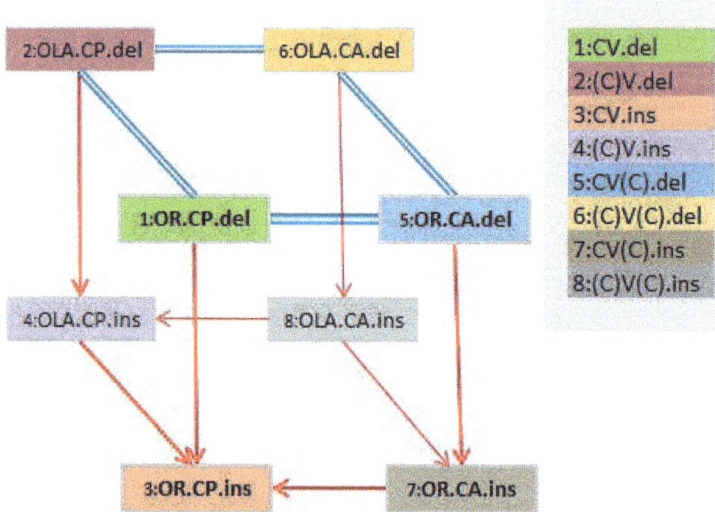

The front face contains the four OR grammars. Vertical merger of front-face elements on the left gives the CP (coda-prohibited) subset of OR languages: all the CV languages. On the right, it gives the CA (coda-allowed) subset: all the CV(C) languages. When we construct these mergers on the EPO-annotated typohedron, the obstruction to typological join emerges as clearly as in the EPO itself.

(10) EPO(f.dep) map with mergers across del/ins divide

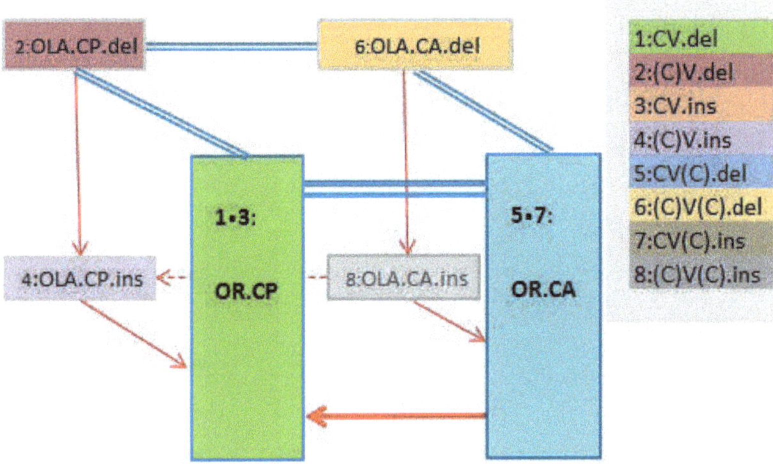

Using familiar EPO-type reasoning, we observe that the OR.CP node cannot be both equivalent to OR.CA and ordered below it on f.dep. More elaborate cycles may also be observed on the left and right faces of the merged typohedron.

Applying the same technique to the 4-Tops typohedron (4), we obtain the following map of the X-EPO.

(11) X-EPOhedron of the 4 Tops

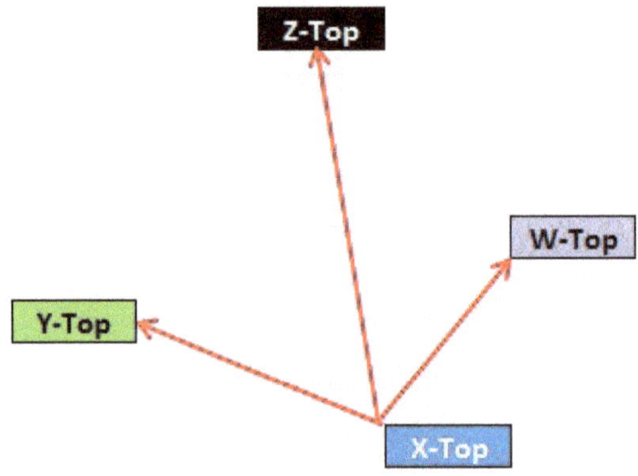

X-Top names the grammar X $\gg$ {Y, Z, W} whose legs are of the form XQ, Q any order on {Y, Z, W}. In X-Top, the choice between languages is decided at X, the first constraint in each of its 6 legs, which allows only one language through. We name the languages of the 4 Tops t_X, t_Y, t_Z, t_W after the constraint that allows them to pass, losing all companions. Any leg of X-Top produces the following filtration, in which decision is immediate.

(12) Filtration by X by any leg λ = XQ of X-Top

$$\{t_{X,}\ t_Y,\ t_Z,\ t_W\} \rightarrow_{\mathsf{X}} \{t_X\}$$

Therefore X may assign any values whatever to t_Y, t_Z, t_W so long as they are greater than the value it assigns to t_X, just as EPO(X) informs us.

The EPOs of the 4 Tops MOAT are all structurally identical and differ only in the grammar that is ordered above all the others. From EPO(X) in (11), it is therefore possible to see that any merger whatever will be acyclic and therefore typologically valid. There is simply no possibility of creating a cycle via node merger.

The situation with the 4 Bots is strikingly different. X-Bot, for example, is the grammar whose legs are of the form PX. The 4 Bots typohedron is isomorphic to that of the 4 Tops, as may be intuited from the fact that the four hexagonal Bot faces lie on the permutohedron in the same spatial relation to each other as the four hexagonal Top faces. Bot and Top may be swapped by exchanging each face of the permutohedron with the one that is opposite to it. We can achieve this effect with the 'antipodal map', globally reversing the internal order of the permutations, as e.g. XYZW → WZYX. Border point pairs transform into border point pairs, so all connectivity between regions is preserved.

The 4 Bots typohedron therefore looks like this:

(13) The 4 Bots

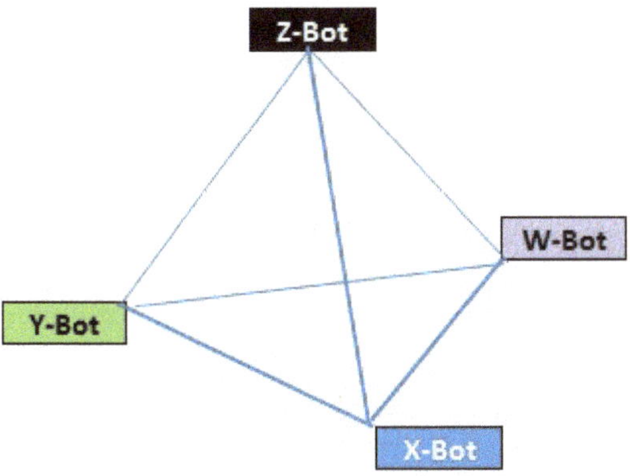

EPO Relations in the 4 Bots do not simply echo those of the 4 Tops. In addition to the expected reversal, whereby there is one node in each EPO that receives a set of incoming arrows rather than sponsoring a set of outgoers, there is a set of equivalences to contend with. Here is the X-EPOhedron of the 4 Bots.

(14) **X-EPOhedron of the 4 Bots**

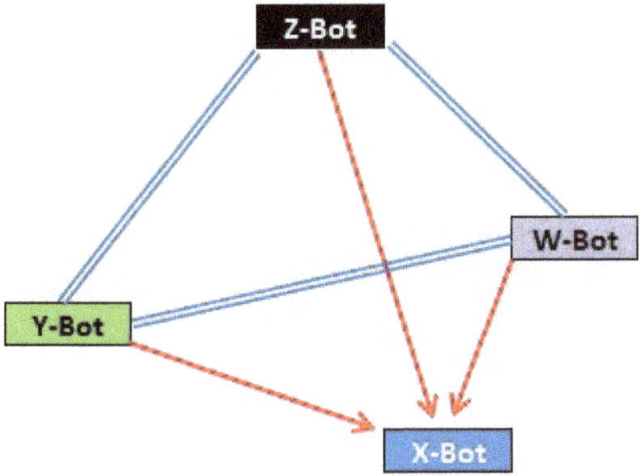

We find equivalence rather than noncomparability because the antipodal map, by inverting the order of constraints, exchanges suffix and prefix. All border crossings in the 4 Tops involve transpositions of the first 2 constraints: for example stepping off Y-Top to arrive at W-Top via the pair {YWZX, WYZX}. By contrast, transiting from one Bot to another always involves the last two constraints in the order. Thus, the pair {XZWY, XZYW}

takes us from Y-Bot to W-Bot. But here, antipodally, both X and Z fall in the prefix, and this ensures that Y-Bot and W-Bot are equivalent in EPO(X) as shown, as well as in EPO(Z).

The filtration patterns in the two typologies are therefore quite different. In X-Top, the constraint X immediately accepts X-Top and forsakes all others, ending the nontrivial part of the filtration. In the 4 Bots, filtration runs through 3 nontrivial steps before settling, extending the pattern we've already seen in the 3 Bots in ex. (81), §4.5.4. Let b_X be the language *ejected* by constraint X, and name the others similarly. Crucially, b_X is the language deemed optimal by the grammar X-Bot, b_Y by Y-Bot, and so on. The one constraint that objects to b_X lies at the bottom of each leg of X-Bot, and sees the candidate set only after it has been winnowed by all the other constraints (see P&S:112 for the first recognition of this pattern).

In the 4 Bots, constraint X not only *ejects* X-Bot but (crucially) accepts all the others. The same is true, *mutatis mutandis*, for constraints Y, Z, W with respect to Y-Bot, Z-Bot, and W-Bot, respectively. This can easily be seen in a UVT.

(15) 4 Bots UVT

4 Bots	X	Y	Z	W
b_X	1	0	0	0
b_Y	0	1	0	0
b_Z	0	0	1	0
b_W	0	0	0	1

Here, for example, is the filtration sequence of the leg YZWX.

(16) Filtration of the leg YZWX in X-Bot

$$\{b_X, b_Y, b_Z, b_W\} \rightarrow_Y \{b_X, b_Z, b_W\} \rightarrow_Z \{b_X, b_W\} \rightarrow_W \{b_X\} \rightarrow_X \{b_X\}$$

To see the equivalences imposed by X from the filtration point of view, we look at legs in which languages pass through X together. Any leg with X in first position will show the pattern: we follow XYZW.

(17) Filtration sequence for the leg XYZW in W-Bot

$$\{b_X, b_Y, b_Z, b_W\} \rightarrow_X \{b_Y, b_Z, b_W\} \rightarrow_Y \{b_Z, b_W\} \rightarrow_Z \{b_W\} \rightarrow_W \{b_W\}$$

Observe that b_Y, b_Z, b_W all pass through X together in the first step, ensuring their equivalence in $\text{EPO}_{\text{4Bots}}$(X), as shown in the X-EPOhedron (14).

The system of equivalences and orders entails that *no* two grammars of the 4 Bots may be typologically joined without creating a cycle in some EPO. X-Bot, for example, cannot be joined with any other grammar because of its status in $\text{EPO}_{\text{4Bots}}$(X). Merging X-Bot and Z-Bot, for example, produces the following cyclic monstrosity.

(18) Merger of X-Bot and Z-Bot in the X EPO.

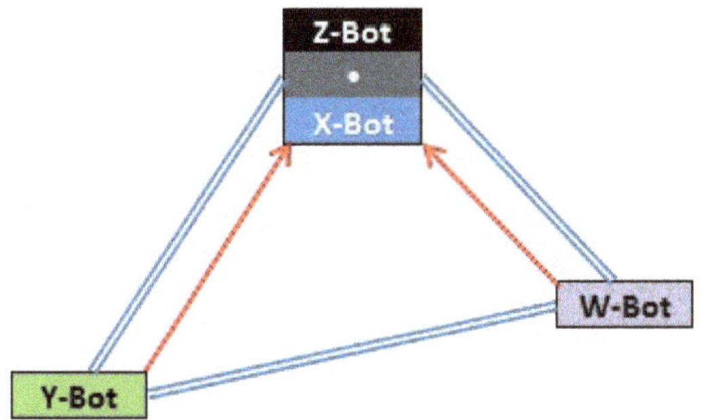

7.3 Putting the metric in geometric

Section contents

The permutohedron is a geometric object in the informal sense that is used of any collection of points and edges – any graph. But a new world of analytic possibilities opens up when a geometry brings with it a notion of *distance*: a metric. Riggle (2012) has proposed a way of assigning distance between vertices of the permutohedron that renders the notion of grammar in metric terms: namely, the thesis is that every shortest path between any two points in a grammar always lies entirely within that grammar, a property he identifies as 'spherical convexity'. In the following sections, we first introduce the Riggle metric, showing how it works through examples (§7.3.1). We then go on to discuss its relationship to the UVT and the MOAT (§7.3.2), showing that the Riggle metric may be derived from the UVT for the Discrete Typology and vice versa, but that the MOAT is not derivable from the Riggle metric in the general setting and therefore remains irreplaceable as a mode of characterizing typologies. In the course of proving basic claims about the Riggle metric (§7.3.3), we provide an algorithm, Recursive Constraint

Promotion (RCP), which produces a shortest path between arbitrary points. This allows us to establish in §7.3.3 that grammars are both connected and spherically convex.

7.3.1 The Riggle metric, spherical convexity, and the Join

Jason Riggle (2012) introduces a concept of great relevance to the present enterprise. In addition to the established techniques for construing orders in terms of adjacency, adopted here, he proposes a notion of *distance* between vertices on the permutohedron. The distance between two adjacent permutations $\mathsf{P\underline{XY}Q}$ and $\mathsf{P\underline{YX}Q}$ is given by $|\mathsf{Q}|+1$, where $|\mathsf{Q}|$ is the number of elements in the suffix Q. This is exactly the number of constraints following the leftmost member of the transposition. The effect, broadly put, is that permutations of higher-ranked constraints result in greater distances than permutations of lower-ranked constraints.

In a 3 element system on $\{\mathsf{X},\mathsf{Y},\mathsf{Z}\}$, the Riggle distance d_R between $\mathsf{\underline{XY}Z}$ and $\mathsf{\underline{YX}Z}$ is 2 because $|\mathsf{Z}|+1=2$. By contrast, $d_R(\mathsf{X\underline{YZ}}, \mathsf{X\underline{ZY}})=1$, because $|\mathsf{Q}|=0$, since Q is empty for this pair.

The notion generalizes in a natural way to define the distance between two arbitrary points, not necessarily adjacent, because we are guaranteed the existence of a path between them that is made up of adjacent points. Consider any such path between points p and q, sum up the distances between the adjacent points along it to get the length of the path, and regard the shortest such path as giving the distance $\mathrm{d}_R(\mathsf{p},\mathsf{q})$.

The geometric effect of imposing the Riggle distance on the permutohedron can be seen directly in the 3 constraint case, shown below. The scale is slightly exaggerated for visual clarity.

(19) 3C Permutohedron with Riggle distances

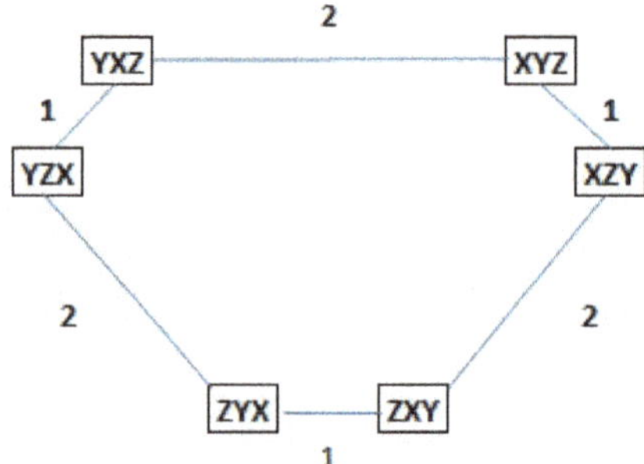

With three elements in the underlying set, there are always just 2 paths between any two points, excluding paths that visit a point more than once.

For example, from **YZX** at the far left to **XZY** on the far right, there's the up-and-over path π_1 = ⟨**YZX**, YXZ, XYZ, **XZY**⟩, and there's the down-and-under path π_2 = ⟨**YZX**, ZYX, ZXY, **XZY**⟩. Writing $|\pi|$ for the length of a path π, we may easily calculate the length of these paths from the diagram:

$$|\pi_1| = 1+2+1 = 4$$
$$|\pi_2| = 2+1+2 = 5$$

The Riggle distance d_R(YZX, XZY) between YZX and XZY is therefore 4, not 5. Both paths use exactly the same set of binary transpositions, but in π_1 they occur in more favorable positions. This may be seen in the following chart, where we use parentheses to demarcate the transposition.

(20) From YZX to XZY: the high road and the low road

Path	Transp.	Leg Map	d_R
π_1	(ZX)	Y(ZX) → Y(XZ)	1
	(YX)	(YX)Z → (XY)Z	2
	(YZ)	X(YZ) → X(ZY)	1
π_2	(YZ)	(YZ)X → (ZY)X	2
	(YX)	Z(YX) → Z(XY)	1
	(ZX)	(ZX)Y → (XZ)Y	2

Determining the point at which a necessary transposition should take place will prove crucial to finding the shortest path. To anticipate, notice that the shortest path starts by moving X to its final position, then proceeds to deal with Y. Crucially, X is the highest-ranked misplaced constraint in the targeted endpoint, and similarly for Y, once X is correctly positioned.

Riggle's main claim is that every shortest path between two points in a grammar always lies *within* that grammar. In the present discrete context, we use the term *geodesic* to mean a shortest path between two points; there may be more than one.[6] A grammar (and equivalently, an antimatroid) is then claimed to be *spherically convex* under the Riggle metric. The related notion of 'geodesic convexity' requires that the shortest path be unique; but like a sphere, any permutohedron based on the orderings of 4 or more elements has many pairs of points that are connected by more than one path

---

[6] In a continuous context, there is a distinction between a 'locally shortest path' and a 'globally shortest path' which does not arise in this discrete context.

of the shortest length.[7] Spherical convexity of a set requires that *all* geodesics between its points reside within it. We establish that a particular shortest path, the one produced by Recursive Constraint Promotion (39), resides within a grammar. We then leverage this result to establish in (51) that all geodesics connecting a pair of points within a grammar reside within that grammar and hence that grammars are spherically convex, yielding a new way of fully characterizing what a grammar is.

The grammatical consequences of convexity can be seen in our example. Consider the leftmost and rightmost points in the 3C permutohedron as we have rendered it.

(21) 3C permutohedron with distances and selected points

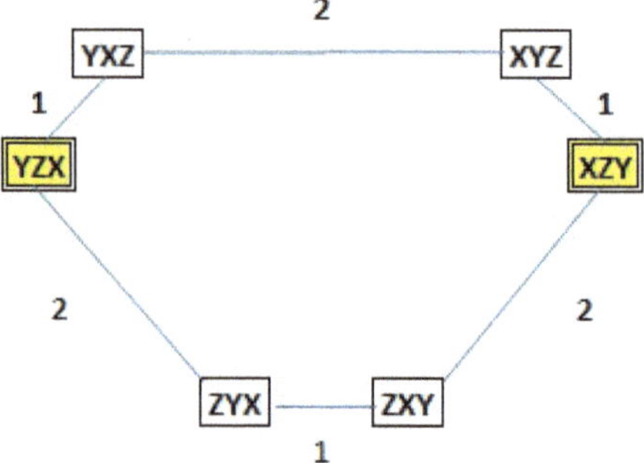

Suppose we wish to find the smallest grammar that contains both YZX (leftmost) and XZY (rightmost). As we've just seen, the (unique) shortest path π_1 between them has length 4 and consists of {YZX, YXZ, XYZ, XZY}. Since this also necessarily contains the shortest paths between all the legs along the path, once it is established that grammars are spherically convex, it follows from metrical reasoning that the smallest containing grammar must include all four of these vertices. By inspection we can see that this set is the grammar {WWL}: 'X or Y dominates Z.'

What then of the other path, π_2, of length 5? If grammars are convex, any grammar containing the legs of π_2 must also contain those of π_1 because π_2 contains the nodes {YZX, XZY}and therefore the shortest path between

[7] On a sphere the shortest path between two points lies on a great circle. (The great circle defines two routes between points; both routes are said to be 'geodesics', a term that is defined locally.) But for antipodal points, like the north and south pole, any great circle including them supplies two geodesic paths of the same, shortest length; and there are many such great circles. The northern hemisphere, by contrast, is *geodesically* convex in that the geodesic between two points is unique. See e.g. Ferreira et al. (2014). See also 'Geodesic' and 'Geodesic convexity' in Wikipedia.

them: π_1. But π_1 and π_2 together exhaust the nodes of the {X, Y, Z} permutohedron. The smallest grammar containing π_2, assuming grammar convexity, is therefore the trivial grammar that includes every leg. This grammar has no restrictive ranking conditions on it at all, and can be rendered by any ERC that contains no L's.

Recall that a join of grammars is said to be *nonconservative* when it is larger than their union. A nonconservative join need not absorb the entire set of legs in the typology, because the join expands on the union only to the point where a valid grammar is reached. To see this effect, it is sufficient to examine a simple 4-constraint case. Consider any typology on {X, Y, Z, W} which happens to contain two one-leg grammars G_1 = {XYZW} and G_2 = {YXWZ}. They sit across from each other on a quadilateral face of the permutohedron. A relevant patch of their local environment looks like this, drawn to reflect Riggle distances.

(22) G_1= {XYZW} and G_2 = {YXWZ} on the measured Permutohedron (local view)

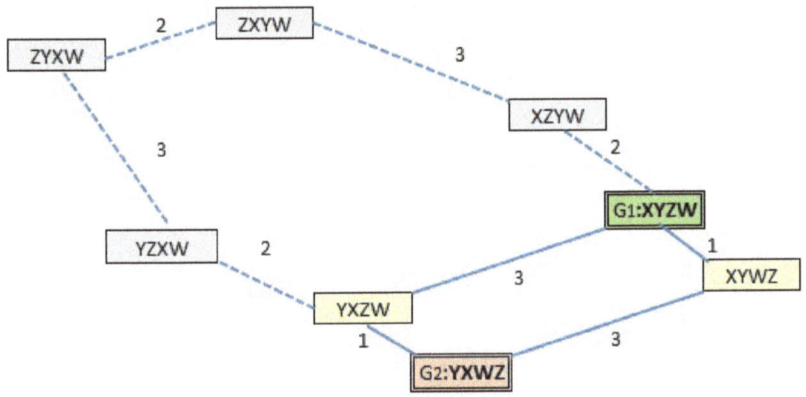

Suppose we wish to *join* the grammars G_1 (green) and G_2 (tan). The shortest distance between them is 4. Since the join is a grammar, it is convex. Convexity asserts that we must include all vertices on any minimal-length path between them. Therefore both YXZW and XYWZ (shaded yellow) must be included. It is also true that the set of four points just amassed constitutes a grammar, namely {W*e*LL, *e*WLL}.

Now consider another path from G_1 to G_2, π_b, which runs left and up from G_1 in the region shown here, and contrast it with the geodesic path $\pi_{a,}$ which runs left and down from G_1.

π_a = **XYZW** - YXZW - **YXWZ** Length $= 4 = 3 + 1$
π_b = **XYZW** - XZYW - ZXYW - ZYXW Length $= 13 = 2 + 3 + 2 + 3 + 2 + 1$
-YZXW - YXZW - **YXWZ**

The minimal path π_a has length 4, while π_b has length 13. It follows that on the left side of G_1 only the leg YXZW will be included in the join $G_1 + G_2$. But since the right descending path from G_1 to G_2 also has length 4, the leg XYWZ must also be part of $G_1 + G_2$. From metric considerations alone we can deduce, without further calculation, that $G_1 + G_2$ = {XYZW, <u>YXZW</u>, <u>XYWZ</u>, YXWZ}, where the legs outside G_1 and G_2 and underlined. The join is nonconservative but not radically so.

This is a typical case where more than one geodesic connects a pair of points. Observe that the path runs from (XY)(ZW) to (YZ)(WZ). Two disjoint flips are required, as shown, but they may take place in either order, since neither affects the Riggle distance induced by the other.

The join of two ERC grammars (§6.1) is the smallest grammar that contains both (Merchant 2008, 2011). We will show that grammars are spherically convex (51). Suppose that the converse could also be shown, so that all spherically convex sets would be guaranteed to be grammars. Then another perspective would emerge on what's happening when two grammars are joined. Given two leg sets, there is a smallest spherically convex set that contains both: the 'convex hull' of the sets.[8] Given two grammars, if the desired converse holds, their join would be exactly their convex hull.

Since the result of joining is a grammar, by convexity (51) it contains all shortest paths between all pairs of its legs. Furthermore, if the conjectured converse holds, there could be no smaller convex set containing both grammars, because it would be a joinard-containing grammar smaller than the join, contradicting Merchant. Thus, under the converse, the join would be the 'convex hull' of its joinards. Among the legs of the join are those coming from either of the two joinards. The join computes an ERC description of the set of all legs that are needed to render the simple *union* of the joinard grammars into a single valid grammar, which under convexity would be all shortest paths between any legs in either, plus all shortest paths between the legs in those paths, and so on.

Spherical convexity of grammars means that all the legs along every shortest route must be included in the join. It is striking that convexity entails that this geometrical calculation can be carried out in ERC space via the purely algebraic join operation with no mention of points or distances

[8] See e.g. Convex hull in Wikipedia.

or permutations. Looking back in the other direction, it is equally striking that the algebraic join can be computed, given the equivalence of grammars and convexity, by the geometric operation of finding the convex hull of a set of points.

The join of two grammars is independent of any typology in which the joinards may be embedded. Whether joining grammars within a given typology leads to another valid, coarser typology is, as we've seen in the Split Bots and the Contradictory Snake examples of section §6.2, contextually determined. At the typological level, the order and equivalence requirements of the MOAT are inescapable, and they may obstruct even a conservative join. We know from the Contradictory Snake (§6.3) there are conservatively joinable sets of disjoint grammars which cannot be embedded in any typology unjoined.

The specific metric proposed by Riggle and discussed here is one of many assignments of value to edges of the permutohedron which could support the spherical convexity property. Compare the fact that the standard Euclidean metric of daily life is unchanged if we double its value, or change from inches to centimeters. Metrics of the Riggle class are even more flexible, in that only the relative order on paths imposed by their length is important, not for example the ratio of distances from one object to another, which is constant in the Euclidean metric no matter what units we express it in.

The essence of the Riggle metric lies in defining distance based on the position of the adjacent flip that distinguishes neighboring points, increasing geometric distance as the flip recedes from the end of the sequence. This gives us spherical convexity, but it does not give us *clustering*, in that the legs inside a grammar are by no means guaranteed to be closer to each other than to legs in another grammar. For example, in the 4 Bots, a flip like PXY → PYX puts a border point from Y-bot at a distance of 1 from a point of X-bot; yet within X-bot, a flip like ZWYX → WZYX puts two X-bot points at a distance of 3 from each other.

It is an interesting project to redefine the Riggle metric as a pseudometric relativized to a typology so that all points within a region are assigned 0 distance from each other. (In a metric per se, points at zero distance must be the same point; in pseudometric, this condition – the coincidence axiom – is dropped.[9]) The idea is that only certain flips would contribute distance, those within border point pairs, which determine the ranking requirements of grammars. On this conception, in the typology we have named Half & Half above, the only flip contributing distance would be the one exchanging

[9] See for example the article 'Metric' in Wikipedia.

adjacent $X \gg Y$ and $Y \gg X$. In the 4 Tops, the only flips contributing distance would be those between first and second position in the orders. We leave this idea for future contemplation.

7.3.2 The Riggle metric, the UVT, and the MOAT

We now have two numerical representations of a typology: the UVT, with its violation values licensed by EPO structure, and the partitioned permutohedron, with its Riggle distances between vertices. Here we investigate their relationship. First, we show how the Riggle metric may be derived from the violation value scheme. This construction also allows us to go the other way, deriving the UVT for the Discrete Typology, in which every grammar has a single leg, from the Riggle metric. Then, moving from the Discrete Typology to the general typological landscape, we find that a parallel method of deriving UVTs from the Riggle metric is not in the offing, because of the way that relations between grammars develop through order-based interactions. This confirms the irreducible centrality of the MOAT in typological analysis.

The Discrete Typology provides an exact image of the permutohedron: each vertex represents one grammar. As always, the Discrete Typology will have many UVTs, but one of them is conspicuously minimal, in the sense that it uses the smallest possible integers for its values. More precisely put, the largest integer that it uses is as small as possible. Furthermore, this minimal UVT is unique up to renaming of rows and columns. For the Discrete Typology $DT^{(n)}$ on n constraints, we will call it $U_0^{(n)}$. Let's begin by settling the layout of $U_0^{(n)}$.

We may view a UVT from two different angles, horizontally or vertically, as it were. Consider first all the n-length row vectors over the integers $\{0, 1, ..., n-1\}$, where each vector contains exactly one instance of each of these integers. Assign each component of the vector to a different constraint in some arbitrary but fixed fashion. Each vector then represents a different permutation of the first n non-negative integers, so that there are $n!$ vectors in total. There are also $n!$ grammars in the Discrete Typology and therefore $n!$ rows in any of its UVTs. Assign each vector to one of the languages as its violation profile. We claim that this gives us the UVT we're looking for.

To see this, consider the filtration process in the VT we have defined. Claim: the language L_k will be selected by the leg λ_k that orders the constraints in such a way that they assign strictly increasing values to L_k.

The highest-ranked constraint in λ_k, call it C_1, assigns 0 to L_k, so L_k survives filtration by it. This means that every survivor of C_1 is assigned 0. The next highest ranked constraint in λ_k, call it C_2, assigns 1 to L_k. Observe that no survivor of C_1 can have a 0 in C_2: this would put two 0s in a violation profile, an impossibility by construction of the profiles. Therefore, 1 is the smallest value that C_2 assigns to any survivor of C_1, and L_k also survives C_2. The same argument replicates, *mutatis mutandis*, down the hierarchy of λ_k, leaving L_k as the only survivor. The argument is generic: it follows that each language will be chosen by some leg, so that every language of the DT is an optimum of this VT. Furthermore, each leg chooses a distinct language. This establishes that we have a UVT for the DT on n constraints.

Now shift perspective to the vertical. Consider any constraint X and some n-constraint leg that it initiates, call it $\lambda_1 = \mathsf{XYZ...W}$. Consider the set of grammars, i.e. single legs, obtained by shifting X downward by a series of adjacent flips:

(23) Leg sequence

$\lambda_1 = \underline{\mathbf{X}\mathsf{Y}}\mathsf{Z...W}$
$\lambda_2 = \underline{\mathsf{Y}\mathbf{X}}\mathsf{Z...W}$
...
$\lambda_{n-1} = \mathsf{YZ...}\underline{\mathbf{X}\mathsf{W}}$
$\lambda_n \; = \mathsf{YZ...}\underline{\mathsf{W}\mathbf{X}}.$

Each pair $\{\lambda_i, \lambda_{i+1}\}$, $1 \leq i \leq n-1$, is a border point pair in the Discrete Typology. Therefore in EPO(X), these grammars form a strictly ordered sequence $\lambda_1 <^{\text{bp.X}} \lambda_2 <^{\text{bp.X}} ... <^{\text{bp.X}} \lambda_{n-1} <^{\text{bp.X}} \lambda_n$. Instantiating these relations numerically in a UVT requires n integers. The set $\{0, 1, ..., n-1\}$ offers the smallest non-negative integers that will do the job. This shows that violation profiles used above to create a UVT for $\text{DT}^{(n)}$ cannot be improved upon by using a smaller maximum integer. We conclude that the UVT is unique, up to renaming the constraints and candidates and is therefore the promised $U_0^{(n)}$.

With 3 constraints at play, the UVT looks like this, labeling each language with mention of the leg that selects it.[10]

[10] It may be observed that the violation profile of a language is the *inverse* of the permutation that selects it, enumerating *positions* in the sequence starting from 0. Thus, in L_{ZXY}, for example, X is in position 1, Y in position 2, and Z in position 0.

(24) UVT for $DT^{(3)}$, the 3C Discrete Typology

$U_0^{(3)}$	X	Y	Z
L_{XYZ}	0	1	2
L_{YXZ}	1	0	2
L_{YZX}	2	0	1
L_{XZY}	0	2	1
L_{ZXY}	1	2	0
L_{ZYX}	2	1	0

Returning now to the n-length leg sequence in (23), consider how values must be assigned to the languages in $U_0^{(n)}$. From ex. (23) and the ordering that it implies, we have $X(L_1) = 0$, $X(L_2) = 1, \ldots, X(L_n) = n-1$. For any L_k, we have $X(L_k) = k-1$, which is exactly the serial position of X in the constraint order, minus 1. This pattern may be easily seen for $n = 3$ in ex. (24). We are close to finding a relationship between violation value and Riggle distance because the Riggle distance is also sensitive to serial position.

Consider that the Riggle distance between any pair $\{\lambda_k, \lambda_{k+1}\}$ is 1 plus the length of the sequence Q following X in λ_{k+1}. The length of that suffixal sequence is given by $n - (k+1)$.

$$\begin{aligned} d_R(\lambda_k, \lambda_{k+1}) &= 1 + |Q| \\ &= 1 + n - (k+1) \\ &= n - k \\ &= (n-1) - X(L_k) . \end{aligned}$$

To state it more genererally, consider any border point pair {P<u>XY</u>Q, P<u>YX</u>Q} and let the constraints assign minimal values in the way described. Then we have:

(25) Riggle distance between adjacent nodes in $DT^{(n)}$. For $|PXYQ| = |PYXQ| = n$.

$$\begin{aligned} d_R(PXYQ, PYXQ) &= (n-1) - X(L_{PXYQ}) \\ &= (n-1) - Y(L_{PYXQ}). \end{aligned}$$

This gives us complete interconversion between the Riggle distances between adjacent nodes and their correlated evaluations in $U_0^{(n)}$. The Riggle metric giving distances between arbitrary nodes is projected from these local distances: the Riggle metric has therefore been successfully interpreted in violation values for $DT^{(n)}$, as promised. Conversely, by juggling the equations of (25), the violation values in $U_0^{(n)}$ can be stated in terms of distances.

At this point, it is natural to imagine that the Riggle distance between points can be generalized to a distance between regions that allows us to derive a UVT in way that parallels or extends the results of (25). But regions interact orderwise in a way that will dash this hope. The first hint of a red flag can be seen in the gross shape of the Snake typology, which imposes in EPO(X) a linear order on its 5 grammars. This will require 5 distinct integers to instantiate it, as indeed is visible in UVT (25), §6.2.2. But there are only 4 Riggle distances in a 4-constraint permutohedron.

To see the source of this effect, it is useful to lay out a flattened version of the permutohedron, running from X-initial orders (top) to X-final orders (bottom), with each vertical thread following the pattern of the leg sequence in (23), where X transposes stepwise through the sequence. (See (123), §4.6.5, for a 3 constraint version of this kind of 'curtain' diagram.)

(26) X-view of permutohedron

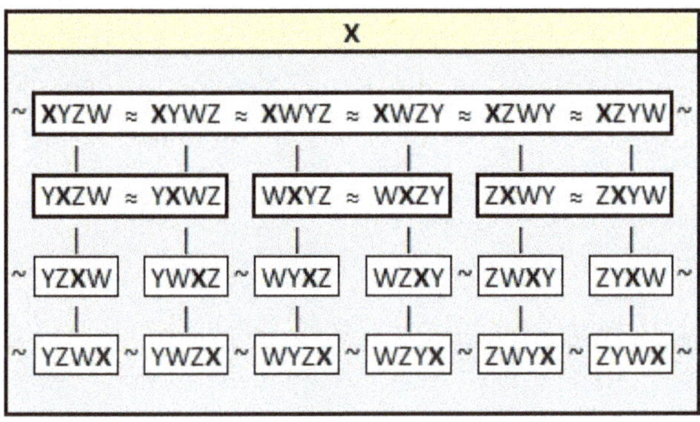

Nodes are connected by ≈ when adjacent and X-equivalent, by the vertical edge | when adjacent and ordered, and by ~ when merely adjacent and non-comparable on X, with the order $<^{bp.X}$ running from top to bottom. Leftmost and rightmost nodes are adjacent in all except the 2nd row from the top. To aid with visual parsing, X-equivalent nodes are boxed in heavier lines.

It is instructive to portray the Contradictory Snake in this format, replacing the crucial vertical links with arrows. Let's re-name the grammars after the colors that mark them.

Pink	= x-Top
Blue	= $S_1 \bullet S_4$
Orange	= S_2
Green	= S_3

(27) The Contradictory Snake

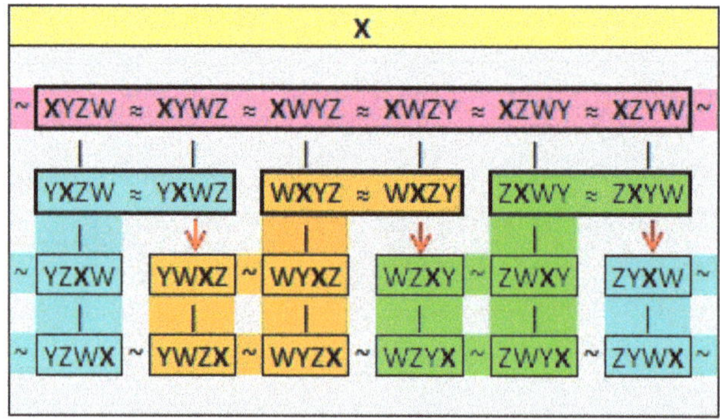

The red arrows indicate the crucial ordering interaction. From left to right, we have

Blue	$<^{\text{bp.X}}$	Orange
Orange	$<^{\text{bp.X}}$	Green
Green	$<^{\text{bp.X}}$	Blue.

This results in the cycle that renders the Contradictory Snake a non-typology. The problem is easily fixed by severing blue into two parts, where Dark-Blue = S_1, interrupting the cycle and yielding the Snake of UVT (25), §6.2.2.

(28) The Snake

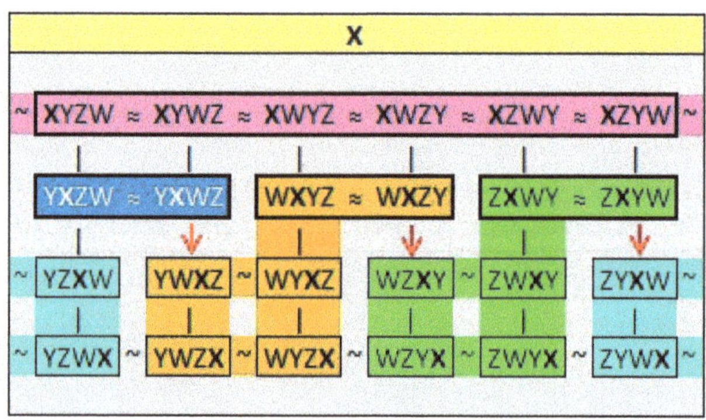

We can now assign coherent X-values to the (languages corresponding to the) grammars, based on the ordering Pink$<^{\text{bp.X}}$ DarkBlue $<^{\text{bp.X}}$ Orange $<^{\text{bp.X}}$ Green $<^{\text{bp.X}}$ Blue.

(29) X-values for the Snake

Language	X
Pink	0
DarkBlue	1
Orange	2
Green	3
Blue	4

The problem is now immediately apparent: the Riggle distance is the same between the border points of pairs of languages linked by the red arrows in diagram.

$$\begin{aligned} d_R(\text{DarkBlue, Orange}) &= d_R(\mathsf{Y\underline{XW}Z}, \mathsf{Y\underline{WX}Z}) = 2 \\ d_R(\text{Orange, Green}) &= d_R(\mathsf{W\underline{XZ}Y}, \mathsf{W\underline{ZX}Y}) = 2 \\ d_R(\text{Green, Blue}) &= d_R(\mathsf{Z\underline{XY}W}, \mathsf{Z\underline{YX}W}) = 2. \end{aligned}$$

Thus there is no hope of translating the local distance between a region and its neighbors into a useful violation value. Any attempt to construct the violation values must be non-local, taking account of the transitivity of order. To see what this amounts to, one must turn to the EPO. But metric considerations are then uninformative and add nothing to what the EPO already says.

7.3.3 The spherical convexity of grammars

In this section we prove the major results asserted in the previous sections. Starting with the notion of adjacency used throughout, we define distance between points on the permutohedron. From this, we obtain the Riggle metric, which we show imposes a metric in the formal sense. We then define a way of creating a path between any two points, Recursive Constraint Promotion (RCP). We prove that this path stays inside any grammar containing the two points it connects; this establishes that grammars are connected. In addition, we show that the RCP path has minimal length under the Riggle metric. We conclude by establishing that grammars are spherically convex regions on the typohedron.

(30) **Definition. Adjacent.** Vertices p_1 and p_2 of a permutohedron are *adjacent* iff p_1 = P$\underline{\text{XY}}$Q and p_2 = P$\underline{\text{YX}}$Q, for constraints X, Y and sequences of constraints P,Q, possibly empty.

This restates the notion of adjacency used throughout. Note that a vertex is not adjacent to itself.

(31) **Definition. Distance between adjacent vertices.** Given adjacent nodes p_1 and p_2, with p_1 = P$\underline{\text{XY}}$Q and p_2 = P$\underline{\text{YX}}$Q, the distance between p_1 and p_2 is adjDist(p_1,p_2) = $|Q| + 1$.

(32) **Definition. Path between two vertices.** Given vertices p_1, p_2, a path $\pi(p_1, p_2)$ between p_1 and p_2 is a sequence of vertices $\pi(p_1, p_2) = (r_1, r_2, ..., r_n)$ where $r_1 = p_1$, $r_n = p_2$, and each pair r_i, r_{i+1}, $1 \leq i \leq n-1$, is adjacent.

(33) **Definition. Length of a path.** Given a path $\pi(p_1, p_2) = (r_1, r_2, ..., r_n)$, the length of $\pi(p_1, p_2)$, denoted Len(π), is the sum of the distances between sequential points on the path.

$$\text{Len}(\pi) = \textstyle\sum_{k=2}^{n} \text{adjDist}(r_{k-1}, r_k)$$

(34) **Definition. Distance between vertices.** Given arbitrary vertices p_1, p_2, the Riggle distance between p_1 and p_2, $d_R(p_1,p_2)$, is the shortest path between the two if they are distinct, and zero if $p_1 = p_2$.

$$\begin{aligned} d_R(p_1, p_2) &= \min\{\text{Len}(\pi) \mid \pi \text{ is a path between } p_1 \text{ and } p_2\}, \text{ if } p_1 \neq p_2 \\ &= 0, \text{ if } p_1 = p_2. \end{aligned}$$

The following lemma justifies our calling $d_R(p_1, p_2)$ a 'distance'.

(35) **Lemma. d_R is a metric.**

Proof. There are four parts to showing that d_R is a metric on the vertices of the permutohedron.

(i.) **Non-negativity**. We need to show that $d_R(p,q) \geq 0$. This is clear from the definition of $d_R(p,q)$ since $d_R(p,q)$ is the smallest value of a set that consists of sums of positive numbers, when it is not zero.

(ii.) **Coincidence**. Next we show that $d_R(p,q) = 0$ iff $p = q$. If $p = q$, then by definition (34), $d_R(p,q) = 0$. Now suppose $d_R(p,q) = 0$. If $p \neq q$, then every path between them contains at least two distinct vertices, p and q. The smallest distance between adjacent vertices is 1, occurring when the shared suffix in the adjacent pair is empty. But this means that $d_R(p,q) \neq 0$. Therefore, $p = q$.

(iii.) **Symmetry**. $d_R(p,q) = d_R(q,p)$. Given a path from p to q, $\pi(p,q) = (r_1, r_2, ..., r_n)$, we can immediately construct a path from q to p, $\pi(q,p)=(r_n, r_{n-1}, ..., r_1)$, by reversing the order of the vertices. Furthermore, these paths have the same length since they contain the same pairs of adjacent vertices. This means that a minimal-length path from p to q is also a minimal-length path from q to p.

(iv.) **Triangle inequality**. We must show $d_R(p,q) \leq d_R(p,s) + d_R(s,q)$. The distance $d_R(p,q)$ gives a minimal path $\pi_{min}(p,q)$ between p and q. Similarly, we have minimal paths $\pi_{min}(p,s)$ and $\pi_{min}(s,q)$. Concatenating the paths $\pi_{min}(p,s)$ and $\pi_{min}(s,q)$ yields a path between p and q; denote this path $\pi(p,q)$. Now

$$\begin{aligned} d_R(p,q) &= \mathrm{Len}(\pi_{min}(p,q)) \\ &\leq \mathrm{Len}(\pi(p,q)) \\ &= \mathrm{Len}(\pi_{min}(p,s)) + \mathrm{Len}(\pi_{min}(s,q)) \\ &= d_R(p,s) + d_R(s,q). \end{aligned}$$ □

We now establish some basic facts about the geometry of points in the permutohedron. First, that the Riggle distance between neighbors is just their adjDist.

(36) **Lemma.** For adjacent p_1 and p_2 where $p_1 = \mathsf{P\underline{XY}Q}$ and $p_2 = \mathsf{P\underline{YX}Q}$, $d_R(p_1,p_2) = \mathrm{adjDist}(p_1,p_2)$.

Proof. First note that because (p_1, p_2) is a path between p_1 and p_2, the distance between the two vertices must be less than or equal to $\mathrm{adjDist}(p_1, p_2)$, that is: $d_R(p_1,p_2) \leq \mathrm{adjDist}(p_1,p_2)$. We claim that there is no shorter path than (p_1, p_2).

To see this, consider any arbitrary path $\pi = (p_1,..., p_2)$ between p_1 and p_2. Note that in π the constraint Y must be transposed from the $|\mathsf{P}| + 2^{nd}$ position to the $|\mathsf{P}| + 1^{st}$ at some step in the path. This incurs a cost of $|\mathsf{Q}| + 1$ which is exactly the value of $\mathrm{adjDist}(p_1, p_2)$. Any additional transpositions will only increase the length of π. Therefore (p_1, p_2) has a length less than or equal to all other paths between p_1 and p_2. In fact, it is the unique least path because all other paths must include other points, adding positive increments to the path length. □

Given arbitrary points *s* and *t* in the same grammar, we construct a path between them that is both minimal and entirely contained within the grammar.

Given two points $s, t \in \mathrm{Ord}(S)$, where S is a set of *n* constraints, there is a first position *k*, $1 \leq k < n$, at which they differ. Therefore, they share a prefix P, possibly empty, with $k = |\mathsf{P}| + 1$. Thus, $s = \mathsf{PQ}$ and $t = \mathsf{PXR}$, with X occurring non-initially in Q. We construct a path (s, t), where *s* is the start point and t the terminus, by a procedure that we call *Recursive Constraint Promotion* (RCP). We outline RCP verbosely here and spell it out immediately below in (39).

RCP: First we find X in s, somewhere in Q, for s = PQ; then we move it up to right below P by pairwise flips, leaving everything else the same, creating a path from s to a new point $f(s) = f^{(1)}(s)$ that now shares PX with t. This first step reduces our problem by extending the shared prefix by one constraint. If $f^{(1)}(s)$ is not t, we reapply the same procedure to $f^{(1)}(s)$ and t, creating a path between $f^{(1)}(s)$ and $f(f^{(1)}(s)) = f^{(2)}(s)$, a point that is identical to t in one more prefixal position. If $f^{(2)}(s)$ is not t, we continue onward, pushing the shared prefix rightward, until the result of the procedure $f^{(n)}(s)$ is identical to t. Pasting together all of the intermediate paths gives us a path from s to t.

Consequences: we show first in Lemma (40) that this path stays within any grammar that includes s and t, and then in Theorem (45) that this is a shortest path between s and t. This gives a geodesic between s and t that is within G. We then go on to consider an arbitrary geodesic between s and t and show via contradiction in (51) that it cannot exit the grammar, thereby establishing that grammars are spherically convex.

(37) **Definition. Start point.** The start point of a path $\pi = (s, ..., t)$ is the total order s.

(38) **Definition. Terminus.** The terminus of a path $\pi = (s, ..., t)$ is the total order t.

We now turn to the definition of RCP. We use the notation p[k] to refer to the kth constraint in the total order p, counting left to right and starting with p[1]. We use the notation π^- to represent the path that results from removing the last point from the path π. We write $\pi_1 + \pi_2$ to denote the path resulting from the concatentation of paths π_1 and π_2 in that order, an operation defined only when the terminus of π_1 is adjacent to the start point of π_2.

(39) Recursive Constraint Promotion. RCP(s, t)

Step 0. Identify the first constraint $t[k]$ at which s and t differ, i.e. where $s[k] \neq t[k]$

Step 1. Find the constraint $t[k]$ in s. This must be in some position $m > k$ in s. Move it up to position k by a series of $m-k$ adjacent flips to create a path $\pi_k = (s, q_1, ..., q_{m-k})$. Constraint $s[m]$ is now in position k in q_{m-k}. Consequently, $q_{m-k}[i] = t[i]$ for all i, $1 \leq i \leq k$.

Step 2. If $q_{m-k} = t$, then RCP(s, t) $= \pi_k$.
Else RCP(s, t) $= \pi_k^- +$ RCP(q_{m-k}, t).

Remark. The algorithm terminates because there are only a finite number of differences between t and s, i.e. k increases strictly with every recursive call to RCP, and $k \leq |s| = |t|$.

To grasp the intuitive sense of RCP, observe that the problem we face is equivalent to that of restoring a permutation s of some sequence t to the order of elements in t. If we code t as a numerical sequence 1234, say, then going from s = 4231 (for example) to t by adjacent transpositions will require a series of steps moving each element frontward over all those that are greater than it numerically.

We now consider the relation between RCP(s, t) and a grammar containing both s and t.

(40) **Lemma.** The path RCP(s, t) lies within any grammar that contains s and t.

Proof. We show by contradiction that the path RCP(s, t) can never stray outside a grammar containing s and t. Let s, $t \in$ G for some grammar G and suppose that s and t first differ in the kth position of t, with $t[k]$ = X. Then we have the following:

s = P...XQ

t = PX...Q

Let s' be the result of applying step 1 of RCP to (s, t). Then we have

s' = PX...Q

where the only difference between s and s' is that X stands in position k, having been moved there through a sequence of adjacent transpositions bringing it always closer to the front.

Consider the path $\pi(s,s')$ of adjacent legs produced by flipping X frontward under RCP. Any such path is associated with a sequence of grammars $\mathcal{P} = \mathrm{H}_1,..., \mathrm{H}_n$, $n \geq 1$, within which the path lies as it proceeds from $s \in \mathrm{H}_1$ to $s' \in \mathrm{H}_n$. Now suppose *per contradictio* that $\pi(s, s')$ exits G. This entails that $\mathcal{P}$ contains more than $\mathrm{H}_1 = \mathrm{G}$. For each sequential pair of grammars H_j, H_{j+1}

in $\mathcal{P}$, there must be a border point pair $\{s_i, s_{i+1}\}$ with X in the transposition. Each pair has this form:

$$s_i = \mathrm{PR}\underline{\mathrm{YX}}... \in \mathrm{H}_j$$
$$s_{i+1} = \mathrm{PR}\underline{\mathrm{XY}}... \in \mathrm{H}_{j+1}$$

From this, it follows immediately that $\mathrm{H}_{j+1} <^{\mathrm{bp.X}} \mathrm{H}_j$. For convenience, we turn this relation around to $\mathrm{H}_j >^{\mathrm{bp.X}} \mathrm{H}_{j+1}$ so that the sequence of relations follows the sequence of the path. Thus, $\mathcal{P}$ is totally ordered by $>^{\mathrm{bp.X}}$.

$$\mathrm{G} = \mathrm{H}_1 >^{\mathrm{bp.X}} \dots >^{\mathrm{bp.X}} \mathrm{H}_{n-1} >^{\mathrm{bp.X}} \dots >^{\mathrm{bp.X}} \mathrm{H}_n$$

By construction of $\mathcal{P}$, we have $s' \in \mathrm{H}_n$. Therefore, H_n contains a leg with prefix PX, namely s', as does G, namely $t =$ PX... . Thus, $\mathrm{G} = \mathrm{H}_1 \sim^{\mathrm{pr.X}} \mathrm{H}_n$. By the theorem 'Equality of Equivalences' (96), §4.6.1, we have $\mathrm{G} \sim^{\mathrm{bp.X}} \mathrm{H}^n$. By hypertransitive inference, then, we have $\mathrm{G} >^{\mathrm{htc.bp.X}} \mathrm{G}$, an impossibility. Therefore, as claimed, $\pi(s, s')$ cannot exit G.

The same argument by contradiction applies *mutatis mutandis* to any step of RCP where the path is assumed to leave G.

Therefore the entire path RCP(s, t) stays within G. □

RCP proves constructively that Ord(S) is path-connected, where by 'path-connected' is meant that there is a path between any $s, t \in$ Ord(S).

(41) **Corollary.** Every grammar G is path-connected.

Proof. Let $s, t \in$ G. RCP(s, t) connects them and Lemma (40) ensures that the entirety of RCP(s, t) lies within G. □

We now show that RCP(s, t) is a shortest path – a length-minimizing geodesic – between any points s and t.

Consider an arbitrary path $\pi = (s,..., t)$ Any given constraint X participates in a certain number of adjacent flips in the path. Each flip defines an edge in π of a certain length. Let the *travel* of X in π, denoted tr(X, π), be the sum of the length of the edges that those flips give rise to.

To define it, we write X[p] for the serial position of constraint X in leg p, and for an enumerated path $\pi = (\mathrm{p}_1,..., \mathrm{p}_n)$, we define X⟨$\pi$⟩ to be the set of indices of the vertices in the path where X changes position between p_i and p_{i+1}

$$\mathrm{X}\langle\pi\rangle = \{i \mid \mathrm{X}[\mathrm{p}_i] \neq \mathrm{X}[\mathrm{p}_{i+1}]\}.$$

With these in hand, we may define the travel of X in π.

(42) **Definition. Travel.** For X ∈ S.Con and $\pi = (\mathrm{p}_1,...,\mathrm{p}_n)$ a path between $\mathrm{p}_1, \mathrm{p}_n \in$ Ord(S.Con), the travel of X in π is the total length of all edges in which X is transposed, that is:

$$\mathrm{tr}(\mathrm{X}, \pi) = \textstyle\sum_{i \in \mathrm{X}\langle\pi\rangle} \mathrm{d_R}(\mathrm{p}_i, \mathrm{p}_{i+1})$$

From this, we may define the *action* $\mathcal{A}(\pi)$ of a path to be the sum over all constraints of their travel in π.

(43) **Definition. Action of a path.**

$$A(\pi) = \Sigma_{X \in S.CON} \, tr(X, \pi)$$

The action of a path π has a simple relationship to its length Len(π). Each flip involves two constraints; therefore, the length of the edge associated with a flip is added to the travel of two different constraints. Thus, the action of a path is twice its length.

(44) **Lemma.** $\mathcal{A}(\pi) = 2$ Len(π)

Proof. As in text above. □

This means that properties of the action translate immediately into properties of path length. In particular, if we find a path of least action, we have found a path of minimal length. We use this fact to show that RCP(s, t) provides a minimal-length path from s to t.

In describing the location of constraints in a leg, we will refer to linear precedence in terms that evoke standard ranking terminology: constraint X is 'above' constraint Y in leg λ if it precedes (dominates) Y in λ, in which case we will also say that Y is 'below' X.

(45) **Theorem.** For any $s, t \in$ Ord(S.Con), RCP(s, t) is a shortest path between s and t.

Proof. Let s, t be points on the permutohedron. Consider any constraint X occurring as $s[i]$ and $t[k]$. We begin by establishing the minimal number of flips that involve X in any path between s and t, as it moves from its initial position i to its terminal position k. We make this calculation without regard to whether there is a path that contains only these flips.

Observe that in s, there is a set of constraints D above X that appear below X in t. In any path from s to t, these constraints must move *down* past X to reach their position in t. Similarly, in s, there is also a set of constraints U below X that appear above X in t. In any path from s to t, these constraints must move *up* past X to reach their position in t.

In addition to these, there is a set A of constraints lying above X in both s and t, and a set B of constraints lying below X in both s and t.

Writing [S, T] for a sequence constructed from all the elements of sets S and T, we can schematize the general situation as follows:

$$s = [A, \text{D}] \text{ X } [B, \text{U}]$$
$$t = [A, \text{U}] \text{ X } [B, \text{D}]$$

This notation is not meant to imply that the mentioned sets of constraints A, B, D, U, lie in separate contiguous subsequences, merely that they are in a sequence with the elements of whatever sets they are bracketed with.

There are |D| constraints that must flip downward past X in any path from s to t. Each of these flips moves X up by one position. Therefore X must minimally flip upward |D| times. Similarly, there are |U| constraints that must flip up past X in any path from s to t. Each of these flips moves X one position downward. Therefore X must minimally flip down |U| times. Since these flips must occur in any path that goes from s to t, every such path, regardless of any other flips within it, must contain at least |D| + |U| flips that involve X.

Claim: for any X, the path RCP(s, t) includes *only* these flips. RCP proceeds by finding the first point at which s and t differ. Each element $u \in$ U will be detected in its position k_u in t, and its avatar in position i_u in s will be flipped up to position k_u. In this process, it passes X exactly once, shifting X down once, so that X is shifted down precisely |U| times in the processing of U. Note that in RCP a constraint is shifted down only when a constraint that must be above it in t is moved up past it. This means that in RCP a constraint X participates in no other down-flips besides those involving the elements of U.

Now consider what happens when RCP reaches X in its left-right sweep of t looking for disparities between t and its current start point s_c. The path under construction currently ends on a point s_X that looks like this:

s_X = [A, D, U] X [B]

At this point, RCP has placed every constraint in A and U – everything in t preceding X – in its correct terminal position. This excludes all of D, because the elements of D follow X in t, and nothing in D has yet been found by RCP. The positions occupied by the elements of A and U are the first |A| + |U| positions in s_X, because they occupy those positions in t. Therefore at this stage *all* of the members of D lie in a sequence that immediately follows [A, U] and immediately precedes X. Thus s_X may be more tightly schematized as follows:

(*) s_X = [A, U] [D] X [B]

Since all of the constraints in D must follow X in t, RCP will flip X up past each of them, with one flip per constraint in D, accumulating |D| flips. After this, there are no other up-flips of X, because everything that must be above it (A, U) and every constraint that must be below it (D, B) is correctly positioned with respect to X.

These arguments establish that RCP flips X exactly |U| + |D| times, which is the minimal number of flips involving X in any path from s to t. Since X is arbitrary, RCP flips every constraint the minimal number of times it must be flipped in any path from s to t. The path RCP(s, t) has therefore the minimal number of points in it.

We now show that the action $\mathcal{A}$(RCP(s, t)) is minimal. We begin by showing that the travel of each constraint in RCP(s, t) is minimal. To accomplish this, we ascertain the best positions, i.e. the least costly positions in terms of distance, in which the necessary transpositions can take place.

First, consider the *best possible set of positions* for the |U| necessary down-flips of X, without reference to any particular path. We start with X in position i = X[s] = $|A| + |\mathrm{D}| + 1$ in s. We know that X must flip down exactly |U| times as it is passed by the elements of U in their ascent. Claim: these down-flips of X contribute minimally to the travel of X if they take place when X is in positions i, $i+1$, ..., $i+|\mathrm{U}|$. Observe that X will occupy each of these positions when the elements of U are flipped up past it without any intervening flips involving X. If this sequence is interrupted by flipping X up, then the length of a necessary down-flip can only be increased, so this option can be dismissed. The only way to decrease the length of any of these down-flips with elements of U would be to move X downward prior to the flip by moving some constraint C $\notin$ U up past X before the flip takes place. However, this is equally futile because the travel of X still includes the length of an edge produced by the flip (with C) at the position it was moved down from. Therefore, to achieve minimal downward travel for X the constraints of U must be moved up past X with no other flips involving X, starting with X in its initial position i =X[s] as claimed. This is precisely what RCP does.

Now consider the *best possible positions* for the necessary |D| up-flips of X, without reference to any particular path. To minimize the up-flip cost, X must start at the lowest position it reaches when the elements of |U| have been flipped up past it. Thus, the sequence of up-flips of X should start at position $i+|\mathrm{U}|$ and proceed up to position $i + |\mathrm{U}| - |\mathrm{D}| = k$, for k = X[t]. This is a general fact. In RCP in particular, X is reached for processing after all its down-flips involving elements of U, and sits in position $i + |\mathrm{U}|$, as may seen from schema (*). It has |D| flips to go. But this means that it is in the best position $i+|\mathrm{U}|$ and arrives at position i + |U| – |D| = k. Therefore RCP incurs the minimal cost for the |D| up-flips.

Now observe that there can be no compensation in down-flip cost for choosing a path that increases the cost of the up-flips, because the down-flip cost cannot be reduced below its minimum. Similarly for attempting a path with supraminimal down-flip cost. Since there is no way to lower either down-flip or up-flip costs associated with RCP, the sum of the two is also minimal. Thus, for each constraint X, RCP(s, t) incurs minimal travel. By the same reasoning just employed, there can be no other less-travel path that has overall less action, to be obtained by raising the cost of one constraint's travel in order to lower the cost of another's: no travel value can be lowered below its minimum. Therefore, RCP(s, t) is the least action path between s and t. Because path length is simply half the action, RCP(s, t) is the shortest path between s and t. □

We have now established two key facts:

i. the RCP path RCP(s, t) lies within any grammar G with $s, t \in$ G, shown in Lemma (40)
ii. the RCP path is a minimizing geodesic, shown in Theorem (45).

This falls short of establishing that grammars are spherically convex, because there might be (and often are) multiple such geodesics between s and t, all of which must lie in G if G is spherically convex. Let us proceed to the general result. It will be useful to enrich our understanding of geodesics before arriving there.

Observe first that the argument of Theorem (45) gives basic information about general geodesics. In particular, it shows that, for any constraint, there is a set of minimally necessary flips and a set of correlated positions where they must occur that contribute minimally to the length of the path. The RCP path meets these conditions. But any path with just these flips in just these positions will have the same length, and therefore be a geodesic.

(46) **Corollary. Flips and Positions.** Every geodesic $\gamma(s, t)$ between points s and t contains the same constraint flips at the same positions.

Proof. Note that $\gamma(s, t)$ must be the same length as RCP(s, t). Since Len(RCP(s, t)) is minimal, any longer path is not a geodesic.

Now consider, for arbitrary X, the flips in $\gamma(s, t)$ in which X participates. Using the schematism as above, we note that every path from s to t, geodesic or not, must include flips of X with the elements of U and the elements of D. Theorem (45) establishes that the path RCP(s, t) contains only those.

The argument of Theorem (45) also establishes the exact positions at which these flips must occur if they are to achieve minimal travel for X. It is then shown that RCP(s, t) contains the flips of X at these positions and no others. Thus, a path exists that contains the flips at these best positions, those which endow X with minimal travel. If the geodesic $\gamma(s, t)$ contains flips involving X with the elements of U and D at positions different from these, or additional flips, then its travel is increased. The argument of Theorem (45) establishes that there are no trade-offs whereby increasing the travel of X can reduce the travel of some other constraint. Since this is generically true for every constraint, any variation in position of the minimally required flips for any constraint will merely increase the length of the path. But no geodesic can be longer than RCP(s, t), so $\gamma(s, t)$ has only the minimally required flips and they occur at the same positions as in the path RCP(s, t). □

(47) **Corollary. Uniqueness.** No geodesic contains two flips involving the same constraints.

Proof. From Corollary (46), we have it that all geodesics between any s, t have exactly the same flips. Using the notation of Theorem (45), observe that in any such geodesic, an arbitrary constraint X flips down once for each constraint in U, up once for each constraint in D, and participates in no other flips. But U and D are disjoint. □

From (47), we immediately obtain the (obvious, but still useful) corollary that no geodesic contains both a flip XY → YX and its reverse, YX → XY.

(48) **Corollary. Up Excludes Down.** If a geodesic $\gamma(s, t)$, understood as running from s to t, contains the edge (P$\underline{\text{XY}}$Q, P$\underline{\text{YX}}$Q), it does not contain an edge (P′$\underline{\text{YX}}$Q′, P′$\underline{\text{XY}}$Q′).

Proof. Since edges (P$\underline{\text{XY}}$Q, P$\underline{\text{YX}}$Q) and (P′$\underline{\text{YX}}$Q′, P′$\underline{\text{XY}}$Q′) involve the same constraints X, Y, it is immediate from Uniqueness (47) that they cannot co-reside in the same geodesic. □

We note in passing that the calculations of Theorem (45) determine the travel of every constraint in $\gamma(s, t)$, and therefore permit algorithmic calculation of the length of every geodesic as well as of the number of legs it contains.

(49) **Corollary. Getting Better All the Time.** If a geodesic $\gamma(s, t)$ contains an edge (P$\underline{\text{XY}}$Q, P$\underline{\text{YX}}$Q) anywhere, containing a flip XY → YX, then Y precedes X in t.

Proof. If not, then there must be another later edge (P′$\underline{\text{YX}}$Q′, P′$\underline{\text{XY}}$Q′) in the path γ to set X and Y on their way to their positions in t. But this cannot be, by (48). □

Corollary (46) also yields information about the order in which the flips are executed in any geodesic path. By working from left to right through t, RCP imposes a convenient order on the operations creating the path between s and t. But Corollary (46) entails that there are strong intrinsic limits on flip order in general geodesics. In particular, for every X, all down-flips of X involving U must proceed any up-flips of X involving D.

(50) **Corollary. Ordnung muß sein.** Let $\gamma(s, t)$ be any geodesic from $s = [A, \mathrm{D}]\,\mathrm{X}\,[B, \mathrm{U}]$ to $t = [A, \mathrm{U}]\,\mathrm{X}\,[B, \mathrm{D}]$, in the schematic notation of Theorem (45). Then, in γ, every (down) flip of X with the elements of U precedes every (up-) flip of X with the elements of D.

Proof. Let i be the position of X in s. By Corollary (46), X in $\gamma(s, t)$ participates in flips with all and only the elements of U and D, at the same positions as in RCP(s, t). By Theorem (45), X flips with an element of D when it is in position $i + |\mathrm{U}|$ in RCP(s, t). But X only reaches that position after every constraint in U has flipped up past it. In γ, therefore, all (down-) flips of X with elements of U precede the (up-) flips of X with elements of D. □

RCP(s, t) provides a kind of universal catalog of flips and correlated positions that are exactly the flips and their positions that occur in every geodesic $\gamma(s, t)$. What can differ among geodesics is only the order in which those flips are executed at their determinate positions, creating a different path. But, as we've seen, even this order is tightly constrained.

We are now in a position to prove the main result. We will do this in two ways. First, we examine a situation parallel to that examined in Lemma (40), which established that the RCP path between two legs of grammar lies inside it. Then we develop a more algebraic perspective, which provides insight into the structure of geodesics and how that leads to convexity.

(51) **Theorem. All grammars are spherically convex.** For any grammar, all geodesics between legs of the grammar lie within it.

Proof. Let G be an arbitrary grammar, situated in some typology. Let $s, t \in \mathrm{G}$ and let $\gamma(s, t) = (\mathrm{p}_0, \ldots, \mathrm{p}_n)$ be a geodesic from s to t, with $s = \mathrm{p}_0$ and $t = \mathrm{p}_n$. Assume that γ exits G at some point. Since exit always creates a border point, we may assume without loss of generality that $s = \mathrm{p}_0$ is itself the border point in question and that γ exits G after p_0. We will show that this leads to a contradiction and therefore that γ lies entirely within G. Thus, no geodesic between points of G can leave G, establishing G's spherical convexity.

Consider the first edge $(\mathrm{p}_0, \mathrm{p}_1) \in \gamma$. By construction, we have that $\mathrm{p}_0 \in \mathrm{G}$ and $\mathrm{p}_1 \in \mathrm{H}_1$ where $\mathrm{H}_1 \neq \mathrm{G}$. Now consider the geodesic produced by RCP from p_1 to t, call this path $\rho(\mathrm{p}_1, \mathrm{t})$. Note that concatenating p_0 with ρ yields a path $\mathrm{p}_0 + \rho$ from G to G that exits G and then returns to G. This need not be the same as $\gamma(s, t)$.

We now turn our attention to ρ and deduce some EPO-relational facts. Since $\rho = (\mathrm{p}_1, \ldots, \mathrm{p}_n = t)$ starts in H_1 and ends in G, there is a sequence of grammars that ρ travels through before entering G. We'll label these grammars H_1, H_2, ..., H_m, $m \geq 1$, where ρ sequentially moves through H_1, then H_2, etc., until it enters G from grammar H_m. This path produces a border point pair for each pair of sequential grammars, bpp_1, bpp_2, ..., bpp_m, where bpp_i exits H_i, spelled out immediately below. As usual P, Q (subscripted below) denote sequences of constraints, possibly empty. We write the transposing constraints in lower case for visual distinctness,

$$bpp_1 = (P_1 d_1 u_1 Q_1,\ P_1 u_1 d_1 Q_1),\ \text{with}\ P_1 d_1 u_1 Q_1 \in H_1,\ P_1 u_1 d_1 Q_1 \in H_2$$
$$bpp_2 = (P_2 d_2 u_2 Q_2,\ P_2 u_2 d_2 Q_2),\ \text{with}\ P_2 d_2 u_2 Q_2 \in H_2,\ P_2 u_2 d_2 Q_2 \in H_3$$
$$\ldots$$
$$bpp_m = (P_m d_m u_m Q_m,\ P_m u_m d_m Q_m),\ \text{with}\ P_m d_m u_m Q_m \in H_m,\ P_m u_m d_m Q_m \in G$$

These are given as pairs ordered by the sense of the path ρ, thereby defining edges which appear, among possibly others, in ρ.

For each flipping pair in bpp_i (d_i, u_i), call u_i the upward-moving constraint and d_i the downward-moving constraint in the sequence of edges of the oriented path. By construction, these total orders and border point pairs all fall along the RCP-produced geodesic ρ from p_1 to t and therefore each upward-moving constraint in each bpp is in fact moving upwards in the RCP algorithm and each downward-moving constraint is moving downwards in RCP, because each total order in each bpp lies along the RCP path. Recall from RCP that once a constraint starts moving upwards it moves uninterruptedly upwards to its target location – its position in t – and once there, no constraints that precede it are moved by RCP.

Consider now bpp_1, crossing from H_1 to H_2 via the transposition $d_1 u_1 \rightarrow u_1 d_1$ in the context $P_1\_Q_1$, focusing attention on the constraint u_1. In the total order $p_1 = P_1 d_1 u_1 Q_1$, the constraint u_1 is the highest-ranked (frontmost) constraint in t that is mispositioned in $P_1 d_1 u_1 Q_1$. This means that once RCP has placed u_1 in its correct position no further transposition will pass u_1, nor will RCP transpose any constraint that precedes u_1. Therefore in all further transpositions after bpp_1 along the RCP path $\rho = (p_1,\ldots,p_n = t)$, whether in border point pairs or not, the constraint u_1 is either upward-moving or prefixal. But this guarantees that in each border point pair of ρ, being among the edges of the RCP path ρ, either u_1 is the constraint moving up, or u_1 is prefixal.

This establishes a series of inequalities and equivalences in the EPO[u_1] between all of the grammars that ρ traverses, including its final grammar G. We can represent it thusly:

$$(*)\quad H_1 >^{bp.u1} H_2 >^{bp.u1} \ldots >^{bp.u1} H_k \sim^{bp.u1} H_{k+1} \sim^{bp.u1} \ldots \sim^{bp.u1} H_m \sim^{bp.u1} G$$

Note that in (*), although the existence of bpp_1 guarantees an order relation on u_1 between H_1 and H_2, there need not be any equivalences, in which case $k = m$. In that circumstance, u_1 would be the only constraint moved by RCP in traversing ρ from H_1 to G.

Crucially, (*) establishes an order relation between H_1 and G.

(**) $H_1 >^{htc.u1} G$

We now turn our attention to the pair of total orders $p_0 \in G$ and $p_1 \in H_1$ that lie along the original geodesic $\gamma(s = p_0, p_n = t)$. By the assumption made for purposes of contradiction, this is the pair that leapt us out of G in γ. These two total orders form a border point pair $bpp_G = (p_0, p_1)$, which we will write out as (PdvQ, PvdQ), with $p_0 = \text{PdvQ} \in G$ and $p_1 = \text{PvdQ} \in H_1$. Note that bpp_G need not be on the RCP path from p_0 to p_n.

Now, bpp_G = (PdvQ, PvdQ) is the first edge in geodesic γ that leaves G for H_1. By our construction, it is also the first edge in the path $p_0 + \rho\ (p_1, p_n)$. Now, the path $p_0 + \rho$ returns somewhere to G, exiting from H_1 at the edge $bpp_1 = (P_1d_1u_1Q_1, P_1u_1d_1Q_1)$.

Let us ask where constraint u_1 might lie in the total orders $\text{PdvQ} \in G$ and $\text{PvdQ} \in H_1$ that comprise bpp_G = (PdvQ, PvdQ). We show that it cannot be positioned anywhere without incurring a contradiction. There are four cases to consider: prefix, transposition (×2), suffix, each of which we dismiss by *reductio*.

Case 1. $u_1 \in P$. In this case, bpp_G = (PdvQ, PvdQ). From this, it follows that $G \sim^{u1} H_1$ which with (**) $H_1 >^{htc.u1} G$, yields a cycle in EPO[u_1] an impossibility by Lemma (49), §4.3.5. So, $u_1 \notin P$.

Case 2. $u_1 = v$. In this case, $bpp_G = (Pdu_1Q, Pu_1dQ)$. This entails that $G >^{bp.u1} H_1$ which with (**) $H_1 >^{htc.u1} G$ leads to a cycle in EPO[u_1], an impossibility by Lemma (49), §4.3.5. So $u_1 \neq v$.

The last two cases involve more elaborate arguments.

Case 3. $u_1 = d$. In this case, $bpp_G = (Pu_1vQ, Pvu_1Q)$. This yields $G >^{bp.v} H_1$. Recall from Corollary (48) that no geodesic ever contains both a flip $xy \rightarrow yx$ and its reverse $yx \rightarrow xy$. Now, bpp_G is an edge of γ, therefore γ contains only the flip $u_1v \rightarrow vu_1$ and must lack the reverse flip.

Consequently, in the subpath γ_1 of γ running from $p_1 = Pvu_1Q \in H_1$ to $t = p_n \in G$, constraint v always precedes u_1. Now consider ρ, the RCP-produced geodesic from $p_1 = Pvu_1Q$ to t. By Corollary (46) 'Flips and Positions', all geodesics running from p_1 to t contain the same transpositions.

Therefore, ρ also lacks the transposition $\mathsf{vu}_1 \rightarrow \mathsf{u}_1\mathsf{v}$, and the constraint v always precedes u_1 in ρ.

Since u_1 is the upward-moving constraint in $bpp_1 \in \rho$ and is therefore either upward-moving or prefixal in any and all subsequent border point pairs in ρ, it follows that v is prefixal in all bpps of ρ. Therefore, $H_1 \sim^{\mathsf{v}} H_2 \sim^{\mathsf{v}} \cdots \sim^{\mathsf{v}} H_m \sim^{\mathsf{v}} G$, so that $H_1 \sim^{\mathsf{v}} G$. Since $G >^{\mathsf{v}} H_1$ from bbp_G, this creates a cycle in EPO[v], which is impossible. Therefore, $\mathsf{u}_1 \neq \mathsf{d}$.

Case 4. $\mathsf{u}_1 \in Q$. In this case, $bpp_G = (\mathsf{PdvQ}, \mathsf{PvdQ})$, with $\mathsf{u}_1 \in Q$. The edge defined by bpp_G is the first step of $\gamma(s, t)$. In it, v moves up. By Corollary (50), v can only move up in any further flips involving v in γ.

We now inquire as to where v sits in t with respect to u_1. Observe that from bpp_G we have $G >^{\mathsf{bp.v}} H_1$. If v precedes u_1 in $bpp_1 = (P_1\mathsf{d}_1\mathsf{u}_1Q_1, P_1\mathsf{u}_1\mathsf{d}_1Q_1)$, then since u_1 is either upward-moving or prefixal in any and all subsequent border point pairs in ρ, it follows that v is prefixal in all border points of $\rho(p_1, p_n = t)$. Since ρ starts in H_1 and ends in G, this gives us $H_1 \sim^{\mathsf{v}} G$, contradicting $G >^{\mathsf{bp.v}} H_1$. Therefore, the only remaining possibility is that u_1 precedes v in t.

However, in $p_1 = \mathsf{PvdQ}$, it must be that v precedes u_1, since by assumption $\mathsf{u}_1 \in Q$. Therefore, in $\rho(p_1, t)$ the transposition $\mathsf{vu}_1 \rightarrow \mathsf{u}_1\mathsf{v}$ must occur. Now consider the subpath γ_1 of γ which runs from p_1 to t. Since every subpath of a geodesic is also a geodesic, we have a geodesic $\gamma_1(p_1, t)$ that runs between that start and terminus of $\rho(p_1, t)$. By Corollary (46) 'Flips and Positions', these two geodesics have the same flips. Therefore, $\mathsf{vu}_1 \rightarrow \mathsf{u}_1\mathsf{v}$, which must occur in ρ, must also occur in γ_1, and consequently must occur in $\gamma(p_0, t)$ as well. But this is a down-flip involving v. We've seen that γ contains no down-flips of v. This contradiction entails that u_1 cannot precede v in t. Since it cannot follow v in t either, the assumption $\mathsf{u}_1 \in Q$ cannot hold and the final case is dismissed, establishing the Theorem.

No geodesic between legs of a grammar can exit that grammar. Grammars are spherically convex. □

We now develop another perspective on the matter, which gives further insight into the result. Understanding how all geodesics must be contained within a grammar is enabled by understanding the crucial configuration that gives rise to multiple geodesics between two points. This can be exemplified by what we will call the Rectangle Grammar, which we first encountered in ex. (22).

Consider the grammar on 4 constraints $\{\mathsf{x}, \mathsf{y}, \mathsf{z}, \mathsf{w}\}$ defined by the following ERC set, which requires, informally put, that both constraints $\{\mathsf{x}, \mathsf{y}\}$ dominate both constraints $\{\mathsf{z}, \mathsf{w}\}$.

(52) **The Rectangle Grammar**

x	y	z	w
W	e	L	L
e	W	L	L

We call this the Rectangle Grammar because on the permutohedron as based on the regular omnitruncated simplex, its 4 legs define a rectangular region under the Riggle metric. It looks like this, with the distance between adjacent points written next to the edge connecting them. For visibility, we insert a period between the internally-permuting sets of constraints. The RCP path we will discuss is marked by double lines.

(53) **The Rectangle**

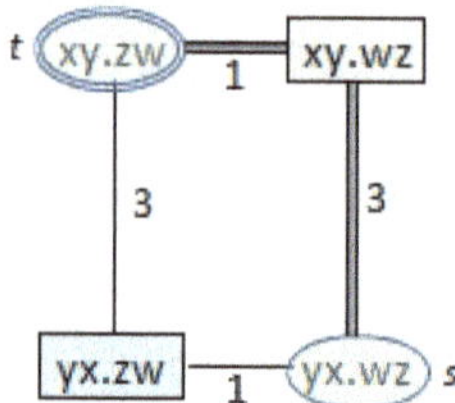

The 4 legs of the grammar are characterized by free permutation of the constraints x, y in the two leftmost positions and free permutation of z,w in the two rightmost positions.

Let $s =$ yx.wz, the lower right corner of the diagram, and let $t =$ xy.zw, the upper left corner. RCP finds x as the highest-ranked constraint in t that is mispositioned in s. Therefore RCP(s, t) proceeds up and over, running from yx.wz to xy.wz (distance 3) and thence to xy.zw (distance 1). The length of the path RCP(s, t) is 4, which is a shortest path between s and t, by Lemma (45), assuring us that there is no shorter path to be found anywhere on the rest of the permutohedron (not shown).

We can immediately see, however, that there is another path γ between s and t of equal length, specifically yx.wz – yx.zw – xy.zw, which runs to the left (distance 1) and then up (distance 3). By contrast, the RCP path runs up first and only then to the left. Furthermore, this path is also contained within the grammar. This exemplifies the multiple geodesic issue. As shown above, RCP(s, t) and $\gamma(s, t)$ contain the same transpositions, namely yx → xy and wz → zw, occurring in the same positions, but in a different order. This difference in order is consistent with Corollary (50) because the provisions of that result refer to flips involving a single constraint, but the flips of RCP(s, t) and $\gamma(s, t)$ pertain to disjoint sets of constraints.

To see what's going on here, it is useful to introduce a new perspective on path descriptions. Rather than regarding a path as a sequence of legs, we represent a path as a sequence of transpositions applied to the start point. In this discussion, by a *transposition* σ_h we mean the exchange of the constraints in positions h and $h+1$. Thus, for any leg λ, $\sigma_1(\lambda)$ flips the content of positions 1 and 2, and so on. It is also convenient to number the positions from the end, so that position 1 is final and holds the last constraint, position 2 is penultimate and holds the next-to-last constraint and so on.

Under these conventions, a four-constraint leg has the positional structure p_4-p_3-p_2-p_1. For example, we have σ_1(xy.zw) = xy.wz, because σ_1 transposes the constraints in positions 1 and 2, final and penultimate, here w and z. Similarly, σ_3(xy.zw) = yx.zw, transposing the constraints in positions 3 and 4, namely y and x. Note that the Riggle distance between s and $\sigma_h(s)$ is exactly h.

This notion of transposition can be given a formal definition as follows. First, we recall the notation that retrieves the content of a position.

(54) **Definition.** Given $\lambda = C_k\, C_{k-1} \cdots C_1$, then $\lambda[h] =_{df} C_h$.
By this, $\lambda[h]$ is the constraint in position h of leg λ, where the final constraint is in position 1.

(55) **Definition.** Transposition σ_h

$$\sigma_h\colon \mathrm{Ord}(S.\mathrm{Con}) \rightarrow \mathrm{Ord}(S.\mathrm{Con}), \text{ where}$$
$$\sigma_h(\lambda) = \lambda' \text{ where } \lambda = \lambda' \text{ everywhere except}$$
$$\lambda'[h] = \lambda[h+1] \text{ and}$$
$$\lambda'[h+1] = \lambda[h].$$

With this, the path $\rho(s, t) = \mathrm{RCP}(s, t)$ from the example (53) becomes

$$\rho = s,\ \sigma_3(s),\ \sigma_1\sigma_3(s),$$

which is entirely deducible from the expression $t = \sigma_1\sigma_3(s)$, which represents t as deriving from s by a sequence of transpositions. For the other geodesic $\gamma(s, t)$, we have

$$\gamma = s,\ \sigma_1(s),\ \sigma_3\sigma_1(s),$$

which is likewise deducible from the expression $t = \sigma_3\sigma_1(s)$.

Observe that in this situation, the RCP path ρ between $s=$ yx.wz and $t=$ xy.zw starts out with σ_3, by transposing the element x, the frontmost misplaced element of t, from its position 3 in s with what precedes it in position 4, and then proceeds to σ_1, transposing the endmost element z (position 1) with its neighbor w (position 2). RCP thus generates one of the two geodesics between s and t.

This example illustrates that transposition is commutative as long as the distance between the indices is 2 or more. Using the notation, we have $\sigma_h\sigma_k(\mathrm{s}) = \sigma_k\sigma_h(\mathrm{s})$ iff $|h-k| \geq 2$. Sequential transpositions σ_h and σ_k commute exactly when the constraints transposed by σ_h are distinct from the constraints transposed by σ_k. In the language of combinatorics, they are *disjoint permutations.*

When indices are sequential, transposition never commutes. For example, let $s =$ xyz and consider $\sigma_2\sigma_1(s)$ and $\sigma_1\sigma_2(s)$.

s	=	xyz	s	=	xyz
$\sigma_1(s)$	=	x<u>zy</u>	$\sigma_2(s)$	=	<u>yx</u>z
$\sigma_2\sigma_1(s)$	=	<u>zx</u>y	$\sigma_1\sigma_2(s)$	=	y<u>zx</u>

Any further manipulations will map the content of position 1 (the final position, by our numbering scheme), for example, into some determinate position $k \in \{1, 2, 3\}$ in the output of the manipulation. But what's in position 1 differs in $\sigma_2\sigma_1(\mathrm{s})$ and $\sigma_1\sigma_2(\mathrm{s})$, and so will differ in position k in the output.

There's nothing special about starting at the bottom. If we interchange two adjacent sequentially indexed transpositions anywhere in a sequence of transpositions, we change the outcome of the entire sequence.

Interchanging a commuting pair $\sigma_h\sigma_k$ with $|h-k| \geq 2$ does not change the outcome of a sequence of transpositions that they belong to, nor does it change the constraints that are transposed in each of the two transpositions, but it does change the path that the sequence generates. Geometrically, this always involves taking a different route around the rectangle. For example, the lower right corner $s =$ yx.wz of the rectangle in example (53) is mapped to its upper left corner $t =$ xy.zw by both $\sigma_1\sigma_3$, following the RCP(s, t) path $\rho(s, t)$, and by $\sigma_3\sigma_1$ which follows the other path $\gamma(s, t)$. The length of the path is unchanged, because the length is merely the sum of the indices of the transpositions. By this method, which we will call *commutative exchange*, a geodesic produced by RCP is mapped into another geodesic. A further commutative exchange will map that geodesic into yet another, and so on.

Crucially, at each step the new geodesic remains in the grammar. Schematically, we are dealing with a generalized rectangle, where $t =$ PxyQzwR and $s =$ PyxQwzR. Note that RCP deals first with x, then with z, due to their positions in t, exactly as in diagram (53), where P,Q,R are empty.

(56) **Lemma. Boxing.** Given total orders s and t, where $t = \sigma_h\sigma_k(s)$, $|h-k| \geq 2$, $k > h$, then any grammar G containing s and t also contains $\sigma_h(s)$.

Proof. Note that $\sigma_k(s) \in \mathrm{G}$, because $\sigma_k(s)$ is on the RCP path $\rho(s, t)$ from s to t, since $k > h$. Note further that since $|h-k| \geq 2$, $t = \sigma_h\sigma_k(\mathrm{s}) = \sigma_k\sigma_h(\mathrm{s})$. Suppose for purposes of contradiction that $\sigma_h(\mathrm{s}) \in \mathrm{G}' \neq \mathrm{G}$. This gives us two border point pairs, $b_1 = \{s, \sigma_h(s)\}$ and $b_2 = \{\sigma_h(s), t\}$. Consider the EPO relations between G and G′ on constraint $s[k]$. From b_1, we have $G \sim^{bp.s[k]} G'$. From b_2, we have that $G <^{bp.s[k]} G'$. Since EPOs are noncyclic, two grammars can't be both equivalent and ordered in any EPO. But this means that the assumption that $\sigma_h(s) \notin G$ is false. □

From this, it immediately follows that *if* the procedure of commutative exchange enumerates *all* geodesics from s to t for any $s, t \in G$, then they all lie within G, giving an alternate proof to (51) that an OT grammar is spherically convex. We conclude with that demonstration.

Consider any two geodesics γ and δ, running from s to t. Our tactic will be to show how the path γ can be transformed into the path δ via commutative exchange, preserving geodesicity and inclusion in any grammar containing γ or δ. Since the RCP path $\rho(s, t)$ has been shown to lie within any grammar G with $s, t \in G$ in Lemma (40), it follows that every geodesic $\gamma(s, t)$ lies within G.

First, we develop a representation of paths which is amenable to transformation. Let's begin by noting that in each case, we have a sequence of adjacent legs running from s to t, each one after the first derived by pairwise transposition of adjacent constraints:

(57) Paths π as a composition of transpositions

$$\pi(s, t) = s, \sigma_j(s), \ldots, \sigma_k \circ \cdots \circ \sigma_j(s) = t$$

The representation of the terminus as a composition of transposition functions beginning at the start point encodes a recipe for producing the entire path that leads to it.

(58) Terminus in terms of start point

$$t = \sigma_k \circ \cdots \circ \sigma_j(s)$$

The path π is reconstructible as the list of every partial composition applied to the start point, from s to $t = \sigma_k \circ \cdots \circ \sigma_j(s)$, moving from j to k.

Since several transposition at the same index may occur in the sequence of compositions, the individual items of the form σ_i are not unambiguous in isolation. But from representations like (58), we may construct sequences of unique items that explicitly record all information about the individual flips: not only their positions, but also the constraints involved.

The key step is to write

$$\sigma_h\langle \mathsf{yx}\rangle(s)$$

for the adjacent transposition that maps $\mathsf{Pyx}|_h\mathsf{Q}$ to $\mathsf{P\underline{xy}}|_h\mathsf{Q}$, starting with x in position h and transposing it with y into the preceding position $h+1$, leaving everything else the same. We use underlining to draw attention to a transposed sequence. In portraying a string schematically, we use the notation $\mathsf{z}|_h$ to indicate that element z occurs in position h, which we count from the end.

The function $\sigma_h\langle\mathsf{yx}\rangle$ can be applied to any leg that has y and x in positions $h+1$ and h, respectively, and to no others. We call this an *Element-Restricted Transposition* (ERT) to distinguish it from the general position-based transposition σ_h as defined in (55), which applies to any total order of sufficient length. A general transposition σ_h is a function with domain Ord(S.Con), as in definition (55). The ERT $\sigma_h\langle\mathsf{yx}\rangle$ is defined as σ_h with its domain restricted to those legs where elements y, x occur in positions $h+1$ and h respectively.

(59) **Definition. Element-Restricted Transposition (ERT).** Let $\mathsf{x}, \mathsf{y} \in S.\mathrm{Con}$.

$$\sigma_h\langle\mathsf{yx}\rangle : \{\lambda \in \mathrm{Ord}(S.\mathrm{Con})\} \mid \lambda[h+1] = \mathsf{y},\ \lambda[h] = \mathsf{x}\} \rightarrow \mathrm{Ord}(S.\mathrm{Con}),$$
where $\sigma_h\langle\mathsf{yx}\rangle(\lambda) = \sigma_h(\lambda)$.

An expression involving composition of general transpositions, like that in (57)

$$t = \sigma_k \circ \cdots \circ \sigma_j(s)$$

can, given the content of a specific s, be rewritten in terms of ERTs. For the Rectangle example (53), where $t =$ xy.zw and $s =$ yx.wz, we have $t = \sigma_1 \circ \sigma_3(s)$ from RCP, which spells out as

$$\mathsf{xy.zw} = \sigma_1 \circ \sigma_3(\mathsf{yx.wz}).$$

With ERTs, this becomes

$$\mathrm{xy.zw} = \sigma_1\langle\mathrm{wz}\rangle \circ \sigma_3\langle\mathrm{yx}\rangle(\mathrm{yx.wz}).$$

The geodesic path $\rho(s,\ t) =$ (yx.wz, $\underline{\mathsf{xy}}$.wz, xy.$\underline{\mathsf{zw}}$) may then be represented unambiguously as a list of single individual ERTs presented in the order in which they apply. Thus, for the Rectangle example, we will have the two-item sequence

$$\rho(s,\ t) = \sigma_3\langle\mathsf{yx}\rangle,\ \sigma_1\langle\mathsf{wz}\rangle$$

The path ρ is constructed by having each ERT apply to the output of the previous, with the first in the list applying to the start point.

This maneuver converts function-composition representations like those in (57) into ordered lists of single items. We write $\Sigma(\pi)$ for the ERT sequence representing the path π in terms of the ERTs that produce it. We call a sequence of ERTs a 'Σ-sequence.'

(60) Σ-sequence: σ_m⟨ba⟩,..., σ_n⟨dc⟩

A general Σ-sequence is just a list of ERTs. Unlike a sequence of position-based transpositions σ_k, a general Σ-sequence need not be interpretable as a description of a path. For that to be the case, the appropriate function compositions must be well-defined, in that the range of any one must be the domain of the next. If a Σ-sequence is derived from a licit path, however, that path may be unambiguously regenerated from the Σ-sequence when the starting point is given.

There are three key observations to be made about the Σ-sequences derived from geodesics between a given start and a given terminus.

i. All such Σ-sequences consist of exactly the same ERTs.
ii. There are no repetitions within a given sequence.
iii. Therefore, all such Σ-sequences are of exactly the same length.

The first follows because by Corollary (46) all geodesics between *s* and *t* have the same constraint transpositions at the same positions: an ERT specifies a constraint transposition at a position. The second follows because for any two constraints, only one transposition involving them may occur in a geodesic, by Corollary (47).

The immediate consequence is that any such Σ-sequence for a geodesic between *s* and *t* is a *permutation* of the Σ-sequence for any other such geodesic. It follows immediately from the Boxing Lemma (56) that we can swap two consecutive ERTs with nonsequential position indices in any such Σ-sequence and arrive at another geodesic between *s* and *t* in the same grammar.

(61) **Lemma. Boxing (ERTs).** Given total orders $s, t \in \mathrm{G}$, let $\pi(s, t)$ be a path between *s* and *t* that lies entirely within G. Suppose, for some $|h-k| \geq 2$, and $\mathbb{P}$, $\mathbb{Q}$ sequences of ERTs, we have

$\Sigma(\pi) = \mathbb{P}$, σ_h⟨ba⟩, σ_k⟨yx⟩, $\mathbb{Q}$

Construct from this another sequence of ERTs

$\mathrm{E} = \mathbb{P}$, σ_k⟨yx⟩, σ_h⟨ba⟩, $\mathbb{Q}$

by transposing the specified ERTs. Then, E denotes denotes a path π' than runs between *s* and *t* and lies entirely within G, so that $\mathrm{E} = \Sigma(\pi')$.

Proof. The ERTs in a specific Σ-sequence denoting a path π from *s* to *t* may each be derived from the general position-based transposition mapping from one adjacent point to the next in π by including mention of the transposing constraints, given the start point *s*. If we replace each ERT with the general transposition at its positional index, we may construct a description of the same path as a sequence of function compositions, where the functions are general transpositions, in the manner of example (57). From this representation, we may conclude that the exchange of disjoint transpositions σ_h and σ_k creates a licit path π' running from s to t, which by Lemma (56) stays within G. The ERT sequence E may then be constructed from that description of π' in terms of general transpositions. E is therefore $\Sigma(\pi')$ and the path it denotes stays within G. □

We now show that this is all that's needed, in the context of earlier results on the form of geodesics, to establish that an arbitrary geodesic $\gamma(s, t)$ lies within the same grammars as every other geodesic between s and t, including of course the RCP-derived geodesic $\rho(s, t)$.

Given geodesics $\gamma(s, t)$ and $\delta(s, t)$, we wish to map γ to δ by operating on $\Sigma(\gamma)$ to arrive at $\Sigma(\delta)$, mapping one Σ-sequence of transpositions into the other, by swapping adjacent ERTs in Σ-sequences. Note that any ERT-swap from $\Sigma(\pi)$ to $\Sigma(\pi')$, as long as function composition of ERTs remains well-defined, will designate an entire new *path* π' between s and t, denoted by the derived Σ-sequence $\Sigma(\pi')$. Contrast the transposition of adjacent constraints in a leg, which produces a new leg, thereby creating or extending a single given path.

We already have at hand a general method for mapping a sequence to any of its permutations: RCP. As laid out in (39) above, RCP works on sequences of constraints, but nothing in the definition depends on the nature of the elements that are permuted. We will refer to this generalized version of RCP as GRCP. Its definition can be exactly as in (39), with the word 'constraint' replaced by 'element' (of the sequence under consideration).

We will now use it here on Σ-sequences, where it swaps ERTs that are adjacent in a Σ-sequence, mapping one Σ-sequence into another. Given two arbitrary paths π and π' where the Σ-sequence of one is a permutation of the Σ-sequence of the other, there is no *a priori* guarantee that GRCP creates intermediate Σ-sequences interpretable as paths. However, geodesics prove to be remarkably well-behaved in this respect. We will find that the only ERT transpositions that GRCP effects, when applied to a pair of geodesics between s and t, are those that i. create a new geodesic, and ii. swap only adjacent pairs of ERTs with nonsequential indices, resulting in commutative exchange. This leads directly to the desired result.

(62) **Theorem. Commutative exchange.** Let $s, t \in \text{Ord}(S.\text{Con})$. Let $\gamma(s, t)$ and $\delta(s, t)$ be geodesic paths between s and t, with no further restrictions other than that they are geodesic. Then in the GRCP-derived sequence of Σ-sequences between $\Sigma(\gamma)$ and $\Sigma(\delta)$, each Σ-sequence is related to the

previous by commutive exchange, that is, transpositions of adjacent ERTs of the form $\sigma_h\langle \mathsf{xy}\rangle$, $\sigma_k\langle \mathsf{zw}\rangle$, where $|h - k| \geq 2$, and therefore denotes a geodesic between s and t.

Proof. Observe first that GRCP applies successfully to map $\Sigma(\gamma)$ to $\Sigma(\delta)$, by virtue of the fact the one is a permutation of the other. At issue is whether the intermediate steps denote licit paths in G from s to t that stay within G. If so, then all must be geodesic, since for any path π, Len(π) is the sum of the position indices in $\Sigma(\pi)$, which does not change under GRCP.

We consider only the first step of the first step of GRCP, making a single ERT transposition, as it applies to Σ-sequences S = $\Sigma(\gamma)$ and T = $\Sigma(\delta)$, where γ and δ are geodesics running from s to t. By the definition of GRCP, it seeks in S the first ERT in T, counting from left to right, which is different from the ERT in the same position in S; then it operates on S to transpose that ERT with the ERT that immediately precedes it in S, creating a new sequence S′. (The case $\gamma = \delta$ is set aside as trivial.)

Let $\sigma_f\langle \mathsf{x}\omega\rangle$ be the first element of T that is not in the same position in S as it is in T, searching T left to right. Note that, parallel to the observation in step 1 of (39), the position of the ERT $\sigma_f\langle \mathsf{x}\omega\rangle$ in S is to the right of its position in T, implying that $\sigma_f\langle \mathsf{x}\omega\rangle$ is never initial in S. Let $\sigma_q(\mathsf{ba})$ be the element of S that immediately precedes $\sigma_f\langle \mathsf{x}\omega\rangle$, so that S has this structure, where $\mathbb{P}$, $\mathbb{Q}$ denote sequences, possibly empty, of ERTs.

$$\mathrm{S} = \mathbb{P}, \sigma_q\langle \mathsf{ba}\rangle, \sigma_f\langle \mathsf{x}\omega\rangle, \mathbb{Q}$$

The first step of the first step of GRCP rearranges S by a single exchange to deliver a Σ-sequence S′ = GRCP(S) of the form

$$\mathrm{S}' = \mathbb{P}, \sigma_f\langle \mathsf{x}\omega\rangle, \sigma_q\langle \mathsf{ba}\rangle, \mathbb{Q}$$

We now show that $|q - f| \geq 2$, deducing from this that S′ denotes a valid path $\gamma'(s, t)$, itself a geodesic. There are three possible contrary cases to consider, which we eliminate by *reductio.*

Case 1. Assume $q = f$.

This, we show, contradicts the assumption that γ is geodesic. Let $\sigma_f\langle \mathsf{x}\omega\rangle$ be the first ERT in T that is not the same position in S as in T With $q = f$, we have for S = $\Sigma(\gamma)$,

$$\mathrm{S} = \mathbb{P}, \sigma_f\langle \mathsf{ba}\rangle, \sigma_f\langle \mathsf{x}\omega\rangle, \mathbb{Q}$$

S denotes a licit path $\gamma(s, t) = (s = \lambda_1, \ldots, \lambda_n = t)$. The ERT $\sigma_f\langle \mathsf{ba}\rangle$ thus outputs a leg $\lambda_i \in \gamma$ in which ba is swapped to ab. Thus, $\lambda_i[f+1] = \mathsf{a}$ and $\lambda_i[f] = \mathsf{b}$. The leg λ_i is the input to $\sigma_f\langle \mathsf{x}\omega\rangle$, which requires $\lambda_i[f+1] = \mathsf{x}$ and $\lambda_i[f] = \omega$. Therefore, $\mathsf{a} = \mathsf{x}$ and $\mathsf{b} = \omega$. Thus, if $q = f$, then S will take this form:

$$\mathrm{S} = \mathbb{P}, \sigma_f\langle \omega\mathsf{x}\rangle, \sigma_f\langle \mathsf{x}\omega\rangle, \mathbb{Q}$$

The ERT sequence $\sigma_f\langle \omega x\rangle$, $\sigma_f\langle x\omega\rangle$ effects the transpositions $\omega x \rightarrow x\omega \rightarrow \omega x$, implying that path γ contains the following leg sequence, where a swapped pair of constraints is underlined:

$$\gamma = ..., P\omega xQ, P\underline{x\omega}Q, P\underline{\omega x}Q, ...$$

However, this path can be shortened by simply eliminating the round-trip detour through $P\underline{x\omega}Q$, replacing the specified trio with just $P\omega xQ$, reducing its overall Riggle length by the amount f. Thus if $q=f$, then γ cannot be a geodesic, contrary to assumption. From this, $q \neq f$.

Case 2. Assume $q = f-1$.

This, we show, contradicts the assumption that δ is a geodesic. Let $\sigma_f\langle x\omega\rangle$ be the first ERT in T that is not the same position in S as in T. In this case $S = \Sigma(\gamma)$ takes this form:

$$S = \mathbb{P}, \sigma_{f-1}\langle ba\rangle, \sigma_f\langle x\omega\rangle, \mathbb{Q}$$

Consider the leg $\lambda_i \in \gamma$ that is the output of $\sigma_{f-1}\langle ba\rangle$, in which ba has been swapped to ab. We have $\lambda_i[f] = a$ and $\lambda_i[f-1] = b$. But $\sigma_f\langle x\omega\rangle$ requires of its input that $\lambda_i[f] = \omega$. Therefore, $a = \omega$. Thus,

$$S = \mathbb{P}, \sigma_{f-1}\langle b\omega\rangle, \sigma_f\langle x\omega\rangle, \mathbb{Q}$$

Therefore, path γ takes the following form

$$\gamma = ... , Pxb\omega Q, Px\underline{\omega b}Q, P\underline{\omega x}bQ, ... = ..., \lambda_{i-1}, \lambda_i, \lambda_{i+1}, ...$$

In the specified subsequence, the constraints x, b, ω occupy positions $f+1$, f, $f-1$. Crucially, ω moves up from $f-1$ to f to $f+1$.

Now apply the GRCP transposition to S, producing a Σ-sequence S′:

$$S' = \mathbb{P}, \sigma_f\langle x\omega\rangle, \sigma_{f-1}\langle b\omega\rangle, \mathbb{Q}$$

There is no general guarantee that S′ denotes a licit path. However, from the fact that it is produced by GRCP, we are guaranteed that further applications of GRCP will eventually map it into T, and crucially, that in T, $\sigma_f\langle x\omega\rangle$ precedes $\sigma_{f-1}\langle b\omega\rangle$, by Corollary (49), which establishes that the sequential order relation between the transposed elements in the output of a GRCP transposition is never changed in further steps of GRCP.

Since δ is a licit path, the Σ-sequence $T = \Sigma(\delta)$ denotes it, and we can follow the trajectory of ω through the legs of that path by following the ERT order in T. The ERT $\sigma_f\langle x\omega\rangle$ sends ω up from position f to $f+1$. Subsequently in T, the ERT $\sigma_{f-1}\langle b\omega\rangle$ sends ω up from position $f-1$ to f. For this to happen in a licit path, ω must descend from $f+1$ to $f-1$ after $\sigma_f\langle x\omega\rangle$ has applied and before $\sigma_{f-1}\langle b\omega\rangle$ applies. But ω's trajectory of rise-fall-rise cannot appear in any geodesic, by Corollary (50). Therefore, the assumption $q = f-1$ contradicts the assumption that δ is a geodesic. This contradiction implies $q \neq f-1$.

Case 3. Assume $q = f + 1$.

This, we show, also contradicts the assumption that δ is a geodesic. Let $\sigma_f\langle \mathsf{x\omega} \rangle$ be the first ERT in T that is not in the same position in S as in T. In this case S = Σ(γ) takes the following form:

$$S = \mathbb{P},\ \sigma_{f+1}\langle \mathsf{ba} \rangle,\ \sigma_f\langle \mathsf{x\omega} \rangle,\ \mathbb{Q}$$

Now consider the leg $\lambda_i \in \gamma$ that is the output of $\sigma_{f+1}\langle \mathsf{ba} \rangle$, in which **ba** has been swapped to **ab**. We have $\lambda_i[f+2] = \mathsf{a}$ and $\lambda_i[f+1] = \mathsf{b}$. But $\sigma_f\langle \mathsf{x\omega} \rangle$ requires of its input that $\lambda_i[f+1] = \mathsf{x}$. Thus, $\mathsf{b} = \mathrm{x}$.

Therefore,

$$S = \mathbb{P},\ \sigma_{f+1}\langle \mathsf{xa} \rangle,\ \sigma_f\langle \mathsf{x\omega} \rangle,\ \mathbb{Q}$$

Since S = Σ(γ), the path γ takes the following form

$$\gamma = \dots,\ \mathsf{Pxa\omega Q},\ \mathsf{P\underline{ax}\omega Q},\ \mathsf{Pa\underline{\omega x}Q},\ \dots = \dots,\ \lambda_{i-1},\ \lambda_i,\ \lambda_{i+1},\dots$$

The trajectory of x in the specified legs descends from $f+2$ to $f+1$ to f. The ERT transposition of GRCP as applied to S yields the following Σ-sequence S′.

$$S' = \mathbb{P},\ \sigma_f\langle \mathsf{xa} \rangle,\ \sigma_{f+1}\langle \mathsf{x\omega} \rangle,\ \mathbb{Q}$$

Since all GRCP transpositions put affected ERTs in the serial order they have in the terminus, by Corollary (49), it must be that in T = Σ (δ), we have $\sigma_f\langle \mathsf{x\omega} \rangle$ preceding $\sigma_{f+1}\langle \mathsf{x\omega} \rangle$ in the left to right scan of T. Therefore, in the path δ, constraint x first descends from $f+1$ to f and then subsequently descends from $f+2$ to $f+1$. Since δ is a licit path, constraint x must ascend from f to $f+2$ in the legs that lie between these two transpositions. But x's trajectory of fall-rise-fall cannot appear in any geodesic, by Corollary (50). Thus, the assumption that $q = f+1$ contradicts the theorem's assumption that δ is a geodesic. Therefore, $q \neq f+1$.

This argument shows that the first transposition of adjacent ERTs imposed by GRCP on S = Σ(γ), setting out toward Σ(δ), can only between ERTs of the form

$$S = \mathbb{P},\ \sigma_q\langle \mathsf{ba} \rangle,\ \sigma_f\langle \mathsf{x\omega} \rangle,\ \mathbb{Q}$$

$$S' = \mathbb{P},\ \sigma_f\langle \mathsf{ba} \rangle,\ \sigma_q\langle \mathsf{x\omega} \rangle,\ \mathbb{Q}$$

Where $|f - q| \geq 2$. It is therefore a commutative exchange, so that S′ is guaranteed to denote a licit path $\gamma'(s, t)$. Furthermore, Len(γ′) = Len(γ) because the length of a path π is the sum of the position indices in Σ(π), which is not altered by commutative exchange. Therefore, $\gamma'(s, t)$ is a geodesic.

The same argument holds of the first exchange of GRCP as applied to the terminus geodesic δ and the new start point γ′, and so on repeatedly until δ is reached, yielding the entire GRCP collection of paths between S = Σ(γ) and T = Σ(δ), all of which are geodesics, and therefore meet the assumptions of the argument given about the first transposition of ERTs in S. This establishes the theorem. □

(63) **Corollary. Spherical convexity of grammars.** Let $s, t \in \mathrm{G}$, a grammar. Let $\gamma(s, t)$ be a geodesic path between s and t. Then every leg of γ lies within G.

Proof. Consider $\rho(s, t)$ the geodesic path constructed by RCP between $s, t \in \mathrm{G}$. From Lemma (40) we have it that ρ lies entirely within G. From Theorem (62), we have it that GRCP constructs a sequence of geodesic paths between γ and ρ, each pair of which is related by commutative exchange. From Lemma (56), if follows that if path $\pi(s, t)$ in G is related to $\pi'(s, t)$ by commutative exchange, then $\pi'(\mathrm{s}, \mathrm{t})$ also lies entirely within G. Thus, all the paths in any sequence of paths pairwise related by commutative exchange to a path in G must also lie in G. Since the arbitrary geodesic γ (s, t) is related to $\rho(s, t)$ by a series of commutative exchanges, γ lies entirely within G. The establishes that G is spherically convex. □

Finally, we note that since any geodesic $\gamma(s, t)$ is related by GRCP to $\rho(\mathrm{s}, \mathrm{t})$, and since commutative exchange is reversible, it follows that all can be enumerated by commutative exchange, as claimed at the outset of this discussion.

It remains to ascertain to whether all spherically convex sets are grammars.

Appendix I

Leg set partition of EST

1:CV.del	m.Ons	≫	m.NoCoda	≫	f.dep	≫	f.max
	m.Ons	≫	f.dep	≫	m.NoCoda	≫	f.max
	m.NoCoda	≫	m.Ons	≫	f.dep	≫	f.max
	m.NoCoda	≫	f.dep	≫	m.Ons	≫	f.max
	f.dep	≫	m.Ons	≫	m.NoCoda	≫	f.max
	f.dep	≫	m.NoCoda	≫	m.Ons	≫	f.max
2:(C)V.del	m.NoCoda	≫	f.dep	≫	f.max	≫	m.Ons
	f.dep	≫	m.NoCoda	≫	f.max	≫	m.Ons
3:CV.ins	m.Ons	≫	m.NoCoda	≫	f.max	≫	f.dep
	m.Ons	≫	f.max	≫	m.NoCoda	≫	f.dep
	m.NoCoda	≫	m.Ons	≫	f.max	≫	f.dep
	f.max	≫	m.Ons	≫	m.NoCoda	≫	f.dep
	m.NoCoda	≫	f.max	≫	m.Ons	≫	f.dep
	f.max	≫	m.NoCoda	≫	m.Ons	≫	f.dep
4:(C)V.ins	m.NoCoda	≫	f.max	≫	f.dep	≫	m.Ons
	f.max	≫	m.NoCoda	≫	f.dep	≫	m.Ons
5:CV(C).del	m.Ons	≫	f.dep	≫	f.max	≫	m.NoCoda
	f.dep	≫	m.Ons	≫	f.max	≫	m.NoCoda
6:(C)V(C).del	f.dep	≫	f.max	≫	m.Ons	≫	m.NoCoda
	f.dep	≫	f.max	≫	m.NoCoda	≫	m.Ons
7:CV(C).ins	m.Ons	≫	f.max	≫	f.dep	≫	m.NoCoda
	f.max	≫	m.Ons	≫	f.dep	≫	m.NoCoda
8:(C)V(C).ins	f.max	≫	f.dep	≫	m.Ons	≫	m.NoCoda
	f.max	≫	f.dep	≫	m.NoCoda	≫	m.Ons

Appendix II

EST: SKBs and Hasse diagrams

(1) 1:CV.del

m.Ons	m.NoCoda	f.dep	f.max
W			L
	W		L
		W	L

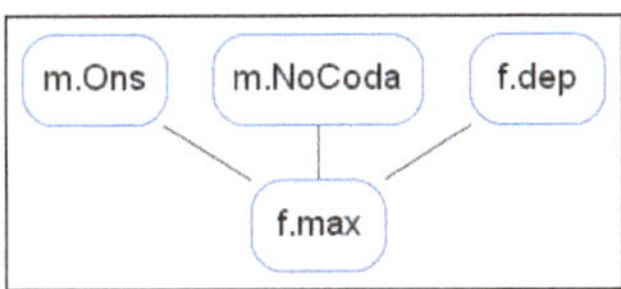

(2) 2:(C)V.del

m.Ons	m.NoCoda	f.dep	f.max
L			W
	W		L
		W	L

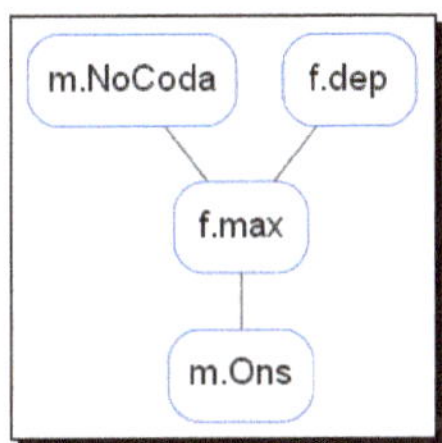

(3) 3:CV.ins

m.Ons	m.NoCoda	f.dep	f.max
		L	W
	W	L	
W		L	

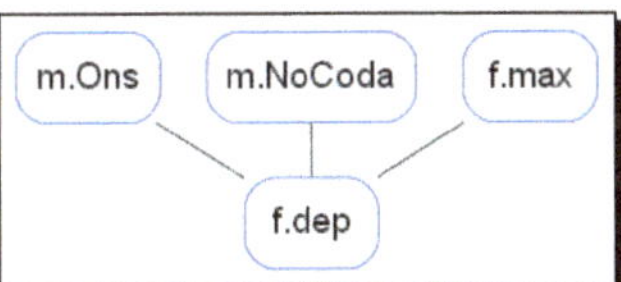

(4) 4:(C)V.ins

m.Ons	m.NoCoda	f.dep	f.max
		L	W
	W	L	
L		W	

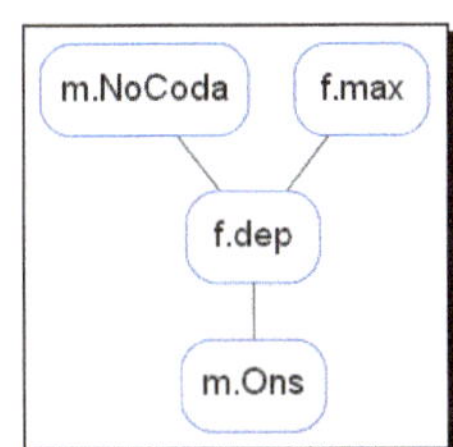

(5) 5:CV(C).del

m.Ons	m.NoCoda	f.dep	f.max
		W	L
	L		W
W			L

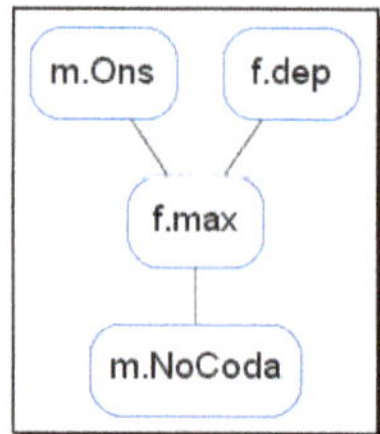

(6) 6:(C)V(C).del

m.Ons	m.NoCoda	f.dep	f.max
		W	L
L	L		W

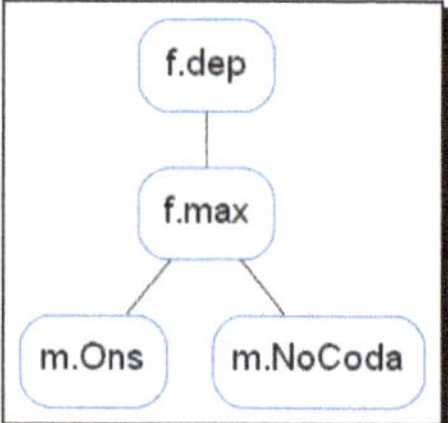

(7) 7:CV(C).ins

m.Ons	m.NoCoda	f.dep	f.max
		L	W
	L	W	
W		L	

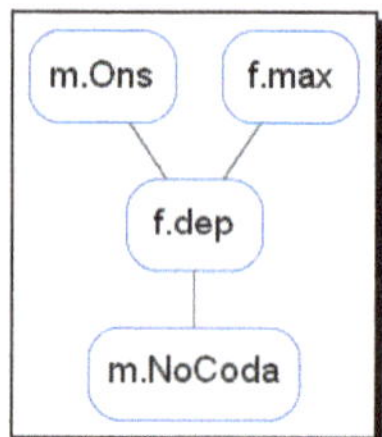

(8) 8:(C)V(C).ins

m.Ons	m.NoCoda	f.dep	f.max
		L	W
L	L	W	

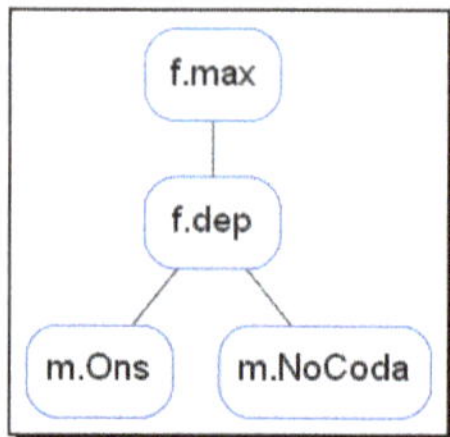

Appendix III

EST.CSys: SKBs and Hasse diagrams

(1) 1∪2:CP.del

m.Ons	m.NoCoda	f.dep	f.max
	W		L
		W	L

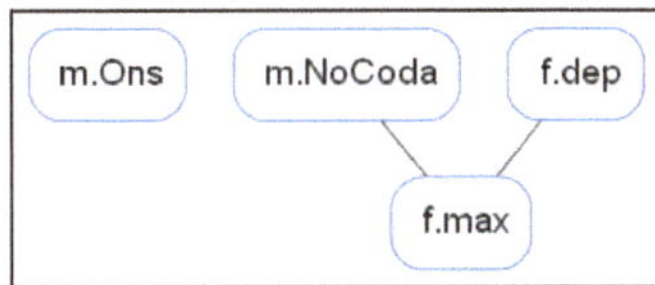

(2) 3∪4:CP.ins

m.Ons	m.NoCoda	f.dep	f.max
	W	L	
		L	W

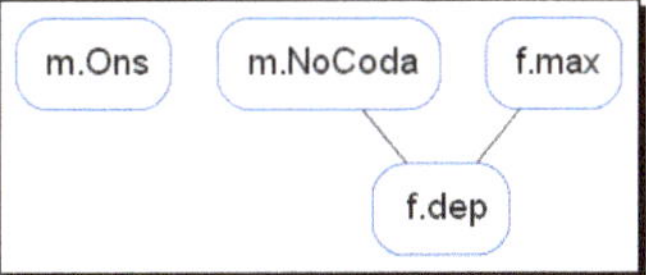

(3) 5∪6:CA.del

m.Ons	m.NoCoda	f.dep	f.max
	L		W
		W	L

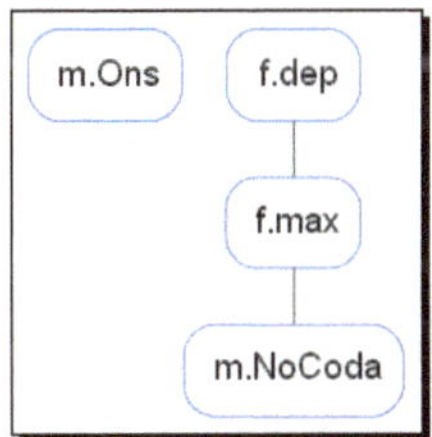

(4) 7∪8:CA.ins

m.Ons	m.NoCoda	f.dep	f.max
	L	W	
		L	W

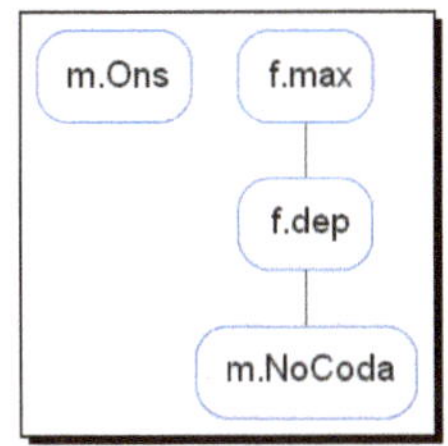

Appendix IV

Notation

Symbol	Meaning		First Use on Page
S.GEN	GEN for a system *S*		7
S.CON	constraints for a system *S*		7
$C_i \gg C_j$	constraint C_i is ranked above C_j		8
$C_i \gg_G C_j$	constraint C_i is ranked above C_j in the set of total orders G		8
Ord(A)	set of all linear orders on a set A		8
cset	candidate set		8
ERC	Elementary Ranking Condition		10
MIB	Maximally Informative Basis		12
SKB	Skeletal Basis		12
leg	linear extension of a grammar		12
AOT	Abstract Optimality Theory		15
UVT	Unitary Violation Tableau		18
T_U	typology associated with UVT U		18
$\mathcal{U}$(T)	set of all UVTs that produce a given typology T		18
G_R(r)	Ranking grammar associated with row r		19
G_E	ERC grammar		19
*x:P(x)	constraint operator yielding number of matches of P(x)		28
∈	element of		28
card(A)	the cardinality of set A		28
Parse-σ	*o	card{σ ∈ out(ϰ)| σ ∉ F}	28
lamb	*$[_F$σ′	card{ $[_F$σ′ ∈ out(ϰ)}	28
AFL	*(σ,F): σ...F	card{(σ,F) ∈ out(ϰ) | σ precedes F}	28
sp	sparse: words taking the form Fo^n or o^nF		29

Symbol	Meaning	First Use on Page
WD	weakly dense: words taking form $F^n(o)$ or $(o)F^n$	29
SD	strongly dense: words taking form F^n	29
$G_1 \bullet G_2$	node merger in EPO bigraph	44
CAND	The set of all candidates for a given system	51
$x \sqsubseteq s$	x is a contiguous substring of the string s	52
m.Ons	number of onsetless syllables in a candidate's output, card{ '[V' $\sqsubseteq$ *out*}	52
m.NoCoda	number of syllables that have a coda in a candidate's output card{ 'C]' $\sqsubseteq$ *out*}	52
f.max	number of input segments that lack output correspondents card$\{x \sqsubseteq in \mid x \in \{C, V\}$ and $\neg\exists y \sqsubseteq out, y = c(x)\}$	52
f.dep	number of output segments that lac k input correspondents card$\{y \sqsubseteq out \mid y \in \{C, V\}$ and $\neg\exists x \sqsubseteq in, y = c(x)\}$	52
OR	onset required	54
OLA	onset lack allowed	54
CP	coda prohibited	54
CA	coda allowed	54
$\oplus$	Minkowski sum	58
$\approx^{C:U}$	equivalence relation induced from UVT, U, for constraint C	63
$\lessdot^{C:U}$	order relation induced from UVT, U, for constraint C	64
u_j	row label for row *j* of UVT U corresponding to grammar G_j	63
$<^{bp.C}$	EPO order relation for constraint C	68
$\sim^{bp.C}$	EPO equivalence relation for constraint C	68
BPP	border point pair	70
C( )	Constraint function for C from CAND to $\mathbb{N}$	102
C[ ]	Constraint filtration function for C from 2^{CAND} to 2^{CAND}	102
P[ ]	OT filtration function for a sequence of constraints P	102
G_v	Grammar associated with row label $v \in U$	104
$\mathcal{U}$(T)	The set all UVTs for typology T	105
P<u>XY</u>Q	A single total order of a BPP with transposition underlined	105
g_U	Bijection from grammars of typology to row labels of U	109

Symbol	Meaning	First Use on Page
$\prec^{bp.C}$	BPP order-related base relation for constraint C	110
$\equiv^{bp.C}$	BPP equivalence-related base relation for constraint C	110
R^{+}	transitive closure of relation R	114
$<^{bp.C}$	the EPO(C) order relation	116
$\sim^{bp.C}$	the EPO(C) equivalence relation	116
R^{refl}	the reflexive closure of the relation R	117
$EPO_T(C)$	the EPO of constraint C in typology T: $\langle T, <^{bp.C}, \sim^{bp.C}\rangle$	118
MOAT(T)	the mother of all tableaux for typology T: $\{EPO_T(C) \mid C \in T.\text{Con}\}$	118
$<^{htc.bp.C}$	hypertransitive closure of EPO(C) order relation $<^{bp.C}$	119
$htcEPO_T(C)$	hypertransitive closure of $EPO_T(C)$: $\langle T, <^{htc.bp.C}, \sim^{bp.C}\rangle$	124
htcMOAT(T)	set of $htcEPO_T$ of MOAT(T): $\{htcEPO_T(C) \mid C \in T.\text{Con}\}$	124
$GEPO_\pi(C)$	Generalized EPO(C) for partition π	126
GMOAT(π)	Generalized MOAT for partition π	126
$\prec^{\pi.bp.C}$	partition order-related base relation for constraint C	127
$<^{\pi.bp.C}$	partition relation transitively closing $\prec^{\pi.bp.C}$	127
$<^{\pi.htc.bp.C}$	partition relation hypertransitively closing $<^{\pi.bp.C}$ and $\sim^{\pi.bp.C}$	127
$\equiv^{\pi.bp.C}$	partition equivalence-related base relation for constraint C	127
$\sim^{\pi.bp.C}$	partition equivalence relation for constraint C	127
htcGEPO	hypertransitive closure of GEPO(C)	130
htcGMOAT(π)	set of hypertransitive closures of GEPOs of GMOAT(π)	130
$P\langle\mathbb{B}\rangle$	Block filtration by prefix sharing for blocks $\mathbb{B}$ in partition π	136
G^U_k	Grammar, G, associated with row u_k in UVT U.	144
$\equiv^{pr.C}$	prefixal equivalence-related base relation for constraint C	147
$\sim^{pr.C}$	prefixal equivalence relation for constraint C	147
$\prec^{pr.C}$	prefixal order-related base relation for constraint C	147
$<^{pr.C}$	prefixal order relation for constraint C	147
$<^{htc.pr.C}$	hypertransitive closure of $<^{pr.C}$ and $\sim^{pr.C}$	147
$PEO_T(C)$	Prefixal equivalence and order structure for C	160
PMOAT(T)	set of PEO(C) for typology T	161
htcPEO(C)	hypertransitive closure of PEO(C)	161

Symbol	Meaning	First Use on Page
htcPMOAT(T)	set of htcPEO(C) for typology T	125
R↾A	Relation R defined on S restricted to the set $A \subseteq S$	169
$\cong$	Isomorphism of PMOATs	181
$\mathbf{a}^{\oplus}$	vector sum of rows $a_1, \ldots, a_n$ from VTs, $V_1, \ldots, V_n$	185
FRed	Fusional Reduction Algorithm	12
ERCoid	a finite-dimensional vector with entries from {W, L, *e*, u}	101
ILR	info loss residue	210
$a \circ b$	fusion of ERCs a and b	209
fu(S)	fusion of the ERC set S	212
$\alpha*\beta$	the weak composition of ERCoids α and β	213
$UBE[\Gamma \sim \Gamma']$	unitary border ERCoid between grammars Γ and Γ'	214
$\partial(G,H)$	set of border point pairs between grammars G and H	213
$[\Gamma \sim \Gamma']_{BP}$	alternate notation for $UBE[\Gamma \sim \Gamma']$	218
$[\Gamma \sim \Gamma']_{M}$	MOAT-derived ERCoid between grammar Γ and Γ'	219
$\Gamma_i \parallel_C \Gamma_j$	grammars Γ_i and Γ_j are noncomparable on constraint C	218
G + H	the join of grammars G and H	265
d_R	the Riggle metric	292
$\lvert\pi\rvert$	length of a path π	293
$DT^{(n)}$	the discrete typology on *n* constraints	298
$U^{(n)}_{\theta}$	the minimal UVT of $DT^{(n)}$	298
RCP	Recursive Constraint Promotion	278
adjDist(p,q)	distance between adjacent vertices p and q in the permutohedron	304
$\pi(p, q)$	path between vertices p and q in the permutohedron	305
$Len(\pi)$	length of a path π	304
$tr(X,\pi)$	travel of X in π	308
$\mathcal{A}(\pi)$	action of path π	309

Bibliography

ROA = Rutgers Optimality Archive, http://roa.rutgers.edu

Alber, Birgit. 2005. Clash, lapse, and directionality. *Natural Language & Linguistic Theory* 23.3: 485–542.

Alber, Birgit. 2017. The Book of BTT. ROA-1327: 37pp.

Alber, Birgit & Alan Prince. 2015–2016. Outline of Property Theory [Entwurf einer verallgemeinerten Eigenschaftstheorie]. Ms. University of Verona and Rutgers University.

Alber, Birgit & Alan Prince. 2017. The Book of nGX. ROA-1312: 50pp.

Alber, Birgit & Alan Prince. 2021, *The Structure of OT Typologies.* Chapter 1: Introduction to Property Theory. ROA-1381.

Alber, Birgit & Alan Prince. 2022. A pseudo-parametric typology at the syntax-prosody interface. ROA-1393.

Alber, Birgit & Alan Prince (in prep.). *The Structure of OT Typologies.* Ms. Free University of Bozen-Bolzano and The ThOT Lab, Seattle, WA.

Alber, Birgit, Natalie DelBusso & Alan Prince. 2016. From Intensional Properties to Universal Support. *Language: Phonological Analysis.* 92.2: e88–e116. ROA-1235.

Atkin, Emily. 2014. First Climate Article On Nate Silver's Data Website Uses 'Deeply Misleading' Data, Top Climatologists Say. *Think Progress*: March 19, 2014.

Bane, Max & Jason Riggle. 2012. Consequences of candidate omission. *Linguistic Inquiry* 43(4): 695–706. ROA-1108.

Bennett, William. G. & Natalie DelBusso. 2017. Typological consequences of ABCD constraint forms. In C. Hammerly, A. Lamont, B. Prickett, & K.A. Teztloff (eds.), NELS 47: Proceedings of the 47th Annual Meeting of the North East Linguistic Society, 1:75–88. Amherst, MA: UMass GLSA. ROA-1307.

Bennett, William G. & Natalie DelBusso. 2018. Typological effects of ABC constraint definitions. *Phonology* 35.1: 1–37. ROA-1326.

Blair, Eric A. (as George Orwell). 1949. *1984.*

Borges, Jorge Luis. 1942. La muerte y la brújula. *Sur*: 92, 27–39. Buenos Aires.

Brasoveanu, Adrian & Alan Prince. 2005/2011. Ranking and necessity: the fusional reduction algorithm. *Natural Language & Linguistic Theory* 29, 3–70. Also: ROA-794.

Chomsky, Noam. 1988. *Language and Problems of Knowledge: the Managua Lectures.* MIT Press. Cambridge, MA.
Crowhurst, Megan J. & Mark Hewitt. 1995. Directional footing, degeneracy, and alignment. In J. Beckman (ed.), Proceedings of NELS 25, Vol. 1, GLSA, Amherst. pp. 47–61, ROA-65.
Danis, Nick. 2014. Deriving Interactions of Complex Stops. Ms. Rutgers University. ROA-1220.
Danis, Nick. 2017. *Complex Place and Place Identity.* Ph.D. dissertation. Rutgers University, New Brunswick, NJ. ROA-1324.
DelBusso, Natalie. 2016. Deriving reduplicants in prosodic-morphology typologies. In A. Albright & M. A. Fuller (eds.), Supplemental Proceedings of the 2014 Annual Meeting on Phonology (AMP 2014). Washington, DC: LSA. ROA-1251.
DelBusso, Natalie. 2018. *Typological Structure and Properties of Property Theory.* New Brunswick, NJ: Rutgers University Ph.D. dissertation.
Descartes, René. 1637. Discourse on Method: Part VI.
Dietrich, Brenda J. 1987. A circuit set characterization of antimatroids. *Journal of Combinatorial Theory,* Series B 43, 314–321 (1987).
Eastwood, Clint & David W. Peoples. 1992. *Unforgiven.* Malpaso Productions.
Ferreira, O. & A. Iusem & S. Németh. 2014. Concepts and techniques of optimization on the sphere. *TOP: An Official Journal of the Spanish Society of Statistics and Operations Research,* Springer; Sociedad de Estadística e Investigación Operativa, vol. 22(3), 1148–1170, October
Gigerenzer, Gerd & Daniel G. Goldstein. 1996. Reasoning the fast and frugal way: models of bounded rationality. *Psychological Review* 103(4): 650–669.
Guilbaud, G. Th. & P. Rosenstiehl. 1963. Analyse algébrique d'un scrutiny. Mathématiques et sciences humaines 4: 9–33. Via Wikipedia article 'Permutohedron.'
Howard, Irwin. 1972. *A Directional Theory of Rule Application in Phonology.* Ph.D. dissertation: MIT, Cambridge, MA.
Hunter, Robert. 1970. Attics of my life. Music: J. Garcia. *American Beauty:* 2:4. Warner Bros.
Hyde, Brett. 2012. Alignment constraints. *Natural Language & Linguistic Theory* 30: 789–836.
Ito, Junko. 1986. *Syllable Theory in Prosodic Phonology.* Ph.D. dissertation, University of Massachusetts at Amherst.
Ito, Junko. 1989. A prosodic theory of epenthesis. *Natural Language & Linguistic Theory* 7:2, 217–250.
Johnson, C. Douglas. 1972. *Formal aspects of phonological description. (Monographs on linguistic analysis).* Mouton: Den Haag. From 1970 UCSD dissertation of same title.
Karttunen, Lauri. 1998. The Proper Treatment of Optimality in Computational Phonology. ROA-258.
Keats, John. 1816. On first looking into Chapman's Homer. *Examiner:* London.
Korte, Bernhard; Lovász, László; Schrader, Rainer (1991), Greedoids, Springer-Verlag, 19–43.

Krugman, Paul. 2014. Tarnished Silver. New York Times: March 23, 10:48am.

Lombardi, Linda. 1999. Positional faithfulness and voicing assimilation in Optimality Theory. *Natural Language & Linguistic Theory* 17:267–302.

McCarthy, John & Alan Prince. 1993. Generalized alignment. In *Yearbook of Morphology 1993*, 79–153, ed. Geert Booij & Jaap van Marle. Boston: Kluwer Academic Publishers. ROA-7.

McCarthy, John & Alan Prince. 1995. Faithfulness and reduplicative identity. In *University of Massachusetts Occasional Papers in Linguistics* 18: *Papers in Optimality Theory*, p. 249–384, ed. Jill Beckman, Suzanne Urbanczyk and Laura Walsh Dickey. ROA-60.

McManus, Hope. 2016. *Stress Parallels in Modern OT*. Ph.D. dissertation, Rutgers University. ROA-1295.

Merchant, Nazarré. 2008. *Discovering Underlying Forms: Contrast Pairs and Ranking*. Ph.D. dissertation, Rutgers University. ROA-964.

Merchant, Nazarré. 2011. Learning ranking information from unspecified overt forms using the join. Proceedings of the CLS 47. ROA-1146.

Merchant, Nazarré. 2018. The Contours of nGY. ROA-1342, ROA-1343.

Merchant, Nazarré & Martin Krämer. 2018. The Holographic Principle: Typological Analysis Using Lower Dimensions. ROA-1340.

Merchant, Nazarré & Jason Riggle. 2016. OT grammars, beyond partial orders: ERC sets and antimatroids. *Natural Language & Linguistic Theory* 34.1: 241–269. As 'Erc Sets and Antimatroids,' ROA-1158.

Mester, Armin & Jaye Padgett. 1993. Directional Syllabification in Generalized Alignment. ROA-1. In *Phonology at Santa Cruz*, Vol. 3, 1994, pp. 79–85.

Miryam, Yeshua bar. ca. 30 CE. Quoted in κατὰ Ματθαῖον εὐαγγέλιον, 7:26 (PC to author).

Prince, Alan. 2002a. *Entailed Ranking Arguments*. ROA-500.

Prince, Alan. 2002b. Arguing Optimality. ROA-562.

Prince, Alan. 2006/7. No More than Necessary: beyond the 'four rules', and a bug report. ROA-882.

Prince, Alan. 2009. RCD – the Movie. ROA-1057. 69pp.

Prince, Alan. 2013. Metrical Theory as a Portal on Theory. Youtube video.

Prince, Alan. 2014a. Act Accordingly: a User's View of Theory. Slides from talk at FLYSM I, St. Petersburg, FL.

Prince, Alan. 2014b. Testing the Boundaries: Aspects of Typological Structure in OT. Slides from talk at Stanford University.

Prince, Alan. 2015a. What is OT? ROA-1271.

Prince, Alan. 2015b. One Tableau Suffices. *Linguistic Inquiry*: rejected. ROA-1250.

Prince, Alan. 2017. Representing OT Grammars. ROA-1309.

Prince, Alan, with Birgit Alber & Nazarré Merchant. 2014. The Structure of OT Typologies: First Steps. Slides from talk at OCP (Old World Conference in Phonology).

Prince, Alan, with Birgit Alber & Nazarré Merchant. 2015. Intrinsic Structure in OT Typologies. Slides from talk at Workshop on the Formal Structure of OT Typologies. Rutgers University.

Prince, Alan, Nazarré Merchant, and Bruce Tesar. 2007–2021. OTWorkplace. Software suite available at https://sites.google.com/site/otworkplace.

Prince, Alan & Paul Smolensky. 2004. Optimality Theory: Constraint Interaction in Generative Grammar. Blackwell. Also: ROA-537.

Riggle, Jason. 2004. *Generation, Recognition, and Learning in Finite State Optimality Theory.* Ph.D. dissertation, UCLA, Los Angeles.

Riggle, Jason. 2010. Sampling Rankings. ROA-1075.

Riggle, Jason. 2012. Spherical Convexity. Talk at the Rutgers Optimality Research Group. Department of Linguistics, Rutgers, The State University of New Jersey, at New Brunswick.

Samek-Lodovici, Vieri & Alan Prince.1999. *Optima.* ROA-363.

Samek-Lodovici, Vieri & Alan Prince. 2005. *Fundamental Properties of Harmonic Bounding.* ROA-785.

Schoute, Pieter Hendrik. 1911. Analytic treatment of the polytopes regularly derived from the regular polytopes. *Verhandelingen der Koninklijke Akademie van Wetenschappen te Amsterdam* 11(3): 87 pp. Googlebook, 370–381. Also online on the KNAW Digital Library.

Silver, Nate. 2016. How I acted like a Pundit and Screwed up on Donald Trump. May 18: FiveThirtyEight.

Steriade, Donca. 1982. *Greek Prosodies and the Nature of Syllabification.* Ph.D. dissertation, MIT, Cambridge, MA.

Stevens, Wallace. 1923. The bird with the coppery, keen claws. *Harmonium.* Alfred E. Knopf.

Wolchover, Natalie. 2013. A new tool to help mathematicians pack. *Quanta Magazine.* Dec. 20.

Wikipedia.

Convex hull
Cycle (discrete mathematics)
Directed graph
Expander Graph
Geodesic
Geodesic convexity
Graph
Graph drawing
Hasse diagram
Lindenbaum–Tarski algebra
Linear extension
Metric
Order
Path (graph theory)
Partition of a set
Permutohedron
Product order
Rooted Graph
Setoid
Transitive closure

La primera letra del Nombre ha sido articulada.

■

Definitions, Facts, Remarks, Lemmas, Theorems and Corollaries

Index

Printed in the USA
CPSIA information can be obtained
at www.ICGtesting.com
JSHW011659220124
55611JS00001B/17